C0-ARE-267

(Recommended for grade 6)

Building Better Health

GOLD LEVEL

TEACHER'S EDITION

Green Level
Red Level
GOLD LEVEL
Silver Level
Aqua Level

McDougal, Littell and Company
Evanston, Illinois
New York Sacramento

Created and Developed by
Contemporary (cpi) Perspectives, Inc.

BETSY R. FLEMING, B.S., M.S.
Teacher Specialist for Health and Drug Education
Anne Arundel County Public Schools
Annapolis, Maryland

CAROLINE PURCELL BARNES, B.A., M.A.
Health Education Specialist
Ector County Independent School District
Ector County, Texas

LILLIAN BILLINGS MORAVA, B.S., M.Ed.
Health and Physical Education Department Chairperson
La Porte High School
La Porte, Texas

MARILYN K. BROWNE, B.S.
Registered Physical Therapist
Somerville Visiting Nurses Association
Somerville, Massachusetts

MERCEDES W. GRANADY, R.N., M.S.
Teacher, Special Education
Formerly Instructor of Nursing
New Rochelle High School
New Rochelle, New York

ARTHUR LEW, M.D.
Director of Training in Child Psychiatry
New York Medical College
New York, New York

GUY JAMES MANASTER, Ph.D.
Professor, Department of Educational Psychology
The University of Texas at Austin
Austin, Texas

EDWARD ANTHONY OPPENHEIMER, M.D.
Assistant Clinical Professor of Medicine
Division of Pulmonary Medicine
Department of Internal Medicine
U.C.L.A. Medical School
Los Angeles, California

ARNOLD C. RATNER, M.D.
Clinical Instructor, Dermatology
Georgetown University School of Medicine
Washington, D.C.

HOWARD L. WARD, F.A., D.D.S., M.A.
Assistant Dean for Clinical Affairs
College of Dentistry
New York University
New York, New York

Contributing Writers and Editors:

Bryan Bunch, Teri Crawford, Eden Force Eskin, Barbara Gentile, Gail M. Griffin, Earle R. Hitchner III, Valerie A. Hurst, Edith Lewis, Charles Miller, Megan Scarpa, Marie C. Smith

ISBN 0-88343-382-6

Contents

Teacher's Edition

This hardcover Teacher's Edition contains the student text reproduced full-size, with additional teaching suggestions printed in blue in the outside margins. These teaching suggestions include ideas for discussion, activities, group projects, assignments, resources, additional information, and sources of free publications. In addition, all answers to exercises are overprinted in blue on the student text pages.

Special Features of the BUILDING BETTER HEALTH Program

BUILDING BETTER HEALTH is designed to help students build and maintain their best potential health and reduce the risk of disease and accidental injury in their lives. The program develops in students

- an *understanding* of major health concepts and issues.
- a sense of *responsibility* for their own health.
- the *skills* needed to implement positive health actions.

Building understanding

. . . with thorough coverage

BUILDING BETTER HEALTH emphasizes total health development—the combination of the physical and the mental/emotional health of the student. Comprehensive in scope, the program develops all major health concepts within strands of spiraling instruction that become progressively more intensive at each level. The nine major concept strands developed at each level are these:

Mental and Emotional Health
Growth and Development
Personal and Dental Health
Nutrition
Safety and First Aid
Disease
Community and Environmental Health
Drugs
Consumer Issues in Health

. . . with basic, readable information

The first step in building and maintaining better health is providing students with accurate and readable information. The readability of the BUILDING BETTER HEALTH series is suited to a wide range of students at each level, and all factual information is provided in a lively, straightforward manner. The concepts explored are appropriate to the maturity, basic needs, and interests of the students.

. . . with features designed for comprehension

While each chapter covers one major instructional strand, concepts are reviewed and cross-referenced throughout. Each chapter is carefully formulated to ensure mastery of four or five key concepts. The following features help to develop students' total understanding of the key concepts:

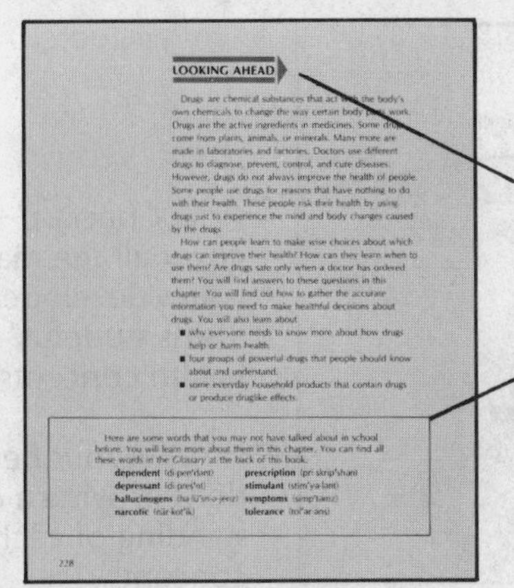

LOOKING AHEAD

Drugs are chemical substances that act with the body's own chemicals to change the way certain body parts work. Drugs are the active ingredients in medicines. Some drugs come from plants, animals, or minerals. Many more are made in laboratories and factories. Doctors use different drugs to diagnose, prevent, control, and cure diseases. However, drugs do not always improve the health of people. Some people use drugs for reasons that have nothing to do with their health. These people risk their health by using drugs just to experience the mind and body changes caused by the drugs.

How can people learn to make wise choices about which drugs can improve their health? How can they learn when to use them? Are drugs safe only when a doctor has ordered them? You will find answers to these questions in this chapter. You will find out how to gather the accurate information you need to make healthful decisions about drugs. You will also learn about

- why everyone needs to know more about how drugs help or harm health.
- four groups of powerful drugs that people should know about and understand.
- some everyday household products that contain drugs or produce druglike effects.

Here are some words that you may not have talked about in school before. You will learn more about them in this chapter. You can find all these words in the *Glossary* at the back of this book.

dependent (di pen'dənt)	**prescription** (pri skrip'shən)
depressant (di pres'ənt)	**stimulant** (stim'yə lənt)
hallucinogens (hə lü'sn ə jenz)	**symptoms** (simp'təmz)
narcotic (när kot'ik)	**tolerance** (tol'ər əns)

228

At the outset of each lesson, the text prepares the students for what they will be learning.

Looking Ahead—content to be covered in the chapter is previewed, highlighting major objectives to let students know what they should expect to learn.

A vocabulary box containing new words used in a context unfamiliar to students appears on every *Looking Ahead* page. A pronunciation guide is given for each word and is repeated in the *Glossary.*

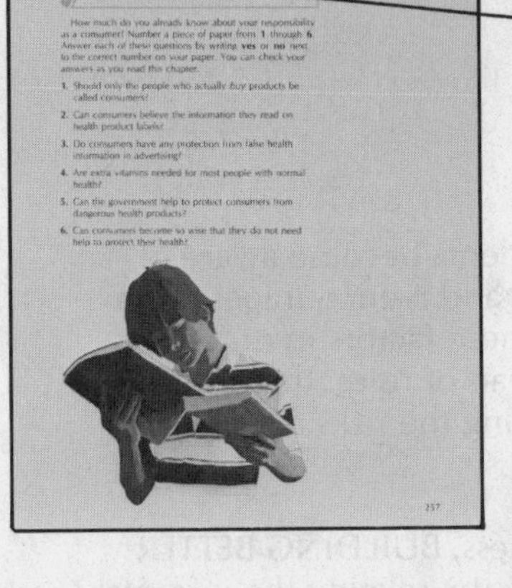

Early Checkup

How much do you already know about your responsibility as a consumer? Number a piece of paper from **1** through **6**. Answer each of these questions by writing **yes** or **no** next to the correct number on your paper. You can check your answers as you read this chapter.

1. Should only the people who actually *buy* products be called consumers?
2. Can consumers believe the information they read on health product labels?
3. Do consumers have any protection from false health information in advertising?
4. Are extra vitamins needed for most people with normal health?
5. Can the government help to protect consumers from dangerous health products?
6. Can consumers become so wise that they do not need help to protect their health?

357

Early Checkup—a brief preview quiz helps to determine how much students know about the concepts covered in the chapter.

Continuous reinforcement throughout each chapter guarantees student mastery.

consumer

YOU CAN BE AN EFFECTIVE CONSUMER

What Is a Consumer?

Anyone who uses or buys products or services is a **consumer**. This means that everyone is a consumer part of the time. Think about just a few of the choices you make as a consumer.

- Which shoes should I wear for the game?
- What should I eat for breakfast and lunch?
- Should I buy the medium or the giant tube?
- Is the bruise serious enough to show to a nurse or doctor?

What was your answer to *Early Checkup* number 1? Should only the people who actually *buy* products be called consumers?

Many consumer decisions can help or harm a person's health. For example, the breakfast cereal you ask your family to buy may contain added sugar. The sugar can help cause tooth decay.

You Can Make Good Decisions

It is not always easy to make the wisest consumer decision. There are so many health questions to keep in mind. Does the product work well? Will it break easily? Is it safe for everyone in the family? Does the health value seem worth the price? Do I need it? Where can I get more information?

Of course, consumers also think about how well they like a product, as well as how healthful it may be. For example, two different brands of fluoride toothpaste may cost about the same amount of money. Both may be approved by the *American Dental Association* (ADA) as being good for preventing tooth decay. In that case, both may be good products. When products are equally good, the consumer may choose the toothpaste that tastes best. This makes building good health more fun, since teeth should be brushed several times a day.

The Better Business Bureau Helps Consumers

People often call the *Better Business Bureau* to find out if it has received complaints about some store, product, or service. The Bureau is supported by local business people who want to stop any unfair or dishonest practices that cheat consumers. Most telephone directories have a listing for "Better Business Bureau."

This shield shows that the American Dental Association has accepted a product for the care of teeth and gums.

Accepted
American Dental Association

258

Each of the Early Checkup questions is repeated at points within the text where the questions are answered.

Vocabulary Tabs—new terms or words used in unfamiliar context are printed at the top of the page on which they are introduced, signalling that these words are phonetically spelled and explained in the *Glossary.*

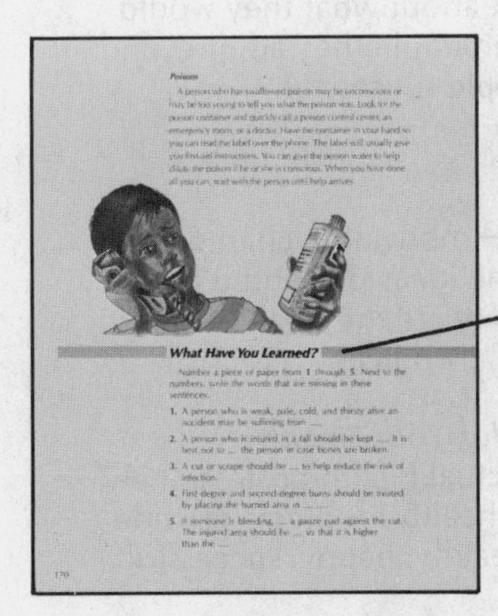

Poisons

A person who has swallowed poison may be unconscious or may be too young to tell you what the poison was. Look for the poison container and quickly call a poison control center, an emergency room, or a doctor. Have the container in your hand so you can read the label over the phone. The label will usually give you first-aid instructions. You can give the person water to help dilute the poison if he or she is conscious. When you have done all you can, wait with the person until help arrives.

What Have You Learned?

Number a piece of paper from **1** through **5**. Next to the numbers, write the words that are missing in these sentences.

1. A person who is weak, pale, cold, and thirsty after an accident may be suffering from ....
2. A person who is injured in a fall should be kept .... It is best not to .... the person in case bones are broken.
3. A cut or scrape should be .... to help reduce the risk of infection.
4. First-degree and second-degree burns should be treated by placing the burned area in ....
5. If someone is bleeding, ... a gauze pad against the cut. The injured area should be .... so that it is higher than the ....

170

What Have You Learned?—brief, periodic questions review specific concepts developed in each section of the chapter.

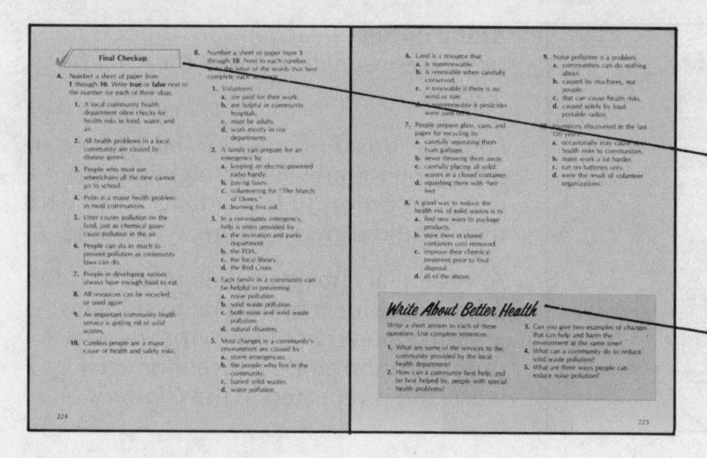

Final Checkup

A. Number a sheet of paper from **1** through **10**. Write **true** or **false** next to the number for each of these ideas.

1. A local community health department often checks for health risks in food, water, and air.
2. All health problems in a local community are caused by disease germs.
3. People who must use wheelchairs all the time cannot go to school.
4. Polio is a major health problem in most communities.
5. Litter causes pollution on the land, just as chemical gases cause pollution in the air.
6. People can do as much to prevent pollution as community laws can do.
7. People in developing nations always have enough food to eat.
8. All resources can be recycled, or used again.
9. An important community health service is getting rid of solid wastes.
10. Careless people are a major cause of health and safety risks.

B. Number a sheet of paper from **1** through **10**. Next to each number, [illegible] the letter of the words that best complete each [illegible].

1. Volunteers
   a. are paid for their work.
   b. are helpful in community hospitals.
   c. must be adults.
   d. work mostly in fire departments.
2. A family can prepare for an emergency by
   a. keeping an electric-powered radio handy.
   b. paying taxes.
   c. volunteering for "The March of Dimes."
   d. learning first aid.
3. In a community emergency, help is often provided by
   a. the recreation and parks department.
   b. the FDA.
   c. the local library.
   d. the Red Cross.
4. Each family in a community can be helpful in preventing
   a. noise pollution.
   b. solid waste pollution.
   c. both noise and solid waste pollution.
   d. natural disasters.
5. Most changes in a community's environment are caused by
   a. storm emergencies.
   b. the people who live in the community.
   c. buried solid wastes.
   d. water pollution.

224

6. Land is a resource that
   a. is nonrenewable.
   b. is renewable when carefully conserved.
   c. is renewable if there is no wind or rain.
   d. [illegible] nonrenewable if pesticides were used [illegible].
7. People prepare glass, cans, and paper for recycling by
   a. carefully separating them from garbage.
   b. never throwing them away.
   c. carefully placing all solid wastes in a closed container.
   d. squashing them with their feet.
8. A good way to reduce the health risk of solid wastes is to
   a. find new ways to package products.
   b. store them in closed containers until removed.
   c. improve their chemical treatment prior to final disposal.
   d. all of the above.
9. Noise pollution is a problem
   a. communities can do nothing about.
   b. caused by machines, not people.
   c. that can cause health risks.
   d. caused solely by loud portable radios.
10. [illegible]ventions discovered in the last 150 years
   a. occasionally may cause [illegible] health risks to communities.
   b. make work a lot harder.
   c. run on batteries only.
   d. were the result of volunteer organizations.

Write About Better Health

Write a short answer to each of these questions. Use complete sentences.

1. What are some of the services to the community provided by the local health department?
2. How can a community best help, and be best helped by, people with special health problems?
3. Can you give two examples of changes that can help and harm the environment at the same time?
4. What can a community do to reduce solid waste pollution?
5. What are three ways people can reduce noise pollution?

225

Final Checkup—chapter-end review tests cover all the major health concepts and issues developed within each chapter, to assess students' comprehension of major health concepts.

Write About Better Health—brief questions provide a check on students' understanding of each chapter's critical health concepts.

Building responsibility

BUILDING BETTER HEALTH helps students become aware of which health factors they can control, and it encourages them to take responsibility for controlling these factors in order to reach their best potential health. Instead of rules, the program suggests positive approaches to reducing the risks of health problems in students' lives.

To develop responsible health awareness, BUILDING BETTER HEALTH focuses on students' own lives by relating the information to their present needs and interests. It encourages a positive self-image and helps students take charge of their own health for everyday success in school, with friends, and in their family and community life. In addition, the program helps students to accept the fact that the health practices they adopt now will have an impact on their future health. Throughout the program students are encouraged to think about what they would like to be like when they are older, the people they admire, and the characteristics that make these people successful.

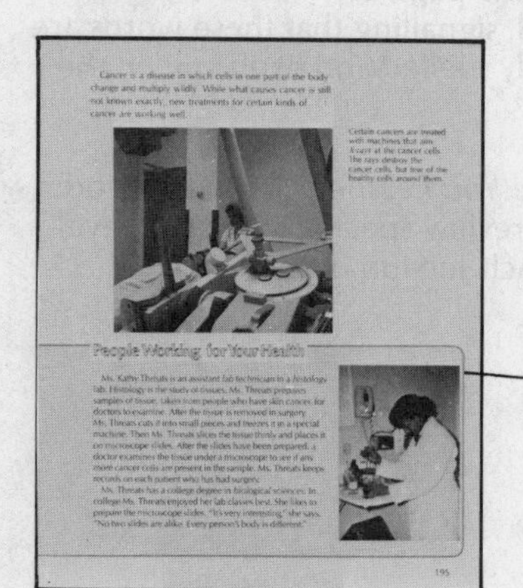

Cancer is a disease in which cells in one part of the body change and multiply wildly. While what causes cancer is still not known exactly, new treatments for certain kinds of cancer are working well.

Certain cancers are treated with machines that aim X-rays at the cancer cells. The rays destroy the cancer cells, but few of the healthy cells around them.

People Working for Your Health

Ms. Kathy Threats is an assistant lab technician in a *histology* lab. Histology is the study of tissues. Ms. Threats prepares samples of tissue, taken from people who have skin cancer, for doctors to examine. After the tissue is removed in surgery, Ms. Threats cuts it into small pieces and freezes it in a special machine. Then Ms. Threats slices the tissue thinly and places it on microscope slides. After the slides have been prepared, a doctor examines the tissue under a microscope to see if any more cancer cells are present in the sample. Ms. Threats keeps records on each patient who has had surgery.

Ms. Threats has a college degree in *biological sciences*. In college Ms. Threats enjoyed her lab classes best. She likes to prepare the microscope slides. "It's very interesting," she says. "No two slides are alike. Every person's body is different."

195

Chapter Opener—motivating chapter openers reflect the ideas presented in the chapter and help relate the health concepts to students' own lives.

People Working for Your Health—interviews with actual health professionals solving everyday health problems provide role models of healthy, happy, successful adults.

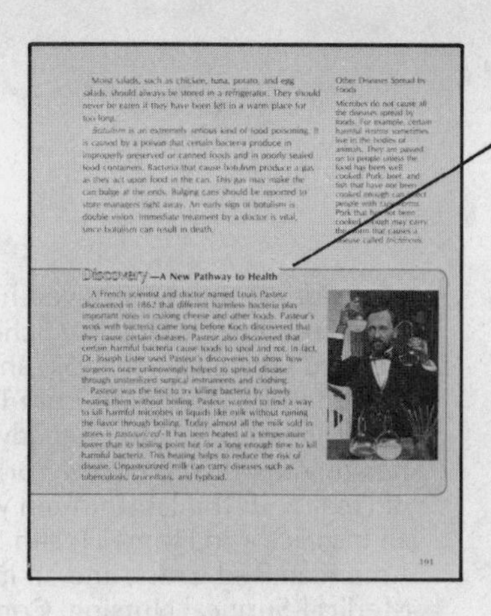

Most salads, such as chicken, tuna, potato, and egg salads, should always be stored in a refrigerator. They should never be eaten if they have been left in a warm place for too long.

Botulism is an extremely serious kind of food poisoning. It is caused by a poison that certain bacteria produce in improperly preserved or canned foods and in poorly sealed food containers. Bacteria that cause botulism produce a gas as they act upon food in the can. This gas may make the can bulge at the ends. Bulging cans should be reported to store managers right away. An early sign of botulism is double vision. Immediate treatment by a doctor is vital, since botulism can result in death.

Other Diseases Spread by Foods

Microbes do not cause all the diseases spread by foods. For example, certain harmful worms sometimes live in the bodies of animals. They are passed on to people unless the food has been well cooked. Pork, beef, and fish that have not been cooked enough can infect people with [illegible]. Pork that has not been cooked [illegible] may carry the [illegible] that causes a disease called *trichinosis*.

Discovery—A New Pathway to Health

A French scientist and doctor named Louis Pasteur discovered in 1862 that different harmless bacteria play important roles in making cheese and other foods. Pasteur's work with bacteria came long before Koch discovered that they cause certain diseases. Pasteur also discovered that certain harmful bacteria cause foods to spoil and rot. In fact, Dr. Joseph Lister used Pasteur's discoveries to show how surgeons once unknowingly helped to spread disease through unsterilized surgical instruments and clothing.

Pasteur was the first to try killing bacteria by slowly heating them without boiling. Pasteur wanted to find a way to kill harmful microbes in liquids like milk without ruining the flavor through boiling. Today almost all the milk sold in stores is *pasteurized*. It has been heated at a temperature lower than its boiling point but for a long enough time to kill harmful bacteria. This heating helps to reduce the risk of disease. Unpasteurized milk can carry diseases such as tuberculosis, *brucellosis*, and typhoid.

191

Discovery—A New Pathway to Health—excitingly portrayed major breakthroughs in health maintenance, disease treatment, and preservation of a healthful environment help to foster student health awareness, which in turn leads to a more responsible attitude.

Building skills

In addition to giving students an understanding of health concepts and the ability to make decisions concerning their own health, BUILDING BETTER HEALTH develops the skills they need to carry out these decisions. The program teaches students the practical steps they can take toward developing sound health habits. An entire chapter at each level is devoted to pulling together all aspects of health—nutrition, exercise, proper sleep habits, and more—into a personal health plan. And special features in each chapter give students the opportunity to apply what they have learned in their daily lives.

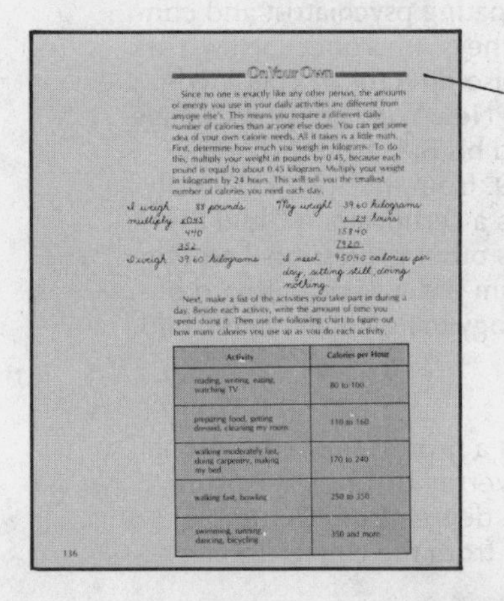

On Your Own

Since no one is exactly like any other person, the amounts of energy you use in your daily activities are different from anyone else's. This means you require a different daily number of calories than anyone else does. You can get some idea of your own calorie needs. All it takes is a little math. First, determine how much you weigh in kilograms. To do this, multiply your weight in pounds by 0.45, because each pound is equal to about 0.45 kilogram. Multiply your weight in kilograms by 24 hours. This will tell you the smallest number of calories you need each day.

I weigh 88 pounds
multiply x0.45
440
352
I weigh 39.60 kilograms

My weight 39.60 kilograms
x 24 hours
15840
7920
I need 950.40 calories per day, sitting still, doing nothing.

Next, make a list of the activities you take part in during a day. Beside each activity, write the amount of time you spend doing it. Then use the following chart to figure out how many calories you use up as you do each activity.

Activity	Calories per Hour
reading, writing, eating, watching TV	80 to 100
preparing food, getting dressed, cleaning my room	110 to 160
walking moderately fast, doing carpentry, making my bed	170 to 240
walking fast, bowling	250 to 350
swimming, running, dancing, bicycling	350 and more

116

On Your Own—an independent activity, related to the topic of the chapter, that helps students apply the concepts on their own.

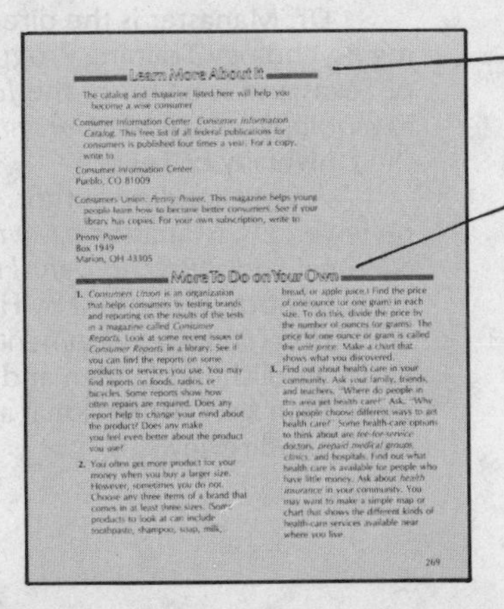

Learn More About It

The catalog and magazine listed here will help you become a wise consumer.

Consumer Information Center. *Consumer Information Catalog.* This free list of all federal publications for consumers is published four times a year. For a copy, write to:

Consumer Information Center
Pueblo, CO 81009

Consumers Union. *Penny Power.* This magazine helps young people learn how to become better consumers. See if your library has copies. For your own subscription, write to:

Penny Power
Box 1949
Marion, OH 43305

More To Do on Your Own

1. *Consumers Union* is an organization that helps consumers by testing brands and reporting on the results of the tests in a magazine called *Consumer Reports.* Look at some recent issues of *Consumer Reports* in a library. See if you can find the reports on some products or services you use. You may find reports on foods, radios, or bicycles. Some reports show how often repairs are required. Does any report help to change your mind about the product? Does any make you feel even better about the product you use?
2. You often get more product for your money when you buy a larger size. However, sometimes you do not. Choose any three items of a brand that comes in at least three sizes. (Some products to look at can include toothpaste, shampoo, soap, milk, bread, or apple juice.) Find the price of one ounce (or one gram) in each size. To do this, divide the price by the number of ounces (or grams). The price for one ounce or gram is called the *unit price.* Make a chart that shows what you discovered.
3. Find out about health care in your community. Ask your family, friends, and teachers, "Where do people in this area get health care?" Ask, "Why do people choose different ways to get health care?" Some health-care options to think about are *fee-for-service doctors, prepaid medical groups, clinics,* and hospitals. Find out what health care is available for people who have little money. Ask about *health insurance* in your community. You may want to make a simple map or chart that shows the different kinds of health-care services available near where you live.

269

Learn More About It—suggestions for further reading and reference materials concerning the chapter topics.

More To Do on Your Own—additional independent activities for students that expand their knowledge of health topics and encourage responsibility for achieving their own ideal health.

The Consultants for BUILDING BETTER HEALTH

Caroline Purcell Barnes received her M.A. from the University of Texas in 1974. She has taught elementary school for twelve years in the Midland Texas Schools and for an additional ten years taught secondary physical education and health education in the Ector County, Texas, School District. Her special educational roles have included the teaching of Bible History and coordination of the Crime Prevention and Drug Education Programs in the Ector County Independent School District.

Among her publications and formal research papers are "Usage Patterns of Nondrug Alternatives" in *The Journal of Drug Education* (vol. 7, no.4, 177-78), and "Adolescent Usage Patterns of Nondrug Alternatives," American Association for the Advancement of Science (1977 presentation).

Ms. Barnes has been chairperson of the Board of Youth Encouragement Service, counseling juvenile delinquents on probation, and president of the Odessa, Texas, Community Services Organization.

Marilyn K. Browne is a registered physical therapist, having been graduated with distinction from the University of Nebraska College of Medicine, where she was the recipient of Awards for Excellence in Service to Education and Excellence in Research. Ms. Browne is a member of the American Physical Therapy Association, and is currently working with the Visiting Nurses Association of Somerville, Massachusetts.

Betsy Fox Fleming holds an M.S. degree in Health Science awarded by Towson State University, Towson, Maryland. She taught junior high school health education for seven years and consults, designs, and conducts drug education workshops in the school district of Anne Arundel County in Maryland. Ms. Fleming has also been a consultant in Montgomery and Calvert Counties and has been an instructor in Health Science at Towson State University. She has also been a consultant to the University of Maryland School of Pharmacy Committee on Drug Abuse Education and the ITV Curriculum Committee for Health Education for the Maryland State Department of Education.

Mercedes Granady received her R.N. diploma from Freedmen's Hospital School of Nursing, Howard University, in 1957, and an M.S. degree in Therapeutics Education from The College of New Rochelle in 1974. Ms. Granady has been a public health nurse for the New York City Department of Health. In the last thirteen years she has been an instructor in Home Health Nursing for the American Red Cross, and an instructor of Medical-Surgical Nursing, Community Health Awareness in the New Rochelle High School, New Rochelle, New York. Most recently she has taught special education classes and has been learning disabilities specialist for the New Rochelle Public Schools.

Between 1970 and 1978, Ms. Granady toured and participated in seminars in hospital facilities in Egypt, Ethiopia, Zambia, Kenya, Italy, Tanzania, Spain, Mexico, Portugal, and Morocco.

Arthur Lew is a participating psychiatrist and consulting psychiatrist to the Mamaroneck, New York Public Schools. He is also director of training in Child Psychiatry at the New York Medical College.

Dr. Lew received his B.A. from Columbia University and his M.D. from the State University of New York. He holds a certificate in Child Psychiatry, and among his other professional credentials are certificates from the American Board of Psychiatry and Neurology in Psychiatry and Child Psychiatry.

Guy James Manaster is a professor of Educational Psychology at the University of Texas at Austin, having received a B.A. degree from Columbia University and a Ph.D. from the University of Chicago.

Dr. Manaster is the director of the Counseling Psychology Training Program at the University of Texas and is editor of the *Journal of Individual Psychology* and of the *Gerontology Newsletter* of the University of Texas.

An outstanding author, researcher, and reviewer, Dr. Manaster has written *Cross-National Social Psychological Research: Problems and Methods,* published by Houghton Mifflin, and *Adolescent Development and the Life Tasks,* published by Allyn and Bacon, along with more than sixty professional articles, reports, books, and reviews.

Lillian Billings Morava is the chairperson, Health and Physical Education Department, and an outdoor education teacher in the La Porte, Texas, Public Schools. With her master of education degree from the University of Houston, Ms. Morava has taught health, biology, and physical education since 1968. Since 1977 she has been instructor for the American Wilderness Leadership School in Jackson, Wyoming.

Ms. Morava is president of the Texas Association for Health, Physical Education, and Recreation, and is a member of the Writers Committee for the Texas Education Agency's Secondary Physical Education Curriculum Guidelines.

In addition to varied officerships in Texas health, physical, and outdoor education organizations, the American Cancer Society, and the American Heart Association, Ms. Morava has been honored as Outstanding Secondary Educator of America (1974), and Texas Outstanding Physical Education Public Information Person, American Alliance for Health, Physical Education, Recreation, and Dance (1979).

Edward Anthony Oppenheimer received his M.D. from the Columbia College of Physicians and Surgeons in 1962. He has been Research Fellow in the Respiratory Unit of the Royal Postgraduates Medical School at Hammersmith Hospital in London, and was Pulmonary Fellow in the Department of Medicine at the University of Chicago.

Dr. Oppenheimer served with the U.S. Public Health Services Heart Disease Control Program, Cardiopulmonary Section, in Tucson, Arizona. He is currently chief of the Pulmonary Medicine Section and assistant chief of the Department of Internal Medicine of the Southern California Permanente Medical Group.

Dr. Oppenheimer is assistant clinical professor of medicine at the UCLA Medical School, and serves on the board of directors of the American Lung Association of Los Angeles County. Among many other professional roles in national health organizations, he is consultant to the National Cancer Institute and has had numerous research articles published in the *American Journal of Medicine*, *British Medical Journal*, and the *American Review of Respiratory Diseases.*

Arnold C. Ratner received his M.D. degree from the Albert Einstein College of Medicine in 1959. He has been a Research Fellow in Dermatology at the University of Oregon Medical Center, consultant in Dermatology to the National Institutes of Health, professor of Dermatology at the University of Georgia School of Medicine, and has taught at Johns Hopkins Medical School and Georgetown University Medical school, where he is at present a clinical instructor.

Dr. Ratner served with the U.S. Public Health Service in the National Cancer Institute of the National Institutes of Health. He has had major articles published in the *International Journal of Dermatology, Skin Care International News, The Journal of Applied Physiology,* and *The New England Journal of Medicine.* He has lectured extensively in the area of continuing medicine education.

Howard L. Ward received his D.D.S. degree from the New York University College of Dentistry and his M.A. in higher education from the New York University School of Education. He is assistant dean for Clinical Affairs of the New York University College of Dentistry., and professor of Periodontics at the same institution. Dr. Ward is the former director of Continuing Dental Education and head of the Division of Health Services Management of New York University.

Dr. Ward's fellowships include the New York Academy of Science, the American College of Dentists, the American Association for the Advancement of Science, and the American Public Health Association. Among his many honors received for distinguished professional contributions are the Harry Strusser Award for contributions to public health education, The Samuel Charles Miller Memorial Award in Oral Medicine, and the American Academy of Oral Medicine's Diamond Pin Award for Outstanding Meritorious Service. Dr. Ward is also the author of several professional texts on preventive dental care and clinical periodontics.

Readability of BUILDING BETTER HEALTH

Most youngsters are fascinated by the myriad topics presented in a health education text. However, the technical terminology and the frequency with which new and sometimes complex concepts appear can become barriers to enjoying learning. Therefore, the authors of BUILDING BETTER HEALTH have chosen several means of enhancing the readability of the materials.

Difficult and new terminology is handled in four ways. Each key concept term in a chapter is introduced twice. The initial introduction is made within the vocabulary box at the beginning of the chapter; there the word and its phonetic spelling appear together. The second introduction occurs in a tab at the top of the page where the term is first used in the text. In the text on this page, the term is printed in boldface, defined, and used several times to reinforce recognition. Third, other technical terms that may be difficult or unfamiliar are *italicized* the first time they appear in a chapter. Fourth, most of the italicized and boldfaced terms appear, with complete definitions, in the *Glossary* at the back of each text.

To help students grasp new and complex information and ideas, the authors have also made wide use of photographs, art, suggested activities, and marginal notes. In addition, they have closely controlled the readability level of each text. In applying the Dale-Chall formula, the authors counted boldfaced and italicized terms once per chapter. The resulting overall readability level for this text is upper fifth grade.

Field-testing of BUILDING BETTER HEALTH

The schools listed below have previewed lessons and activities in BUILDING BETTER HEALTH. Students and teachers evaluated the chapters appropriate to their grade levels. Students responded to the various test items (*Early Checkup, What Have You Learned?*, and *Final Checkup*). Teachers responded to an evaluative questionnaire.

Ector County Independent School District
Ector County, Texas
Burleson Elementary School

Sacramento Public Schools
Sacramento, California
Susan B. Anthony Elementary School
Ethel I. Baker Elementary School
John Bidwell Elementary School
Camelia Basic Elementary School
Isador Cohen Elementary School
Elder Creek Elementary School
Golden Empire Elementary School
Thomas Jefferson Elementary School
William Land Elementary School
James W. Marshal Elementary School
Nicholas Elementary School
Sequoia Elementary School
A. M. Winn Elementary School

Professional Articles on Health

Developmental Profile of the Students: The Beginnings of Adolescence

by Arthur Lew

To be meaningful, topics related to health must be presented in ways that are appropriate to students' ages and developmental levels. The authors of *Building Better Health* have made every effort to match content and approach to the level of maturity of the students who will be using the series. Following is a general profile of the developmental stages being experienced by most of the youngsters for whom this book is intended. The profile may help you to fit the material in the text to the special needs of your students.

By about eleven years of age, most youngsters are entering either adolescence or a preparatory phase sometimes referred to as early adolescence or preadolescence. Maturational changes begin to occur in virtually all body systems at about this time. However, there is a fairly wide variation in the timetable of pubescent changes. This variability often occasions intense interest and comparisons by the youngsters involved. The observations and comparisons youngsters make—together with their personal experiences—sometimes result in anxiety about being "ahead" or "behind" in growth and development. In the long run, however, the awareness of changes in themselves leads to satisfaction and pride. The youngster's sense of sexual identity—the feeling of being a boy or girl—will be influenced by observing, experiencing, and comparing maturational changes.

In addition to physical and hormonal changes of early adolescence, changes will occur in the way the youngster feels. This is true, first of all, of physical sensations. The young adolescent becomes capable of experiencing sensations different from and more intense than those of earlier years. It is also true of emotional states, which may seem wholly new because of their quality and strength. An example quite common at this age is the first "crush," often experienced by the young adolescent as something new and different from anything he or she has known before.

Although youngsters entering adolescence undergo the physical and emotional changes just described, the way they react to and manage these changes varies greatly from one to another. A few common kinds of response are described here. Girls are more likely than boys to express openly their interest in the opposite sex. In contrast, boys often go through a period in which they react to the changes of adolescence with a marked and defensive avoidance of girls, even restricting their activities to all-male groups. Youngsters of either sex, who previously were model students, may become so preoccupied with their physical development that they become harder to deal with and less accessible to their teachers. Similarly, patterns of behavioral control established earlier may become destabilized under the influence of intense sensations and emotions.

Some youngsters will attempt to deal with this new phase of life by doing their best to ignore it. Instead of being preoccupied with themselves, these young adolescents channel their attention into intellectual pursuits. The result may be remarkable scholastic or artistic achievement, although perhaps at the cost of social isolation and loneliness.

Regardless of how the adolescent reacts to pubertal changes, this phase of development usually marks the beginning of a new kind of privacy—privacy from parents in particular. The youngster is likely to become modest physically and to show a similar reticence at revealing his or her emotional life. This desire for privacy and independence often conflicts directly with the adolescent's continuing need for parental support, guidance, and love. Frequently, young adolescents cut themselves abruptly off from their parents, only to replace them with a teacher, another adult, or an older adolescent. Such sudden separations are usually painful to children and parents alike, and an oscillating pattern of closeness and separation is not unusual. In order to bolster their attempts to achieve privacy, some adolescents turn their earlier feelings of love and dependency into their opposites, hatred and contempt, as if burning their bridges would ensure a permanent advance.

Cognitive advances also accompany the beginning of adolescence. As Piaget has demonstrated, a qualitative change in the thinking process occurs around this time. Increasingly the adolescent is able to think beyond the restrictions of the concrete. Abstract and hypothetical ideas become manageable, opening the way for new levels of learning, but also giving rise to new kinds of problems. Youngsters who a short time earlier were taking pride in their accomplishments may become troubled by such questions as "What will I become?" "Will anyone love me?" or "Who am I?"

Two new worlds—an inner world of sensation, emotions, and ideas, and an outer world of bodily changes and new social relationships—begin to open up for the individual entering adolescence. It is a time of great change and excitement, but also one of conflict and apprehension. It is hardly surprising that the expression "adolescent turmoil" is as familiar as it is.

Drug Education:

A Preventive Approach

by Betsy Fleming

The widespread use of drugs by young people makes evident the importance of an effective drug program in the schools. While the specific content of such a program will differ according to the age of the students, the major goals should be the same: (1) to build a healthy respect for chemical substances of all kinds; (2) to foster understanding both of the therapeutic value of drugs and of their potential for misuse.

The idea that drugs have a legitimate purpose as health tools but are dangerously inappropriate when used for other purposes should become part of each student's process of discrimination. Thousands of chemical substances are in approved use today to prevent or cure undesirable physical or mental conditions. Students should understand the difference between the proper use of drugs for medical purposes and their abuse for other reasons. Cultivating a respect for the potential good or ill of chemical substances enables the student to establish a positive rather than a negative framework within which to make wise decisions on the use of any drug.

A sound program in drug education provides students with basic knowledge of drugs and their effects, with the specific information presented being appropriate to the age and needs of the class. Students should be encouraged to investigate the reasons that lead people to the abuse of drugs and to explore more healthful behavioral alternatives.

As a teacher preparing to launch a program of drug education, you will find that a working knowledge of the pharmacology of drugs can be acquired without great effort and affords a valuable resource. (The National Institute on Drug Abuse, 5600 Fishers Lane, Rockville, MD 20857, is a valuable source of information.) You may also wish to explore the role that representatives of community health agencies can play in your program. Enlisting this kind of help can bring welcome expertise and variety of presentation to your drug education program.

Besides a general knowledge of drugs and their effects, it is highly desirable that you have an awareness of possible signs of their use or abuse. The following chart indicates certain general behavior characteristics of drug users, as well as some signs of the possible effects of specific substances. It should be remembered, however, that no one of these signs can be considered proof of drug use. The conclusion that a student is using drugs should be based on more facts than the presence of one or more of these signs.

Education about drugs that is carefully planned and effectively presented can become a major force in preventing drug abuse, in upgrading the quality of health instruction, and in improving the life and health of today's young people.

General Behavior

- abrupt change in attendance, quality of work, or attitude
- unusual flare-ups or outbreaks of temper
- deterioration of appearance and grooming
- furtive behavior

Possible Signs of Use of Specific Drugs

Glue

- odor of glue on breath and clothes
- excess nasal secretion; watering eyes
- poor muscular control
- drowsiness
- increased preference for being with a group rather than alone

Stimulants (amphetamines, cocaine, "speed," "ups")

- enlarged pupils
- dryness of mouth and nose
- loss of appetite
- restlessness; nervousness; excitability
- tension and anxiety
- inability to sleep

Depressants (barbiturates, tranquilizers, "downs")

- slurred speech
- staggering or stumbling
- falling asleep unexpectedly
- lack of interest in school or family activities

Narcotics (heroin, morphine)

- lethargy; drowsiness
- constricted pupils
- impaired thinking
- false sense of well-being

Marijuana

- giggling and hilarity (in early stages)
- drowsiness (in later stages)
- enlarged pupils; inflamed whites of eyes
- odor on clothing or breath

Promoting Good Posture

by Marilyn K. Browne

Good posture is such an important aspect of the physical development of young people that you, as a teacher, will want to do all you can to promote it. In addition to making students aware of how much good posture contributes to their health and appearance, you can help them recognize their postural strengths and weaknesses through the exercises featured in the text.

Good standing posture generally has these characteristics:

- head erect
- upper back erect
- abdominal wall flat
- lower back slightly curved forward
- hips level
- kneecaps straight ahead
- feet pointing straight ahead or toeing out slightly

Each of the exercises suggested in the text is mainly intended either to relax and stretch muscles or to contract and tighten them. To keep the body in good alignment, opposing muscle groups must be balanced between strength and flexibility. Stretching exercises maintain flexibility, while strengthening exercises develop muscle tension. Each exercise session should include both kinds of exercise so that the working muscle has an opportunity to relax and maintain its normal flexibility.

The objective of a balanced program of exercises is good posture. If a youngster has a serious posture problem, the program may need to be modified. It is, therefore, important that teachers conducting exercise sessions be able to demonstrate good posture, recognize faulty posture, and modify exercises to fit specific needs.

As you work with posture, you will find your ability to observe characteristics of both good and poor posture increasing. Such observational skill is important, for the sooner a posture problem is recognized, the easier it will be to correct.

Poor posture typically includes one or more of the following characteristics:

- head forward or tilted to one side
- rounded shoulders
- uneven shoulders
- rounded upper back (kyphosis)
- spine curved to one side (scoliosis)
- spine curved forward with protruding abdomen (lordosis)
- uneven hips

In habitual poor posture, the length-tension ratio of opposing muscle groups is unbalanced. It is important, therefore, to emphasize exercises that will counteract the posture fault, and to omit those that will stretch an already weak muscle or strengthen one that is already too tight. Thus, a pupil with a tendency toward lordosis (forward curvature of the spine) should be given exercises to tighten the abdominal wall and stretch out the lower back. An appropriate exercise would be a slow-curl sit-up, with knees bent and arms folded across the chest. Back-extension exercises, such as back bends, should be avoided. Similarly, a student exhibiting kyphosis (rounded upper back) should work on exercises that strengthen the upper back and avoid those—such as toe-touching and recumbent bicycling—that would accentuate the faulty posture.

Serious posture problems, of course, require prompt professional attention. Many schools have scoliosis screening programs for early detection of lateral curvature of the spine. However, children with scoliotic tendencies may exhibit drastic changes in their spinal curve during periods of rapid growth. The sooner scoliosis can be detected, the better the prognosis. For this reason, you should be on the lookout for such telltale signs as uneven hips or shoulders or clothes that hang unevenly. If you notice an abnormal change in posture or a poor posture that is becoming habitual, be sure to notify the student's parents, who should be encouraged to discuss the problem with a physician.

The development of good posture is of lifelong importance to young people. An obvious contributor to good physical health, good posture also plays a major role in the development of a positive self-image. You are in an excellent position to promote good posture and detect possible problems at the time in your students' lives when such attention means the most.

Preventive Dental Care

by Howard L. Ward

Teachers who work with young people in health education programs are in a position to share the overriding responsibility of all dental-health professionals: shifting the dental-health emphasis from treatment, cure, and control to *prevention.*

Signs of Gum Disease and Critical Ages

Unfortunately, gingival and periodontal diseases—generally, diseases of the *gingiva*, or gums, and the underlying tissue—are considered by many to affect older adults only. Symptoms of gingivitis, however, can often be easily detected in people at any age. Normally, the gingival tissue is pale pink in color and holds tightly to the tooth on all sides. With the onset of gingivitis, this pale, pink tissue becomes swollen and inflamed—blood-red in color, softer and looser around the tooth. These changes are due to the dilation of capillaries in the tissue, bringing dramatically greater amounts of blood to the site of the local infection. The tissue becomes engorged with blood. This condition is called *hyperemia.*

Diseased gingiva then become enlarged. The surface of the gum appears shiny, wet, and tense. Papillae—those small, pointed peaks of gum tissue between the teeth—may swell and become red-colored nodules that stand out more prominently.

Prompt treatment of gingivitis by a dentist or periodontist is of special importance in preventing premature degeneration of the tissues, severe dental problems, and unnecessary tooth loss in later years.

The age of highest risk and severity in children seems to differ between the sexes. Among girls, the peak age of severity usually occurs at around ten-and-one-half years. For boys, the severity peak most often occurs between twelve- and thirteen-and-one-half years. In the adolescent years the severity of gingivitis declines rapidly, and beyond the age of sixteen, remains pretty much level.

Gingival and periodontal diseases begin when the primary teeth of many very young children are appearing. Yet it is in early childhood that the mouth is best constructed for vigorous function. Throughout the remaining growth and development of childhood, the jaws will change dramatically. Between the ages of five and twelve, 20 primary teeth are shed and 24 permanent teeth appear. The process by which teeth have cut through a child's gums does little damage to healthy, young gum tissue. The wound produced by the eruption of each primary tooth heals in a matter of hours and rarely becomes infected.

From this point forward, however, regular daily care of teeth and gums becomes central to children's future dental health. Equally crucial is the responsiveness of families and teachers to early signs of gingival disease in children, and the establishment of regular professional examinations for every young person.

How Can Teachers and Families Help?

Preventive dentistry, if it is to be effective, must be a *system* for sharing health responsibilities among dentists, their personnel, health teachers, patients, and their families. It must be seen as a cooperative venture at all levels:

1. *Prepathogenic level:* Teaching young people and their families the health value of eating a wide variety of well-balanced, nutritious foods; regular fluoride brushing and flossing techniques to prevent plaque accumulation; and early correction of defects in tooth occlusion.
2. *Early recognition and treatment level:* Teaching young people and their families the need to watch for signs of disease and to report any symptoms during regular dental examinations, and early treatment of diseases.
3. *Advanced recognition and treatment level:* Teaching young people that loss of teeth and painful oral diseases can only be prevented by proper dental treatment.

Parents, teachers, and children can learn to share a variety of responsibilities for building and maintaining the health of teeth and surrounding tissues. These responsibilities begin with the families and teachers of very young children who can learn—and look for—the early warning signs of gingivitis. As children grow toward adolescence, they should be encouraged to accept greater responsibility for detecting these signs on their own. Most importantly children must learn that preventive daily tooth and gum care can reduce the risk of future mouth disease more than any understanding of symptoms on their part, and more than any treatment they can receive from dentists.

Above all, families must, by example, demonstrate the importance of home dental care; of nutritionally balanced, thoughtful food planning; and of regular dental checkups every year.

CHAPTER NOTES

CHAPTER 1 YOUR EMOTIONS AFFECT YOUR HEALTH

Chapter Overview

This opening chapter explores with the students ways in which emotions, personal relationships, and stress affect a person's overall health. The first section develops the concept of total health—physical, mental, and emotional—and examines the needs that are common to all people. The second section covers the development of individual personality traits and their importance in forming, building, and maintaining personal relationships. The concluding section introduces some of the ways stress may affect health and suggests ways of coping with stress. It emphasizes the importance of acknowledging and understanding one's emotions as an avenue for controlling stress.

Objectives

After completing this chapter, students should be able to

- identify certain emotional needs common to all people.*
- describe the importance of communication in human relationships.*
- enumerate ways of building trust, dependability, and other personal qualities.*
- suggest appropriate ways of handling anger, fear, and disappointments that can cause stress.*

Suggested Activities and Discussions

Chapter Opener (pp. 10–11).
Most students have some experience with being an "outsider" and should be able to empathize with Eddie. You might point out that anger is only one of many possible ways people try to cover up feelings of loneliness and insecurity. Encourage students to suggest other ways in which young people may try to hide insecurity. Being a smart aleck, showing off, appearing aloof, and putting down other people are a few they may mention. Help students recognize that often such attitudes do little to help young people handle their uncomfortable feelings or gain acceptance.

Ask students how someone can make a newcomer feel welcome. (Introduce yourself to the person. Invite the person to a party, or to join in a project or game. Ask the newcomer about his or her old home. Introduce him or her to your friends.)

Ask students what they would do to make friends in a new place. (Introduce yourself and say you are new. Sit with a group during lunch and talk with them. Participate in after-school activities. Ask someone to tell you what is interesting about your new neighborhood. Join local clubs that have members your age.)

Looking Ahead (p. 12).
Before students go further in this chapter, have them locate the glossary in the back of the book and use the pronunciation key to determine how each term is pronounced.

Early Checkup (p. 13).
After students have completed this checkup, you may find it helpful to review the answers to determine which portions of the chapter may require particular emphasis.

THINKING ABOUT TOTAL HEALTH (pp. 14–19).

Good Health Is Balanced Health (pp. 14–15).
Call attention to the words in the box on page 14. Explain that a box like this is on each text page where new vocabulary words are introduced. If students have not done so previously, have them look up the words in the glossary and discuss their meanings.

*These objectives are stated in age-appropriate terms on page 12 of the student text.

The text and photos on pages 14 and 15 introduce three dimensions of health and some of the numerous ways in which they interact to affect one's total health. You may wish to diagram the dimensions on the chalkboard to illustrate their interrelatedness. Three interlocking circles, each one representing one of the three dimensions, can represent the relationships.

You might recall Eddie as a focus for the class's discussion of balanced health. Point out that even though Eddie was worried about being short, his physical health was good. His interest in making new friends attests to his social health. However, because of his memories and feelings, Eddie's level of emotional health was temporarily reduced. His total health, therefore, was a little off balance. When Eddie realized this, he was then able to think about his emotions, to determine quickly that they were not appropriate in this new situation, and to take action. Unless he was rejected by the group, his action probably led to improved emotional health.

You may want to ask the class what Eddie might do to keep all parts of his health in balance if he was rejected by this group. (Look for other new friends and for activities, clubs, or groups that draw people together on the basis of interests and skills that can be shared.)

On the chalkboard, write "A stranger is a friend you haven't met yet." Encourage students to discuss ways in which a whole group can benefit by welcoming new members.

People Have Emotional Needs (pp. 16–17).
You might suggest to students that just as a balance of rest and exercise is essential to physical health, a balance of social activity and solitude is important to emotional health. Time alone is important for evaluating our needs and behavior, for setting goals and planning ways of achieving them, and for simply relaxing and resting our minds and emotions.

On Your Own (p. 17).
After they have completed their individual descriptions of themselves, students might enjoy writing a description nominating a Man or Woman of the Year. The person they choose might be a historical figure, a person who at present is nationally or internationally known, a character from a book or play, or someone from their own families or community. The nominations should specifically state the qualities that make the person worthy of the nomination.

Your Decisions Can Affect Your Health (pp. 18–19).
In the course of the discussion, try to elicit the idea that students should be patient with themselves when they are learning new skills. Everyone has different natural abilities. What may come quite easily to one person may require significantly more time, effort, and practice for another.

Students may discuss some specific situations in which going along with the group is an unwise decision. Encourage them to suggest as well some appropriate ways of expressing their disapproval, without attacking or "putting down" others.

What Have You Learned? (p. 19).

Each section of each chapter concludes with a short fill-in quiz reviewing the contents of the section. Students should review the text for any material they may have difficulty answering.

YOU AND OTHERS (pp. 20–27).

Families and Friends Try To Understand (pp. 20–21).
Students might share their ideas about ways of making and keeping friends. After discussing their ideas, they might collaborate in small groups on posters illustrating what friendship means to them.

Families and Friends Share Feelings (pp. 22–23).
Students might enjoy experimenting with the ways in which tone of voice can affect communication. Write on the board a perfectly neutral statement such as "This is my report." Ask students to change the meaning of the communication by using their voices to express the following feelings: happiness, sadness, anger, fear, surprise, disbelief.

You might elicit the notion that in family relationships and friendships alike, a balance between communication and respect for another's privacy can be of great importance. Students themselves will have had the experience of not wanting to talk about a problem at some time or another, and will understand that they should not press another to do so. Have them suggest ways of showing support and caring for a troubled relative or friend without invading that person's privacy. (Helping with chores, offering to do a favor for a friend, lending a book or record, or sending a note are some possibilities.)

People Try To Build Their Personal Qualities (pp. 24–27).
Many of the things we call "good manners" are really signs of respect for others. Saying "please," "thank you," or "excuse me," rising when an older person comes into a room, and using the titles *Mr., Mrs., Ms.,* and *Miss* for adults are all conventions that have their roots in expressing respect for another person. Encourage students to suggest other practices that show respect and consideration.

The ability to keep a confidence is an important, and sometimes awkward, element of trust. It is a demonstration of loyalty that is important to everyone, and seems to be especially important to young people. Encourage students to discuss their feelings about this aspect of trust and when and if a confidence may ever justifiably be violated.

STRESS AND YOUR EMOTIONS (pp. 28–34).

How Can Stress Affect You? (pp. 28–29).
If you have students list stressful situations as suggested in the annotation on page 28, you might also ask them to try to think of healthful ways to handle the stress. The stress related to leaving friends and moving to a new place, for example, may be reduced by planning decorations for a new bedroom, investigating the recreational facilities of the new community, finding ways to make new friends, and the like.

Throughout the discussions, *discourage* the idea of using activities as a way of escaping one's true emotions. *Reinforce* the importance of first acknowledging the emotions and then finding constructive outlets for them.

People Learn To Handle Stress (pp. 30–31).
Although a wide range of activities can be useful in reducing and handling stress, those involving other people are perhaps the most beneficial. Solitary activities often serve to reinforce stress by affording people too much time to dwell on their problems. Activities such as volunteer work or tutoring, by contrast, not only channel excess energy and take the person outside his or her own problems, but also enhance a person's feelings of self-worth.

In discussing this material, do not overlook the role that older friends can play in helping to relieve stress and solve problems. A sympathetic teacher, a religious leader, a scout leader or sports coach, or an older relative can often prove to be a good sounding-board and a valuable source of constructive suggestions for solving problems.

Understanding Your Emotions Helps Control Stress (pp. 32–34).
Be sure students understand the difference between stressful conditions that they can change and those that they cannot. Stress over an upcoming test, for example, can be controlled by thorough preparation, including extra help, if needed, and by getting adequate rest the night before. The unemployment or serious illness of a family member, on the other hand, is beyond the student's control. Suggest that when students feel stress, they take extra pains to pace themselves appropriately: take frequent breaks for reading, exercise, or conversation; and allow themselves occasional treats to boost their morale—such as having a special snack, going to a movie, or buying a record they have been wanting.

Anger is one of the stress-inducing emotions that can often be successfully handled by talking about it. You might caution, however, that if the angry person is to feel better, the discussion of his or her feelings should be reasonable and controlled so as not to be hurtful to the other person who is involved. (Saying hurtful things in the heat of anger often only compounds stress by adding guilt feelings to the existing emotions.) Point out that it is frequently better to wait before discussing one's angry feelings until one has calmed down, or to "let off steam" through exercise or talking about the situation with an uninvolved party.

People Working for Your Health (p. 33).
Invite students who have had experience with scouting to share with the class. Guide the discussion to emphasize the learning experiences and service activities of scouting rather than the purely social aspects. Interested students might learn about the origin of the Boy Scouts and Girl Scouts and report to the class on the founders and the goals they had in mind for scouting.

Learn More About It (p. 35).
In addition to the titles listed in the text, you can recommend the following books to your students:

Adams, Barbara. *Like It Is: Facts and Feelings About Handicaps From Kids Who Know.* New York: Walker & Company, 1979. Disabled youngsters talk about what it is like to have a handicap and how youngsters with handicaps would like to be treated by others.

Bernstein, Joanne E., and Gullo, Stephen V. *When People Die.* New York: E.P. Dutton, Inc. 1977. Explains the reasons for death, old age, grief, and the naturalness of death in the chain of life. Many beautiful photos of people, young and old.

Naylor, Phyllis Reynolds. *Getting Along With Your Family.* Nashville, Tenn.: Abingdon Press, 1976. This book deals with personal involvement, problems, feelings, privacy, love, and more.

Stolz, Mary Slattery. *The Bully of Barkham Street.* New York: Harper & Row, Publishers, Inc., 1963. Something happens to change a tough neighborhood bully with a secret desire to be liked.

Thomas, Marlo, et al. *Free To Be You and Me.* New York: McGraw-Hill Book Company, 1975. A book of stories, songs, and adventures about feelings, people, and meeting new people.

Wilder, Laura Ingalls. *Little House in the Big Woods.* New York: Harper & Row, Publishers Inc., 1932. One in a series of books about a log-cabin family in Wisconsin in the 1800's; others include *Little House on the Prairie* and *On the Banks of Plum Creek.*

For your own reading, you may be interested in the following books:

Beauchamp, Tom L., and Perlin, Seymour, eds. *Ethical Issues in Death and Dying.* Englewood Cliffs, N.J.: Prentice-Hall, Inc., 1978. The issues of dying, suicide, life, and death are considered by many famous writers.

Newton, David E. *Understanding Mental Illness.* Portland, Maine: J. Weston Walch, Publisher, 1979. This book discusses different kinds of mental illnesses, their causes, how they are dealt with, and how studying mental illnesses has increased understanding about the mind in general.

Scott, Gwendolyn, and Carlo, Mona. *Learning—Feeling—Doing: Designing Creative Learning Experiences for Elementary Health Education.* Englewood Cliffs, N.J.: Prentice-Hall, Inc., 1978. This book contains suggestions for teaching social, mental, and physical health. Various areas are looked at in terms of these three dimensions.

If time permits, you may wish to use one or more of the following audiovisual materials with this chapter:

Developing Self-Discipline. Boulder, Colo.: Learning Tree Filmstrips, 1981. 4 filmstrips, 4 cassettes, and guide. Self-discipline as a means of accomplishing goals is examined.

Family Life Around the World. Chicago, Ill.: Coronet Films, 1980. 40 study prints. These color photographs show the daily lives of 40 families around the world.

Understanding Your Feelings. Boulder, Colo.: Learning Tree Filmstrips, 1981. 4 filmstrips, 2 cassettes, and guide. Emotions and how to deal with them are explained.

More To Do on Your Own (p. 35).
Like the "On Your Own" activities, these are intended for the students to do independently as desired. Some students may want to do several such projects in each chapter; others may select only a few in the book. Student involvement will depend on a student's ability, your preference, and time constraints.

Final Checkup (pp. 36–37).
Each chapter ends with two tests, usually in the form of ten multiple-choice and ten true-false questions. Answers are shown on the student's page *only* in this *Teacher's Edition.*

Write About Better Health (p. 37).
The short-answer questions that conclude each chapter allow students somewhat greater latitude in expressing their grasp of the chapter's content. Although there is room for creativity and individual expression, students' answers to the questions on page 37 should reflect an understanding of the following concepts:

1. All people share the needs to do something well, to have friends, and to give and receive love.
2. Communication helps people to know and learn more about each other and themselves, to share feelings and ideas, and to clear up misunderstandings.
3. Some ways of showing responsibility are doing homework completely and on time, helping with household chores, being on time for appointments, being loyal to friends, and taking care of one's own and others' belongings.
4. Some ways of dealing with anger include working off anger through physical activity, taking time out to "cool down" if necessary, and talking about one's feelings.
5. People can help themselves deal with disappointments by accepting blame for their mistakes, thinking about their good qualities, trying to learn from their mistakes, and avoiding comparing themselves to others.

CHAPTER 2
PEOPLE GROW...
PEOPLE CHANGE

Chapter Overview

In this chapter, students explore the processes of growth, development, and aging and the various factors that influence them. Although the material examines the influences of heredity and environment, it emphasizes the importance of personal choices in ensuring maximum growth potential and life expectancy.

Objectives

After completing this chapter, students should be able to

- specify times of life when growth spurts typically occur.*
- state ways in which they can help promote their own physical, mental, and personality development.*
- describe how to maximize the body's growth plan.*
- describe some changes that occur in the body during aging.*

Suggested Activities and Discussions

Chapter Opener (pp. 38–39).
Using the photo essay and the suggestions in the accompanying annotations, have students make a chart listing characteristics of each age. Changes for each stage of life may be listed under the headings *Physical Development* and *Mental/Social Development.* Have the students save their charts so that they can be taken out for reference during the chapter discussions.

Looking Ahead (p. 40).
Encourage students to discuss the ideas they have about the aspects of growth and development listed in the objectives.

*These objectives are stated in age-appropriate terms on page 40 of the student text.

YOUR BODY'S GROWTH (pp. 42–49).

Everyone Grows at a Different Rate (pp. 42–43).
Generally people today are taller and have larger frames than people of centuries past. Assign some students to research average heights over the last two or three hundred years and chart them at fifty-year intervals. In discussion of the resulting charts, encourage students to speculate on the possible reasons for increased height and size. (Better nutrition and improved general health care are two possible contributing factors.)

Body Parts Grow at Different Rates (pp. 44–45).
Emphasize the control that students *do* have over their own health as their bodies grow. When the body gains a few pounds before or during a growth spurt, the student can control overall weight gain by maintaining a balanced diet. A person who develops poor eating habits during a growth period is less likely to return to a desired weight after the spurt is over. Many kinds of exercise can help a person overcome clumsiness. Rest is especially important for someone who is growing very fast. Scientists have found that most of the growth hormone is secreted during sleep.

Bodies Grow Because Cells Divide (pp. 46–47).
After completing this section, students should be able to identify these parts of a cell: cell membrane, cytoplasm, and nucleus.

What Controls Your Growth? (p. 48).
Note that the description of the endocrine glands omits the testes and ovaries, although the effects of hormones from these reproductive glands are touched upon in the text. Any discussion of sexual changes occurring at puberty and beyond should be at the option of the teacher and within the instructional guidelines and policies of your local school district.

Your students may know that insulin is connected with diabetes and with sugar in some way. Students will learn more about *diabetes* (the general name for several related diseases) in Chapter 7.

People Working for Your Health (p. 49).
Interested students may want to learn more about some of the specific disorders of the glands and present methods of treating them.

HEREDITY, ENVIRONMENT, AND BEHAVIOR INFLUENCE GROWTH (pp. 50–55).

How Did You Get To Be *You*? (pp. 50–51).
Much of what is known about how people are influenced by the environment and by their own behavior was learned through studying twins. Because identical twins have the same heredity, studies of identical twins who have been reared apart have been very important in determining the influence of heredity, environment, and behavior on people.

How Does Heredity Work? (pp. 52–53).
After reading about dominant and recessive genes in the Discovery story, interested students may wish to research and develop a list of other traits known to be dominant or recessive. Some possibilities include straight and curly hair, left- and right-handedness, skin color, and eye color.

Discovery—A New Pathway to Health (p. 52).
Interested students might be asked to learn more about Mendel and his work and share their findings with the class.

Is Heredity All That Matters? (pp. 54).
Human heredity is very complicated. As a result, it is often presented with many oversimplifications that cause misunderstandings. Emphasize that while certain traits are inherited, the person's environment may not give him or her the chance to use or express the trait.

For example, traits for intelligence and the ability to learn quickly may be inhibited and never noticed in people economically or culturally deprived of the opportunity or motivation to go to school. They may never be exposed to problems and situations that sufficiently challenge their intellect. Therefore, the environment and opportunity to express traits are often as important as heredity. Not all traits need be inherited; some may appear later in life. An example would be a person who develops a limp as a result of a war wound or other injury.

Some students may be interested in learning more about hereditary diseases.

HOW DOES THE BODY AGE? (pp. 56–58).

What Is Aging? (pp. 56–57).
Certain aspects of aging seem to be hereditary. Interested students might find out whether graying hair and wrinkling are inherited traits, the result of physical changes, or a combination of both.

Can People Help Themselves Live Longer and Age More Slowly? (p. 58).
Students are often confused by life expectancy. For example, it is not immediately obvious why, as you get older, your life expectancy should increase. Explain that a person who has already lived to be forty-five has a better chance of living to be seventy-five than a person who has just been born.

Similarly, the concept of average length of life can be confusing. A numerical example may help. If the age at death of five persons is five, fifteen, forty-five, seventy-five, and eighty-five, then the average age would be forty-five. In general, you would expect of a population with a life expectancy of forty-five that more than half the persons in the population would live to be older than forty-five. In the United States today, more than a quarter of the population that is in sixth grade now can expect to live to be older than eighty-five.

Learn More About It (p. 59).
In addition to the titles listed in the text, you can recommend the following books to your students:

Brindze, Ruth. *Look How Many People Wear Glasses.* New York: Atheneum Publishers, 1975. This book presents the history of eyeglasses, along with information about how glasses are made, how eyes are examined, how eyes work, and how eyes should be cared for.

Cobb, Vicki. *How To Really Fool Yourself—Illusions For All Your Senses.* Philadelphia: J.B. Lippincott Company, 1981. The text and illustrations show how the senses work and how they can be fooled.

Sobol, Donald. *Encyclopedia Brown's Record Book of Weird and Wonderful Facts.* New York: Delacorte Press, 1979. A fascinating collection of miscellaneous, lesser-known information about the human body and physical feats and records.

For your own reading, you may be interested in the following books:

Dunbar, Robert E. *Heredity.* New York: Franklin Watts, Inc., 1978. The author describes the research of Mendel, Darwin, and others; clearly explains DNA and hereditary structures within cells, and discusses the relationship of heredity and environment.

Fincher, Jack. *The Human Body: The Brain.* Washington, D.C.: U.S. News Books, 1981. A clear and fascinating description of the brain—its physical structures, the organization and interrelatedness of its parts, and the functions it performs.

Fries, James F. and Crapo, Lawrence, M. *Vitality and Aging.* San Francisco: W. H. Freeman and Co., 1981. A study on aging—the reasons for it, ideas about it, attitudes toward it in our culture.

Kuhne, Paul, M.D. *Home Medical Encyclopedia.* New York: Fawcett Books Group, 1980. This guide offers much information that will help readers understand and care for their bodies.

Wertenbaker, Lael. *The Human Body: The Eyes.* Washington, D.C.: U.S. News Books, 1981. Content includes such subjects as the anatomy of the eye, mechanics of vision, color, optical illusion, and eye safety.

If time permits, you may wish to use one or more of the following audiovisual materials with this chapter:

For the Sake of Your Heart. Pleasantville, N.Y.: Sunburst Communications, 1980. 3 color filmstrips, 3 record/cassettes, guide. Structure, function, problems, and diseases of the heart are explored.

Mechanics of Life: Blood and Circulation. Santa Monica, Calif.: BFA Educational Media, 1981. Color film. The composition of blood and the function of each part of the blood are explained.

The Human Body. Pleasantville, N.Y.: Imperial Educational Resources, Inc., 1981. 12 transparencies. The structure and function of various systems are presented.

Write About Better Health (p. 61).
Although students' answers will vary in length and detail, they should demonstrate an understanding of the following content:

1. A balanced diet, exercise, and adequate rest are important at all times, but especially during a growth spurt.
2. During the growing years, the pituitary gland produces large amounts of growth hormone, which is carried by the blood to body cells. The hormone seems to direct the cells to divide, so that one cell becomes two, two become four, and so on.
3. A well-balanced diet, adequate rest, regular exercise, friendships, interests, and activities can help students make the most of inherited traits. However, students can do little to actually change such traits as skin and eye color, or height.
4. After the body stops growing, the changes that are part of aging include loss of brain cells and reduction of brain size, less ability to take air into the lungs, loss of calcium from the bones, loss of ability to tell patterns of light and dark, and skin wrinkling.
5. The ways in which the average length of life has been increased include vaccinations (which have eliminated formerly fatal diseases), improved sanitation, better diet, fewer smokers, better health care, the discovery of antibiotics, and other life-saving medical discoveries (not mentioned in the chapter).

CHAPTER 3
YOUR AMAZING BODY

Chapter Overview

In this chapter, students are introduced to the organizational pattern of the human body—cells grouped together to form tissues, tissues grouped together to form organs, organs functioning together as systems, and systems interacting with and controlling each other. Next, they are given a detailed look at the structure and functions of the circulatory system, the respiratory system, and the nervous system. As students learn about the organs that make up the systems and how they function together, they also discover what kinds of measures responsible people can take to maintain the health of these important body systems.

Objectives

After completing this chapter, students should be able to

- describe how organs work together in the circulatory, respiratory, and nervous systems.*
- state ways of providing body systems with the fuel and energy they need for health, growth, strength, and repair.*
- describe the role of the senses in maintaining the health of body systems.*

Suggested Activities and Discussions

Chapter Opener (pp. 62–63).
Students may or may not be able to name the body parts described on this page. They should be more familiar with the function and location of each of these organs after reading this chapter. The following organs are described:

(a) brain	(g) heart
(b) nerves	(h) arteries
(c) ear	(i) veins
(d) eye	(j) capillaries
(e) nose	(k) muscles
(f) stomach	(l) lungs

Looking Ahead (p. 64).
You might provide a more in-depth preview of the content by naming the three systems the chapter will focus on and defining in broad terms the function of each. The circulatory system controls the flow of blood throughout the body. The respiratory system controls breathing. The nervous system controls thinking, movement, and other body functions. Write the names of the three systems on the board, and have the students turn back to the diagram of the body on page 62. Invite them to make educated guesses about which body parts might belong to the nervous system (a through e), the respiratory system (l), and the circulatory system (g through j).

FROM CELLS TO SYSTEMS (pp. 66–71).

Healthy Cells Build Healthy Tissues (pp. 66–67).
All the cells in a human body are very small. The largest cells, barely visible without the aid of a microscope, are egg cells in the ovaries of females. Although some nerve cells may be more than three feet long, they are too slender to be seen individually without a microscope.

If a microscope is available, have students examine prepared slides of blood tissue and cells. (Note that red blood cells have no nucleus.)

Discuss with students the importance of a balanced diet to the maintenance and growth of healthy cells. Different kinds of cells require different combinations of nutrients in order to function efficiently. If a balanced diet is not maintained, one

---

*These objectives are stated in age-appropriate terms on page 64 of the student text.

or more types of cells are likely to be less healthy. (Nutrition is treated in greater depth in Chapter 5.) Emphasize that body tissues work together in a healthy body. For example, tissue that forms the eye and other sense organs would be of no value if it were not working with healthy nerve, brain, and blood tissues. The heart and lungs are made up of muscle and other tissues working with blood tissue, and so on.

Organs Work Together as Systems (pp. 68–69). Have students look for veins in their hands or along the inside of their elbows. Veins look blue because the blood moving through them does not contain as much oxygen as the blood in arteries. (Oxygen helps give red blood cells their color.)

Students should be able to find the pulse in their wrists. It is usually easier, however, to find the pulse in the large artery in the neck below and in front of the angles in the jaw. Be sure students understand the difference between pulse and blood pressure. With respect to the latter, ask students why they think blood keeps moving in the same direction, even when it must move against gravity, as in the legs and feet. (The force of blood pressure and a series of flaps, or valves, in the veins that hold back the blood between heartbeats keep blood moving properly.)

If students have trouble remembering the direction in which blood flows through the arteries and veins, point out that *artery* and *away* both begin with the letter *a*; arteries carry blood away from the heart.

Assign interested volunteers to research some of the surgical procedures developed to repair damage to the circulatory system. Their topics might include implanting artificial valves, artificial pacemakers, and coronary bypass surgery. Have the students share with the class the ways in which these procedures offer a second chance at life to people who have disorders that were once fatal.

Organ Systems Work Together (pp. 70–71). Call for volunteers to collect more information about emphysema and other respiratory disorders such as asthma, pneumonia, chronic bronchitis, and black-lung disease. Ask them to report their findings to the class. Reports should include information about the causes, symptoms, and treatment of each disorder, as well as the specific effects each has on the respiratory and other body systems.

Initiate a discussion of other ways in which body systems work together to protect vital organs. For example, the skeleton is more than a framework. The eye socket in the skull is designed to protect the eye and optic nerve from blows. The skull also completely encloses and protects the brain. The heart and lungs, too, are protected by a skeletal structure, the rib cage. In general, the more critical the organ to life, the tougher the protective covering.

WHAT MAKES BODY SYSTEMS WORK? (pp. 72–76).

Some Systems Are Automatic (p. 72). Have the students list some observable involuntary responses such as blinking, swallowing, ducking an approaching object, and the like. Point out that even though these actions can be controlled to some extent, they usually occur automatically.

The Nervous System Controls the Body (pp. 72–73). The spinal cord sometimes directs actions *before* informing the brain what it is doing. These actions are called *reflexes.* If you touch a hot stove, for example, your muscles will pull your hand away even before you realize what you have done. When the signal for "touching hot stove" reaches the spinal cord, it sends the signal for "move hand" on its own. Since signals do not travel very quickly through the nerves, this shorter route from hand to spinal cord and back gets your hand out of danger faster than if the signal had traveled from hand to brain and back.

Despite the fact that nerve tissues do not regenerate, today doctors are able to reconnect through microsurgery some nerves that have been cut. For example, if someone loses a finger in an accident, there is a fair chance that it can be made to work again by sewing the blood vessels and muscles together and by reconnecting the nerves. In such accidents, people should know that time and the protection of the severed part are extremely important. The severed part should be preserved in ice, and both the injured person and the severed part should be rushed to the hospital.

The Nervous System Links You to the World (pp. 74–75). During class discussion of these pages you may wish to encourage students to share their knowledge of (1) health practices that promote the health of sense organs and (2) ways in which healthy organs help people to protect or improve their total health. Have someone record the information and ideas that are presented. Then, if time permits, have small groups of students work together to develop a chart, graph, or diagram that clearly shows the interrelatedness of health practices, healthy sensory organs, and total health.

You Have Health Responsibilities (p. 76).
You might mention to students that rest is important for replacement of damaged cells as well as for cell growth.

Ask students to suggest what they can do to protect their bodies besides the recommendations in the first paragraph on page 76. Possibilities include dressing properly, protecting the skin from sun, wearing shoes that fit properly, and using safety belts.

On Your Own (p. 76).
Before students begin the activity, explore with them the five senses they are already fimiliar with. You might enlist your librarian's assistance in locating some books that show optical illusions and some recordings of sound effects, and see how many items students can identify. Then, with students blindfolded, have them identify by taste and/or smell such foods and spices as lemon, licorice, onion, peanut butter, a strong cheese, and the like. Have students identify by touch such common items as a pine cone, moss, a pear, marbles, and a damp sponge. The exercise should be done with students blindfolded or with eyes closed.

Learn More About It (p. 77). In addition to the titles listed in the text, you can recommend the following books to your students:

Brown, Paula S. *The Incredible Body Machine.* New York: Random House/Children's Television Workshop, 1981. All about the body—various organs, tissues, functions, and so forth. Includes many diagrams, pictures, and cut-outs.

Elgin, Kathleen. *The Heart.* New York: Franklin Watts, Inc., 1982. The function of the heart is explained in this book.

For your own reading, you may be interested in the following books:

Davis, Goode P., Jr., and Park, Edwards. *The Heart: The Living Pump.* Washington, D.C.: U.S. News Books, 1981. This book examines the structure, function, disorders, health, and repair of the heart.

Fincher, Jack. *The Brain: Mystery of Matter and Mind.* Washington D.C.: U.S. News Books, 1981. Many aspects of the brain are discussed in this book.

If time permits, you may wish to use one or more of the following audiovisual materials with this chapter:

Everybody's Skin Makes Everybody Kin. Northbrook, Ill.: Hubbard Scientific Co., 1982. 3 color filmstrips, 3 cassettes, and 3 guides. Information about the skin and its care are presented.

Person Power: The Value of Personal Hygiene. Pleasantville, N.Y.: Imperial Educational Resources, Inc., 1981. LP/cassette and filmstrip. The necessity of good personal hygiene is examined in relation to overall health and personal relationships.

Posture: Thinking Tall. Santa Monica, Calif.: BFA Educational Media, 1981. Color film. The importance of good posture is examined.

Write About Better Health (p. 79).
Despite individual differences, the students' answers should reflect an understanding of the following material:

1. Your body depends on you to provide it with the foods it needs in order to function. You must also decide how much rest and exercise to provide in order to help your body grow and develop properly.
2. Most of the nutrients from food are in a form the body cells can use by the time the food is in the small intestine. The nutrients move into the blood through capillaries in the small intestine. The blood picks up oxygen from the air sacs in the lungs.
3. The circulatory and respiratory systems work together to supply all of the cells of the body with oxygen. The respiratory system supplies oxygen through breathing (lungs). The oxygen moves into capillaries in exchange for gaseous cell wastes.
4. Ways of preventing disease of the circulatory system include avoiding overweight; keeping salt, sugar, and fat to a minimum; not smoking; and exercising regularly.
5. The sense organs are special parts of the nervous system. When nerve endings within the sense organs (the eyes, ears, nose, tongue, and skin) are stimulated by, for example, chemicals, sound or light waves, pressure, and rises and falls in temperature, responses occur within the nerves. These responses create signals that are carried to the spinal cord and brain, warning the body of outside threats and changes such as heat, cold, and other phenomena.

CHAPTER 4
WORKING FOR YOUR OWN HEALTH

Chapter Overview

In Chapter 3 students learned more about why people need to assume responsibility for keeping their body systems healthy. In this chapter, students examine specific measures that people can take to achieve that end. The first section of the chapter describes in detail four aspects of health maintenance: diet, rest, exercise, and hygiene. The second section emphasizes the importance of planning for good health by organizing a health routine and regimen and by having regular checkups as a preventive measure. The last section discusses dental hygiene and the importance of dental health to the health of the entire body. As the chapter title suggests, the emphasis throughout is on students' own responsibility for health planning.

Objectives

After completing this chapter, students should be able to

- list sleep, nutrition, exercise, and hygiene as the four basic steps to good health.*
- describe ways of keeping the body in better health.*
- develop and follow a personal health-care plan.†
- state the importance of regular medical checkups.*
- identify and describe appropriate procedures for care of teeth and gums.*

*These objectives are stated in age-appropriate terms on page 82 of the student text.

†Although this objective is the desired outcome of the entire chapter, it is one you will not be able to assess in measurable terms.

Suggested Activities and Discussions

Chapter Opener (pp. 80–81).
List on the board students' suggestions for exercise activities they find particularly enjoyable. Point out that *exercise* is not limited to sports and calisthenics. Exercise also includes driving a bike, gardening, walking or hiking, and many activities that students are involved in without thinking in terms of exercise. Discuss with the class the importance of selecting exercise-related activities that are enjoyable to them. A form of exercise that is tedious and unappealing is usually quickly eliminated from a person's health plan.

Point out to students that both Samantha and her grandfather stop swimming when they feel they are getting tired. Discuss with the class how the body signals its own limitations. People build up to vigorous exercise gradually, they prepare their bodies for exercise with warm-ups, and they respond to signs of tiring by cool-downs and resting.

Looking Ahead (p. 82).
Ask the class to list other people they can think of who help them with health care and who can answer questions they have about their health. You might have them begin a list of health-related services offered in your community.

In previewing the objectives with the class, guide the discussion to find out what ideas students already have about what they can do to promote better health.

SOME STEPS TO BETTER HEALTH (pp. 84–97).

Being Well Is a Good Feeling (pp. 84–85).
In discussion of these pages, reinforce the idea that how a person *feels* is a strong hint of how well the person is. Students should begin to grasp the principle of being in tune with their own bodies

and taking its suggestions for when to rest, eat, exercise, and the like. Also reinforce the concept that people who take responsibility for building and maintaining their health stand a far better chance of staying healthy than those who neglect the needs of their bodies and take unnecessary risks.

What Happens When You Sleep (pp. 86–88).
Remind students that most cell growth and replacement occurs during sleep. This fact explains the importance of getting plenty of sleep—extra sleep, in fact, during an illness, even a minor illness such as a cold.

Students might enjoy exploring the theory held by some scientists that we sleep because we need the *dreams*, not because we need rest. This theory holds that dreams are a way the brain processes recent events, although events may appear in dreams in somewhat distorted forms.

Discovery—A New Pathway to Health (p. 89).
In addition to insomnia and apnea, mentioned in the teacher's annotation, *narcolepsy* is a serious sleep disorder affecting some people. It is characterized by sudden and uncontrollable attacks of deep sleep. Students may be assigned to investigate these three sleep disorders, what is known about them, and what measures can be taken to try to correct them. Encourage students to share their research with the class.

How Can Staying Healthy Help You Look Your Best? (p. 90).
Skin care takes on increasing importance as youngsters enter adolescence and their glands become more active. Blackheads and some kinds of pimples are caused by clogged oil glands. Careful cleansing can minimize such clogging. Keeping one's hair clean contributes to one's overall appearance and also reduces the possibility of oil and dirt clogging pores on the forehead and cheeks. Clean, trim fingernails both improve appearance and reduce the risk of spreading germs from dirt trapped under the nails.

Diet, rest, and exercise also contribute to good appearance since they affect the general health of all body cells. Healthy cells result in better skin color and tone, healthier-looking hair, and brightness of the eyes—all of which make people look more wholesome.

What Is Healthful Eating? (p. 91).
Well-balanced diets are discussed in greater detail in Chapter 5. The photograph on this page is intended to be a springboard for class discussion of the great variety of nutritious, good-tasting meals and snacks available on any budget.

Students this age often enjoy contests. Perhaps a class contest for the "recipe of the week" would motivate students to look at magazines and recipe books that can be nutritionally helpful. Emphasize that varying the foods we eat helps us get a balance of necessary nutrients.

Caution students against dieting without the specific advice of a health professional who is familiar with their medical background and growth history. Dieting during the years of maximum growth may adversely affect attainment of maximum height. Diets that commonly appear in magazines and bestsellers are intended for adults who have completed their growth. Such diets could be seriously damaging to a young person in a period of rapid but uneven growth.

What Is the Best Way To Keep Fit? (pp. 92–97).
You might want to have students review what they learned about circulation and respiration in Chapter 3 as background to exploring the importance of exercise—particularly aerobic exercise directed at strengthening the cardiovascular system.

Be sure students understand that suddenly beginning daily strenuous exercise can be a serious health *risk* for people whose lifestyle has been sedentary. Ask students to suggest ways people can increase their exercise program without endangering their health. Students should be able to express the following ideas in their own terms. Begin gradually and build up stamina and strength. "Listen to" your body and stop exercising if you become too tired, feel excessively short of breath, or feel pain. Heed these warning signals even after you have worked up to a more fit state.

Warm-ups (essentially stretching and flexing exercises) may be done either for their own sake or as a preparation for more strenuous exercise. When done as preparation, they ease the transition from a resting state to a condition of vigorous activity. In the same way, cool-downs make a good transition back to the resting state. Aerobic exercises work chiefly to strengthen the heart and lungs and to gradually increase a person's cardiovascular endurance.

You might set aside some class time for students to try out the exercises illustrated on pages 96–97. You might also invite a physical education instructor to class to discuss and demonstrate warming-up and cooling-down exercises.

PLANNING YOUR OWN HEALTH RESPONSIBILITIES (pp. 98–103).

Take Charge of Your Own Health (pp. 98–99).

Students this age are becoming more aware of their bodies and should be encouraged to assume increasing responsibility for their health. The trick, often, is to help them to be aware of their health needs and the problems that may arise without making them overly concerned. Probably the best advice is to suggest that if they notice something unusual about their health, they should discuss their observations and questions with an adult family member. Students with chronic or recurrent health problems should, of course, learn to be alert to the symptoms.

On Your Own (p. 99).

Before students work out their specific health-care schedules, recall the Chapter 1 discussion about the importance of balancing the physical, social, and mental/emotional dimensions of health. In addition to the four basic elements of health care (sleep, nutrition, exercise, and hygiene), students should be sure their daily schedules allow some time for study, relaxation, and socializing. Encourage them to consider ways to consolidate activities (e.g., exercising to music with a friend), and remind them not to overlook situations that combine the dimensions of health quite naturally. Soccer, basketball, and other team sports combine social and physical dimensions; taking a walk with a friend while talking over a problem combines all three.

Checkups Are Part of Every Health Plan (pp. 100–103).

Be sure students understand that routine checkups will sometimes vary because of what a doctor observes or because a patient has mentioned a particular problem or asked a specific question. Guide discussion of these pages to bring out and reinforce the following points. Routine checkups:

- can confirm the patient's general good health.
- can sometimes lead to discovery of unobserved health problems before such problems become more serious.
- can be a learning experience, as they allow youngsters to ask about weight or skin problems and to discuss any concerns they may have about their health and physical development.

Most students will recognize that going to the same physician or clinic year after year means that earlier health records are available for important checks, such as comparing growth and reviewing family and personal health histories. However, in today's mobile society, many families are not able to establish continuity of health-care providers. If students express concern about this, you may want to explain that health records—including reports of tests and x-rays—belong to the patient, not to the health-care provider. If there is a need to change physicians or clinics, the patient's records can be transferred to the new provider. (A written release from a parent or guardian is required.)

HEALTHY TEETH HELP KEEP YOU HEALTHY (pp. 104–108).

Make Tooth Care Part of Your Health Plan (pp. 104–105).

Although proper care of primary teeth is known to contribute to the health of the permanent teeth, once all the permanent teeth are in, proper dental care is absolutely essential to a healthy mouth. Remind students that the teeth they have now are theirs for life and must be cared for thoroughly and regularly.

You might invite your school nurse or a dental hygienist to class to demonstrate the proper brushing and flossing procedures on a model set of teeth.

Teeth Can Be Straightened (p. 106).

Invite students who wear braces or who anticipate wearing them in the future to do extra research on the work of orthodondists and report their findings to the class. Encourage them to include the following points in their report:

- Orthodontic work not only improves a person's appearance but also helps the teeth work as well and efficiently as possible.
- The amount of time a person spends wearing braces or having other orthodontic work done is usually very short, and the improvement in appearance and in dental health will last for the rest of the person's life.

Reduce the Risk of Tooth Decay (p. 107).

If students express strong antipathies toward dental checkups, remind them that regular checkups enable the dentist to locate cavities when they are small. The smaller the cavity, the less painful the repair to the tooth—and the less damage to the health of the tooth!

Point out the importance of gum-line brushing, and particularly of flossing, in reducing the risk of periodontal disease. Flossing can remove harmful calculus between teeth, where toothbrush bristles don't reach.

Try To Prevent Tooth Injuries (p. 108).
The most common causes of tooth *loss* for young people this age are sports-related accidents, automobile accidents, and careless play with sticks and other pointed objects. In class discussion, have students develop a list of ways to avoid or reduce the risk of accidental tooth loss. For example, wearing protective mouthpieces while playing certain sports may prevent injury to teeth. Fastening safety belts in automobiles may also help. Being aware of these possible outside dangers to the teeth may help students take preventive actions.

Learn More About It (p. 109).
In addition to the titles listed in the text, you can recommend the following books to your students:

Hoopes, Ann, and Hoopes, Townsend. *Eye Power.* New York: Alfred A. Knopf, Inc., 1979. Clearly presented information on how to improve eyesight; how eyesight works and affects the rest of the body; eye care; practical eye-training exercises.

Lewis, Nancy, and Lewis, Richard. *Keeping in Shape.* New York: Franklin Watts, Inc., 1976. Text includes exercises for boys and girls, and tips on physical fitness; information on the importance of keeping the heart, muscles, and other body parts in good shape.

Meyer, Carolyn. *Being Beautiful.* New York: William Morrow & Co., Inc., 1977. All about personal care of the skin, hair, and body, and having a good attitude toward oneself.

For your own reading, you may be interested in the following books:

Association for the Advancement of Health Education. *Yes, You Can Teach Dental Health.* Lanham, Md.: AAHPERD Publications, 1976. This is a guide to teaching the subject of dental health in ways that help students realize its importance.

Donahue, Parnell. *Sports Doc.* New York: Alfred A. Knopf, Inc., 1979. Focus is on taking care of the body through fitness programs and through avoiding alcohol, drugs, and tobacco. Care of injuries is also included.

Lebo, Fern. *The Every Other Day Exercise Book.* Briarcliff Manor, N.Y.: Stein & Day Publishers, 1977. Presents simple exercises to help individuals get in shape and stay there; areas of the body are dealt with through specific exercises.

Wells, Howard, gen. ed. *Start Living Now.* Secaucus, N.J.: Chartwell Books, Inc., 1979. Content covers easy and effective exercises, child development, diet and nutrition, and other health-related areas.

If time permits, you may wish to use one or more of the following audiovisual materials with this chapter:

High Blood Pressure. Pleasantville, N.Y.: Imperial Educational Resources, Inc., 1981. Cassette. High blood pressure and its effects on the circulatory system and the body are explained.

How Blood Clots. Santa Monica, Calif.: BFA Educational Media, 1981. Color film. The functions of the circulatory system, including the formation of a blood clot, are explained.

The Human Body. Pleasantville, N.Y.: Imperial Educational Resources, Inc., 1981. 12 filmstrips. A comprehensive set of filmstrips that discusses the major body systems and individual organs.

Write About Better Health (p. 111).
Although answers will vary somewhat, they should include the following points:

1. Proper sleep, good nutrition, good hygiene, and regular exercise are important in reducing health risks.
2. Warm-up and cool-down exercises stretch and flex muscles so that vigorous exercise will not injure the muscles, bones, and joints.
3. A regular medical checkup usually includes a check of pulse, blood pressure, reflexes, condition of ears, nose, and throat, and the condition of the glands and other internal organs.
4. A person who is healthy and fit as a result of following a regular health-care plan is better able to participate in activities at school, at home, and in the community, and to feel more self-confident.
5. Regular tooth brushing and flossing can help prevent or limit tooth decay and gum disease. (Although gum disease can develop without tooth decay, tooth decay can lead to gum disease.)

CHAPTER 5
NUTRITIOUS FOODS FOR BETTER HEALTH

Chapter Overview

This chapter treats in detail the relationship of sound, appropriate food choices to growth, development, and overall health. The first section details the various types of nutrients required by the body and the specific uses to which the body puts them. The second section describes how to achieve a balanced, nutritious diet by choosing from the basic food groups. It also discusses the importance of reading package labels and the functions of the digestive system. The concluding section deals with differing energy requirements and with weight control. The emphasis throughout the chapter is on making positive choices to maintain the health and growth of the body.

Objectives

After completing this chapter, the students should be able to
- identify the nutrients in food that are necessary for good health.*
- list selections from among the basic food groups to provide a balanced diet.*
- describe ways of achieving and maintaining their ideal weight.*

Suggested Activities and Discussions

Chapter Opener (pp. 112–113).
Have the students identify as many of the pictured foods as they can. Encourage students to talk about different food customs and preferences they have experienced or have read or heard about. (For example, some people stuff their Thanksgiving turkey with oyster dressing. Others traditionally eat sauerkraut soup on Christmas Eve. Some Southerners serve black-eyed peas on New Year's Day to ensure good luck.) Throughout the discussion, elicit the concept that eating habits, preferences, and traditions are acquired and that we can all learn to enjoy new foods if we are exposed to them.

*These objectives are stated in age-appropriate terms on page 114 of the student text.

Looking Ahead (p. 114).
This is a good opportunity to determine to what extent your students assume responsibility for their food choices. You might have students make a private list of all the foods—including snacks—that they have eaten during the last day or two. You might get them started by suggesting that they list *breakfast, lunch, snacks, dinner* across the top of their paper and then list individual foods in the appropriate column. (Suggest that they be as specific and all-inclusive as possible. Sugar added to cereal, butter spread on toast, and salt sprinkled on a celery stick, for example, should be listed as separate foods.) Have students (1) count the total number of food items, (2) check off and count the food items they chose themselves, and (3) report the ratio—"I chose 15 out of 21 foods," for example. Use their findings as a springboard for a discussion of how important it is for them to learn about their nutritional needs so that they can make healthful choices.

NUTRITION—USING FOOD FOR GROWTH AND ENERGY (pp. 116–125).
Be sure students understand that both growth and activity determine the amount of energy the body uses, a fact that explains why the body's nutritional needs are different at different times of life. People in the age group eleven to twelve—a period of extremely rapid growth—require more energy than at any other time in life.

Healthful Meals Have Balanced Nutrients (p. 118).
Explain to the students that many Americans eat a food diet that provides too many of some nutrients and too few of others. For example, some meals served in fast-food restaurants (e.g., hamburger, French fries, and a milk shake) appear to be balanced (meat, vegetable, dairy) yet are really extremely high in salt, fat, and sugar in comparison to the other nutrients in the foods. Ask the students for their ideas on how a diet that consisted almost exclusively of fast foods could affect a young person's growth, energy, and success in school. Make the point that occasional fast-food meals are not harmful, provided people maintain an overall

balance in their food choices. (The youngster should not be made to feel guilty—or, worse yet, to protest to his or her parents—if the family's traditional Friday night treat is dinner at McDonald's!) As the discussions progress, help the students to see that balance over the course of a day can be achieved in a number of ways.

Carbohydrates Are Nutrients (pp. 118–119).
Explain to the students that cutting down on obvious sugar foods does not always lessen the amount of sugar in a diet. Many packaged foods contain sugar. Have the students read package nutrition labels, looking for the words *sugar, maltose, sucrose, glucose, dextrose, lactose, fructose,* or *syrup.* These are all forms of sugar. Also remind the students that cutting down on sugar includes brown and raw sugars, honey, and syrups.

Proteins Are Nutrients (p. 120).
You might explain to the students that people who do not get enough protein may be constantly sick and tired and may be slow to heal if they have been injured. Children who do not get enough protein will not grow straight and tall and may have underdeveloped nervous systems. The students may be interested to know that too much protein can overwork the kidneys, which handle the waste left over from protein digestion.

Fats Are Nutrients (p. 120).
Call for volunteers to research and report to the class on cholesterol. Have them organize their reports to answer the following questions: What is cholesterol? How does the body use it? Does the body itself produce cholesterol? What are some other sources of cholesterol? What health problems are related to having too much cholesterol in the blood? Can cholesterol levels be controlled by careful choices of food or by exercise?

Vitamins Are Nutrients (pp. 122–123).
To reinforce the notion that a balanced diet provides adequate vitamins without supplements, you might have students begin collecting nutrition labels from different processed foods (including milk, bread, flour, cereal, and other grain products) to see how many are fortified with vitamins and minerals. (The collected labels can also be used with the discussion on page 130).

On Your Own (p. 122).
As a follow-up activity, you might have students plan a full day's menu basing their choices on vitamin requirements alone. Mention that of course other factors must be considered in menu planning, but vitamins are one key consideration.

Minerals Are Nutrients (p. 124).
Have the students become salt detectives investigating their own diets for two days. Tell them not to add salt to any of their food and to read the labels on any packaged foods they buy, such as snacks and beverages. After the two days are up, lead a discussion about how foods tasted without added salt. Explore the idea that eating foods without adding salt gives people a better idea of how the foods taste. Point out, too, that other seasonings—pepper, oregano, basil, lemon juice, and the like—can often enhance a food's flavor better than salt can.

Water Is a Nutrient (p. 124).
Discuss with students food sources that contain relatively high amounts of water: fruits and vegetables, in addition to such obvious foods as soups, sauces, gravies, and juices. Point out that these sources supply *some* of the water the body needs, but that the body must process the foods in order to extract the water. For this reason it is still important to drink several large glasses of water every day.

CHOOSING AND USING FOODS (pp. 127–133).

Food Groups Make Choices Easier (p. 127) and **You Can Make Your Own Food Plan (pp. 128–129).**
Weekday lunches are limited either by the cafeteria menu choices or by what can be easily and safely brought from home; yet these are also frequently the meals over which young people exercise more choice. Obtain a copy of a week's menu from your school's food service staff. (It need not be current.) Divide the class into two groups. One group is to plan a week's menu of bag lunches to be carried from home; the other is to list their week's selection from the school menu. Have the groups exchange menus and evaluate the nutritional balance.

Read the Label (p. 130).
If students did not previously (p. 122) collect nutrition labels to compare, have them do so now. When sorting the labels, have students identify the types of packaged foods that seem to provide the most nutritional value. Then have them look at the lists of ingredients. Explain that ingredients are listed in descending order of quantity from the most to the least abundant within the food product. The FDA is considering requiring companies to list milligrams of sodium per *serving* rather than per 100 grams.

Discovery—A New Pathway to Health (p. 131). Students might be assigned to investigate various kinds of food contamination—*salmonella, botulism,* and *staphylococcus*—and how they can be detected. Students who elect to do this research should be encouraged to report their findings to the class.

How Does Your Body Use Food? (pp. 132–133). This material should not pose any particular problem for students. Interested students might be assigned to learn more about the structure and functions of the individual organs in the digestive system.

PEOPLE HAVE DIFFERENT FOOD NEEDS (pp. 134–140).

How Much Energy Do You Need? (p. 134) and **How Is Food Energy Measured? (p. 135).** Expand on the text material through a discussion of the importance of nutrition during illnesses. Guide students to express the following ideas in their own terms: Even though a sick or convalescing person may be using less energy in physical activity, the body still requires nutrition for repair of damaged cells and tissue. A sick person's diet should include all the same nutrients as a well person's but in simpler, more easily digested forms: meat broths, fruit juices, toast and crackers, puddings and custards, and applesauce or stewed fruits, for example.

On Your Own (pp. 136–137). Before students begin to compute their individual caloric needs, you might work out the sample in the book at the board as a demonstration, completing the rest of the day's schedule. Although the computation is not difficult, students may feel more confident if you have been through it together step by step.

Some People Weigh More Than They Should (p. 138). Explain to the students that overweight and obesity (being excessively fat) are major forms of malnutrition in America. Americans have a tremendous variety of food choices. However, because foods high in sugar and fat taste good and are convenient, these foods make up a major part of the diet. This leads to several kinds of health problems. Too much fat can cause overweight and heart disease. Too much salt in the diet can contribute to high blood pressure. Americans also get less evercise than they used to. They do not eat less, though, to compensate. Have the students write some TV commercials that inform young people of the problems resulting from too much fat, sugar, and salt.

Now Is the Time To Watch Your Weight (pp. 139–140). In any discussion of ideal weight, stress individual differences. Remind students that weight charts are based on *averages.* Ideal weights for young people are also hard to determine because the young people are still growing. They often experience periods of physical growth when they are temporarily light or heavy for their age.

Caution students that diets that are not directed or approved by an individual's physician are particularly dangerous during a period of rapid growth—which students are currently going through. Weight gain or loss during growth spurts is often uneven and unpredictable. Students who feel they may be heavier than they want to be should eliminate the "empty calories" found in junk foods and increase their exercise.

Discuss with the students what they may have read or heard about ways to lose or gain weight. Ask the students where they got their information and whether they think the methods sound healthful based on what they have been learning about nutrition. Point out that weight adjustments made slowly and steadily are more healthful and offer a better chance of keeping the weight on or off. Diets that promise quick gain or loss may harm health and usually lack nutrients.

You may wish to talk over weight problems with any student who seems excessively heavy or thin and suggest counseling and a medical checkup. However, singling out such a student may compound a problem that is already highly charged emotionally for many young people. To avoid this, you might set up individual nutritional conferences for the whole class, affording everyone an opportunity to raise questions or concerns.

Learn More About It (p. 141). In addition to the titles listed in the text, you can recommend the following books to your students:

Earle, Olive, and Kantor, Michael. *Nuts.* New York: William Morrow & Co., Inc., 1975. The 33 kinds of edible nuts and their value, use, and preparation.

Noad, Susan Strand. *Recipes for Science Fun.* New York: Franklin Watts, Inc., 1976. Simple recipes accompanied by explanations of the scientific processes that occur during cooking.

Parenteau, Shirley, and Douglas, Barbara. *A Space Age Cookbook for Kids.* Englewood Cliffs, N.J.: Prentice-Hall, Inc., 1979. Various recipes with zany, space-age names like "skywheel omelet," and "sloppy joe volcanoes."

Selsam, Millicent E. *The Plants We Eat.* New York: William Morrow & Co., Inc., 1981. The development of food plants, how we use them, simple directions for growing, and the value of vegetable foods.

For your own reading, you may be interested in the following books:

Guthrie, Helen Andrews. *Introductory Nutrition.* St. Louis, Mo.: The C. V. Mosby Company, 1979. This resource is an introduction to the principles of nutrition.

Makris, Dimetra, et al. *The First Prize Cookbook.* Brattleboro, Vt.: Stephen Greene Press, 1982. A compilation of prizewinning recipes that are nutritious and easy and that often show how to be imaginative in cooking and in diet.

Seddon, George, and Burrow, Jackie. *The Natural Food Book.* Skokie, Ill.: Rand McNally & Company, 1980. How to prepare foods—methods and recipes—and the value of whole foods in nutrition.

Smith, Lendon. *Feed Your Kids Right.* New York: McGraw-Hill Book Company, 1979. Advice on nutrition for the prevention and cure of ailments, allergies, and imbalances.

Winick, Myron. *Growing Up Healthy.* New York: William Morrow & Co., Inc., 1981. Practical advice on nutrition for children of all ages: nutritious eating patterns, healthful diet, avoidance of obesity.

More information on nutrition can be obtained by writing to the following addresses:

Consumer Information Center
Pueblo, CO 81009

National Institutes of Health
9000 Rockville Pike
Bethesda, MD 20014

International cookbooks and food books can be obtained from the following address:

The U.S. Committee for UNICEF
331 East 38th Street
New York, NY 10016

If time permits, you may wish to use one or more of the following audiovisual materials with this chapter:

Good Nutrition: The Foods Platform. Boulder, Colo.: Learning Tree Filmstrips, 1981. 4 filmstrips, 4 cassettes, guide. This series explores the body's needs for nutrients that can bring better health.

Nutrition. Pleasantville, N.Y.: Imperial Educational Resources, Inc., 1981. 20 transparencies with overlays. A complete analysis of nutritional requirements and the sources and function of various nutrients.

Snack Facts. Culver City, Cal.: Health Education Services, 1982. Color filmstrip, cassette, guide. The five nutrients are presented, together with examples of nutritious snack foods.

Write About Better Health (p. 143).
Here more than in some other chapters, you will find variety in the students' answers, particularly regarding Question 2. However, students should demonstrate an understanding of the following content:

1. Anyone preparing a healthful lunch should be sure that food, hands, and utensils are clean; that refrigerated food that was cooked has been reheated; and that foods are kept at the proper temperatures (in thermos bottles).
2. Students' menus will differ greatly, but each should include a balance of foods from the four basic food groups and an adequate balance of vitamins and minerals.
3. Their meals are usually high in fat, salt, and sugar and low in other nutrients. The body stores excesses of fat and sugar as fat.
4. A person who is underweight may be lacking important nutrients and may feel unattractive.
5. Anyone planning to gain or lose weight should consult a doctor to determine the best weight for him or her and to be sure there is no health problem that a diet may worsen. Following the doctor's advice, the person should discuss the diet plan with his or her family to be sure the daily plan includes foods from all the food groups and meets the body's nutritional requirements. He or she should also plan to slowly and steadily increase the amount of daily exercise.

CHAPTER 6
YOU CAN LEARN THE SAFETY HABIT

Chapter Overview

The three sections of this chapter are addressed to ways of reducing safety risks and being prepared for emergencies. In the first section, students examine safety on wheels, in sports, in the water, and on hikes. In the second section, they consider ways of dealing with such emergency situations as fire, natural disasters, and home accidents. In the third section, students learn procedures for administering first aid when emergenices do arise.

As the title suggests, the emphasis of the chapter is on safety as a habit. Students begin to develop the habits of being alert to hazards and foreseeing consequences and, as a result, to become confident about their ability to act appropriately and responsibly.

Objectives

After studying this chapter, students should be able to

- list ways of remaining safe at home or at play.*
- describe appropriate responses to fire and weather emergenices.*
- suggest safe and appropriate ways of dealing with strangers.*
- describe some emergency first-aid procedures.*

Suggested Activities and Discussions

Chapter Opener (pp. 144–145).
The photograph covers several aspects of kitchen safety. Among other kitchen safety considerations are knives (proper cutting techniques and proper storage reduce the risk of cutting oneself or others accidentally), floors (spills should be wiped up and food picked up to avoid anyone's slipping on floors; in addition, floors should be kept clean to avoid attracting vermin); appliances (when instruction booklets for appliances are available, they should be read and comprehended; in the absence of instruction booklets, proper use of appliances can be learned from a knowledgeable person; plugs and outlets should be kept dry to avoid electrical shock; fingers should be kept away from working parts until the appliance is unplugged); household cleaners (should be kept away from food areas, carefully and tightly covered, and out of reach of young children to avoid poisoning; should be held away from face when opening).

Students will, no doubt, be able to add other kitchen safety considerations.

Looking Ahead (p. 146).
Have students share their ideas about what causes accidents: carelessness, taking unreasonable risks, not foreseeing the consequences of an action. Invite comments on the following statements: *Most accidents could be avoided if people got into the habit of stopping to think about what they are about to do and what may happen if they do it. Another way to avoid accidents is to be alert to what is going on around you and especially to the actions of others.*

YOU CAN REDUCE SAFETY RISKS (pp. 148–155).

Your state motor vehicles department can supply you with a complete set of highway and traffic safety signs. It is a good idea to be sure all students can interpret these signs correctly. You might then divide the class into groups and have each group devise similar signs to alert people to other kinds of safety risks. Possible categories include water safety, safe and unsafe play areas, safe and unsafe water sources, and so forth.

---

*These objectives are stated in age-appropriate terms on page 146 of the student text.

Stay Safe on Wheels (p. 150).
Have the students list the kinds of clothing that are the safest to wear when biking. Encourage students to discuss the serious dangers of showing off or trying to perform stunts on bikes and/or skateboards. The sequences they see in movies and TV shows are performed by highly trained professional stuntspeople, and the scenes themselves are carefully staged (sometimes even with photographic tricks) to minimize the risks.

Stay Safe on the Ball Field (p. 151).
This might be an opportunity to discuss appropriate behavior for spectators at sporting events. The discussion could include considerations of choosing safe and unsafe places from which to observe the game, not interfering with the play, not littering or throwing objects onto the field, and the like.

Stay Safe in the Water (pp. 152–153).
Be sure students understand the importance of remaining calm and conserving their energy in water emergencies.

Stay Safe on a Hike (pp. 154–155).
Your state parks department can undoubtedly provide you with a complete list of trail markings for students to study. If you prefer, you might assign students to research the signs on their own and report to the class.

You might discuss with students other possible risks on the trail and ways of avoiding them. Interested students may do extra research on topics such as how to remain safe during a rainstorm; how to reduce the risk from lightning; how to prevent and/or treat heat exhaustion; how to recognize poison ivy, oak, and sumac; and how to distinguish between dangerous and harmless snakes.

YOU CAN BE PREPARED FOR EMERGENCIES (pp. 156–163).

Know What To Do When You Are Alone (pp. 156–157).
Talk over reasons for not giving information over the phone. Students may not consider that a caller could have dialed a number by mistake. If the child hangs up, the stranger may not be able to call again. If the caller keeps calling back within a short span, the child has the option of not answering the phone or not speaking into the answered phone.

In dealing with strangers on the telephone, students are best advised not to let the caller know if they are alone in the home. A response such as "My mother [or other adult] can't come to the phone right now" is true even if the adult is not in the home, but suggests that he or she may just be temporarily busy. The same kind of evasion may be used with a stranger at the door.

Be Ready for Fire Emergencies (pp. 158–159).
If a fire extinguisher is not available, baking soda or salt can be used to put out grease fires. Smothering the fire with either substance extinguishes flames by cutting off the oxygen. Water should never be poured on a grease fire. The grease will float on the water and continue to burn. It may also spread more quickly as the water spreads.

Discovery—A New Pathway to Health (p. 158).
Assign students to do some comparison shopping for smoke detectors or to find out more about them from *Consumer Reports.* Have students report to the class on several makes and models that seem to offer the best value.

Avoid Dangers in Weather Emergencies (pp. 160–161).
Discuss with the class ways of reducing risks from other weather conditions and natural disasters that occur in your area. In an extremely cold climate, for example, students should know how to protect themselves from frostbite and hypothermia. If mud or snow slides are common seasonal occurrences, students should be made aware of the dangers and the appropriate responses.

Use a Checklist for Home Safety (p. 162).
Encourage students to add to the checklists in each of the categories. Some possibilities are suggested below:

- *Falls:* Wear shoes instead of walking in stocking feet.
- *Poisoning:* Learn which house plants are poisonous; keep cigarettes and ashtrays out of reach of small children. (Many children die each year of nicotine poisoning from eating cigarettes and/or cigarette butts.)
- *Small Children:* Keep *any* objects that can fit into their mouths away from small children; be sure stuffed toys and dolls with buttons have the buttons securely sewn on so that they cannot be bitten off or swallowed; do not leave children unattended in highchairs, infant seats, or near water.

- *Fires/Burns:* Turn off stove burners before removing pots; do not leave hot foods or liquids within reach of young children.

On Your Own (p. 163).
Before students work out their individual lists with their families, you might spend some class time discussing the types of phone numbers to include. If someone in the household has a serious ongoing health problem (diabetes, chronic heart condition), the number of his or her specialist should also be listed.

YOU CAN LEARN FIRST AID (pp. 164–170).

Learn To Use a First-Aid Kit (pp. 164–165).

Discuss with the class ways in which prompt first aid can reduce the amount of damage an injury might cause. For example, if a cut is cleaned and bandaged immediately, it is less likely to become infected. You might mention, too, that bleeding itself can be useful in cleansing a wound and that it is excessive and prolonged bleeding that is dangerous.

People Working for Your Health (p. 164).
The discussion of the paramedic's job might well lead to a discussion of appropriate uses of ambulance services and emergency rooms. These services are designed for use in emergencies, not to obtain routine medical treatment.

Learn When First Aid Is Needed (p. 166).
A "medic alert" bracelet can be critical to many people with serious health problems or with allergies to foods and/or drugs. Using medical practice that is standard for most accident victims could be fatal to persons, with certain conditions, and a "medic alert" bracelet can prevent such tragedies.

Discovery—A New Pathway to Health (p. 167).
The procedure for helping a choking victim is different when the victim is very overweight or pregnant:

- First, place your arms under the victim's armpits and around the chest.
- Next, place the thumb side of the fist against the middle, not the lower tip, of the breastbone.
- Grasp your fist with your other hand.
- Squeeze the victim's chest quickly with your arms. Do this four times.

Burns (p. 169). There are two reasons for not rupturing burn blisters. First, most blisters will heal more quickly from the inside out as new skin grows beneath the blister. Second, the skin around the edges of the blister is particularly susceptible to infection.

Poisons (p. 170). If a patient has ingested a dangerous substance that did not come in a container, the caller should still try to have a sample available. The poison center or doctor may ask for a description of the leaf, plant, or other substance.

Learn More About It (p. 171).
In addition to the titles listed in the text, you can recommend the following books to your students:

Berger, Melvin. *Bionics.* New York: Franklin Watts, Inc., 1978. An introduction to this science, which provides new parts for the human body: artificial limbs, organs, and sense organs. This book will help develop an awareness of safety and of how fortunate people are to have healthy bodies.

Fichter, George. *Bicycles and Bicycling.* New York: Franklin Watts, Inc., 1978. The history, accessories, and repair of bicycles are described as well as safety tips for bicycle driving.

For your own reading, you may be interested in the following books:

Annarino, Anthony A., and Kahms, Frederick. *Study Guide to First Aid, Safety, and Family Health Emergencies.* Minneapolis, Minn.: Burgess Publishing Co., 1979. A useful and practical guide and handbook with which to learn about all sorts of emergency situations and how to deal with them.

Fritsch, Albert J., gen. ed. *The Household Pollutants Guide.* Garden City, N.Y.: Anchor Books, 1978. Various types of pollutants found in common household products, and how to avoid exposure to and accidents with them.

Smith, Bradley, and Stevens, Gus. *The Emergency Book—You Can Save A Life.* New York: Simon & Schuster, 1978. First aid and how to handle emergencies: heart attack, choking, drowning, and more common accidents and situations.

If time permits, you may wish to use one or more of the following audiovisual materials with this chapter:

Playing It Safe... In the Home. Pleasantville, N.Y.: Imperial Educational Resources, Inc., 1981. 2 filmstrips, 2 cassettes. The many safety hazards existing in the home are discussed.

Safety in Your Home. Santa Monica, Cal.: BFA Educational Media, 1981. Film. Students are shown how to prevent falls, poisoning, electric shock, and other common household accidents.

Winter Safety. Boulder, Colo.: Learning Tree Filmstrips, 1981. 2 filmstrips, 2 cassettes, guide. Safety hazards of the winter months are discussed.

Write About Better Health (p. 173).
Despite individual differences, students' answers should include the following information:

1. A person who is upset is often not thinking about what he or she is doing. The person's mind is busy being upset, and the person may forget about safety. A person who is tired is usually less alert than a well-rested person and may not react as quickly to potential hazards.
2. A group planning a hike should study a map of the area in which they will be, decide what trails they plan to take, and figure out how long the hike should last. They should then leave all this information with someone who is not going on the hike, so that if they get lost someone will know where they planned to go and can send out a search party. Proper food and clothing should be planned for every hike.
3. A family needs to have an emergency fire-escape plan so they will know what to do and will not panic if there is a fire in their home. The plan should include two ways out of every room in the home and an outside meeting place. The first person out should be responsible for calling the fire department to report the fire.
4. A storm watch is announced when conditions suggest that a storm may be forming. A storm warning is announced after a storm has formed and when its general location and path are known.
5. The family can prepare for the storm by bringing in all loose objects from the yard and porch. Often people board or tape up windows. Then the family should gather emergency equipment, including matches, candles, flashlights, batteries, a portable battery-operated radio, canned food, and bottled water.
6. If someone is bleeding heavily, press gauze pads or a clean cloth over the wound to stop the bleeding. If these become soaked with blood, add another cloth. Then tie the compress over the wound and try to get help. If possible, the bleeding part should be raised higher than the heart to slow the flow of blood.
7. It is important to have the poison container or other source in hand when calling the poison control center in order to be able to read the label or describe the substance to the person at the center.

CHAPTER 7
PREVENTING AND CONTROLLING DISEASE

Chapter Overview

In this chapter, students become increasingly aware not only of ways in which they can personally minimize risks of disease to themselves and others but also of the ways in which scientists and health professionals work to find new methods of minimizing health risks in the entire population. Certainly, however hard people work at it, not all risks can be eliminated. Thus students also learn some of the ways in which diseases can be treated, cured, or controlled.

Objectives

After studying this chapter, the students should be able to

- identify some causes of disease and explain why some diseases spread.*
- suggest some ways to prevent the spread of disease.*
- describe how some diseases can be prevented and controlled.*
- list ways of minimizing the risks of contracting certain diseases.*

Suggested Activities and Discussions

Chapter Opener (pp. 174–175).
Suggest that students interview their parents, grandparents, or other adults of their acquaintance about epidemics of other diseases that have now been virtually eliminated. Polio, scarlet fever, diphtheria, and whooping cough are some possibilities.

Looking Ahead (p. 176).
Allow some time for students to discuss the ideas they already have about the list of topics they will learn about in the chapter.

---

*These objectives are stated in age-appropriate terms on page 176 of the student text.

PREVENTING DISEASES (pp. 178–183).

What Is Disease? (pp. 178–179).
Have students look up the two key vocabulary terms. Discuss the definition of *microbes* with them in some detail. Be sure they understand that some microbes are beneficial and make positive contributions to health.

Is Reducing Disease Risks a New Idea? (p. 180).
The idea of folk remedies will probably intrigue students. Some might interview older relatives about home cures that were common when they were children. Others might read more about folk remedies and the uses of herbs and plants for healing. (If you can arrange to do so, you might assemble some books in the classroom for students to browse through.) Have students devise ways to share what they have learned through their interviews or research.

Discovery—A New Pathway to Health (p. 181).
Today cultures are used not only to isolate and identify specific germs but also to determine appropriate treatment. Once the germs have begun to grow, each individual Petri dish is treated with a different drug to determine which drugs the germs are sensitive to and which will be ineffective in treating the disease.

Doctors Have Learned To Prevent Some Diseases (pp. 182–183).
Be sure students understand that not all immunizations are permanent and that some, such as the tetanus immunization, require periodic boosters. You might suggest that it is a good idea to keep a record of immunizations and the dates they were given. Then if a question arises in the course of medical treatment (for a puncture wound, for instance), it can be quickly determined whether or not a booster is needed.

COMMUNICABLE DISEASES (pp. 184–193).

Microbes Cause Communicable Diseases (pp. 184–185).
The terms *communicable* and *contagious* merit thorough discussion. They will be used repeatedly in the rest of the chapter, and it is important for students to understand the distinction.

Some Diseases Are Spread by Animals (p. 186).
Besides getting in touch with a doctor immediately after being bitten by a dog, it is also important to keep track of the animal to determine whether it is developing rabies. If the animal does develop the disease or cannot be traced, a doctor will normally inoculate the bitten person against rabies.

Discovery—A New Pathway to Health (p. 187).
Interested students might learn more about the lives and work of Drs. Finlay and Reed and report to the class some of the highlights of their reading.

Some Diseases Are Spread by Water (pp. 188–189).
There are two known forms of hepatitis. The one that is transmitted by water or personal contact is called either *hepatitis A* or *infectious hepatitis.* The other form is known as *hepatitis B* or *serum hepatitis.* The latter name results from the fact that this type of hepatitis is often transmitted in blood transfusions or in the use of a hypodermic needle previously used by someone with the virus. *Hepatitis B* is the more serious disease, but a vaccine has recently been approved for use against it.

Some Diseases Are Spread by Food (pp. 190–191).
Salmonella is the name for a group of bacteria that cause food poisoning. In the case of salmonella bacteria, the term *poisoning* may be a bit of an overstatement, for salmonellosis is seldom fatal, although the symptoms and discomfort may last for 24 to 28 hours after the contaminated food has been eaten. Strains of salmonella may be found in some raw meat, fish, poultry, eggs, and milk, but they are easily destroyed by heating food to 165°F. Pasteurization kills the bacteria in milk, and heating soups and stews to a boil ensures that they will not be contaminated, a particularly valuable precaution when eating leftovers.

Discovery—A New Pathway to Health (p. 191).
Pasteur was one of the key figures in the early studies of microbes. His work had both commerical and medical application. He accomplished far more than development of the sterilizing process that bears his name. One of his main accomplishments was development of the rabies vaccine, which has saved countless lives.

Some Diseases Are Spread Through the Air (p. 192).
One of the roadblocks scientists have encountered in trying to develop an effective vaccine to prevent colds is the large number of viruses that cause them—over 100. Although some progress is being made, elimination of the common cold still seems very far away.

Be sure students understand the importance of covering the nose and mouth when they sneeze or cough. Point out that this is one way in which *everyone* can contribute to stopping the spread of disease.

On Your Own (p. 193).
You might compare the experiment here to the phenomenon students experience when they "see their breath" on a cold day. The warm drops of moisture condense when they hit the cold air—or, in this case, the mirror.

NONCOMMUNICABLE DISEASES (pp. 194–198).

Some Diseases Are Not Spread by Microbes (pp. 194–195).
Make sure the class understands the difference between controlling a disease and curing it. When a disease is controlled, the person with the disease still has the underlying problem, but medication or some other treatment may be used to slow the progress of the disease or to remove or diminish distressing symptoms.

People Working for Your Health (p. 195).
Students may be interested in learning more about the treatment of skin cancer. Its causes and prevention might also be discussed at this time.

Diabetes Can Be Controlled (pp. 196–197).
Many noncommunicable diseases have the following features:

- They are wholely or partly hereditary.
- They may be initiated by a virus.
- They may be caused by a defect in the body's metabolism.
- They have few symptoms in the early stages.
- They often can be prevented or controlled by diet and exercise.
- They can result in death if not controlled.

Diabetes has all these features (explained in simpler language in the text).

Discovery—A New Pathway to Health (p. 197).
Be sure students understand that dosages of insulin must be carefully regulated according to a doctor's instructions for each individual case. An overdose of insulin or the use of insulin by a nondiabetic person can cause serious, sometimes fatal, insulin shock.

Heart Disease Is Our Number One Killer (p. 198). Review with students what they learned in Chapters 3 and 4 about the workings of the circulatory system and the importance of exercise. The most common cause of heart attacks is a *coronary thrombosis,* a blood clot that closes off a coronary artery, depriving the heart of food and oxygen. The symptoms usually include a severe tightness or pain in the chest, sometimes spreading to the shoulder, arm, back, neck, or jaw. This primary symptom may or may not be accompanied by the additional symptoms of shortness of breath, sweating, nausea, vomiting, or loss of consciousness. If you can arrange it, have someone from the community—a doctor, nurse, or paramedic—come to class to discuss cardiopulmonary resuscitation (CPR), a procedure that can make the difference between life and death for many heart attack victims.

Other types of cardiovascular problems include *stroke* (a blockage of blood to the brain), *congestive heart failure,* and *atherosclerosis.* Assign students to research and report on these disorders.

Learn More About It (p. 199). In addition to the titles listed in the text, you can recommend the following books to your students:

Knight, David C. *Your Body's Defenses.* New York: McGraw-Hill Book Co., 1975. About the body's various natural defenses against disease and how to keep them working.

Nourse, Alan E. *Viruses.* New York: Franklin Watts, Inc., 1976. What viruses are, how they were discovered, the diseases they cause, and the vaccines available to fight them.

Silverstein, Alvin, and Silverstein, Virginia. *Heart Disease.* Chicago: Follett Publishing Co., 1976. About the heart, what could go wrong with it, how to take care of it through exercise and diet, and why disease occurs.

For your own reading, you may be interested in the following books:

Combs, Murphy C., ed. *Illustrated Family Medical Encyclopedia.* New York: Consolidated Book Publishers, 1976. Extensive list of medical terms, illnesses, and anatomical parts and clear explanations of them.

Stiller, Richard. *Pain.* Nashville, Tenn.: Thomas Nelson, Inc., 1975. Headaches, backaches, and other expressions of pain are discussed, along with reasons and treatments for them.

The American Heart Association Heartbook. New York: E. P. Dutton, Inc., 1980. The risks, causes, and treatments of heart disease are dealt with here, and advice on maintaining a healthy heart is given.

If time permits, you may wish to use one or more of the following audiovisual materials with this chapter:

Disease and Health. Culver City, Cal.: Health Educational Services, 1982. 12 color transparencies, 4 spirit duplicating masters. Information about causes and prevention of disease.

Enemies of the Body. Pleasantville, N.Y.: Imperial Educational Resources, Inc., 1981. 4 filmstrips, 4 cassettes. Cancer, hypertension, heart attack, and diabetes are explained in nontechnical language. Symptoms and precautionary measures are also discussed.

For the Sake of Your Heart. Pleasantville, N.Y.: Sunburst Communications, 1981. Three-part color filmstrip program. Explains the structure of the heart, heart disease, and ways to help the heart stay healthy.

Write About Better Health (p. 201). Despite individual differences, students' answers should reflect an understanding of the following content:

1. The risk of disease can be reduced by a balanced diet, plenty of rest and exercise, immunization, and sanitation of various kinds.
2. Communicable diseases can be spread by animals, by water, by food, and through the air. Noncommunicable diseases can result from microbes, defects in parts of the body due to malnutrition or misuse, environmental conditions, or heredity.
3. The microbe must be obtained (in a blood or tissue sample) from a person or animal infected by the disease. It is then grown in a pure culture and used to infect an experimental animal. If the animal gets the same disease, the microbe has been proven to be the cause.
4. Four ways that a disease can get from one person to another are through the air, through water, by way of an animal, or in food. Disease may also be spread by direct contact with skin or mucous membranes.
5. Noncommunicable diseases are often wholely or partly hereditary, sometimes (perhaps often) started by a virus infection, involve a defect in the way the body handles a substance, start with very few symptoms, and can be prevented or controlled with diet and exercise in many cases. (Note that the question asks for only three features.)

CHAPTER 8
COMMUNITY ACTION FOR HEALTH AND SAFETY

Chapter Overview

This chapter explores some ways in which local communities and the global community work to promote and protect the health of their members. In addition it suggests that students, as members of local and world communities, have a responsibility to promote health care and protect the environment and that they *can* make a difference. The emphasis in this chapter is on the positive measures that can be taken to guarantee a safe and healthful world and reduce risks of harm from the environment.

Objectives

After completing this chapter, the students should be able to

- describe ways in which people in a community help to protect each other's health.*
- identify the means communities use to keep their environments cleaner, quieter, and more healthful.*
- explain how a community deals with health emergencies and any special health problems that may arise.*
- list some people whose jobs involve reducing a community's health and safety risks.*

Suggested Activities and Discussions

Chapter Opener (pp. 202–203).
Have students list as many other types of workers as they can whose jobs involve contributions to the health and safety of the community. (Some possibilities include motor vehicles department personnel who license drivers and inspect vehicles; Red Cross workers, visiting nurses, physical education instructors, and dietitians.)

*These objectives are stated in age-appropriate terms on page 204 of the student text.

Looking Ahead (p. 204).
Ask students to consider the emotional/psychological aspects of life on a desert island, keeping in mind what they learned about the health of the total person in Chapter 1.

COMMUNITIES WORK FOR HEALTH (pp. 206–213).

Local Communities Help You Protect Your Health (pp. 206–207).
Different kinds of emergencies occur with greater frequency in specific parts of the United States. If your area is vulnerable to tornadoes, hurricanes, earthquakes, or floods, you can discuss (or review from discussions in Chapter 6) that particular type of emergency.

People Support Their Community Services (pp. 208–209).
Encourage students to investigate the organizations in your community that rely heavily on volunteers. Perhaps your fire department or ambulance service relies heavily on volunteers, or volunteers may staff a swap shop or thrift store that benefits a hospital or a particular disabled group or charity. Many religious groups have social-action or outreach committees that work to improve the lives of the elderly or disadvantaged members of their community. Be sure students understand the importance of supporting community services by sharing their time and talents.

Health Care Goes Beyond the Local Community (pp. 210–213).
In the average developing country, each person eats about 400 pounds (180 kg) of cereal and bread a year. It takes almost a ton of grain each year to feed the average American. A large part of this grain is fed to animals that supply milk, meat, eggs, and cheese (foods that are seldom, if ever, eaten by many people in developing countries).

Students can investigate and report on the work of various agencies that have programs for assisting people in developing countries.

Discovery—A New Pathway to Health (p. 210). Ask students to obtain leaflets from the organizations mentioned in the text and from other volunteer health organizations.

YOU CAN HELP PROTECT THE ENVIRONMENT (pp. 214–222).

What Is the Environment? (pp. 214–215). Begin by asking students to consider their present environment: the school. Ask them to think about various aspects of their school environment: visual appearance, lighting, space, cleanliness, noise level, safety. Then have them list those parts of the school environment they find comfortable and those that require improvement. Ask them to suggest ways improvements could be made simply and at low cost. (If any suggestions merit attention, ask the students to submit them to the principal.)

Protecting the Environment Is a Community Job (pp. 216–217). Review the terms *pests* and *pesticides* as they refer to animals and insects that destroy part of the environment and spread diseases. Discuss the concept of *trade-offs.* A trade-off is a situation in which one thing is sacrificed to protect another. A pesticide is often needed to eliminate causes of disease (such as mosquitoes and rats), to protect parts of the environment, to keep agricultural products free from damage, or to kill weeds so that desired plants can grow. Often the pesticide kills living things other than the pests at which it is aimed. People may consequently risk pesticide pollution of the land, air, water, and living things.

Today many people think that it is possible to get the benefits of pesticides by using them in smaller amounts and less often. (This is called *integrated pest management.*) Such methods reduce the risks from pesticides and make the trade-off a better bargain for people.

Other examples of trade-offs involve nuclear power, which is a good source of energy but produces radioactive wastes that are very hard to dispose of; and modern technology, which makes our lives much easier but often relies on manufacturing processes that can produce pollution. (More and more industries, however, are finding ways to cut down on pollution from manufacturing.)

People Can Prevent Solid Waste Pollution (pp. 218–219). Additional ways that families can help prevent pollution include conscientiously recycling paper, glass, and aluminum and (in appropriate situations) composting organic solid wastes. Assign some students to find out about recycling centers in your area, the hours they are open, and the materials they accept. Other students can research and report on composting vegetable parings, coffee grounds, eggshells, and leaves for use as fertilizer.

Have the students find out whether or not your state has a "bottle law" requiring that beverage bottles and cans carry a deposit, to encourage buyers to return them to the store. Ask students to discuss the law's merits in reducing solid waste pollution in the form of littering. Ask them also to consider the possible disadvantages of such a law.

Noise Can Be a Health Risk (pp. 220–221). Noise pollution has serious health consequences. Hearing loss has been shown to be connected with exposure to noise. The stress caused by noise aggravates ulcers and other gastrointestinal conditions. Noise also causes changes in heart rate, hormone secretion, and blood pressure, contributing to cardiovascular disease.

Young people can control some of their exposure to noise. Radios, tape recorders, and headsets can be played at a volume that does not damage hearing. Earplugs can be worn at skating rinks and other places where loud music is played.

Much of the worst noise pollution, from a health point of view, is beyond young people's control. Now that the health effects of noise pollution are understood, major noise polluters, such as construction companies, airports, and factories, are taking steps to ease the problem. The sharing of responsibility for solving community problems such as noise should be emphasized as the main message of this chapter.

Have the students list all the noise pollution sources they can think of and decide who is responsible for each source—themselves, the school, or the community. Have them choose a problem in each category and decide how something can be done to solve it.

On Your Own (p. 222). This activity can be used to initiate a discussion of the positive and negative aspects of modern technology.

Students may also compare these problems with some problems that existed 150 years ago: horse manure on the streets, spoiled food, difficulty in getting from one place to another, no electric-powered labor-saving devices, poor lighting, and so forth.

Learn More About It (p. 223).
In addition to the titles listed in the text, you can recommend the following books to your students:

Kavaler, Lucy. *The Dangers of Noise.* New York: Thomas Y. Crowell, 1978. How noise affects people and the environment.

Lewis, Alvin. *Water.* New York: Franklin Watts, Inc., 1980. How we harness water, use it, and depend on it; how we must keep it clean and available for the future.

Olney, Ross R. *Keeping Our Cities Clean.* New York: Julian Messner, 1979. Describes various ways to keep our cities clean and safe for the people who live in them.

Savitz, Harriet M. *Wheelchair Champions: A History of Wheelchair Sports.* New York: John Day, 1978. shows various wheelchair sports and the athletes who participate in them.

For your own reading, you may be interested in the following books:

Black, Hallie. *Dirt Cheap—The Evolution of Renewable Resource Management.* New York: William Morrow & Co., Inc., 1979. Renewable natural resources (air, soil, water, forests) in the United States and the need to care for them.

Eisenberg, Arlene, and Eisenberg, Howard. *Alive and Well: Decisions in Health.* New York: McGraw-Hill Book Co., 1979. The need for care on both community and personal levels so that the individual and the environment are both healthy.

Willgoose, Carl E. *Environmental Health: Commitment for Survival.* Philadelphia: W. B. Saunders Co., 1979. Explains the great need to care for our environment and maintain its health for our safety.

If time permits, you may wish to use one or more of the following audiovisual materials with this chapter:

Energy Monsters: How To Starve Them. Santa Monica, Cal.: BFA Eductional Media, 1981. Film. This story illustrates ways to improve a family's use of energy.

Learning About Conservation. Chicago: Coronet, 1982. Filmstrip. Describes resources and ways to conserve them.

Old Age. Pleasantville, N.Y.: Imperial Educational Resources, 1981. 2 filmstrips, 2 cassettes. Examines old age and society's rejection of the elderly. Ways to improve the lives of older people are presented.

Write About Better Health (p. 225).
Students' answers should reflect an understanding of the following points:

1. A local health department immunizes people against disease; checks food, air, and water for cleanliness and healthfulness; provides hospitals or clinics; sometimes tracks down sources of disease in the community; provides services for the disabled, including regulations that permit access to public facilities.
2. A community may provide resources for disabled people, including job training, physical therapy, and transportation. Communities also pass laws that help disabled people get around in schools and other public buildings more easily. Many communities provide educational programs to teach people more about dealing with their own health.
3. Changes that help and hurt the environment at the same time include spraying with pesticides, packaging foods, construction, and mowing the lawn with a noisy power mower.
4. A community works to prevent solid waste pollution by disposing of trash and garbage, providing sewer lines and sewage treatment plants, and campaigning against and picking up litter. Some communities encourage recycling projects.
5. People can reduce noise pollution by making quieter machines, by keeping radio and television volume down, and by avoiding shouting and loud playing.

CHAPTER 9
MAKING DECISIONS ABOUT DRUGS

Chapter Overview

This chapter discusses the following categories of drugs: over-the-counter (OTC), prescription (Rx), mind/mood altering (both legal and illegal), and hidden (nicotine, caffeine, alcohol, and inhalants). The text makes clear the health risks posed by the use, misuse, abuse, or overuse of various drugs.

Objectives

After studying this chapter, students should be able to

- give reasons for having clear, complete information on the effects of drugs on health.*
- describe the effects on the body and/or mind of stimulants, depressants, narcotics, and hallucinogens.*
- describe the effects of nicotine and alcohol on the body.
- identify the serious health dangers that result from the use of marijuana and other illegal drugs.*

Suggested Activities and Discussions

Chapter Opener (pp. 226–227).
Ask the students to evaluate some current print or television ads for over-the-counter medications. Which ads suggest that consumers should have appropriate information? ("Use only as directed." "Check with your doctor.") Which take the approach of "Trust us" or "Trust so-and-so, who uses this drug"? Which ads are more appealing? Which are more common?

Looking Ahead (p. 228).
Ask students for examples of drugs that have helped make it possible to cure some diseases, to relieve pain, and to improve the quality of life for many people.

CHOOSING DRUGS FOR HEALTH (pp. 230–236).

Can Drugs Change Disease Symptoms? (pp. 230–231).
Reinforce the importance of adult intervention in children's illnesses.

*These objectives are stated in age-appropriate terms on page 228 of the student text.

What Is the Difference Between OTC and Prescription Drugs? (pp. 232–233).
Allergic reactions to drugs are commonly signaled by symptoms such as intestinal problems (cramps, nausea, diarrhea), breathing difficulties, and/or rashes. Students should alert an adult if such symptoms occur and discontinue the medication until a doctor can be consulted. People with known allergies to medications should wear "medic alert" bracelets.

Why Should You Follow Directions? (pp. 234–235).
Stress the importance of following directions on the stickers many pharmacies now affix to containers for certain medications: "Do not take dairy products, antacids, or iron preparations within 1 hour of taking this medication." "Take medication on an empty stomach: 1 hour before or 2 to 3 hours after a meal."

Discovery—A New Pathway to Health (p. 236).
Ask a student to look up Hippocrates in an encyclopedia and explain to the class why he is called the "Father of Medicine."

UNDERSTANDING MORE ABOUT DRUG DANGERS (pp. 237–243).

Explain to the class that some illegal drugs are not lawfully manufactured or sold for *any* purpose. Others have some lawful uses under medical supervision, but are also used illegally without medical sanction.

The use of illegal drugs can lead to problems including malnutrition, poor coordination, impaired heart and/or brain function, and even death, depending on the particular drug and the extent of use. Illegal drugs can control a person's whole life. For many, using the drug becomes the main goal in life. Family relationships, jobs and career goals, and even social activities lose their importance. Users may be unable even to function in normal life situations.

How Do Stimulant Drugs Affect People? (pp. 237–238). Make sure that students understand that this section is about both legal and illegal stimulants. Amphetamines are illegally used by many people. Some who use caffeine or nicotine heavily are not aware that they are using stimulant drugs—albeit legal drugs.

Assign students to research and list the amounts of caffeine in various beverages. Have them report as well on the effect that different brewing methods have on the caffeine content of tea and coffee.

How Do Depressant Drugs Affect People? (pp. 238–239). Drug dependence takes two forms. *Physical* dependence occurs when the body adjusts to the effects of a drug and needs the drug continuously in order to function. *Psychological* dependence occurs when a person thinks the drug is needed in order to cope with the stresses he or she faces. Researching and reporting on the two types of dependence might be assigned to interested students at this point.

Methaqualone produces effects similar to those of large doses of alcohol. Users can quickly become both physically and psychologically dependent on the drug. Withdrawal from methaqualone is more difficult and more dangerous than withdrawal from heroin and other narcotics. Without medical care, a person who overdoses on or who tries to withdraw from methaqualone may die of convulsions and stomach hemorrhaging. Some common names for methaqualone include *quaaludes, ludes,* and *soapers.*

How Do Narcotic Drugs Affect People? (p. 240). Interested students may wish to research and report on the following questions: (1) Where do illegal drugs come from? (2) What does research tell us about the people who sell illegal drugs? (3) Who makes a profit on the sale of illegal drugs? (4) What are the penalties for selling illegal drugs?

How Do Hallucinogens Affect People? (pp. 240–241). Many students are aware that LSD and PCP are extremely dangerous, but most regard marijuana as "tame," if not altogether harmless. The research recommended in the annotation on page 241 may help to disabuse them of this notion. Point out that marijuana today has been found to be up to 20 times more potent than marijuana sold even a few years ago. The dangers of long-term marijuana smoking are discussed in the notes for pages 244-245.

On Your Own (p. 242). This is a good time to discuss what to do if one discovers a friend is "doing drugs." A young person may be torn between a genuine desire to help a friend and a dislike of snitching. A drug counselor may be invited to the class to participate in this discussion.

People Working for Your Health (p. 243). Begin a discussion with your students about what factors or information might keep them from taking drugs. What kind of speaker would they be most likely to find compelling? If possible, get such a person to speak to the class.

DIFFICULT DECISIONS FOR THE FUTURE (pp. 244–250).

What Should You Know About Smoking? (pp. 244–245). Nicotine causes the body to develop first a tolerance, then a physical dependence. People who stop smoking experience withdrawal symptoms such as headaches, nervousness, decreased ability to concentrate, and irritability.

Students may be aware of laws requiring separate seating for nonsmokers and smokers in movie theaters, restaurants, and airplanes. Initiate a class discussion about the rights of nonsmokers versus the rights of smokers.

People who use smokeless tobacco also run the risk of physical dependence and serious diseases.

Many people think that because it does not contain nicotine, marijuana is safe to smoke. Recent research has shown that two carcinogens are 50 to 70 percent higher in concentration in marijuana smoke than in tobacco smoke, that people who had smoked 2.2 marijuana cigarettes a day for 5 years had 25 percent less ability to exchange carbon dioxide for oxygen than tobacco smokers who averaged 16 cigarettes a day, that marijuana is harmful to the entire pulmonary tree, from sinuses to lungs, and that marijuana smoke is even more dangerous to lungs than tobacco smoke.

On Your Own (p. 246). Despite smokers' protestations that they can quit anytime they want to, many find it nearly impossible to do so alone. Have students write for and discuss the following pamphlets:

Quitter's Guide: 7 Day Plan To Help You Stop Smoking Cigarettes. Write to

American Cancer Society
777 Third Avenue
New York, NY 10017

Clearing the Air: A Guide To Quitting Smoking. Write to

National Cancer Institute
9000 Rockville Pike
Bethesda, MD 20205

What Should You Know About Alcohol? (pp. 247–249).
Point out that alcohol dependence has a devastating effect on a dependent person's life.

Young people often feel it is inconsistent for adults to urge teenagers not to drink when so much drinking occurs among adults. Drinking involves risks for adults as well as for young people. There are irresponsible adult drinkers, and young people should not follow their example.

What Should You Know About Chemicals That Act Like Drugs? (p. 250).
One way of minimizing the risk of inhalants in aerosol cans is to avoid purchasing aerosol deodorants, fixatives, and oven cleaners if these products are available in other forms.

Learn More About It (p. 251).
In addition to the titles listed in the text, you can recommend the following books to your students:

Madison, Arnold. *Smoking and You.* New York: Julian Messner, 1975. The history of cigarette smoking; its bad effects on one's body and mind and on the health of others.

Manatt, Marsha. *Parents, Peers and Pot.* Rockville, MD: National Institute on Drug Abuse. This booklet is an informative, straight-forward discussion of marijuana use. It is available through Prevention Branch, Division of Resource Development, National Institute on Drug Abuse, 5600 Fisher Lane, Rockville, MD, 20851.

Sonnett, Sherry. *Smoking.* New York: Franklin Watts, Inc., 1977. The history of smoking; how smoking affects the smoker.

For your own reading, you may be interested in the following books:

Association for the Advancement of Health Education. *Learning About Alcohol: A Resource Book for Teachers.* Reston, Va.: AAHPERD Publications, 1974. Practical information for teachers about alcohol education.

Association for the Advancement of Health Education. *The Drug Alternative.* Reston, Va.: AAHPERD Publications, 1974. Countering the self-destructive behavior of taking drugs through developing and reinforcing self-esteem.

Modell, Walter, ed. *Drugs in Current Use and New Drugs.* New York: Springer Publishing Co., Inc., 1982. A list of drugs, their actions and uses, how they are prepared and administered, and the antidotes.

Richard C. Schroeder Congressional Quarterly, Inc. *The Politics of Drugs: An American Dilemma.* Washington, D.C., 1980. A look at the use of drugs in the United States, the reasons, and the possible ways in which it can be changed.

If time permits, you may wish to use one or more of the following audiovisual materials with this chapter:

Alcohol and Alcoholism. Pleasantville, N.Y.: Imperial Educational Resources, Inc., 1981. 4 filmstrips, 4 LPs/cassettes. The cultural, historical, and medical aspects of alcohol.

Drugs: Values and Decisions. Pleasantville, N.Y.: Sunburst Communications, 1981. 3 color filmstrips, 3 cassettes, guide. Personal-value issues associated with drug use and abuse are examined.

Smoking... or Health? and *Alcohol: Fun or Folly?* Pleasantville, N.Y.: Imperial Educational Resources, Inc., 1981. 2 LPs/cassettes, 2 filmstrips, 2 booklets. Stresses the physical dangers of smoking tobacco and drinking alcohol.

Write About Better Health (p. 253).
Despite individual differences, students' answers should contain much of the following content:

1. Products such as vegetable sprays, hairsprays, paints, glues, lighter fluid, and window cleaners are sometimes inhaled so that people can experiment with the effects. Inhalants can damage the brain, nervous system, and respiratory system. Large amounts can impair motor skills; cause permanent brain damage; and lead to heart failure, suffocation, or sudden death.
2. Cigarettes do not really taste good. They do not help people relax because nicotine is actually a stimulant drug. Smoking does not make people look attractive but discolors their teeth and fingers. People cannot just stop when they want because they become psychologically and physically dependent.
3. Cigarette smoke in the air can increase the heart rate, blood pressure, and carbon monoxide levels of nonsmokers in the room.
4. Some people think that drugs will make them feel happier, more relaxed, or freer.
5. Other activities, such as exercising, walking or talking with a friend, playing a game, reading a book, going to a movie, or having a snack are better ways of temporarily escaping a problem or getting a lift than using drugs.

CHAPTER 10
BETTER HEALTH FOR CONSUMERS

Chapter Overview

In this chapter students learn that many decisions they and their families make as consumers affect their health. The first section of the chapter examines ways of making responsible decisions about products; the second describes laws and agencies that protect consumers. Students of this age are becoming increasingly responsible for buying food (snacks, lunches, sometimes even food for family meals), clothing, and personal health-care products. This chapter gives them some criteria to use as a basis for decision making.

Objectives

After studying this chapter, students should be able to

- cite some health values to look for in products and services.*
- describe how consumers can make use of product labels.*
- discuss ways in which advertising can help consumers.*
- name ways that consumers can protect themselves against unsafe products and services.*
- identify some laws and government agencies that protect consumers.

Suggested Activities and Discussions

Chapter Opener (pp. 254–255).
Students may enjoy sharing stories of difficulties they have had with products and measures, if any, they have taken to try to resolve the problems.

Looking Ahead (p. 256).
Ask the students to consider the kinds of things they purchase in a three-month period and to decide which of them have an effect on their health.

---

*These objectives are stated in age-appropriate terms on page 256 of the student text.

YOU CAN BE AN EFFECTIVE CONSUMER (pp. 258–265).

What Is a Consumer? (p. 258).
Ask the students to think about consumer decisions they make or help their families make that may affect their own health. Some possibilities include the purchase of a school lunch; the selection of footwear; the use of protective clothing; the purchase of candy, gum, or soft drinks (with a negative effect on health); the following of a doctor's instructions in taking medication; the careful use of certain chemicals, such as paint thinner, airplane glue, and window cleaners; the telling of an adult about a health-related problem. If possible, some health services should be included in the list: visits to doctors, dentists, the school nurse, or other health professionals.

School lunches are often a good subject for discussion, as are snacks. For a school lunch, how well the product works becomes how well the food helps the body grow and develop. For snacks, how safe a product is becomes how it may affect teeth or weight.

You Can Make Good Decisions (pp. 258–259).
Check to see whether students realize that the same brand-name item may be sold at different prices in different stores. Price comparison is usually advisable. There are times, however, when factors other than the lowest price should be considered. Sometimes the additional cost of traveling to get an item at a lower price may make the price difference totally irrelevant. Occasionally an item is needed immediately, and a convenience store may be the only available outlet.

Read Your Labels (pp. 260–261).
An important item of information included on dairy products, processed meats (bacon, luncheon meat, etc.), and baked goods is a freshness date or last-sale date. Consumers can get the best value and most freshness by buying products with the latest last-sale or freshness date.

Have students make a "Learn To Read Labels" poster showing labels from different kinds of health products. Be sure to include some labels that give nutritional information on foods and some labels that have health warnings.

What Does Advertising Tell You? (pp. 262–263). Have students test some advertising claims. Ask them to find magazine advertisements for three brands of peanut butter and list the major claims and appeals of each. Then have them conduct a blind taste test. (Either mask the labels or repackage the contents.) How does each brand measure up to the claims of its advertisement?

On Your Own (p. 263). Students who have participated in this activity may benefit from a discussion of the reasons for their ratings. They can try to identify the ways advertisers try to appeal to consumers.

Some People Believe Myths About Products (pp. 264–265). There is nothing wrong with electric toothbrushes, but they cost more to buy and use than regular toothbrushes do. Scientific studies have shown that brushing with a regular toothbrush is just as effective as brushing with an electric one.

A mouthwash strong enough to kill all the germs in the mouth would also be so strong that it would harm the lining of the mouth. Furthermore, a few seconds following use of this mouthwash, the mouth would have its normal complement of germs back (since there are millions of bacteria in every breath of air).

Although the protein in eggs, milk, and certain other foods can coat hairs so that they become more glossy, even the growing hair in the follicles cannot be fed by external nutrients.

Vitamins are organic chemicals that the body cannot make sufficiently for itself. Most excess vitamins are simply excreted. The fat-soluble vitamins, A, D, E, and K are stored in the body, and an excess of these vitamins can make a person ill. Students should be discouraged from taking extra vitamins unless their parents or doctor believe they need them.

WHO PROTECTS THE CONSUMER? (pp. 266–268).

Health Products Must Be Safe and Effective (p. 266). Students should understand that in addition to food and drugs, the safety of beauty-care products (excluding soap) is also a responsibility of the FDA. The FDA's authority to require that the safe-and-effective standard be applied *before* marketing refers only to products making health claims. Such products are technically classified as drugs. If the FDA has reason to suspect that a cosmetic is unsafe, it will test the cosmetic even though it is not classified as a drug. Even mechanical devices, such as belts for "spot-reducing," are classified as drugs if their manufacturers claim that they make specific changes in the body.

People Working for Your Health (p. 266). Have students make a list of the consumer reporters in your area—on radio or television or in local newspapers. Assign the students to observe the topics the consumer reporters discuss. If there are topics your students would like to see covered, ask class members to write to these reporters with their suggestions.

Consumers Are Protected by Their Government (p. 267). Actions by the FTC, FDA, and the U.S. Consumer Products Safety Commission are often news items. Have students clip articles on actions these or other groups have taken to help consumers.

Health Professionals Must Be Licensed (p. 268). Some young people may feel that they have outgrown the family pediatrician and are ready for an adults' doctor. Discuss with students some *responsible* ways of suggesting such a change to their families and of getting sound information to guide their choice of a new physician. Some pediatricians in fact have a maximum age for retaining patients. Many physicians are happy to make referrals in such circumstances.

Often young people will switch to the physician the family adults use. There are some definite advantages to having the same primary-care doctor take care of an entire family. In some cases, however, it is best to select a physician who is particularly attuned to the health needs of adolescents.

Whenever possible, the first visit should be made when there is no urgent health problem.

Learn More About It (p. 269). In addition to the titles listed in the text, you can recommend the following books to your students:

Encyclopedia Britannica, Inc. *Webster's Beginning Book of Facts.* Springfield, Mass.: G. & C. Merriam Co., 1978. Information and facts about science and nature, products and objects are given here.

Papallo, George. *What Makes It Work?* New York: Arco Publishing, Inc., 1976. Explanations of how all kinds of things—microwave ovens, lasers, consumer products—work.

Sobol, Harriet Langsam. *Cosmo's Restaurant.* New York: Macmillan Publishing Co., 1978. A story about a boy whose family owns and runs a restaurant, shown through a typical day there.

Sullivan, George. *How Do They Package It?* Philadelphia: The Westminster Press, 1976. About containers; consumers and the way they consume; products; and environmental concerns in packaging.

Students can write to the Food and Drug Administration for the following free pamphlets:
More Than You Ever Thought You'd Know About Food Additives; And Now a Word About Your Shampoo; In Pursuit of a Summer Tan.
Write to
Office of Consumer Communication
Food and Drug Administration
5600 Fishers Lane
Rockville, MD 20857

For your own reading, you may be interested in the following books:

Dorfman, John. *Consumer Tactics Manual.* New York: Atheneum Publishers, 1980. Ways to become a more informed consumer are presented.

The Editors of Consumer Report Books, *Consumer Reports Buying Guide Issue.* Mt. Vernon, N.Y.: Consumer Reports Books. All sorts of products are examined and reported here. Each year a new issue is published.

Myerson, Bess. *The Complete Consumer Book.* New York: Simon & Schuster, 1979. Information about products and services and ways to become a better consumer.

Root, Waverly. *Food.* New York: Simon & Schuster, 1982. One of the foremost experts on food and cooking discusses a wide range of topics, including food products, current myths and ideas on food, and the history and consumption of food in America and in the world.

Shipley, Roger, and Plonsky, Carolyn D. *Consumer Health: Protecting Your Health and Money.* New York: Harper & Row, Publishers/Inc., 1981. Information for buying all kinds of health products and avoiding dangerous or unhealthful products.

If time permits, you may wish to use one or more of the following audiovisual materials with this chapter:

Being a Consumer. Boulder, Colo.: Learning Tree Filmstrips, 1981. 4 filmstrips, 4 cassettes, guide. Ways to become a better consumer are explored.

Health Fads and Facts. Culver City, Cal.: Health Education Services, 1982. 2 color filmstrips, 2 records/cassettes, guide. Health quackery and worthless products are examined.

Write About Better Health (p. 271).
Allowing for some reasonable variations, answers should include the following basic information:

1. Good reasons for making consumer choices include the products' or services' effectiveness, safety, economy, and ability to suit the individual's taste. For health products, safety and effectiveness are the two most important reasons for making a consumer choice.
2. Labels commonly include a list of ingredients and nutrients, warnings, directions for use, and directions for care.
3. Advertising alerts the public to new products, describes what products are supposed to do, and suggests why one brand may be better than another.
4. Consumers may become more aware by reading advertisements responsibly and critically and by reading consumer-interest columns and publications. They can also share their consumer experiences—positive or negative—with others.
5. The U.S. Department of Agriculture checks the quality of poultry and meat shipped from one state to another. The FDA checks other foods, including pet foods; it checks medicines to see that they are safe and effective and reviews other products for which health claims are made. The U.S. Consumer Products Safety Commission works to keep products that might be unsafe from being sold. The U.S. Postal Service can refuse to accept products that are unsafe or that make false claims.

Building Better Health

Green Level
Red Level
GOLD LEVEL
Silver Level
Aqua Level

The information contained in this book is considered by the American Dental Association to be in accord with current scientific knowledge, 1982.

The publisher would like to thank the National Safety Council, without whose help completion of portions of this publication would not have been possible.

A complete list of organizations whose contributions made this series possible is found on page 288. The authors and editors are especially grateful to the following organizations for the quality and timeliness of their suggestions, participation and/or contributions of illustrative materials.

- Armed Forces Institute of Pathology
- Centers for Disease Control, Atlanta
- Girls Clubs of America, Inc.
- Girl Scouts of the U.S.A.
- Greater New York Councils, Boy Scouts of America
- Junior Achievement
- National 4-H Council of America
- National Science Foundation

The authors and editors express their appreciation to the students and teachers of the schools that previewed lessons and activities from BUILDING BETTER HEALTH. The names of those schools appear in the Teacher's Editions.

Building Better Health GOLD LEVEL

Teacher's Edition

CAROLINE PURCELL BARNES, B.A., M.A.
MARILYN K. BROWNE, B.S.
BETSY R. FLEMING, B.S., M.S.
MERCEDES W. GRANADY, R.N., M.S.
ARTHUR LEW, M.D.
GUY JAMES MANASTER, Ph.D.
LILLIAN BILLINGS MORAVA, B.S., M.Ed.
EDWARD ANTHONY OPPENHEIMER, M.D.
ARNOLD C. RATNER, M.D.
HOWARD L. WARD, F.A., D.D.S., M.A.

McDougal, Littell and Company
Evanston, Illinois
New York Sacramento

Created and Developed by
Contemporary (cpi) Perspectives, Inc.

BETSY R. FLEMING, B.S., M.S.
Teacher Specialist for Health and Drug Education
Anne Arundel County Public Schools
Annapolis, Maryland

CAROLINE PURCELL BARNES, B.A., M.A.
Health Education Specialist
Ector County Independent School District
Ector County, Texas

LILLIAN BILLINGS MORAVA, B.S., M.Ed.
Health and Physical Education Department Chairperson
La Porte High School
La Porte, Texas

MARILYN K. BROWNE, Registered Physical Therapist
Somerville Visiting Nurses Association
Somerville, Massachusetts

MERCEDES W. GRANADY, R.N., M.S.
Teacher, Special Education
Formerly Instructor of Nursing
New Rochelle High School
New Rochelle, New York

ARTHUR LEW, M.D.
Director of Training in Child Psychiatry
New York Medical College
New York, New York

GUY JAMES MANASTER, Ph.D.
Professor, Department of Educational Psychology
The University of Texas at Austin
Austin, Texas

EDWARD ANTHONY OPPENHEIMER, M.D.
Assistant Clinical Professor of Medicine
Division of Pulmonary Medicine
Department of Internal Medicine
U.C.L.A. Medical School
Los Angeles, California

ARNOLD C. RATNER, M.D.
Clinical Instructor, Dermatology
Georgetown University School of Medicine
Washington, D.C.

HOWARD L. WARD, F.A., D.D.S., M.A.
Assistant Dean for Clinical Affairs
College of Dentistry
New York University
New York, New York

Contributing Writers and Editors

Bryan Bunch, Teri Crawford, Eden Force Eskin, Barbara Gentile, Valerie A. Hurst, Charles Miller, Megan Scarpa, Marie C. Smith

Teacher's Edition
ISBN 0-88343-382-6

ISBN 0-88343-381-8

CHAPTER 3

63 YOUR AMAZING BODY

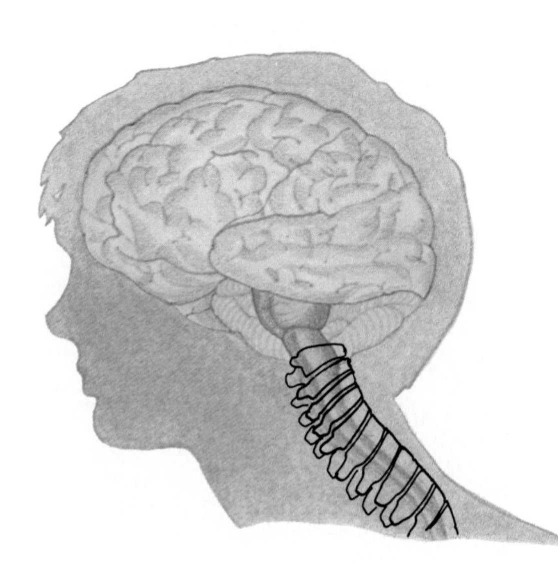

CHAPTER 4

81 WORKING FOR YOUR OWN HEALTH

CHAPTER 5

113 NUTRITIOUS FOODS FOR BETTER HEALTH

CHAPTER 6

145 YOU CAN LEARN THE SAFETY HABIT

NATURAL

24

1 YOUR EMOTIONS AFFECT YOUR HEALTH

See the teaching notes on page 12.

The Choice

Eddie was not very happy. He was "the new kid in town." Walking to school this morning, he had felt nervous about meeting new friends. He wished his old friends were still with him. By the end of the school day, Eddie was feeling no better. In fact, he was very lonely.

As he was leaving school, Eddie noticed a group of boys and girls gathered around the bicycle stand. Some of them were kicking a soccer ball. Eddie walked toward them to get his bicycle from the stand. His heart was pounding. Most of them are my own age, he thought, but they are all taller. If I ask them to play soccer with me, they may call me a "shrimp." That's what some of the smaller kids at the old school were called.

Eddie tried not to look at the boys and girls as he unlocked his bike. He felt, however, that *they* were looking at *him.* This made him uneasy, which caused him to lose his grip on the bike. It fell over, making a loud noise. Still not looking at them, he quickly picked up his bike and rode off.

Riding toward home, Eddie was upset. He asked himself, Why am I angry at *them*? How can I stop feeling lonely if I don't *try* to make some friends? Besides, soccer is my best sport! Eddie suddenly knew he was not angry with anyone else. He was angry with himself. It was his own fault that he was lonely. He was so afraid of making new friends that he never gave himself—or them—a chance.

Eddie turned his bike around at the corner and headed back toward school. Watching TV at home, he said to himself, isn't going to change being lonely, or small, or nervous, or anything else. When he saw the same group of girls and boys walking toward the school's soccer field, Eddie smiled. He put his bike in the stand again and ran over to them.

"Hi," Eddie called to the tallest boy in the group. "Can you use another player?"

Ask students to identify the changes in Eddie's thoughts, feelings, and actions that occur in the story. Discuss why Eddie, who felt lonely, did not immediately try to join a group of people his own age. What made Eddie realize that his own feelings might be working against his real needs? (*He suddenly realized that his feelings of anger and fear were really connected with past experiences rather than with the new situation.*) Emphasize for students the point that once Eddie correctly identified some of his feelings, he was able to choose and carry out an action that might both eliminate his loneliness and reduce his fear and anger.

LOOKING AHEAD

Almost everyone wants to be part of a group of friends. Almost everyone has also felt hurt or lonely by not being part of such a group. Sometimes people are left out by others who do not know they want to be friends. Sometimes people feel they do not know how to make friends, or even how to be liked. Perhaps they feel they are somehow different and not likely to be accepted as friends. Often this feeling is not shared by the people they would like to know better. When you would like to know others better, it is first important to know *yourself* better.

This chapter will help you learn more about yourself and about other people. You will find out more about

- the emotional needs of people.
- communicating with family and friends.
- building trust, dependability, and other personal qualities.
- handling anger, fear, and disappointments that cause stress.

Here are some words that you may not have talked about in school before. You will learn more about them in this chapter. You can find all these words in the *Glossary* at the back of this book.

communication (kə·myü'nə·kā'shən)
dependable (di·pen'də·bəl)
emotions (i·mō'shənz)
goals (gōlz)
physical (fiz'ə·kəl)
quality (kwol'ə·tē)
social (sō'shəl)
stress (stres)
trust (trust)

Early Checkup

Number a sheet of paper from **1** through **5.** Answer each of these questions by writing **yes** or **no** next to the correct number on your paper. You can check your answers as you read this chapter.

1. Does good health involve more than taking care of your body? yes
2. Is having friends an important part of good health? yes
3. Do people share thoughts and feelings only by talking? no
4. Will hiding your mistakes make your friends think better of you? no
5. Can understanding your thoughts and feelings help you handle stress? yes

An *Early Checkup* appears toward the beginning of every chapter in this book. Each of these ungraded quizzes is designed to meet three objectives. First, it introduces some of the health principles covered in the chapter. Second, it motivates students to read the chapter for information. Third, it helps dispel some mistaken beliefs that students may have, and encourages them to develop the habit of checking reliable sources to find out about sound health principles.

You may want to discuss some of the ideas covered in the *Early Checkup.* Assure the students that they will learn the answers as they read the chapter.

emotions
physical

Discuss the need to balance all aspects of one's health—physical, emotional, and social—by referring to the opening story again.

Often a person feels angry at others for leaving him or her out. However, the others may think the person is not interested in joining them. What can this person do to get along better with others? Can being friendly toward others affect a person's health?

THINKING ABOUT TOTAL HEALTH

Good Health Is Balanced Health

The way you take care of your body affects your **physical** health. Good physical health means having a body that is as healthy as possible. Did you know that being healthy also helps you to think better? People who are tired or hungry often do not do their best in school. They also may be more easily upset with friends, families, and teachers. This is because the health of your body can also affect your **emotions**.

All the ways you feel about different people and different events are called emotions. Sadness, happiness, fear, excitement, jealousy, anger, pride, and love are all emotions. Can you think of other emotions you feel from time to time?

Just as the health of your body affects your emotions, your emotions also affect your body. People who are unhappy about some problem are not likely to play at their best or have their usual energy. They may find it hard to get enough sleep, or to eat what they should for good health.

Building and keeping your best physical and emotional health are also important in getting along with other people. People who feel good about themselves usually feel better about their families and friends. They enjoy being with other people. Their minds are often clearer. They may be better able to deal with the problems that often come up between people who live, play, or work together.

What was your answer to *Early Checkup* number 1? (Does good health involve more than taking care of your body?)

social

Your Social Health Is Important, Too

Most doctors agree that physical and emotional health affect each other. Both can also affect your **social** health. The abilities to make new friends and get along with others are part of social health. Having good social health does *not* mean always agreeing with others or always joining the crowd. People with good social health enjoy spending some time alone.

goals

Students may suggest other needs associated with good physical, mental/emotional, and social health. You may wish to list their suggestions on the chalkboard and invite discussion of how meeting or not meeting each need could affect a person's total health.

People Have Emotional Needs

You know that everyone needs nourishing food and a balance of rest and exercise for the best physical health. People also have needs for emotional health. For example, most people need to feel successful. They feel better when they have **goals** they can keep trying to achieve. The goals may be activities they would like to try, or things they would someday like to own. Goals can be learning new skills, like building model boats or airplanes. Many people can feel successful even when they do not reach their goal. By just trying to reach it, they may make new friends or learn new skills.

Another emotional need is to be loved by family and friends. Almost all people live in families when they can. People who live together can share love by helping and supporting each other. People also need to find friends with whom they can share fun and some of their day-to-day problems. This does not mean that people need to be with others all the time. Most people also like to be by themselves at times.

People need to feel wanted by others. People need to share love, thoughts, and feelings.

What was your answer to *Early Checkup* number 2? (Is having friends an important part of good health?)

On Your Own

Every person is different from every other person. You can explore your own needs and learn more about who you are by writing a description of yourself. First, describe what you look like. Next, write down some skills you think you may have. Here are some questions to consider as you write about yourself. This is your own description, and you do not need to show it to anyone else.

1. What are your goals—what would you like to own, or become, or be able to do better?
2. Who are the people you like? What qualities of theirs do you admire?
3. Who are the people who like being with you? What do you think they like about you?
4. What do you like best about yourself?
5. What do you want most to improve about yourself?
6. What kinds of activities do you enjoy?

Keep your description in a safe place. In a few months, read it again. See if you want to add something to your description or change it in any way. Perhaps reading it every few months will show you some ways you are growing and changing.

People need to feel successful and have others recognize their success. People need to think of how others feel.

Your Decisions Can Affect Your Health

Some people will always be better at some things than other people. However, friends help each other to learn new skills. This helps to make them like each other and to like themselves.

What other people think of you is important. What you think of yourself, however, is even more important. Often the more content you are with yourself, the more others seem to like you. This is one reason people should spend some time thinking about their own good characteristics and abilities. They should also take the time to evaluate what they would like to improve. For example, you may be happy about the skills you are learning in some sport or hobby. You may find, however, that you get upset with others on

your team who do not play as well. Finding ways to help others do better may keep you from getting upset. You might also find that you can accept people for what they are.

It is important to decide how far you are willing to go to make or keep your friends. There may be times when a friend needs your help but you have something else you want to do. Sometimes you may decide to put aside your own interests to help your friend. Sometimes you may decide to do what you had planned to do. It is good to help others. Sometimes, though, it is also right to say *no* when you have to follow plans that are important to you.

At other times your friends may want to do something that you think is wrong. It may be something that can hurt your health, or annoy or harm someone else. These are the times when you must be able to tell your friends exactly how you feel.

What Have You Learned?

Number a piece of paper from **1** through **4**. Next to the numbers, write the words that are missing in these sentences.

1. Good health is a combination of good physical and ___ health. Healthy people seem to be better able to get along with ___ .

2. Getting along with people can be called ___ health.

3. Everyone needs a family and ___ to share problems and fun.

4. Getting to know your own abilities can help you ___ yourself.

Answers to *What Have You Learned?*
1. emotional (social, mental); others
2. social
3. friends
4. like (understand, help)

YOU AND OTHERS

Families and Friends Try To Understand

Most young people are friendly with others their own age. Friends, however, can often be different ages and different sizes, and enjoy doing different things. Some friends are quiet, while others talk a lot. Some are not very active, while others are always involved in an activity. Each friend has different skills and abilities.

Families, too, are made up of different people, with different needs and interests. Most members of a family expect each other to act in *courteous* and helpful ways. At times, your family may expect you to do certain things or behave in certain ways, even when you do not completely agree. Since they probably are helpful to you in ways that are not always easy for them, it is fair that you sometimes go out of your way for your family, too.

Different friends like you for different reasons. They may share some of your interests and not others. Some like certain characteristics you have, but may not like all of them. Good friends, however, always care about what you think and feel, even when what they think and feel is different.

To have good friends, you must be a good friend. You must be able to share your time with others in ways that often help them more than yourself. For example, a good friend must be a good *listener.* Friends need to be able to talk to each other about their thoughts, feelings, and needs. By talking about how their feelings may be the same or different, friends often find new ways to help and enjoy each other. Friends can be honest and open with each other while still showing they care about each other's health and well-being.

Tony likes Fred, but will not smoke a cigarette to keep Fred's friendship. At first, Fred called Tony "chicken," but now he seems to understand how his friend feels. Tony hopes Fred will change his own mind, and not smoke.

communication

Discuss the idea that nonverbal behavior, such as actions and facial expressions, can have several meanings. (*One person will raise a fist to signal encouragement. Someone else uses the raised fist to imply a threat. A frown can mean a person is deep in thought, or it can communicate anger.*)

Older and Younger Friends

People do not have to be the same age to be friends. Often you may feel friendly toward younger boys and girls who need your help and sometimes your protection. In the same way, you probably know adults who can help you because they care about you. Older people have had more years to build *wisdom* and skills they can teach their younger friends. Wisdom is knowing how to think through hard problems and dealing with them in the best possible way. Talk with older members of your family and others when something troubles you. Older friends can be wise and helpful.

Invite interested students to pantomime such emotions as concern, happiness, sadness, fear, anger, grief, surprise, approval, pride, worry, and shyness. Have the class guess which emotion is being shown. Answers may vary considerably. This is a good time to make the point that asking questions and listening can help you to keep from misunderstanding another person's expressions and actions.

Families and Friends Share Feelings

People get to know each other by sharing thoughts and feelings. This sharing is called **communication**. Talking and writing are two ways people can communicate. They also communicate how they feel by what they do. For example, people who are angry may frown or slam the door. Sad people may cry or walk with their heads bent downward. Some people show they are happy to see you by waving and smiling.

Families and friends who care about each other often communicate how they are feeling without saying a word.

What was your answer to *Early Checkup* number 3? (Do people share thoughts and feelings only by talking?)

Sometimes people are thinking so hard about their own feelings that they forget to think about the feelings of someone else. Often the adults in a family may have problems with the health of a relative, or in paying certain bills, or in getting along with someone important to them. Younger people in the family may also have problems that seem just as important to them. At these times it can be hard for younger and older people to communicate as well as they might. In the same way, friends sometimes have a problem communicating with each other. These are the times when people who care for each other need to be as patient, courteous, and understanding as they can.

A good way to open up communication is to tell people how you see them and then see if they agree. The girl in the picture is doing just this, saying, "You look awfully unhappy sitting there with a serious expression. Are you feeling unhappy?"

Listening carefully is part of good communication. Listening well means paying close attention. It means asking questions to make sure you understand what the other person thinks and feels. Someone who is looking around usually is not listening well. Someone who is thinking about what he or she will say next often is not listening well either. Being a good listener helps you to know your family and friends better. Sometimes listening may be asking what is wrong when a parent, some other adult you love, or a friend has not said a word. How might you know if people need some kindness when they have not asked for it?

Although smiles, frowns, and many other facial expressions may differ only slightly from one culture to another, some societies may encourage more or less expression of emotions in people's faces. If any of your students are familiar with other cultures, they may be able to share their knowledge with the class. "Body language" might also be included in such a discussion.

quality

People Try To Build Their Personal Qualities

People who are *considerate* show their friends they care by calling when they are going to be late for an activity. Considerate people try not to interrupt others who are talking. They try not to make noise or disturb others who are reading, studying, or working hard. Considerate people also find ways to let others know it is nice to have them as friends. Being considerate toward others is a personal **quality** that most people expect in friends.

There are other qualities people look for in friends. They want friends who are good sports and who show *respect* for others. A good sport enjoys winning a game and sharing the credit with others who helped. Good sports show others respect. They can enjoy winning without making fun of the people who tried but lost. Good sports also know how to accept losing a game. They do not try to blame themselves or others for losing. They think about what they did well and how they can do even better next time.

There are many more ways to show people you respect them. Respect can mean leaving others alone when they want to be by themselves. Respect is listening politely to someone even when you do not agree. Being careful with something you have borrowed and returning it promptly show your respect for others. Telling people how much you enjoy being their friend is also a way of showing them respect.

Many movies, television programs, and books have done an excellent job of presenting the problems, achievements, optimism, and courage of people who have different kinds of disabilities. Invite students to tell the class what they respect and admire about people with handicaps whom they have seen, read about, or know personally.

Discuss with students the need to be considerate of another person's time. Invite students to give other examples of ways to be considerate of others.

Being Considerate on the Telephone

"Hi, Juanita. Are you busy? Oh, you're having dinner? What's the best time to call you about the science project? Seven-thirty? Fine with me. Thanks!"

Writing a letter can be an excellent way to communicate your respect for another person. This is especially true when the letter mentions some of the things you appreciate about the person and about the experiences you have shared.

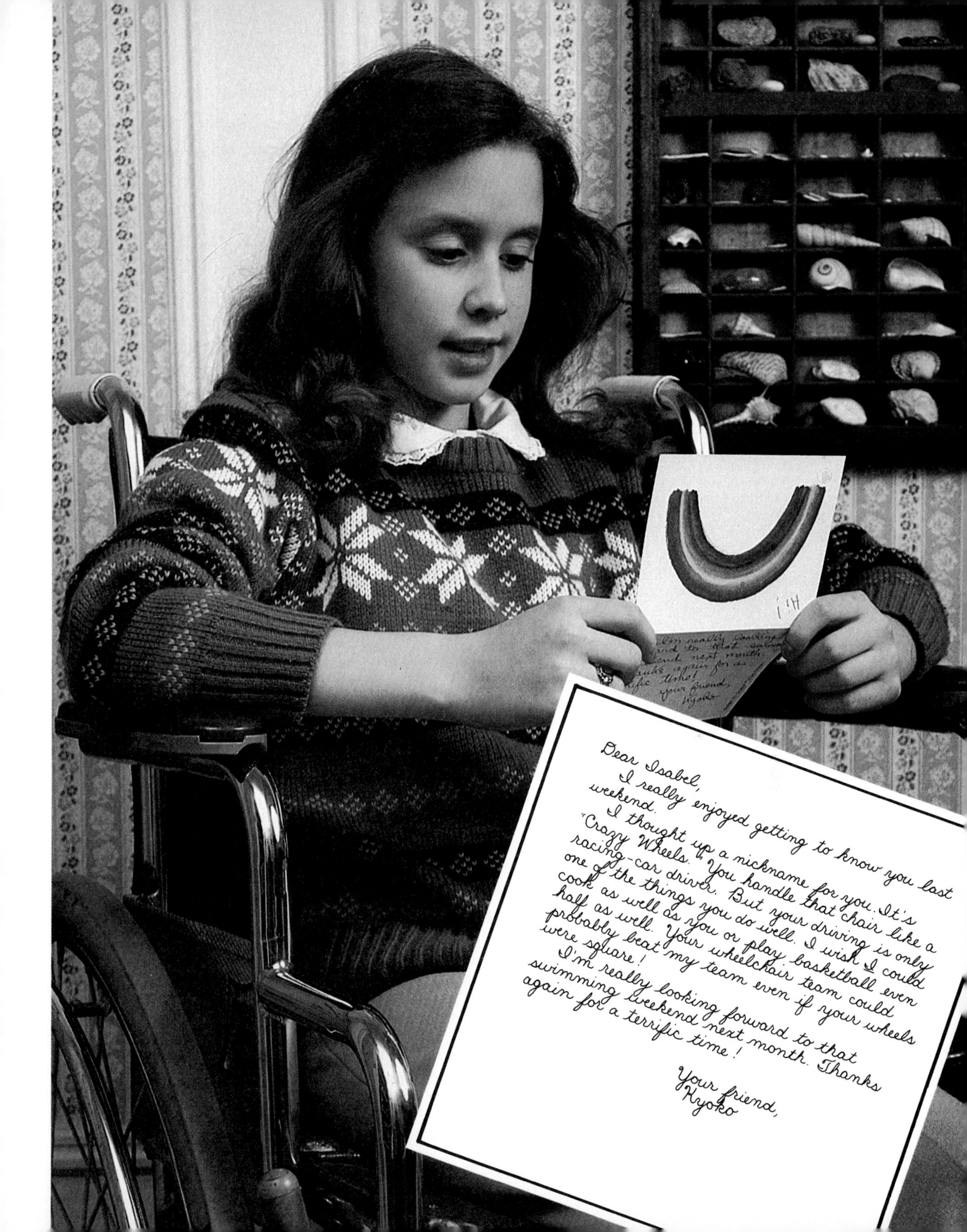
Dear Isabel,
I really enjoyed getting to know you last weekend.
I thought up a nickname for you. It's "Crazy Wheels." You handle that chair like a racing-car driver. But your driving is only one of the things you do well. I wish I could cook as well as you or play basketball even half as well. Your wheelchair team could probably beat my team even if your wheels were square!
I'm really looking forward to that swimming weekend next month. Thanks again for a terrific time!

Your friend,
Kyoko

dependable
trust

Another quality that people expect in friends is that they be **dependable**. Dependable people can be relied on to do what they say they will do. There are many ways to be dependable. You can show your family you are dependable by being on time for meals and by doing chores and homework without having to be reminded. You show classmates you are dependable by doing your part of a group project well—and on time. What are some other ways you show your family and friends that you are dependable?

Sometimes it is difficult to be dependable. Without realizing it, people may agree to do more than they really can. They may not have the time to do something as well as they should. They may have to put off doing what they have promised others they would do. To be dependable, people must think about how much time they really have. They must think of what else they have agreed to do before promising to do something new. By honestly telling friends why you cannot do what you said you would, you may be able to work things out. Making excuses for forgetting can make others think you are not dependable.

To be trusted, friends try to be more than dependable. When you have **trust** in people, you have confidence in them. You believe in them. To be trusted, people try to be honest and truthful, even when this seems hard to do. People *earn* trust by not talking badly about friends to others, even just for fun. They are *loyal* to their friends. However, this does not mean they will support them even when they think their friends are wrong. Good friends and family members can be trusted to help others make better, more healthful decisions.

Ask students to identify qualities they would like in a friend. In addition to those already mentioned in the text, they might suggest *a sense of humor, honesty,* and *truthfulness.* Have students tell why each quality is important. Then have each student write a "want ad" for a person to fill the position of his or her friend. The ad should include a description of their own qualities as well as the qualities they would like the "applicants" to have. Have students keep their ads in a safe place for a few months and take them out for revisions later.

The photo provides students with an example of a healthful way to work out an overscheduling problem. One friend made plans without stopping to think about previous agreements and admits the oversight, suggesting an alternative. This helps friends understand, even though they may be disappointed. A friend's honesty lets others know he or she is an important friend. A friend's understanding and willingness to make new plans say "I am still your friend."

What was your answer to *Early Checkup* number 5? (Will hiding your mistakes make your friends think better of you?)

"I know I said I'd play, but I forgot
I promised to clean my room. I'm sorry
I didn't remember sooner."

"That's OK. Sometimes I
forget, too. How about
Saturday?"

What Have You Learned?

Number a piece of paper from **1** through **5**. Next to the numbers, write the words that are missing in these sentences.

1. To have good —, you must be a good — yourself.

2. Families and friends share their thoughts and feelings by — with each other.

3. Being a good — means paying close attention to what other people are saying. It also means asking — to make sure you understand what they are thinking and feeling.

4. Caring about others and being a good sport are personal — people like in their friends.

5. Showing — and admiration, and being —, are all personal qualities that help to build strong friendships.

Answers to *What Have You Learned?*
1. friends; friend
2. communicating (communication, talking)
3. listener; questions
4. qualities
5. respect; dependable (courteous)

stress

Ask students to mention situations in which a person might experience stress that could be harmful. Write their ideas on the chalkboard. If it is necessary, start the list with examples such as *moving to a new place, having too much to do, arguing with a friend, worrying about someone who is ill,* and *being in trouble with parents about grades.*

STRESS AND YOUR EMOTIONS

How Can Stress Affect You?

Do you ever feel so excited about something that you have trouble sleeping? Do you ever feel nervous before doing something you think will be difficult? These kinds of feelings are caused by **stress**. Stress comes from any activity, problem, or thought that makes people feel tense or strained. Stress can cause a strain on your body. It can also strain your mind.

Stress often helps people to do their best. Their brains signal their bodies to get ready for some special, new challenge. This may start with a surge of energy. Their muscles get tense and ready to move quickly. Their hearts

Each of these racers wants to win. They are all using stress to concentrate their energy for their best effort.

beat faster, sending more blood and oxygen to their brains. All parts of the body tune up to help them meet the challenge.

Stress can be harmful when people cannot quickly make use of it and cannot reduce the strain. People who are unable to handle their stress may become physically ill. The stress has made them ready for action, but they must be able to think of some action to take. For example, the student who gets a poor report card can feel great stress. The student's family may get upset, and that can add to the *tension.* The student can find a way to use this stress by taking action.

One kind of action is to make a plan to get better grades. The student can set up study time and homework time. If it is necessary, the student can ask for help in understanding schoolwork. By taking sensible steps to make the next report card a better one, the student can reduce the stress.

Stress Can Harm You Physically, Emotionally, and Socially

Physical Effects
tiredness; upset stomach; headache; no appetite; cannot sleep; fast heartbeat

Emotional Effects
worry; nervousness; cannot think clearly; fear; frustration; forgetfulness; anger

Social Effects
cannot listen well; irritable with others; impatient with others; critical of others

Then have students list the kinds of emotions a person may have in each stressful situation. Record their responses beside the first list. Explain that the first step in handling stress in a healthful way is to identify all of the feelings involved.

Most people think of stress exclusively as a health risk. In reality, students should learn that people experience stress every day. Often the stress helps them accomplish what they want or need to do. Whenever they set goals, people create challenging and stressful situations. How well and how rapidly the goals are accomplished depend in part on how well people handle the stress they create.

Not everyone in a given situation experiences the same kind or amount of stress. Physical health and other factors, such as one's self-image, also influence the ways an individual handles stress.

In this text, students are given an unusually clear explanation of why stress becomes harmful. The authors do not expect them to develop an in-depth understanding of the subject. The text is designed merely to help them recognize when they are experiencing stress—both helpful and harmful. It also introduces healthful ways to handle thoughts and emotions associated with stressful situations.

Some people find it helpful to write about the stress they are feeling. Simply describing their thoughts and feelings seems to reduce the strain.

Some people are helped more by exercise or sports when they feel stress. Exercise helps to loosen tight muscles. It helps take people's minds off their problems for a while.

People Learn To Handle Stress

In the story, "The Choice," that opened this chapter, Eddie was under a lot of stress. Part of this stress came from moving to a new home. He had not yet made new friends. Another part of Eddie's stress came from remembering an unhappy experience. He worried that he might have the same problem with some people in this new school. Eddie was feeling strong emotions—sadness, loneliness, and fear. These emotions added to the stress.

Eddie made a healthful decision to do something about the stress he felt. First, he *identified* the problem. He tried to understand his own thoughts and feelings. He found that they were caused more by what happened in the past than by what was happening now. This helped him decide to take the risk that his new friends might tease him.

As Eddie walked toward the group, he was probably still feeling stress. Now, however, stress was helping him to reach his goals. He wanted to make some friends and to play soccer. His earlier thoughts and feelings were still with him, but his new thoughts and feelings were stronger. His stress had become helpful rather than harmful.

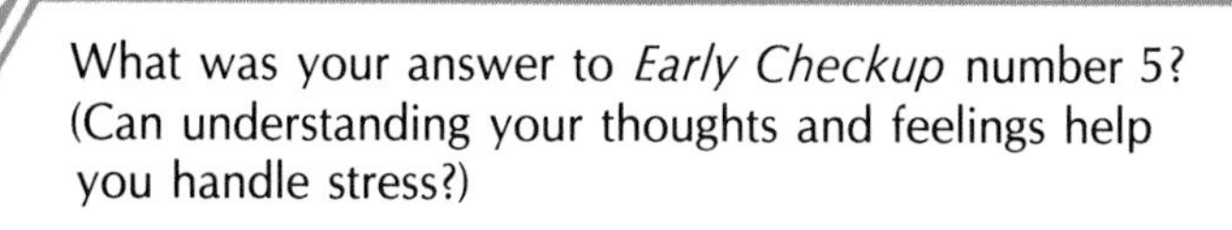

What was your answer to *Early Checkup* number 5? (Can understanding your thoughts and feelings help you handle stress?)

By this point, students should begin to realize that often people's thoughts and feelings amplify the stress they feel. List some thoughts and feelings on the board that may be barriers to handling stress in a healthful way. Then have students suggest helpful thoughts and feelings that they might choose to replace those on the first list. You might begin with the following:

I can't do that.
I'm nervous.
I'm really stupid.
I can't help it.
I'm ugly.

I will do my best.
I'm excited.
I need to learn more.
I think I could change this.
I have a nice smile.

Understanding Your Emotions Helps Control Stress

Strong, unpleasant emotions, such as anger, disappointment, and fear, can cause stress in people. For example, the unhappiness people feel when a family member is ill can cause stress in the rest of the family. Families and friends often find that stress makes it harder to communicate and get along well together. Long periods of stress can affect their health. This is why people must learn to deal with their unpleasant emotions *before* they lead to harmful stress.

The first step in handling your emotions and reducing stress can be to talk about how you feel when you are upset. It is often best to do this when you are *not* feeling upset.

"Anger makes me feel like I'm exploding."

"My stomach gets tied up in knots."

"When I feel angry, I want to yell."

"I feel shaky all over."

"I feel disappointed with my pen pal when she doesn't answer my letters."

"I feel disappointed when I'm not home and my grandparents telephone our family."

"I feel disappointed with myself when I strike out at bat."

People Working for Your Health

Aline Lemmons is a Girl Scout leader in Forth Worth, Texas. She helps the seventh and eighth grade girls in her troop learn about other cultures, about what it is like for people to have a disability, and about themselves. The troop has a lot of fun and helps other people to have fun, too.

There are many reasons why Ms. Lemmons enjoys being a Girl Scout leader. Through Girl Scouting, she gives young people opportunities they might not have had otherwise. She has a chance to encourage them to accept people who are different from themselves. As Ms. Lemmons says, "Girl Scouting lets me help young people believe in themselves and what they can do."

Fear is another emotion that causes stress. Sometimes people are afraid with good reason. For example, seeing a fire in the kitchen would cause anyone to feel afraid. It is important, however, to deal with an emotion like fear by taking some form of action. In the case of a fire, warning your family, getting out of the house, and calling the fire department are actions that help to reduce fear. Changing the unpleasant emotion can reduce stress.

Sometimes people have different fears that others may not have at all. Some people are afraid of dogs. Most of these people would like to be less afraid. They might try taking some small steps to help themselves.

Looking at pictures of dogs or reading a book about them is a good first step. Visiting a friend who has a small dog or visiting a pet shop to look at puppies in their cages might help also. By learning about dogs and spending time with them, people may get used to being near dogs. As their fear of dogs changes, such people should feel less stress.

How might people with a fear of speaking in front of the class use some "small steps" to change their fear?

You might suggest these other ways for handling stress. *Get enough sleep and rest.* Someone who is not well rested may be irritable and unable to think clearly. *Avoid comparing yourself to others.* Every person learns and grows at his or her own rate.

What Have You Learned?

Number a piece of paper from **1** through **3**. Next to the numbers, write the words that are missing in these sentences.

1. Certain problems and unpleasant emotions can cause ___ in people.

2. Stress often ___ people in reaching their goals. If it lasts too long, it can ___ their health.

3. Learning to ___ their emotions can help people to handle stress.

Answers to *What Have You Learned?*
1. stress
2. helps; harm (hurt)
3. handle (control, understand)

Learn More About It

Do you want to learn more about people's feelings? You might look for some of these books in your library.

Herman, Charlotte. *Our Snowman Had Olive Eyes.* New York: E.P. Dutton, Inc., 1977. This is the story of a young girl and the loving relationship she develops with her grandmother.

Stein, Mark L. *Good and Bad Feelings.* New York: William Morrow and Co., Inc., 1976. This easy-to-read book tells about people's feelings of love, anger, fear, happiness, sadness, and more.

Wilder, Laura E. *Little House in the Big Woods.* New York: Harper & Row Publishers, Inc., 1932. This is one in a series of stories about a log-cabin family in Wisconsin in the late 1800's. Others in the series include *Little House on the Prairie* and *On the Banks of Plum Creek.*

More To Do on Your Own

1. People's faces can communicate their feelings. Cut out pictures of people's faces from old magazines. You might want to draw the faces instead. What messages do their faces communicate to you? Write these messages as captions.

2. What can you do to show you are responsible? You might help with more chores in your home. Here are some ideas. Offer to help with a younger brother or sister. Help with the dishes after a meal. Clean one room besides your own. These are ways you can show your respect for your family. What other ideas do you have? Write them down. Try to do at least one of them every day.

Final Checkup

A. Number a sheet of paper from **1** through **10**. Next to each number, write the letter of the words that best complete each sentence.

1. A person's emotional health can affect his or her
- **a.** physical health.
- **b.** social health.
- **c.** mental health.
- **d.** all of the above.

2. To be happy with yourself,
- **a.** think about your failures.
- **b.** think about other people's abilities.
- **c.** think about your good qualities.
- **d.** think about other people's failures.

3. Good friends should
- **a.** talk about their feelings.
- **b.** try to act the same.
- **c.** compare themselves to each other.
- **d.** always be with each other.

4. An example of communication is
- **a.** thinking about what you will say as the other person is talking.
- **b.** not telling your friend what is bothering you.
- **c.** hugging someone in your family.
- **d.** watching TV while someone is trying to talk to you.

5. To handle stress,
- **a.** do more activities all at the same time.
- **b.** do some exercise.
- **c.** try to ignore it.
- **d.** refuse to do your chores.

6. Responsible people
- **a.** hold in their feelings.
- **b.** do what is expected of them.
- **c.** make excuses for their mistakes.
- **d.** always succeed in whatever they do.

7. The first step to solving any problem is to
- **a.** identify the problem.
- **b.** think about how to solve it.
- **c.** keep trying solutions.
- **d.** talk to someone else about it.

8. When you feel angry at others,
- **a.** try to hold in your feelings.
- **b.** discuss your feelings with the people involved.
- **c.** make the people angry so they will know how you feel.
- **d.** scream at them.

9. When you have failed at something,
- **a.** blame it on someone else.
- **b.** give up.
- **c.** think of ways to improve.
- **d.** try to cover up your mistakes.

10. Fears may be overcome by
- **a.** ignoring them.
- **b.** trying to understand them.
- **c.** exercising and getting enough rest.
- **d.** eating healthful foods.

B. Number a piece of paper from **1** through **10**. Write **true** or **false** next to the number for each of these ideas.

1. To be a good friend you must do everything your friends do. false
2. Being loved helps people feel good about themselves. true
3. Everyone's mental picture is the same. false
4. Group members must share the same interests. false
5. Trust is something that must be earned. true
6. Stress is always helpful. false
7. Nothing is as important as what others think of you. false
8. People should always compare themselves with others in order to feel better. false
9. Everyone has fears. true
10. Some fears come from a person's past experiences. true

Write About Better Health

Write a short answer to each of these questions. Use complete sentences.

1. What are some ways that most people are alike?
2. How can good communication help people?
3. What are some ways to show that you are a responsible person?
4. What should you do when you feel angry?
5. What can people do to get over disappointment?

Model answers to *Write About Better Health* are provided in the chapter notes at the front of this *Teacher's Edition.*

2 PEOPLE GROW... PEOPLE CHANGE

Use the photograph as a springboard to discuss some of the details that indicate age: *size, smooth or wrinkled skin, hair (to an extent), distribution of fat and muscles, etc. Note that in some families, people of different ages also dress differently—certainly babies will be dressed differently from adults. Some less obvious—or nonvisible—indicators should also be noted: development of teeth, learning acquired in school, job skills, social development, and the accumulation of life experiences and wisdom.* Encourage students to think about the nonphysical and physical clues to an individual's age.

This chapter deals with three closely related major concepts: growth, heredity, and aging. The authors have placed earlier emphasis upon growth concepts, since students of this age can most easily understand and identify with the changes taking place in their own bodies. The chapter begins with the dynamic nature of growth. It covers those factors that the individual can help control through more healthful living, and those factors that the individual cannot control but must learn to accept and turn to positive value.

When you look at the people in a family, you can usually make a pretty good guess at their ages. Even when you cannot guess their exact ages, you can tell children from parents. Usually you can tell parents from grandparents. Your mind usually thinks "baby," "child," "teenager," "adult," or "elderly person." What you may not think about are the clues that help you to recognize the differences.

Look at the photograph of the family you see here. Think about the clues that lead you to decide about a person's age. Think about what stages of growth each person has probably experienced and what stages each has yet to experience.

Some differences among people of different ages cannot be seen. Can you think of any? These inner, hidden differences will be discussed in this chapter.

LOOKING AHEAD

As a person grows, the size of one part of the body may change, compared with the rest of the body. For example, how big is a baby's head compared with the rest of the baby's body? Does this change as the baby grows? What happens to the neck, shoulders, legs, and arms?

As people age, or grow older, they are constantly changing. Even after their bodies stop growing, they are still becoming different in various ways from day to day.

In this chapter, you will learn that there is no "just right" size for people at any age. Everyone grows differently. You will also learn

- how you will grow more slowly or quickly at different times of your life.
- what you can do to help the way your body, mind, and personality grow.
- how you can make the most of your body's growth plan.
- how you will change as you age.

Here are some words that you may not have talked about in school before. You will learn more about them in this chapter. You can find all these words in the *Glossary* at the back of this book.

cells (selz)
chromosomes (krō'mə·sōmz)
dominant (dom'ə·nənt)
endocrine glands (en'dō·krən glandz)
gene (jēn)
growth spurt (grōth spėrt)
heredity (hə·red'ə·tē)
hormones (hor'mōnz)
recessive (ri·ses'iv)
traits (trāts)

Early Checkup

How much do you already know about growth and aging? Number a piece of paper from **1** through **6**. Answer each of these questions by writing **yes** or **no** next to the correct number on your paper. You can check your answers as you read this chapter.

1. Does your height today tell you how tall you will be as an adult? no
2. Do all parts of the body grow at the same speed? no
3. Once the body stops growing in size, does it still need nutritious food and exercise? yes
4. Is the size you will be as an adult determined only by the size of your parents? no
5. If a child has two parents with blond hair, will the child also have a trait for blond hair? yes
6. Do the health choices you make now have anything to do with how you will age when you are older? yes

growth spurt

Most children, especially in the years just before they reach their teens, are concerned about growth. They worry that they will be too short or too tall, too fat or too thin. Help them to understand that growth rates vary and that their final height and weight may be very different from what their relative height and weight are now.

You can use the students' interest in this topic to introduce some of the main themes of the chapter. If there is no way to know people's final height and weight, how can people help themselves to grow in their own best way? What controls each person's final size? Student responses should include the following:

1. *A nutritious diet, regular exercise, and adequate rest all promote healthful growth.*
2. *The height and weight of parents and previous generations in a family set a pattern for the growth of each new generation.*

Students may also venture the myth that cigarette smoking makes people shorter. While there are a number of health risks in cigarette smoking, stunted growth is *not* a direct consequence of smoking. Also, there is no evidence that exercises designed to stretch the body do actually increase height.

YOUR BODY'S GROWTH

Everyone Grows at a Different Rate

Whatever your height is now, you have been growing every day of your life. Many of your bones have become longer, thicker, and heavier. Many of your muscles have also grown, and your skin has grown to cover your growing body.

Your body will continue to grow in size for years. Growth is slower in some years of your life than in others. At the age when you have a **growth spurt**, your body will grow very quickly. A growth spurt can occur at a different age for different people. Many girls may have their growth spurt between ages nine and thirteen. Many boys have a later growth spurt, taking place between ages eleven and fifteen.

After the spurt, growth slows down. Many girls stop getting taller around sixteen years of age. Many boys continue getting taller until they are around twenty years old. Different people also gain weight faster at different ages. Babies usually grow so fast that their weight triples between birth and the age of one year. By the age of eleven, people may weigh from seven to more than ten times their weight at birth.

It is hard for someone your age to know what size you will be years from now. For example, these people are the same age. Are they the same size? Their height and weight will most likely change a lot in the next ten years. The tallest and heaviest at this time may be the smallest and lightest in the future.

What was your answer to *Early Checkup* number 1? (Does your height today tell you how tall you will be as an adult?)

The photographs on these pages present a dramatic view of the growth of a person from birth to adulthood. Ask children why the stages shown are progressively further apart. (*Growth rates change with time. They become slower as the person grows older.*)

Body Parts Grow at Different Rates

You know that different people grow in different ways, at different times, and at different rates of speed. Even different parts of the same body grow differently. Arms and legs may grow faster than the rest of the body. Hands and feet may be their adult size long before the rest of the body.

What was your answer to *Early Checkup* number 2? (Do all parts of the body grow at the same speed?)

Young people often worry about the way they look at a certain age. They may feel their feet are too big. They may feel "too short" or "too tall." They may worry about some extra weight they have gained during a growth spurt. It often takes time for different parts of the body to "catch up" with each other. The right amount of *nutritious* food and exercise will help people finally reach the best weight for their bodies.

A newborn baby's head is large compared with the rest of the baby's body. Nutritious foods, together with crawling and kicking exercise, will make the baby's soft bones harder.

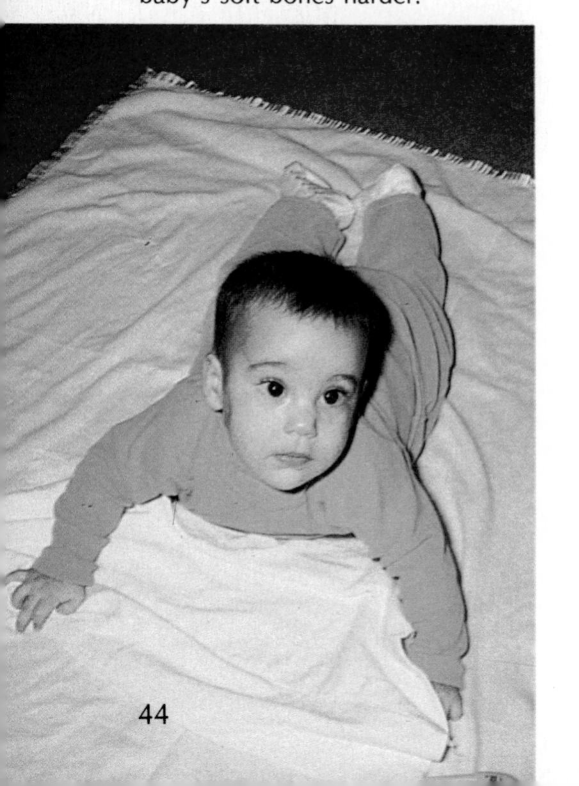

The body of a two-year-old has grown much larger. Hair and *primary,* or "baby," teeth have grown. Soft bones have become harder and longer. The child is walking and may be talking now.

At age six, healthy children may be twice the height they were at birth. Primary teeth should be cared for until they fall out and are replaced by *permanent teeth*. Healthful foods, daily brushing, and flossing will help keep these final teeth healthy and strong.

By age twelve, young people may have fully grown hands and feet on bodies that are still growing. There is no one "right" height or weight. Usually all the permanent teeth are in place. Daily meals must be well balanced for stronger muscles and bones. Exercise and rest are especially important in these quick-growth years.

By age twenty-five, body growth has caught up with fully grown hands and feet. The body has stopped growing. Nutritious food, exercise, and rest each day will maintain a healthy body as it grows older.

cells

Bodies Grow Because Cells Divide

You know that **cells** are the smallest living parts of a body. They are so small that they cannot be seen without a microscope. The human body is made up of more than 50 thousand billion, or 50 *trillion,* cells. This is what makes the bodies of people larger than the bodies of small animals like ants or mice. Most body cells are the same size, but larger bodies contain many more of them.

Cells multiply by dividing. This dividing body cell is seen through a microscope. A *cell membrane* surrounds the cell. Oxygen and food *nutrients* pass through the membrane from the blood into the *cytoplasm*—living, jelly-like material within the cell. Every cell also has a "control center" called the *nucleus.*

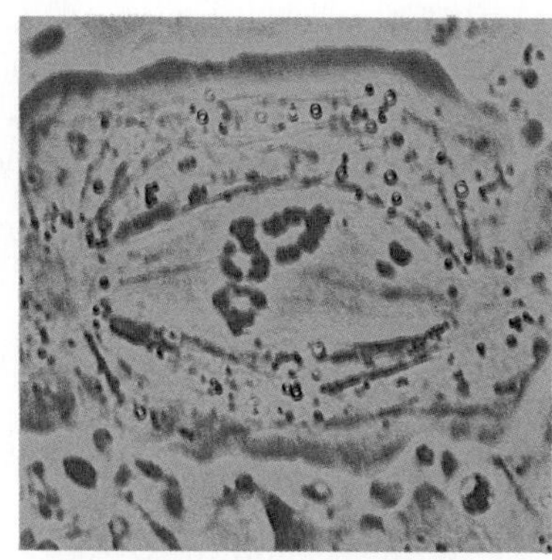

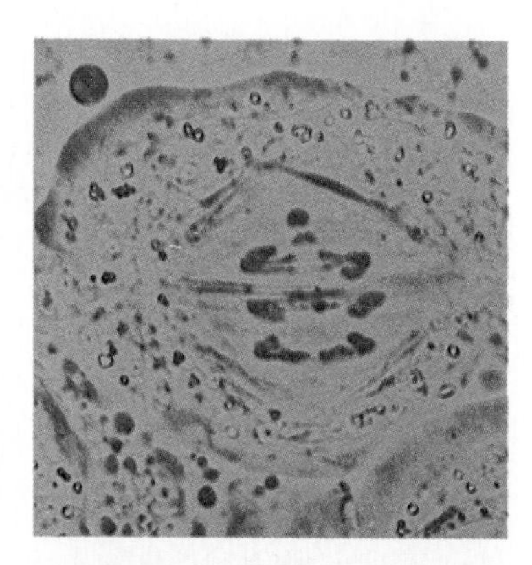

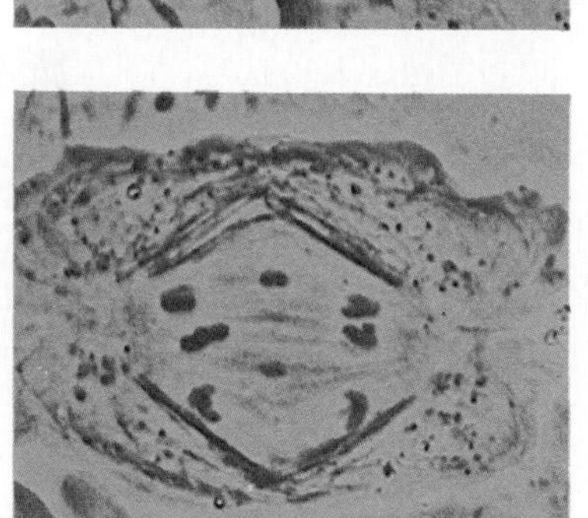

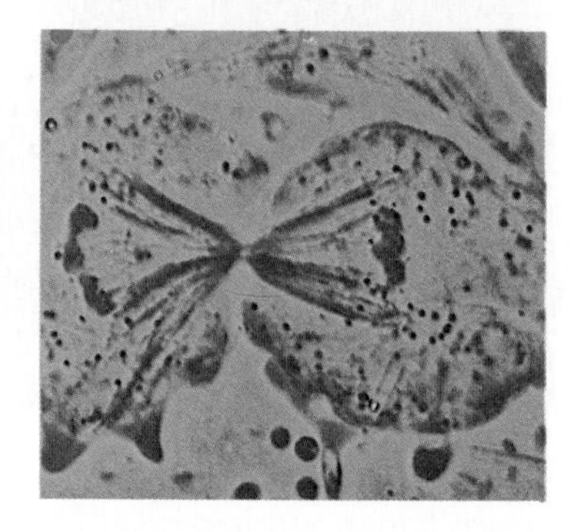

The human body is made up of thousands of different kinds of cells. Remind students that most organs are made of many different kinds of cells. For example, there is no such thing as a "small-intestine cell." Instead, three layers of the small intestine contain different kinds of cells, and even one of those layers contains more than one kind of cell.

If a microscope is available, students may enjoy seeing some of their own cells. A good source of cells is the lining of the inside of the cheek. These cells can be scraped off easily and seen on a glass slide with no further preparation.

Most of your body grows because cells divide, making new cells. One cell splits to become two cells. The two cells split to become four. The four become eight, and so on. Body parts that grow quickly are made of certain kinds of cells that divide quickly. A few kinds of cells, like brain and *nerve* cells, grow in size. However, most of your body grows because each kind of cell makes more cells just like itself.

The body is made up of many kinds of cells. Each kind looks different from the others.

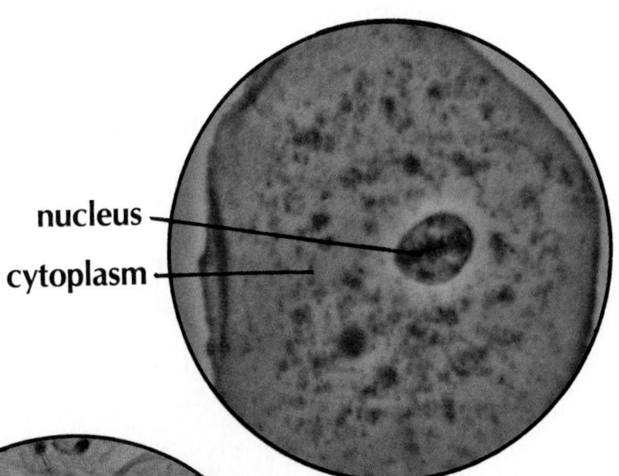

skin cell

fat cells

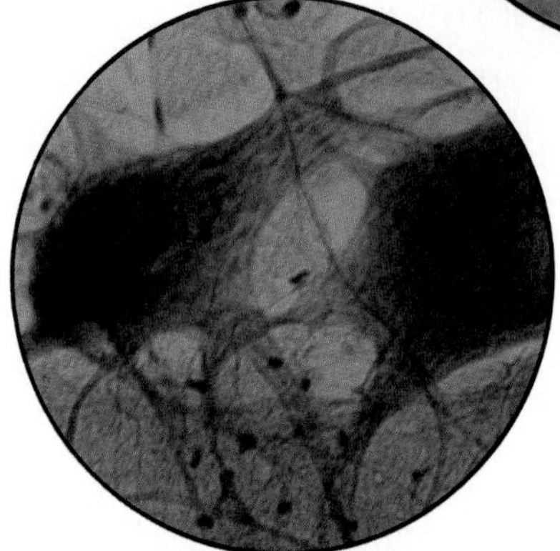

nerve cells

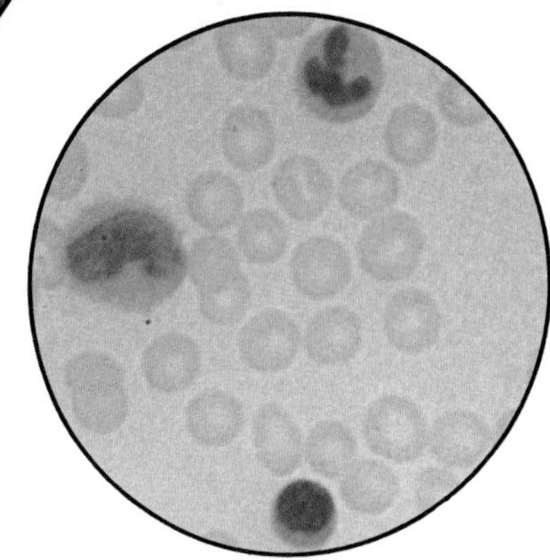

blood cells

All through life, the body continues to make healthy, new cells to take the place of older ones. Some kinds of cells are replaced after a short time, such as *red blood cells,* which are replaced after about 120 days. Other body cells, such as some nerve cells and liver cells, are not replaced once they reach their full growth. By eating nutritious foods and by bringing more oxygen into the blood through plenty of exercise and rest, people supply body cells with the energy and materials they need to divide, grow, and do their work.

What was your answer to *Early Checkup* number 3? (Once the body stops growing in size, does it still need nutritious food and exercise?)

Strictly speaking, not all human cells reproduce by cell division. Red blood cells, for example, are produced in the bone marrow. However, cell division is the most important process and thus the one focused upon in the text.

The cytoplasm and other internal parts of the cell were originally called *protoplasm.* The term *protoplasm* is rarely used by scientists today.

endocrine glands
hormones

Not all glands are endocrine glands. Some glands have tubes (called *ducts*) that carry the hormone directly to where it will be used. These are called *exocrine glands*. Endocrine glands are ductless. They release hormones directly into the bloodstream. Some glands, such as the pancreas, have both endocrine and exocrine hormones.

What Controls Your Growth?

Why do young people grow and then stop growing when they get older? Why does a person grow faster or slower at different times? Why does a healthy body grow better than a less healthy body? The answer to each of these questions includes the word **hormones**. Hormones are chemicals produced by special parts of the body called **endocrine glands**. These chemicals travel through the blood and cause changes in other parts of the body.

An endocrine gland that directs body cells to divide and grow is called the *pituitary gland*. When the pituitary gland makes a lot of *growth hormone*, people have growth spurts. The pituitary gland makes less growth hormone as people get older. Doctors are now sure that most growth hormone is produced by the pituitary gland during sleep.

Even after adults grow taller, they can still grow heavier. The healthful eating habits and exercise plans you start now help your growth in at least two ways. They help to keep your pituitary gland and other body cells healthy for your best growth. They also help to keep your body from becoming too heavy later in life.

Boys and girls produce some different hormones. The difference between their voices, between the hair that will grow on their faces and bodies, and between the size of their breasts, shoulders, and hips is caused by the difference in their hormones.

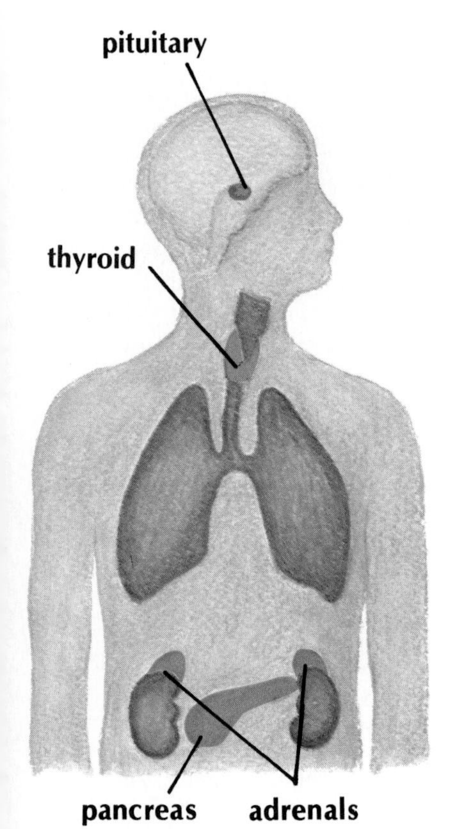

Healthy glands produce different hormones that keep the body working and growing. *Insulin,* a hormone produced in the *pancreas,* helps the body use carbohydrates. A hormone from the *thyroid* helps the body use energy from food. *Adrenal* hormones help control blood pressure and other body activities.

People Working for Your Health

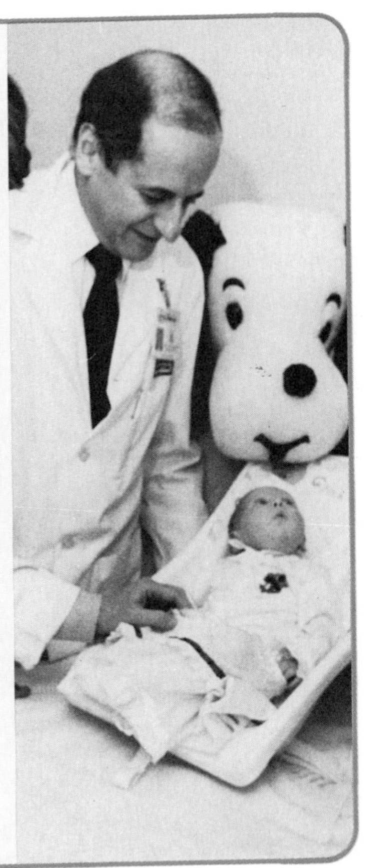

Dr. Raphael David is a *pediatric endocrinologist* at Bellevue Hospital in New York City. He treats children who have problems with their endocrine glands. Dr. David's patients may have growth disorders because their pituitary glands are not functioning properly. They may have disorders of their adrenal or thyroid glands. Dr. David says, "If the disease can be related to an endocrine disorder, the chances for help are very good." The young patient is given a replacement of the hormone that is not being produced in the correct amount. This treatment continues throughout the patient's life. Some of these hormones, such as the thyroid hormone, are *synthesized.* Dr. David says that in the near future, scientists will be able to synthesize more and more hormones, including the growth hormone.

After Dr. David graduated from a university in Switzerland, he came to the United States to study medicine. Now, Dr. David is a professor of pediatrics and the director of the Pediatric Endocrinology Division at New York University.

"Working with children is fun," Dr. David says. "It makes me happy to see the children get well."

What Have You Learned?

Number a piece of paper from **1** through **4**. Next to the numbers, write the words that are missing in these sentences.

1. Many — between the ages of nine and thirteen have a growth —, while — often have theirs a bit later.

2. In a newborn baby, the — is large compared to the body.

3. Food and — help the — to divide and make the body larger. Daily food, exercise, and — help keep the body growing at its best.

4. Growth is controlled by a — from the pituitary gland.

Answers to *What Have You Learned?*

1. girls; spurt; boys
2. head
3. oxygen; cells; sleep (rest)
4. hormone (chemical)

heredity

HEREDITY, ENVIRONMENT, AND BEHAVIOR INFLUENCE GROWTH

How Did You Get To Be *You*?

Have you ever wondered what makes you different from other people? Have you ever wondered why some of your friends look something like their parents? All the answers to these questions are still not completely known. However, you can learn some of the answers by finding out more about **heredity**.

The development of specific traits is caused by a combination of heredity, environment, and behavior. The balance among these influences varies widely. For example, the shape of the nose is almost entirely determined by heredity, unless something in the environment breaks it or unless a plastic surgeon alters the shape. Even a trait that seems to be caused by a disease, such as polio, or by a personal decision, such as starvation on a macrobiotic diet, is also influenced by heredity. How the body reacts to the disease or to the decision is part of the genetic pattern.

Every mother and father has received one set of traits from each of her or his parents. Every mother and father passes along this set of traits to her or his children. Do you see any traits shared by members of this family?

Heredity is the passing along of **traits** from parents to children. Eye color, hair color, certain health problems, height, and the shape of the nose, ears, and lips are a few of the millions of traits that families pass from one generation to the next. These traits are all locked into threadlike bodies called **chromosomes**, which are located in the nucleus of each body cell. Half of the set of chromosomes in any cell comes from a mother. The other half comes from a father.

chromosomes
traits

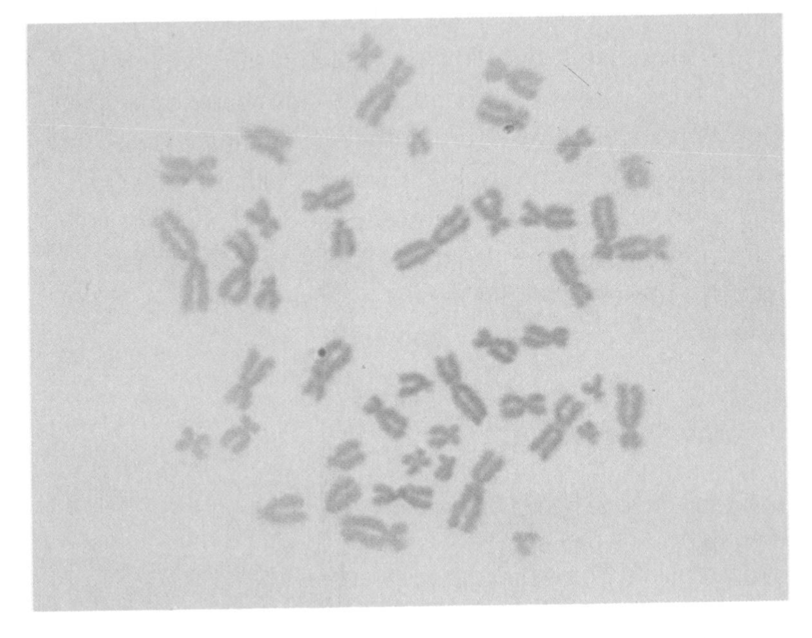

This picture, taken through a powerful microscope, shows the chromosomes within a cell. A set of chromosomes has the blueprint, or plan, for every person's growth.

Heredity helps to set every person's own growing plan. However, people cannot grow as well as their plan allows if they do not make the right choices for health. For example, without choosing a balanced daily diet and without getting enough exercise and rest, people risk losing the full growth they can achieve from their heredity. Can you see how people help to shape their own bodies by the health choices they make?

What was your answer to *Early Checkup* number 4? (Is the size you will be as an adult determined only by the size of your parents?)

Brothers and Sisters Have Different Heredity

Because only half of each parent's chromosomes are passed along to each child, brothers and sisters get many different chromosomes from their parents. This is why brothers and sisters may be like each other in some ways, but different in many other ways. Only *identical twins* are certain to have the same set of chromosomes. This is because identical twins come from the very same *fertilized egg cell* in the mother.

dominant
gene
recessive

Mendel also investigated other aspects of heredity, but his work on dominant and recessive genes is best known. In this discussion, the authors try to get across the basic idea without getting involved in the mathematics. If students are curious, however, you can tell them that in the first generation of a cross between tall and dwarf pea plants, the plants will all be tall (as noted in the text). In the second generation of a cross between plants from the first generation, approximately three out of four of the plants will be tall, but the fourth will be short.

How Does Heredity Work?

Traits that are passed along from parents to their children are called *inherited* traits. Each trait you inherited from your parents is in a **gene** that is part of a chromosome. Genes and chromosomes contain a substance called *deoxyribonucleic acid,* usually abbreviated as *DNA*. This DNA forms the individual plan that makes you the person you are. It is different for every person. You have genes that determine eye color, hair color, body size, skin color, special skin marks and dimples, certain gland problems, blood type, right- or left-handedness, and many other traits.

A baby receives two chromosomes containing genes for each trait. One chromosome is from its father's cells, and one is from its mother's. Normally, the child will receive 23 different chromosomes from its father and 23 from its mother. These 46 chromosomes arrange themselves in 23 pairs that are part of every body cell.

Discovery —A New Pathway to Health

In 1865, the world learned more than anyone had ever known about a mystery of life called heredity. An Austrian named Gregor Mendel was working with pea plants. Some of his seeds grew into tall plants. Others grew into shorter ones. Mendel found that when he crossed the tall plants with the short plants, their seeds all grew into tall plants. Mendel decided that tallness must be a **dominant** gene in determining height. Dominant genes, he felt, must have greater influence over certain traits. Shortness, he decided, must be a **recessive** gene. Recessive genes have less influence in determining a trait, such as body size.

However, when Mendel raised another generation of plants from the seeds with genes for tallness and shortness, he got a surprise. Some of the new plants were tall and some were short. Mendel decided that the short plants would not be short if one of their two inherited genes for height were dominant. Therefore, short plants show the recessive trait for height only because *both* genes they inherit are recessive.

Mendel at work in his garden

Today we know that genes for dark hair are dominant to genes for blond hair. A dark-haired father may have two genes for dark hair or one gene for dark hair and one for blond hair. The dominant dark-hair gene would influence the trait for hair color. If his wife is a blond-haired woman, you know that both of her hair-color genes are for blond hair. What color hair will their baby have?

Students should understand that possessing the pattern for a trait does not necessarily mean that you will have the trait. For example, some people have a pattern for one color of hair, but can dye it with another color. It is also possible that some other factor in the environment may cause the trait not to follow the pattern.

Each parent has two genes for hair color.

Father

Gene 1: Dark hair (dominant)
Gene 2: Dark hair (dominant)
or
Blond hair (recessive)

Mother

Gene 1: Blond hair (recessive)
Gene 2: Blond hair (recessive)

The baby will inherit one recessive trait from its blond-haired mother. If the baby inherits the father's dominant gene, the baby's hair will be dark. If the father does have a recessive gene and the baby inherits it, the baby's hair will be blond. *Two* blond parents would have only blond children. Why?

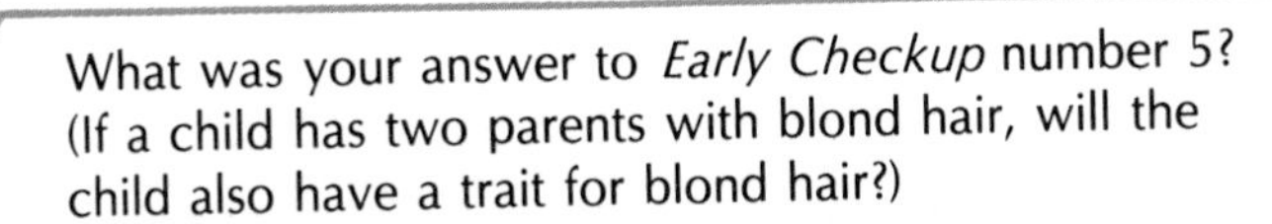

What was your answer to *Early Checkup* number 5? (If a child has two parents with blond hair, will the child also have a trait for blond hair?)

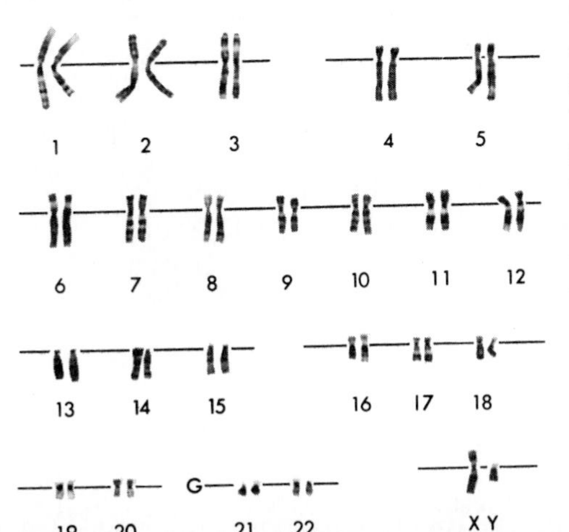

Each of these pairs of chromosomes contains genes, so each inherited trait is formed by a pair of genes. Look at the last pair of chromosomes. They do not match. It is called an XY pair. Males have this XY pair. In females, chromosomes in this pair match each other. It is called an XX pair.

Some Diseases Are Inherited

Some diseases are passed on through recessive genes. Both parents would have to carry such genes before their child could be born with the disease. When neither parent actually has the disease, only about one in four of their children may be born with it. These *hereditary* diseases—*sickle-cell anemia, hemophilia, Tay-Sachs disease,* and others—may also skip a generation or two before they appear in a family that has the genes.

Is Heredity All That Matters?

Heredity may provide your growing plan, but it is not the only reason you become the person you are. The health choices you make help your body to make the most of your heredity. The friends you make will help to determine your personality. How much you learn and decisions about what you will be are more or less under your control. The health choices you make help your body to make the most of your heredity. The friends you make will help to determine your personality. How much you learn and decisions about what you will be are more or less under your control. This means that the person you become is mainly up to *you*. How will you use your heredity?

Because they come from the same egg cell, identical twins inherit the same traits. However, they may choose to develop those traits differently. *Fraternal twins* come from different egg cells. They may not look any more alike than any other brother or sister.

On Your Own

Draw a chart like the one pictured. Use it to solve the heredity puzzle below.

The gene for brown eyes is dominant, while the gene for blue eyes is recessive. Call the gene for a brown-eye trait **B**. Call the blue-eye gene **b**. If the father has blue eyes, you know he has two **bb** genes. The brown-eyed mother may have **BB** or **Bb** genes. If the mother has **Bb** genes, show how the genes might combine to produce children with brown eyes and children with blue eyes.

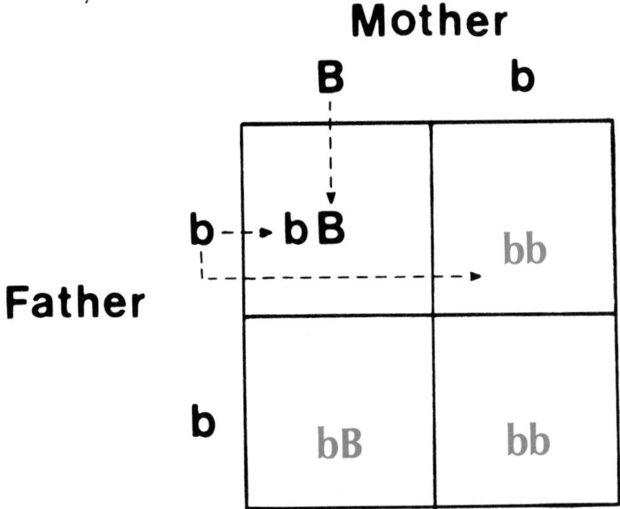

As noted earlier, this is a simplified presentation of human heredity. If only combinations of chromosomes occurred, then it would be possible for people to have the same heredity even if they did not come from the same fertilized cell. In looking in depth at heredity, however, scientists have discovered that genes sometimes cross between pairs of chromosomes in cell division. Since there are about 100,000 different human genes (as opposed to only 46 different chromosomes) in each cell, crossing over makes the number of possible combinations so great that only identical twins could, with any reasonable probability, share exactly the same genes.

Some students may have difficulty filling in the squares because the idea of combining genes is new to them. Here is the complete grid. You can display it on the board so that the students can compare it with their work.

What Have You Learned?

Number a piece of paper from **1** through **3**. Next to the numbers, write the words that are missing in these sentences.

1. People inherit pairs of — from their parents. These are part of the chromosomes, and each pair passes on a different — to children.

2. By itself, — cannot determine how healthy you will be. Each person makes many — that will make the best of his or her inherited —.

3. If you have a dominant gene and a recessive gene for some trait, the trait people will see is the — one.

Answers to *What Have You Learned?*

1. genes; trait
2. heredity; choices (decisions); traits
3. dominant

Aging and Calcium

As people age, their bone cells lose *calcium*. People who exercise daily often lose less calcium. Their bones stay stronger. People who have always exercised can usually continue to exercise throughout their lives.

Many changes associated with aging are actually caused by development. For example, loss or graying of hair, farsightedness, and the diseases of old age are not, strictly speaking, the products of aging itself. Aging is a continuous process throughout a person's life. Farsightedness, for example, starts at about age forty and usually gets no worse after age sixty. One does not gradually get more and more farsighted from the cessation of physical growth until death.

HOW DOES THE BODY AGE?

What Is Aging?

From the first moment of their lives, people begin to grow older. Cells grow old and die or become damaged. Some are replaced by new cells, but many are not replaced. As people grow older, their bodies change in many ways. These body changes, called *aging*, are most clearly seen after the size of the body stops growing.

No one knows exactly why the body ages. What doctors do know is that people who reduce health risks while they are young often age more slowly than those who make fewer good health choices.

What was your answer to *Early Checkup* number 6? (Do the health choices you make now have anything to do with how you will age when you are older?)

Brain cells actually become smaller in number as people age. However, people who stay interested in important activities and who do not drink a lot of alcohol stand a better chance to keep all their intelligence and memory for life.

As people grow older, their lungs may hold less air. Regular exercise can improve their lungs' ability to hold air. By not smoking, people can also help maintain healthy lungs as they age.

The eyes of older people sometimes change, making it more difficult to see patterns of light and dark. People who have eaten a balanced diet, containing vitamin A, often have less trouble with their eyes as they age.

One sign of aging is wrinkling of the skin. The skin seems looser and does not stretch the way it once did. Protecting young skin from getting too much sunlight now can help keep the skin from wrinkling as much when you are older.

Can People Help Themselves Live Longer and Age More Slowly?

At one time, few people lived to be more than forty-five years old. Today, the average person lives to be more than seventy years old. As people have learned to protect their health, they have gained the promise of longer, happier, and healthier lives.

Vaccination programs now prevent many of the diseases that once took the lives of young people. Better sanitation stops the spread of diseases in communities. Many more people avoid the health risks of smoking and drinking too much alcohol. Better diets and exercise plans help people prevent many forms of heart and lung disease.

What Have You Learned?

Number a piece of paper from **1** through **3**. Next to the numbers, write the words that are missing in these sentences.

1. When physical growth stops, it is easier to notice changes caused by __.

2. Young people can help protect their skin from wrinkling later on by protecting their skin from the __ now.

3. People live longer today by taking fewer health __ than they once did. Young people get __ to prevent many diseases. People also eat better foods and get more active daily __.

Answers to *What Have You Learned?*

1. aging
2. sunlight (sun)
3. risks; vaccinations (immunizations); exercise

Learn More About It

These books will help you to find out more about growth, heredity, and aging.

Allison, Linda. *Blood and Guts: A Working Guide to Your Own Insides.* Boston: Little, Brown & Co., 1976. Discover all the different parts that compose your body. Experiments and tests will help to reveal the way your body works.

Engdahl, Sylvia, and Roberson, Rick. *Tool for Tomorrow: New Knowledge About Genes.* New York: Atheneum Publishers, 1979. You will learn about genes and the various ways scientists are using them to help people.

Tully, Marianne, and Tully, Mary-Alice. *Facts About the Human Body.* New York: Franklin Watts, Inc., 1977. Many questions you may have about the body and its functions will be answered in this book.

More To Do on Your Own

1. If there is a senior citizen center near your school, it may be possible to set up or join a "Big Grandchild" program. In such a program, you and members of your class are paired with older people from the center. Once a week, you can meet for activities, such as going to the zoo or just learning about what life was like a long time ago.
2. Can you curl your tongue? Curling is forming a "U" shape at the tip of your tongue. Tongue curling is an inherited trait. Find out how many members of the same family have inherited this trait from their parents and grandparents. Are there other inherited traits you can try to trace?
3. Use an almanac to find out how the average length of life has changed in the nation since 1900. Make a graph showing the average length of life for each ten-year period; that is, show 1900, 1910, 1920, and so forth. What can you predict for the year 2000? Make a poster version of the graph for display in class.
4. If you have never kept a chart of your own growth, you can begin one now. Record in some permanent place your height and weight every six months. It is interesting to see how you grow.

Final Checkup

A. Number a sheet of paper from **1** through **10**. Next to each number, write the letter of the words that best complete each sentence.

1. A growth spurt usually occurs
- **a** earlier for boys than girls.
- **b.** earlier for girls than boys.
- **c.** at the same age for girls and boys.
- **d.** for children from large rather than small families.

2. You can be sure how tall you will become
- **a.** if you know your height at the age of twelve.
- **b.** if you know how tall your parents are.
- **c.** by looking at how tall your oldest brother or sister is.
- **d.** when you stop growing.

3. The parts of the body that often grow faster than the rest of the body during the growth spurt are
- **a.** the arms, legs, hands, and feet.
- **b.** the head and eyes.
- **c.** the brain and nerves.
- **d.** the ears and nose.

4. You begin to get permanent teeth around the age of
- **a.** two.
- **b.** six.
- **c.** twelve.
- **d.** sixteen.

5. The major reason people grow is that
- **a.** the cells get larger.
- **b.** the skin stretches.
- **c.** the fat increases.
- **d.** the cells divide.

6. To stay alive and work for growth and health, each cell needs
- **a.** food.
- **b.** oxygen.
- **c.** both food and oxygen.
- **d.** food, oxygen, and recessive genes.

7. The hormone insulin controls
- **a.** the use of carbohydrates.
- **b.** growth.
- **c.** blood pressure.
- **d.** breathing.

8. People inherit
- **a.** most chromosomes from their mother.
- **b.** most chromosomes from their father.
- **c.** half their chromosomes from each parent.
- **d.** chromosomes from their mother only.

9. If you have only one recessive gene for some trait, you will
- **a.** probably show that trait.
- **b.** probably not show that trait.
- **c.** always grow tall.
- **d.** never grow tall.

10. As people get older, they are most likely to
- **a.** lose their hair.
- **b.** lose calcium from their bones.
- **c.** lose part of their memory.
- **d.** lose their ability to speak.

B. Number a sheet of paper from **1** through **10**. Write **true** or **false** next to the number for each of these ideas.

1. Boys often continue growing until they are in their late teens or early twenties. true
2. In no way can you affect your growth. false
3. Some parts of the body form new cells all the time. true
4. Every cell in a person's body is replaced every seven years. false
5. The pituitary gland makes the growth hormone throughout your entire life. true
6. If you have a brother or sister, you both probably received exactly the same chromosomes from your parents. false
7. Your genes determine what you will finally be. false
8. Some inherited traits can skip a generation. true
9. The way you care for your body now can alter the speed at which aging changes your body. true
10. Avoiding such health risks as smoking and severe sunburns can help you prevent diseases you may get when you are older. true

Write About Better Health

Write a short answer to each of these questions. Use complete sentences.

1. What are three health practices you can perform to help your body's growth during a growth spurt?
2. How does the body grow larger while people are young?
3. Describe what people can and cannot do to make the most of their traits.
4. After your body stops growing, what are four changes that happen to it as a part of aging?
5. What are three ways by which the average length of life has been increased?

Model answers to *Write About Better Health* are provided in the chapter notes at the front of this *Teacher's Edition.*

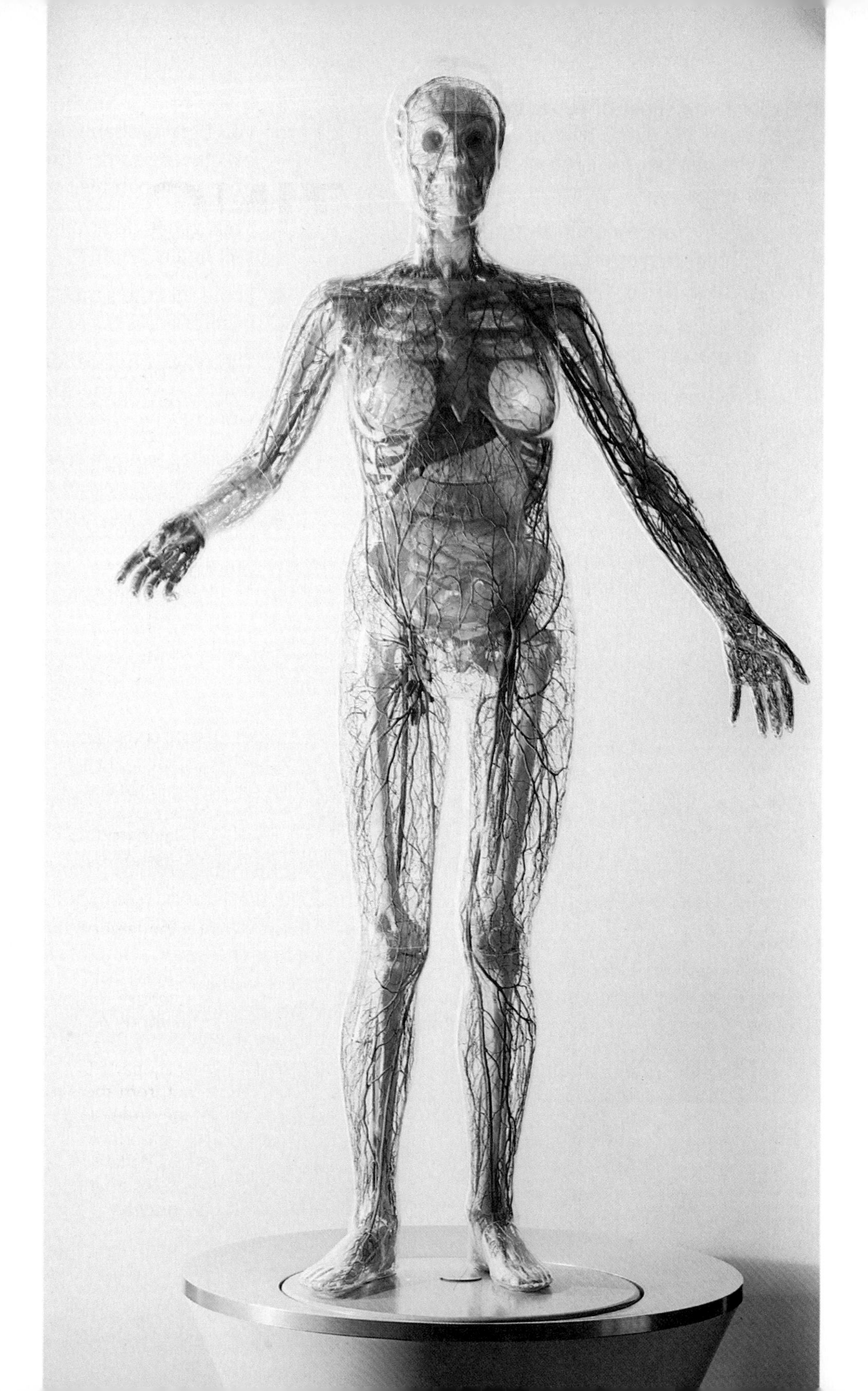

3 YOUR AMAZING BODY

Your body is more complex and wonderful than any machine ever designed. It is made from more than 10 trillion, or 10 million million, cells—each cell so tiny it cannot be seen without a microscope. If all your blood vessels were straightened and placed end to end, they would stretch for about 100,000 miles (160,000 km)—4 times around the earth's equator. Arteries, capillaries, and veins carry blood from the heart, throughout the body, and back to the heart in just one minute. This trip is repeated 1,440 times every day, without stopping, for as long as you live.

Read each description. On a piece of paper, write the name of each body part described. If you do not know the name of a part, fill it in after you read about it in this chapter.

a) This "control center" of the body weighs about 3 pounds (about 1.4 kg). Nerve fibers connect it with every part of the body.

b) These carry signals to and from the brain by way of the spinal cord.

c) This body part senses sound vibrations.

d) This body part senses light waves.

e) This body part senses odors in the air.

f) This body part helps to change food so it can be used by cells in the body.

g) This part of the body acts as a pump. During your lifetime it will beat between two and three billion times.

h) These blood vessels have thick, elastic walls and carry oxygen-rich blood to the body.

i) These large blood vessels have thin walls. They carry blood that contains carbon dioxide and other wastes from cells.

j) These very narrow blood vessels connect the larger blood vessels to each other.

k) Some of these connect and move bones. Exercise, oxygen, and nutritious foods help these become strong.

l) These body parts bring oxygen to the blood from the air outside the body. They release carbon dioxide from the blood into the air. They inflate and deflate because of the movement of a large muscle called the *diaphragm*.

LOOKING AHEAD

People who make cars start with thousands of small parts. They put the small parts together to make larger parts. The larger parts are then assembled into groups called *systems.* Each system performs a special job. When all the systems are connected and supplied with fuel, the car is able to run. All it needs now is an owner who will fuel it, drive it carefully, and keep it in good repair.

In some ways, your body is similar to a car. In this chapter you will learn more about how you fuel your body and how you can keep it working in its own best way. You will learn

- how body parts work together in systems.
- how you can help supply body systems with the fuel and energy they need for health, growth, strength, and repair.
- how healthy body systems stay in touch with each other and keep you in touch with the world.

Here are some words that you may not have talked about in school before. You will learn about them in this chapter. You can find all these words in the *Glossary* at the back of this book.

arteries (är'tər·ēz)
capillaries (kap'ə·ler'ēz)
cells (selz)
circulatory system (sėr'kyə·lə·tôr'ē sis'təm)
nervous system (nėr'vəs sis'təm)
organ (ôr'gən)
respiratory system (res'pər·ə·tôr'ē sis'təm)
tissues (tish'üz)
veins (vānz)

Early Checkup

Number a piece of paper from **1** through **5**. Answer each of these questions by writing **yes** or **no** next to the correct number on your paper. You can check your answers as you read this chapter.

1. Can you make decisions that help to keep body cells healthy? yes
2. Can exercise help to keep your heart healthy? yes
3. Can healthy blood vessels help to make up for unhealthy lungs? no
4. Are there parts of your body that keep working even when you do not think about them? yes
5. Does your body automatically take care of itself, no matter how you decide to live? no

cells
organ
tissues

Living cells take in oxygen, food, and water through the thin *cell membrane.* The *nucleus* in a cell controls all of the cell's activities. In the jellylike *cytoplasm* of the cell, oxygen, water, and food nutrients are changed to energy and to materials needed to make new cells.

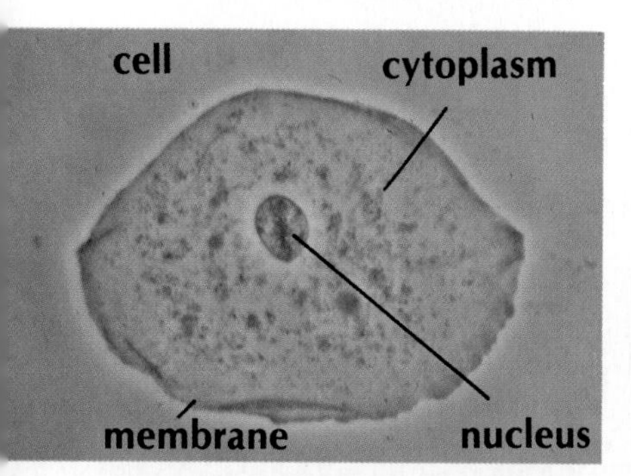

FROM CELLS TO SYSTEMS

Healthy Cells Build Healthy Tissues

Every part of your body is made of millions of tiny **cells**. Cells are so small that they cannot be seen without a microscope. When you look at yourself in a mirror, the skin you see is really a huge group of skin cells. Groups of the same kind of cells that carry out a certain function are called **tissues**. Tissues grow as the cells divide to form new cells.

There are five main kinds of tissue in the body. Together, different kinds of skin cells form *skin tissue.* Together, different kinds of muscle cells form *muscle tissue.* The same is true of *nerve tissue, bone tissue,* and *blood tissue.*

bone tissue

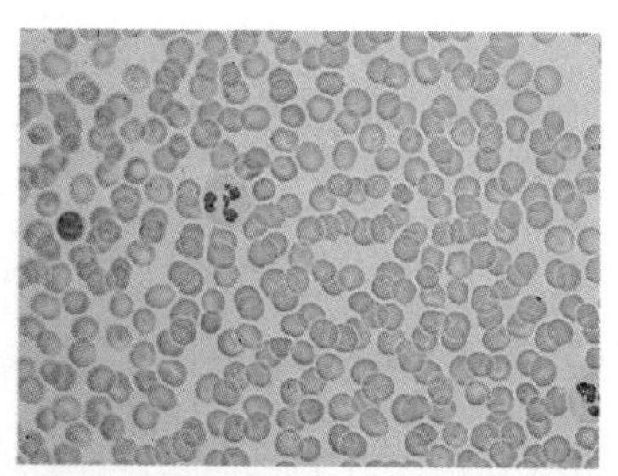
blood tissue

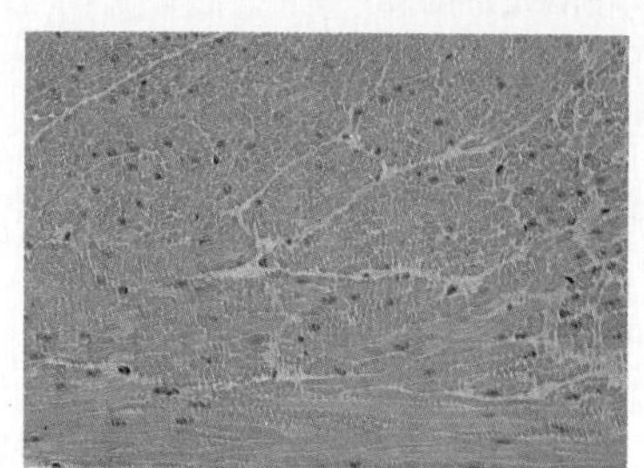
muscle tissue

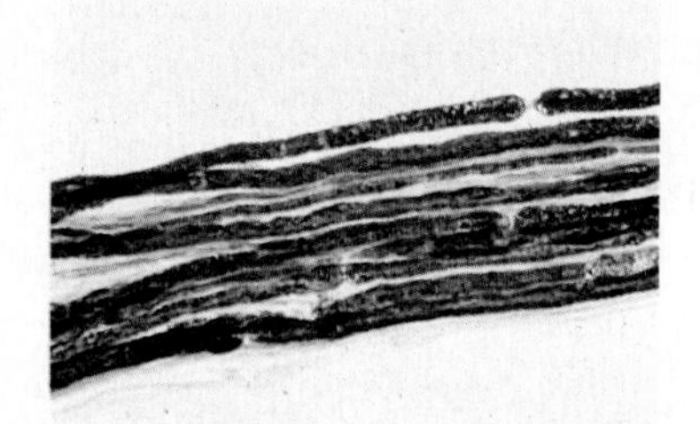
nerve tissue

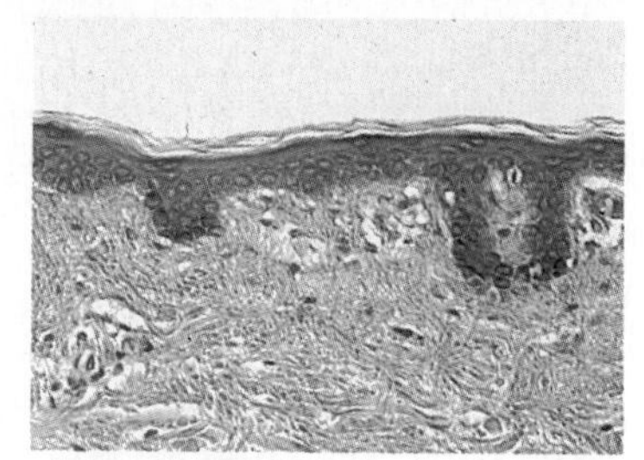
skin tissue

Review with students the health practices that help keep skin healthy. Students may suggest *keeping clean, protecting skin from cuts and abrasions, cleaning and otherwise taking care of injuries, using sun screens,* and *eating a balanced diet.*

A group of tissues that work together is called an **organ**. For example, the skin is an organ. It is made of skin tissue working together with blood tissue and nerve tissue. Some other organs you may know about are the heart, brain, eyes, and lungs. Can you think of the different kinds of tissues that each of these organs needs to keep your body working well?

cross-section of skin

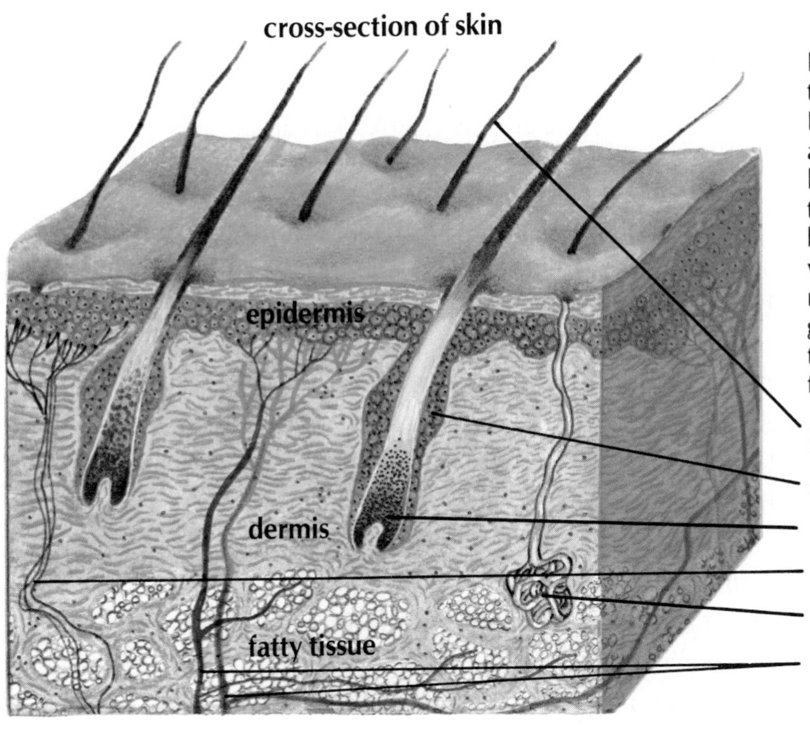

Many organs have more than one health function. For example, healthy skin and healthy sweat glands help control the temperature inside the body. Skin helps make vitamin D, which is needed for healthy bone growth. Skin protects all the organs of the body from disease germs.

Skin tissue receives oxygen, water, and nutrients from blood tissue. Nerve cells in the skin help warn the body about heat, cold, and painful injury. Oil glands help to lubricate the skin. Healthy skin cells produce a protective, waterproof covering. Cells in the *epidermis* age and die. They are replaced by healthier, new cells that divide in deeper levels of the epidermis. The outer layer of skin is replaced about every 28 days.

Besides eating well-balanced meals, people can do several things to help keep their skin healthy. Skin cells should be protected from very strong sunlight. Skin should also be kept clean. Removing collected dirt and oil helps to remove harmful germs that could cause disease. Getting enough sleep each day is important, too. During sleep, cells grow and tissues are repaired.

Can Exercise Help Skin Health?

Doctors who specialize in care of the skin are called *dermatologists.* Many dermatologists report that daily exercise seems to reduce skin wrinkling as people age. One reason may be that exercise increases the heart rate. During exercise blood moves through the body faster, bringing more nutrients and oxygen to skin tissue. Strong exercise also causes heavy sweating. This seems to help make skin thicker, stronger, and more elastic.

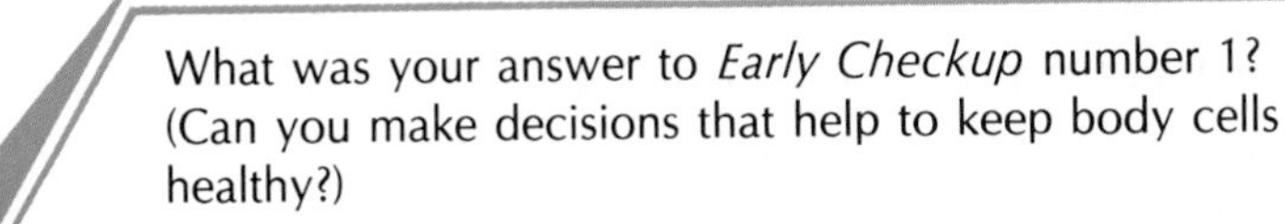

What was your answer to *Early Checkup* number 1? (Can you make decisions that help to keep body cells healthy?)

arteries
capillaries
circulatory system
veins

Heart disease and related circulatory-system diseases continue to be the major cause of death in the United States. Control of diet, more aerobic exercise, and abstention from smoking are the best ways to prevent such diseases. Chapter 4 describes exercises that enhance the health of the circulatory system.

Organs Work Together as Systems

The heart is made chiefly of muscle tissue. However, it is more than just a muscle. The heart is an organ made of several kinds of tissue.

The heart, blood, and blood vessels form the **circulatory system**. In a system, each organ works with tissues and with other organs to keep the body healthy. The circulatory system carries blood containing nutrients, water, and oxygen to each cell of the body. Cell wastes are carried away by the circulatory system. Your heart probably beats about 85 to 95 times a minute to keep blood moving through your body.

You can help keep your heart strong and healthy by exercising daily and by eating nutritious foods. The healthier and more *fit* your heart is, the more blood it pushes with each beat. This means your heart must beat fewer times to supply the body with blood.

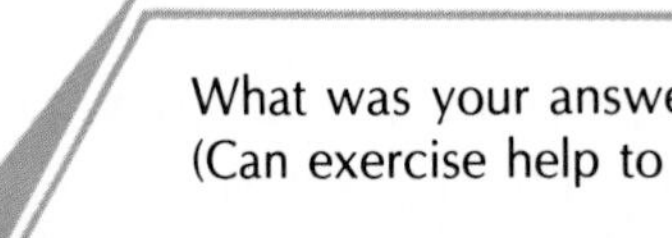

What was your answer to *Early Checkup* number 2? (Can exercise help to keep your heart healthy?)

With each heartbeat, blood is pushed into the arteries. Each push of blood stretches the thick, elastic walls of the arteries. After each stretch the artery wall moves back to its normal shape. These movements in artery walls can be felt as beats in the wrist or neck. The beating is called the *pulse*. Each beat of the heart causes a beat of the pulse.

As the heart beats, it pushes blood against the blood vessel walls. The force of this blood pressing against these walls is called *blood pressure.* The greater the blood pressure is, the harder the heart must work to pump blood. High blood pressure can cause damage to the heart and to the rest of the circulatory system. Being seriously overweight and eating too much salt are among the causes of high blood pressure. A doctor usually measures both blood pressure and pulse when checking the health of the circulatory system.

Fat and Your Health

Overeating or following a poorly balanced diet can cause people to become overweight. Food energy not used by the body is stored as fat. Existing fat cells enlarge to store the unused food energy and blood is needed to supply these new cells with oxygen, food, and water. New blood-carrying capillaries must be produced by the body. This makes the heart work harder to pump more blood. Overwork can damage the heart.

A healthy circulatory system is needed for the health of all the body's tissues, organs, and systems. Deciding not to take risks with the circulatory system can mean better health. Deciding not to smoke, for example, will lower the risk of heart and blood vessel disease. Tobacco smoke in the body makes it harder for the blood to deliver oxygen needed by body tissues. Eating foods low in salt, fats, and oils helps to keep the circulatory system healthy and lowers the risk of high blood pressure. Exercise also helps to keep the circulatory system healthy.

The heart is slightly larger than your fist. A bundle of nerve tissue called the *pacemaker* receives signals from the brain. The signals tell the heart how fast to beat. Each beat pushes blood away from the heart through **arteries**, then into **capillaries** that supply body cells with oxygen and nutrients, and then on to **veins** that bring blood and dissolved cell wastes back to the heart.

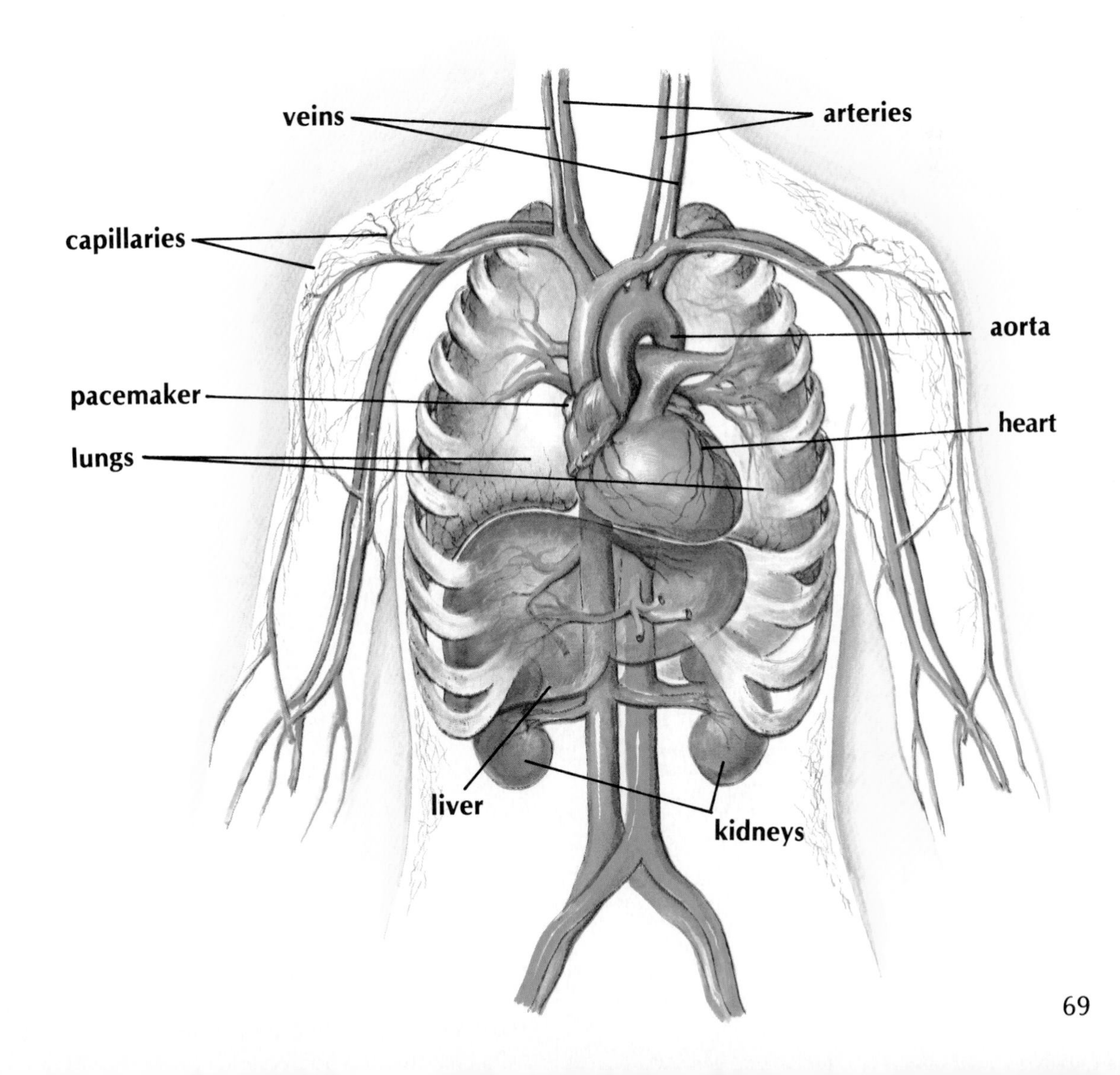

respiratory system

Call for volunteers to explain what happens as the blood circulates through the body. (*It leaves the heart, picks up nutrients from the small intestine, discharges wastes through the kidneys, picks up carbon dioxide and gives up oxygen all along the way, returns to the heart, goes to the lungs and exchanges carbon dioxide for oxygen, and returns to the heart.*)

Students should understand that each system is made up of several different tissues and organs. (*For example, the digestive, or alimentary, system is made up of the teeth, tongue, pharynx, esophagus [gullet], stomach, small intestine, large intestine [colon], rectum, and many different glands. The urinary system is made up of the kidneys [the organs that extract wastes from the blood], the bladder, and urinary tubes.*

Organ Systems Work Together

The circulatory system depends on the **respiratory system** to remove carbon dioxide, which is a waste product, from the blood. The respiratory system also supplies the blood with fresh oxygen.

Fresh air, warmed and filtered as it passes through the nose, travels down the *trachea,* or windpipe, through the *bronchial tubes,* and then to the lungs. Oxygen from the air moves into the blood. To do this, oxygen must go through the walls of capillaries that surround tiny elastic air sacs in the lungs. As the blood picks up oxygen, the carbon dioxide leaves the blood, moves through the capillary walls, enters the air sacs of the lungs, and then leaves the body through the mouth and nose.

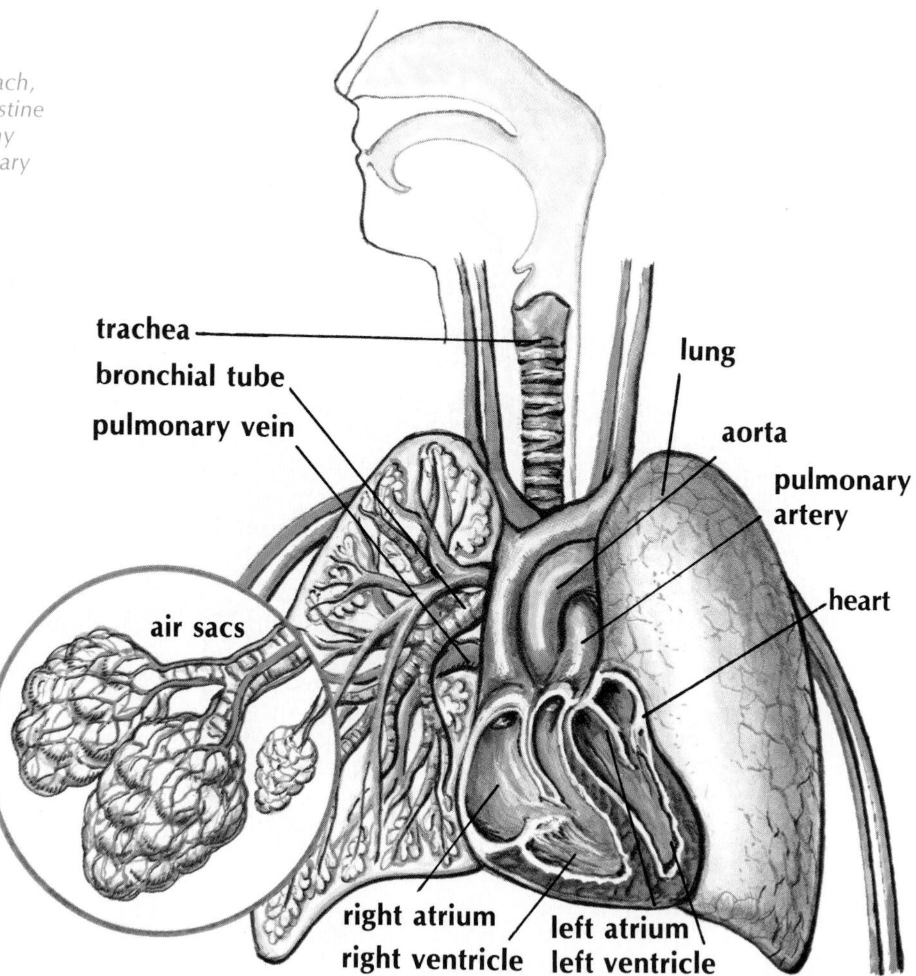

When the heart beats, blood carrying oxygen from the lungs is pushed from the left *ventricle* into the arteries. At the same time, blood carrying carbon dioxide moves from veins into the right *atrium.* This blood is then pushed into the right ventricle. From there it moves through a large artery, called the *pulmonary artery,* to the lungs. In the lungs, the carbon dioxide leaves the blood and the oxygen enters. The oxygen-rich blood departs from the lungs and moves through the *pulmonary vein* to the left atrium of the heart. From there the blood is pushed into the left ventricle. The oxygen-rich blood then begins its trip all over again.

Air pollution and tobacco smoke may make breathing more difficult, especially in people with a crippling lung disease called *emphysema.* This disease causes thick mucus to cover the tiny air sacs, making it hard for carbon dioxide to leave the lungs. Pollution and smoke can damage air sacs and lung tissue even more. If the lungs are not healthy, the circulatory system cannot keep the body healthy.

When Is Blood Red?

Red blood cells get their color from the combination of oxygen and *hemoglobin,* a substance that has red coloring matter in it. Most arteries carry oxygen-rich blood, so it is bright red. Most veins carry blood with carbon dioxide and 20 percent less oxygen, so it is a dark, almost bluish red. However, blood in the pulmonary vein is redder than blood in the pulmonary artery. Can you figure out why?

The pulmonary artery has deoxygenated blood, and thus the color of the blood in it is dark red. The pulmonary vein, however, has the oxygen to give the blood a bright red color. The pulmonary artery carries deoxygenated blood from the heart to the lungs. In the lungs, the excess carbon dioxide is lost and an increased amount of oxygen is absorbed. The blood returns from the lungs to the heart via the pulmonary veins.

What was your answer to *Early Checkup* number 3? (Can healthy blood vessels help to make up for unhealthy lungs?)

What Have You Learned?

Number a piece of paper from **1** through **4**. Next to the numbers, write the words that are missing in these sentences.

1. Tissues are made up of groups of __. Groups of tissues working together are called __.

2. Organs and tissues that work together form body __.

3. In the circulatory system, the __ pumps __ carrying oxygen and __ to all cells of the body.

4. Smoking and air __ can harm the lung tissue in the __ system.

Answers to *What Have You Learned?*
1. cells; organs
2. systems
3. heart; blood; nutrients
4. pollution; respiratory

nervous system

Both halves of the brain are involved in thought. Recently it has been found that in most people the left half of the brain (which controls the right side of the body) does most of the work of language and abstract thinking, while the right half (which controls the left side of the body) is involved in recognizing shapes and music. Some educators believe that children tend to be either more "left brained" or more "right brained," and that slightly different teaching techniques should be used for each group. In other words, "left-brained" children can be expected to deal better with language, but "right-brained" children might learn more from pictures.

WHAT MAKES BODY SYSTEMS WORK?

Some Systems Are Automatic

Most of the bones in your skeletal system are attached to muscles. In order for people to move an arm, all they have to do is decide to move it, and they can make their arm move. What is it, however, that makes your *digestive system* work to change the foods you eat? Do you have to make any decisions in order to make your stomach and intestines work? The digestive system, the circulatory system, the respiratory system, and most parts inside your body work *automatically.* You do not have to think about them to make them work. (See Chapter 5 for more information about the digestive system.)

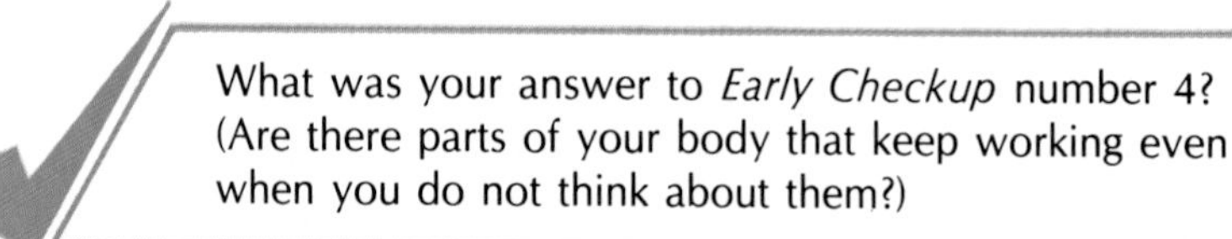

What was your answer to *Early Checkup* number 4? (Are there parts of your body that keep working even when you do not think about them?)

Automatic or not, all the body systems are kept working together by the **nervous system**.

The Nervous System Controls the Body

The Brain and Spinal Cord

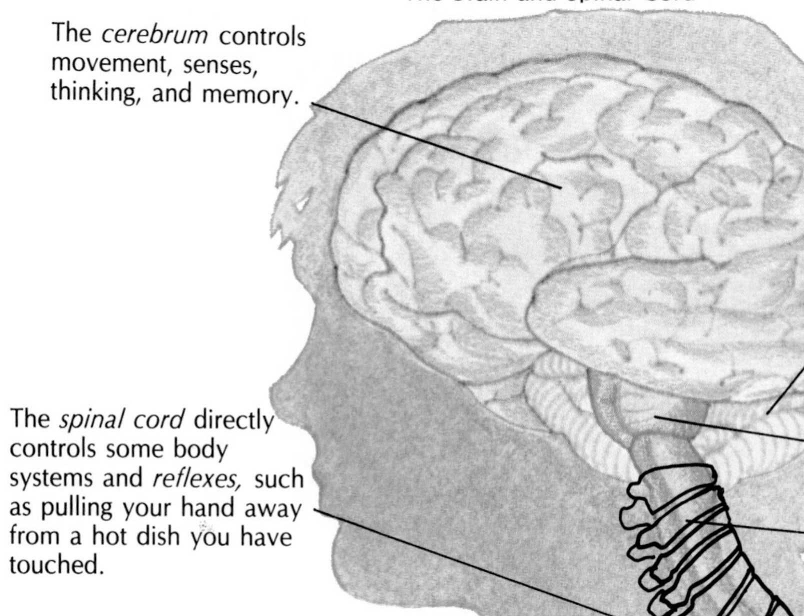

Unlike some other body tissues, brain and nerve tissues do not repair themselves. Most cells of the nervous system are not replaced when they are lost or damaged. This makes it important to protect your brain and spinal cord from possible injury. Wearing a helmet for rough sports or games in which it is easy to fall or get hurt can help protect your nervous system. Wearing a safety belt can keep you from injuring your head or spine when a car suddenly stops or hits another object.

Getting enough sleep is also important for your nervous system. Sleep seems to give the nervous system and the senses a chance to rest and refresh themselves. People who do not get enough sleep often become irritable. They also find normal tasks and body movements more difficult. Many doctors believe that sleep and dreams allow people to ease the stress and strain caused by everyday problems.

The authors have used the term "signal" in place of "message," which is often used to describe nerve actions. "Signal" is not likely to leave students with the impression that nerves deal in words.

Nerves carry signals by a combination of electrical and chemical means. A nerve cell "fires" an electrical or chemical impulse in a fraction of a second. In another fraction of a second, the nerve cell is ready to fire again. Although no one is sure exactly how the nervous system works in totality, in some instances it has been shown that the rate of firing is important in transmitting the signal.

Nerve cells carry signals between the organs and the "control center" called the brain. Many of the signals travel through bundles of nerve fibers called the spinal cord. The spinal cord runs through an opening that extends downward through the middle of the surrounding bones that make up the spine.

The Nervous System

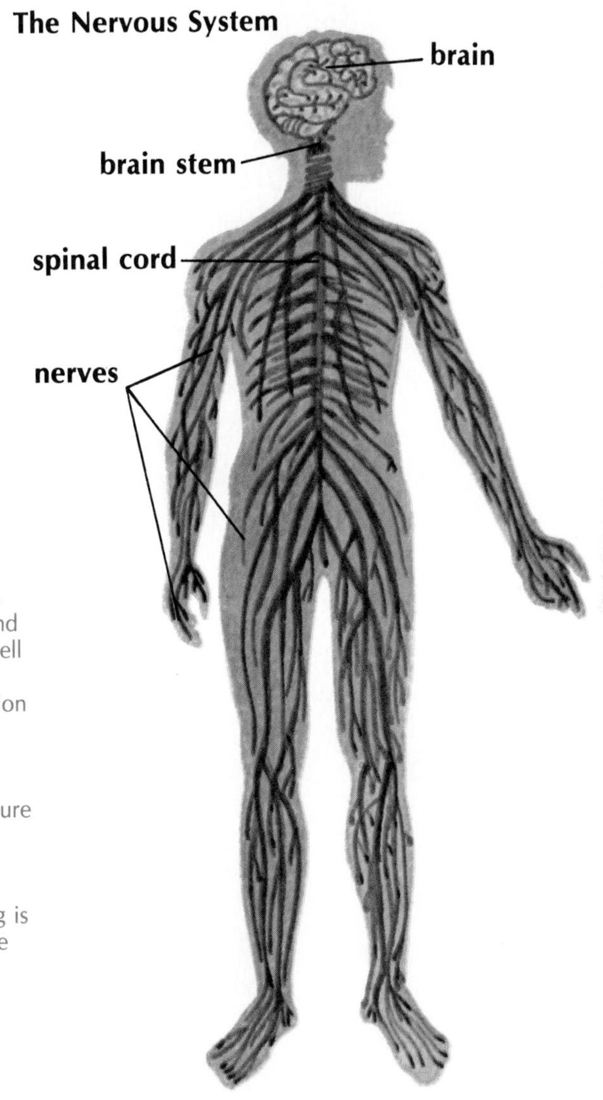

The Nervous System Links You to the World

Your nervous system does far more than direct and control other body systems. It keeps you in touch with the world around you. It helps you to avoid risks to your health and safety.

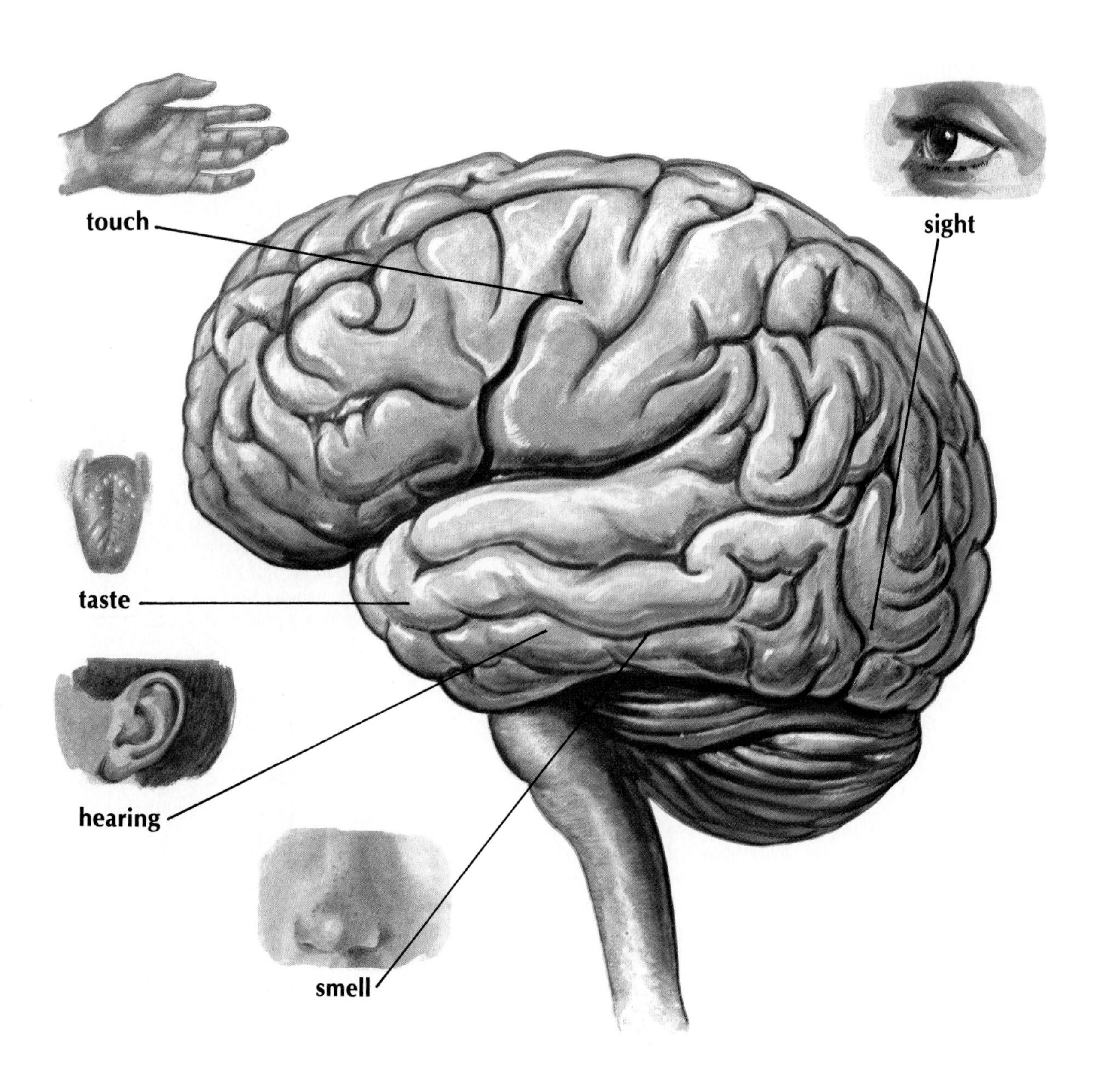

Nerve cells in your eyes respond to light reflected from objects and people around you. The signals of light are instantly passed on to the cerebrum, which identifies them. Do you protect your eyes with safety glasses when you work with certain tools? Do your glasses have safety lenses for sports? Do you go to a doctor if you have trouble seeing or have pain in your eyes? About 95 percent of blind people have lost their sight from disease or accident.

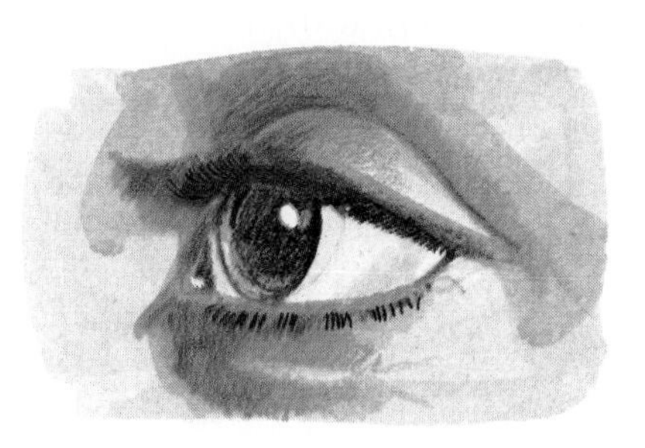

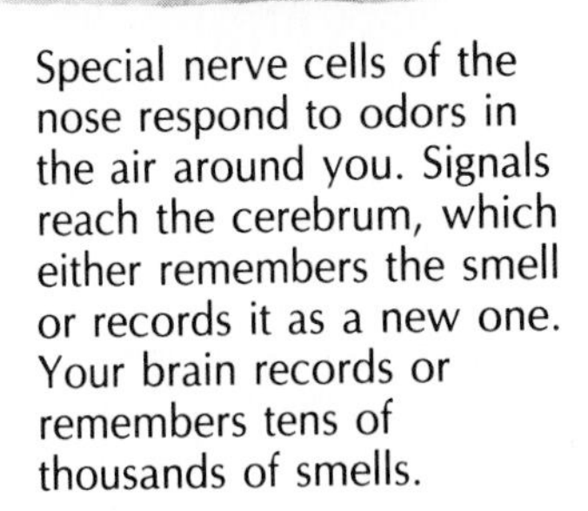

Special nerve cells of the nose respond to odors in the air around you. Signals reach the cerebrum, which either remembers the smell or records it as a new one. Your brain records or remembers tens of thousands of smells.

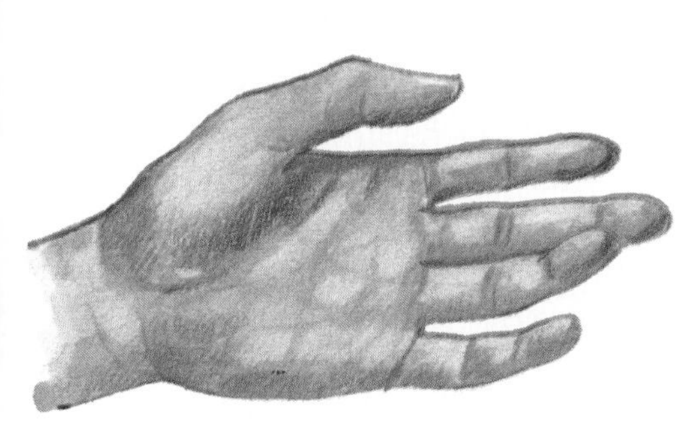

One sense organ covers your entire body. Parts of it are not located near the brain. This sense organ is the skin. Nerves in the skin sense temperature, pressure, and pain. When you automatically pull your hand away from something hot, the action is called a reflex.

Sound waves cause your eardrum to vibrate. The vibrations move along tiny, connected bones, and then through liquid in your inner ear to nerve cells. These signal the cerebrum, which tries to identify the sounds from its sound memory. Are you careful to clean only the outer ear? Are you careful never to put anything in your ear canal? Did you know that very loud noise, even very loud music, can cause permanent hearing loss?

Clusters of nerve cells, or *taste buds,* in small bumps on the tongue respond to different chemicals in your food. Different parts of the tongue respond to different tastes—sweet, sour, bitter, or salty. There are about 3,000 separate taste buds in your tongue. The brain uses signals from these and from nerves in the nose to identify the foods you eat.

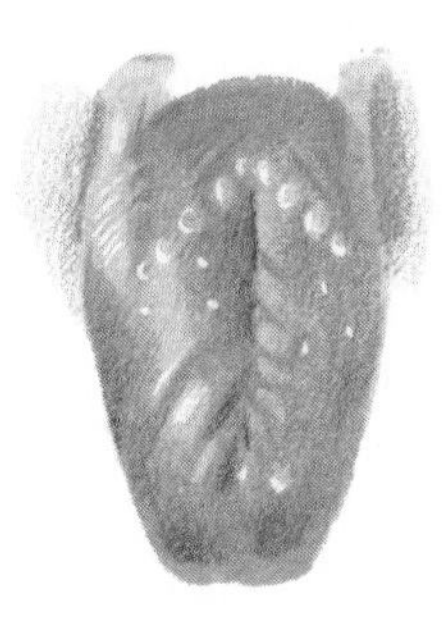

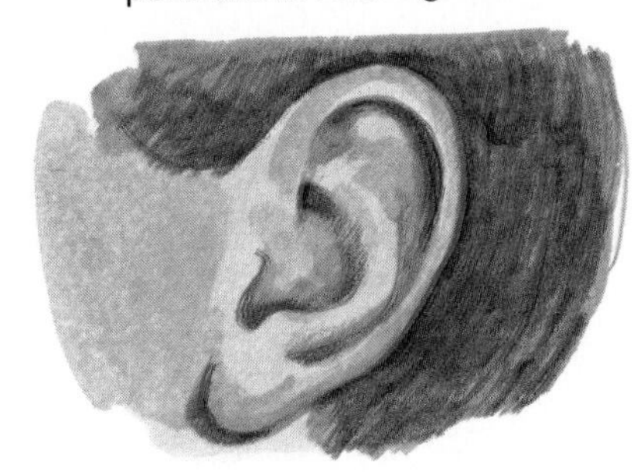

Exploring those senses other than the traditional five completes the study of the way the nervous system informs the body about the environment and about itself. *Heat and cold* are considered separately because the nervous system has different receptors for heat and for cold; in other words, cold is not simply treated as the absence of heat. The ability to sense the position that parts of the body take is called the *kinesthetic sense.* The *sense of equilibrium or balance* is mediated by inner-ear organs called the semicircular canals.

This catalog of additional senses is not complete; for example, nerve endings in the bladder produce sensations that could also be labeled another sense. Many scientists consider pain a separate sense, although some believe that it is caused by overloads in any part of the nervous system. The criterion for a separate sense is that there be nerves whose function is to detect a particular phenomenon and report the phenomenon to the brain.

You Have Health Responsibilities

Perhaps the most amazing feature of the human body is that it can help to repair and protect itself. However, your body cannot take care of itself on its own. You are responsible for eating well-balanced meals, exercising, and getting enough rest every day. Only you can decide not to smoke and not to use drugs that keep your body systems from working at their best.

What was your answer to *Early Checkup* number 5? (Does your body automatically take care of itself, no matter how you decide to live?)

On Your Own

You know that your amazing body is equipped with five senses—sight, hearing, smell, taste, and touch. However, your health also depends on other body senses.

Touch your arm with a metal coin. Now put the coin in hot water and touch it to your arm again. Repeat this with cold water. What senses tell you the coin feels different? How can these senses help your health?

Close your eyes and hold your arm straight out from your body. Now bend it at the elbow. Do you have a sense that tells you the position of your body parts?

What Have You Learned?

Number a piece of paper **1** and **2**. Next to the numbers, write the words that are missing in these sentences.

1. People must protect the ___ from accidental injury, because it is the control center of the body's ___ system.

2. Body senses, such as touch, help to ___ the body from injury. The sense of ___, which depends upon signals of light to the brain, also helps to do this job.

Answers to *What Have You Learned?*
1. brain; nervous
2. protect; sight (seeing)

Learn More About It

These books will help you find out more about your body, its systems, and your senses.

Brown, Paula S. *The Incredible Body Machine.* New York: Random House, Inc., 1981. The major body systems are explained in this book.

Cobb, Vicki. *How To Really Fool Yourself.* Philadelphia, Pa.: J.B. Lippincott Co., 1980. This interesting book will help you to understand the different ways in which parts of your body function.

Daly, Kathleen N. *Body Words: A Dictionary of the Human Body, How It Works, and Some of the Things That Affect It.* New York: Doubleday & Co., Inc., 1980. You can learn still more about your body by reading this book.

More To Do on Your Own

1. Measure your pulse while you are resting. Then exercise (running or bicycling) for a while, and stop to measure your pulse again. Stop exercising when your pulse reaches 150. Record your resting pulse and the time it took for your pulse to reach 150. Repeat this for 20 to 30 minutes a day, three times a week, for a month. What happens to your resting pulse? After a month of regular exercise, does it take the same time for your pulse to reach 150 as it first did? What do you think the effect of exercise has been on your circulatory system?
2. Invent a slogan for an advertising campaign intended to promote better health for the circulatory system. You can use your slogan in a poster or bumper sticker.
3. Find your own *blind spot.* Everybody has one. The blind spot is the point where all the nerves from the eye join to form the *optic nerve*—the nerve that sends signals of light to the brain. On a piece of paper, draw a solid black circle that is about the size of a nickel. Draw an "X" that is about the same size three or four inches (7.6 or 10.2 cm) to the right of the circle. Hold the piece of paper with your arms out straight. Close your left eye and stare at the circle. You should see the "X" even though you keep staring at the circle. Slowly bring the piece of paper closer to you while you stare at the circle. There will be a point where you cannot see the "X." This is your blind spot.
4. Build a model of either the circulatory and respiratory systems or the nervous system. Most of the model can be made with wires, but several organs may have to be made of heavy paper or cardboard.

Final Checkup

A. Number a sheet of paper from **1** through **10**. Next to each number, write the letter of the words that best complete each sentence.

1. Cells of the same kind increase by dividing to form
- **a.** organs.
- **b.** systems.
- **c.** cytoplasm.
- **d.** tissues.

2. For growth and energy, cells need
- **a.** sunlight and moisture.
- **b.** carbon dioxide and other wastes.
- **c.** nutrients, oxygen, and water.
- **d.** exercise and rest.

3. The heart is fit when
- **a.** it works as hard as possible.
- **b.** it pumps the most blood with the least effort.
- **c.** it can add oxygen and nutrients to blood.
- **d.** it beats very slowly.

4. The heart is
- **a.** a big muscle tissue.
- **b.** an organ.
- **c.** a total system of blood supply.
- **d.** a nerve.

5. Blood vessels that take blood from parts of the body to the heart are called
- **a.** arteries.
- **b.** capillaries.
- **c.** veins.
- **d.** ventricles.

6. High blood pressure is
- **a.** caused by too much exercise.
- **b.** a sign that your heart is healthy.
- **c.** cured by taking more salt in foods.
- **d.** one reason the heart works too hard.

7. Capillaries pick up oxygen for blood in the
- **a.** cells.
- **b.** lungs.
- **c.** heart.
- **d.** diaphragm.

8. Smoking is harmful because it
- **a.** makes breathing more difficult.
- **b.** prevents mucus from building up in the lungs.
- **c.** stops the division of cells.
- **d.** kills brain cells.

9. It is important to protect the nervous system because
- **a.** the body continues to replace nerve cells.
- **b.** it requires the most oxygen.
- **c.** the body does not repair nerve cells.
- **d.** it makes new blood cells.

10. A daily well-balanced diet is important for
- **a.** protection from pollution.
- **b.** the health of all cells.
- **c.** stopping the death of skin cells.
- **d.** preventing emphysema.

B. Number a sheet of paper from **1** through **10**. Write **true** or **false** next to the number for each of these ideas.

1. Cells are nearly always too small to see without a microscope. true
2. The diaphragm is a large bone. false
3. A tissue is made from many different kinds of cells. false
4. The skin is both a group of tissues and an organ. true
5. Your pulse tells you how many times a minute your heart beats. true
6. Food, water, and oxygen pass through the walls of arteries into the cells. false
7. Being overweight puts a strain on your circulatory system. true
8. The brain does much of its work without your being aware of it. true
9. Oxygen and carbon dioxide are exchanged in the lungs only when you think about breathing. false
10. All of the sense organs are located in the head so that they are near the brain. false

Write About Better Health

Write a short answer to each of these questions. Use complete sentences.

1. If the body can protect itself so well, why do you have to take care of it?
2. How does blood get food and oxygen?
3. How can two body systems work together for health?
4. What are four ways to prevent diseases of the circulatory system?
5. How does the nervous system help to protect your body?

Model answers to *Write About Better Health* are provided in the chapter notes at the front of this *Teacher's Edition.*

4 WORKING FOR YOUR OWN HEALTH

See the teaching notes on page 82.

Fitness Is for Always

"I'm on our school swimming team," Samantha told her grandfather as they stood near the pool.

"Have you been in any races yet?" her grandfather asked.

"Yes," Samantha answered, looking down at her feet. "I race, but I never win. I'm thinking of quitting."

"I see," said her grandfather. "Well, I never got to be a fast swimmer either, when I was your age. But I did get to be one of the *strongest* swimmers in my school."

Samantha was puzzled. Didn't "strongest" mean "fastest"?

"Lots of people could swim faster than I," her grandfather explained. "But I could swim for a longer time than most, without getting tired. I always thought being fit was even more important than being fast."

"I never thought of it that way," Samantha said, looking at the pool. "This pool is smaller than the one I use at home. I wonder how many laps I can do." She dove into the water.

Samantha's grandfather counted as she swam 46 laps. "That was pretty good," he told his tired granddaughter. "Now you count for me."

Samantha could hardly believe it. She counted 50, then 60, then 70 laps. Her grandfather stopped at 75, but it looked as though he could have gone on swimming.

"How did you do that?" she asked him. "I thought older people couldn't do such hard exercise."

Samantha's grandfather laughed. "Many people who have exercised all their lives don't slow down all that much as they age. When I wasn't swimming, I did other kinds of exercise every day. I've kept in the best shape I could since I was younger than you are now. Of course, I never did get much faster."

"Grandpa," Samantha said, smiling, "I think you're telling me something without saying it. Speed champion or not, I'll stick with my swimming. Maybe I can beat your record when I'm your age!"

Today many people are aware of the desirability of keeping healthy and fit. Fitness—a measure of how little work the heart must do to get life-giving oxygen and nutrients in the blood to all parts of the body—is a lifetime endeavor to more people than ever before. Exercise is one critical element in keeping fit. Some people will always enter sports activities in order to win. However, many more people are active in sports not just to win, but to test and stretch their own limits. For example, the goal of many people in entering a marathon or bicycle race is merely to complete the course. They recognize that it requires skill and fitness to do so.

A major focus of this chapter is that any serious physical exercise program—whether to have fun, to win, or simply to keep fit—requires a commitment of time and persistence.

LOOKING AHEAD

An important part of growing up is finding out how you can help to keep yourself healthy and fit. This starts with learning how your body signals its need for more rest, more exercise, or more healthful food. When you understand your body's needs, you can take more responsibility for its care.

Of course, people can never be completely responsible for their own health care. Young people should discuss their health ideas with their families. Doctors, dentists, school nurses, and others will usually have helpful answers to many of your health questions. The adults you feel close to and who care about you can often help with problems that worry you.

Still, there are many important ways to help yourself stay healthy and fit as you continue growing up. This chapter can give you ideas for building better health. It will teach you

- four basic steps to good health.
- how to know your body better and follow your own health-care plan.
- why regular health checkups are important.
- what you can do to keep your teeth and gums healthy.

Here are some words you may not have talked about in school before. You will learn more about them in this chapter. You can find all these words in the *Glossary* at the back of this book.

aerobic exercise (er'ō'bik ek'sər·sīz)
cavities (kav'ə·tēz)
cool-downs (kül-dounz)
flex (fleks)
hygiene (hī'jēn')
muscle tone (mus'əl tōn)
permanent teeth (pėr'mə·nənt tēth)
posture (pos'chər)
preventive medicine (pri·ven'tiv med'ə·sən)
REM sleep (rem slēp)
warm-ups (wôrm-ups)

Early Checkup

Number a piece of paper from **1** through **8**. Answer each of these questions by writing **yes** or **no** next to the correct number on your paper. You can check your answers as you read this chapter.

1. Is the time people spend sleeping wasted time? no
2. Does the brain rest by shutting itself off while you sleep? no
3. Do all people of the same height and weight need the same amount of food to feel their best? no
4. To be physically fit, must people do special exercises and play sports? no
5. Does exercise strengthen your lungs? yes
6. Do you need to prepare your body for vigorous exercise? yes
7. Should a person who feels healthy skip a medical checkup? no
8. Can you do anything to reduce the risk of cavities? yes

A person who begins fitness training as a child and who keeps up some form of exercise throughout adulthood need not give it up later in life. In fact, most physicians advise such people to continue exercising for the maintenance of their health.

You may want to initiate a class discussion about the range of health—that is, from the peak of health, through the various feelings of not being quite at one's healthiest, to being actually sick. Students should understand that there is a spectrum of health, not just the extremes of healthy and sick. It is important to stress that there are many diseases—contagious and other—that an individual may not be able to avoid, no matter how carefully that individual observes the basic rules of good health.

The four basic rules for health can shorten the duration of many diseases and minimize the consequences of others.

SOME STEPS TO BETTER HEALTH

Being Well Is a Good Feeling

How did you feel when you awoke this morning? Did you get up feeling full of energy for the day ahead? Did you feel lots of energy as you washed and dressed? Were you hungry enough to eat a full breakfast?

If you felt that way, then you know what feeling well really means. Feeling well is being as healthy as you can be. It feels good to be well.

You can help yourself feel well more often. Even if you cannot always prevent illness, you can help yourself to be sick less often. When you catch a cold, you can help make it last a shorter time. Being well starts with at least four basic steps to good health.

Step 1. Eating well-balanced meals and snacks helps you feel well. Breakfast is especially important. Try something nutritious but a bit different for breakfast every day. You can find some healthful food ideas in Chapter 5.

Step 2. Daily exercise is necessary for good health. What are your favorite exercises?

Step 3. Keep your skin clean. After you play hard, wash well with warm water and soap. Wash your hands before handling food. Why is this important?

Step 4. Getting enough sleep every day is important. When you do not feel your best, you may need a little more sleep than you usually get.

Some "Getting to Sleep" Ideas

Once in a while, some people cannot fall right to sleep at bedtime. Here are some "getting to sleep" ideas many young people say work for them.

1. One by one, tighten and relax each muscle that you can.
2. Think of the most pleasant place you know. Imagine you are there.
3. Drink a glass of warm milk before bedtime.
4. Read for a half hour before bedtime.

Although most of us know from practical experience that we need sleep, scientists have not yet discovered exactly what the body does to restore itself during sleep. Therefore, the authors have emphasized the "symptomatic" need for sleep and how a person who has not had enough sleep might feel. Ask students to draw their own idea of how a person lacking sleep might look. Use the pictures to initiate a discussion of how a person usually feels without enough sleep or rest. Try to elicit suggestions of when students feel that a good night's sleep is particularly important (*before any stressful situation, such as a test; before participating in sports; when one wants to look one's best*). Students should also be aware that different people require different amounts of sleep. The "eight hours a night" rule applies to many people, but some individuals need more and some need less. Most important is that people respond to what their own bodies signal they need.

What Happens When You Sleep?

Did you ever stop to think about how much time people spend sleeping? Most people sleep for about one third of their lives. Scientists are trying to learn more about sleep. They now know that sleep time is not wasted. Sleep refreshes your body and mind. Important changes take place in your body when you are asleep. The body goes on working even though many parts slow down. While you sleep, the heart muscle and other muscles keep working, but more slowly than when you are awake. One part of the body seems to work harder during sleep. The *pituitary gland* produces more *growth hormone* while you are sleeping. You can learn more about this in Chapter 2.

What was your answer to *Early Checkup* number 1? (Is the time people spend sleeping wasted time?)

Breathing slows down and the body's temperature lowers when you sleep. The brain relaxes, but it continues to control the heart, lungs, and other organs.

Scientists are still trying to find the answer to why the body must have rest and sleep. Until they do, there is one certain fact about sleep. People feel less fit and less alert when they do not get enough sleep. Too little sleep seems to affect the way people feel about themselves and others. Lack of sleep often makes people nervous and more easily upset by small problems.

Do these people look well rested? You, too, can see the effects of sleep. Look at yourself in the mirror each morning. What might be the signs that you need more sleep?

GIRL
WANTED

REM sleep

Everyone Dreams

Whether or not you can remember dreams, sleep scientists are now sure everyone has them. Those that happen during REM sleep are the easiest to remember. Dreams are usually about yourself, your family and friends, and your own experiences. They may be happy or frightening, but many scientists now believe dreams help relax your mind and ease the day's worry and stress.

Sleep laboratories have provided us with information on the different stages of sleep. An electroencephalograph records brain waves on an electroencephalogram (EEG). This EEG enables scientists to measure the brain's activity during each stage of sleep. REM sleep is detected by sensors on the closed eyelids.

Sleep Changes Through the Night

In the first stage of sleep, your breathing slows down. You move around and turn over often. In the second stage of sleep, the organs of your body slow down a bit more. There are short bursts of activity in the brain. The third stage is a deeper stage of sleep. Your body moves less. Brain waves are longer, showing that the brain is not working as hard, even though it is still controlling every part of the body. In the fourth stage of sleep, it is hard to be awakened. **REM sleep** (''REM'' stands for ''rapid eye movement'') is the fifth and last stage. It is very different from the other stages. The eyes move quickly under the lids as if they were watching something. The body is relaxed, but the heart rate and breathing quicken. Dreams that occur during REM sleep are easier to recall when a person is awakened than dreams during other sleep stages. The five stages, from the first stage through REM sleep, form a cycle that people go through as they sleep.

What was your answer to *Early Checkup* number 2? (Does the brain rest by shutting itself off while you sleep?)

Record of Brain Activity

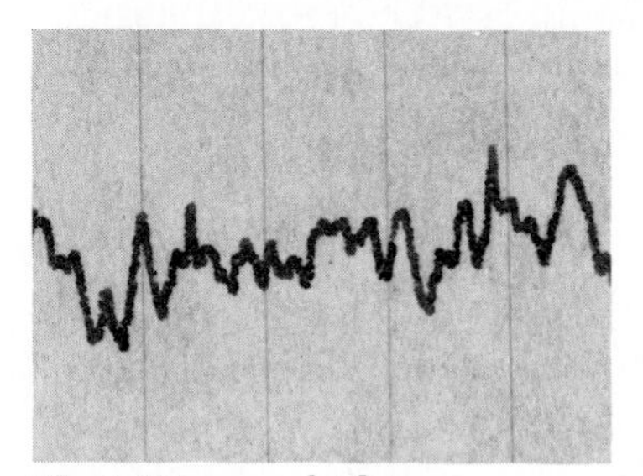

First Stage of Sleep

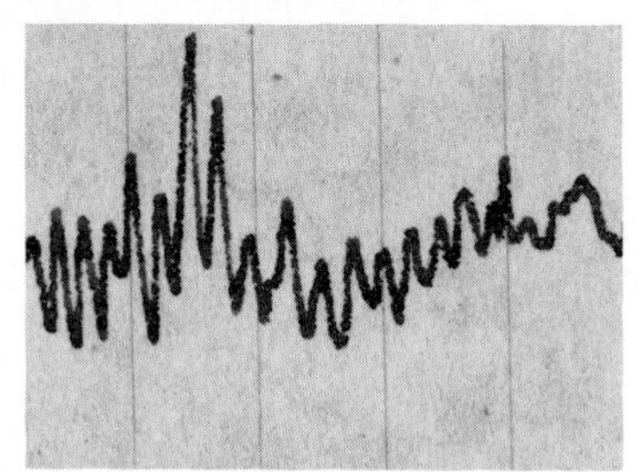

Second Stage of Sleep

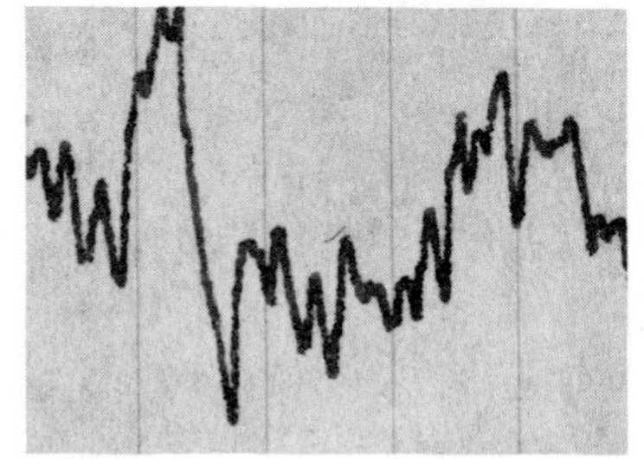

Third Stage of Sleep

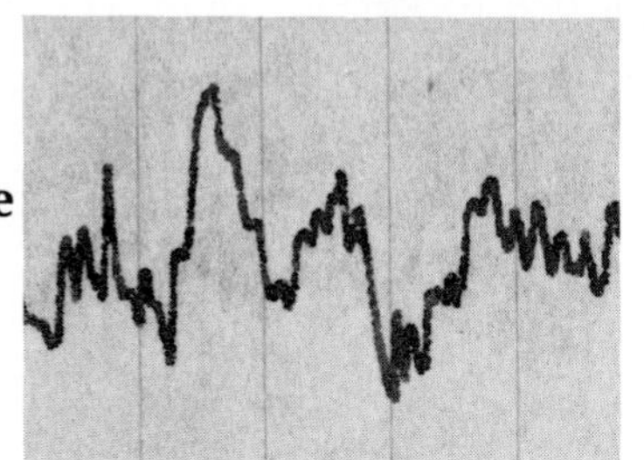

Fourth Stage of Sleep

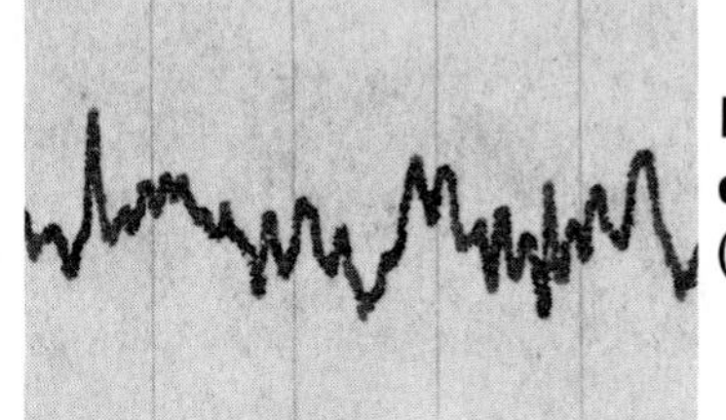

Fifth Stage of Sleep (REM)

Discovery—A New Pathway to Health

Very little was known about sleep until the 1950's. At that time, three doctors at the University of Chicago—Dr. Nathaniel Kleistman, Dr. Eugene Aserinsky, and Dr. William C. Dement—asked people to volunteer for a special study of sleep. Some who volunteered had sleep problems. Others who volunteered slept normally.

The doctors wired people to special machines that measured the brain's electrical activity during sleep. Other machines measured the people's heartbeats, eye movements, and muscle activities.

Today many doctors believe that dreams may be important to the health of the mind. They find that people who sleep enough hours but are awakened every time REM sleep begins often feel nervous and upset in the morning.

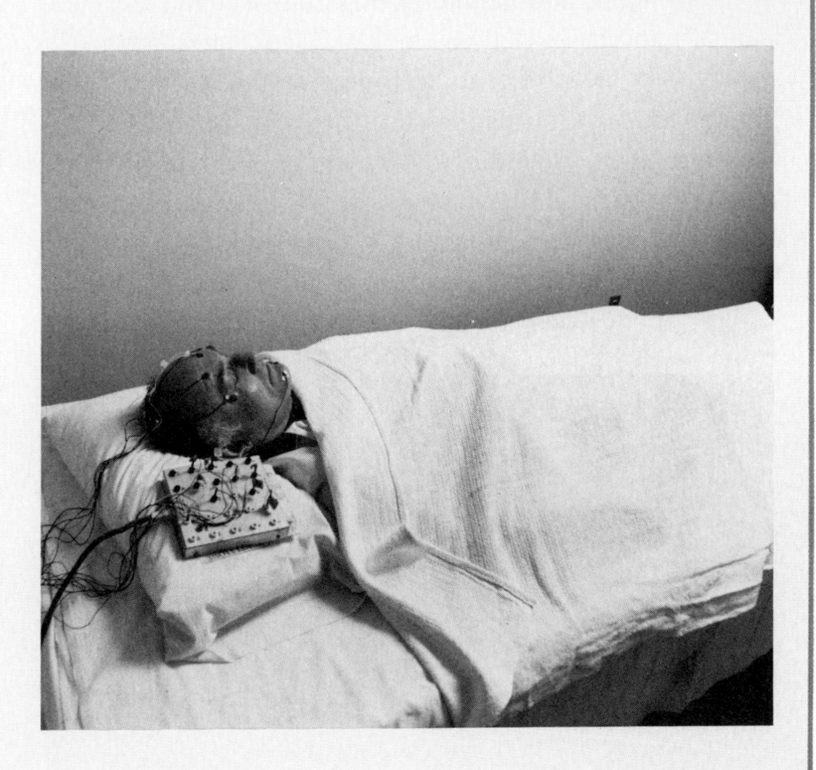

Many people who believe that they never dream have been surprised to learn that they do dream. Researchers have awakened such sleepers toward the end of a REM sleep period, and the sleepers were able to recall dreams they had been having.

All sleep-study measurements are made with instruments that are wired to the surface of the skin. There is no pain or danger to the volunteer in a sleep laboratory. The information gained from these laboratories has been very useful in understanding and treating people with such sleep difficulties as insomnia (*a continuing inability to fall asleep or stay asleep easily*) and apnea (*a potentially serious problem in breathing while asleep*). Interestingly, sleep-study volunteers who have lived in total isolation for many weeks began to organize their activities around a day that is closer to 25 hours than to 24. Many adults seemed to require fewer than 8 hours of sleep.

Emphasize to students that getting enough sleep during their fast-growth years is especially important.

hygiene

Students of this age are often concerned about their appearance. It is sometimes effective to approach the subject of personal hygiene as much from the standpoint of appearance as from its value in helping to reduce health risks. It is important for students to understand that everyone cannot have a perfect face or shape. Most people can make the most of their appearance by following a plan of daily personal hygiene. Good hygiene practices affect not only our physical health, but also our mental health. A positive feeling about oneself is an important element in good mental health.

Many preteen and teenage students cultivate a look of studied carelessness. This choice can still be made without sacrificing personal hygiene.

How Can Staying Healthy Help You Look Your Best?

How do you look to yourself? How do you look to others? The way you take care of your health can make a big difference in the way you answer these questions. For example, the more people care for their personal **hygiene**, the fewer health risks they take. Hygiene is all the steps people take to keep themselves clean. The cleaner your body, clothing, school, and home are, the smaller your risk of disease is. Personal hygiene is also a way of making yourself look better to yourself and others.

Just as litter can keep a school or neighborhood from looking its best, dirt can keep people from looking their best. Soap and water remove extra oils, sweat that produces unpleasant odors, and harmful germs from skin and hair. Clean skin and hair make you look and feel better, too. Brushing your teeth helps to keep your mouth smelling clean.

Clean clothing is also important. Dirty clothing can carry odors and germs. Help the person who does the family laundry by placing dirty clothing where it belongs. People do not need clothing that costs a lot in order to look good. Clothing that is clean makes any person look better.

What Is Healthful Eating?

Students should be encouraged to evaluate whether their food intake is too high, too low, or just right. Students should understand that their bodies may require more food during a period of rapid growth. After the growth spurt ends, their bodies may signal a return to former eating habits.

Even people who seem to be about the same size may need different amounts of food to feel well. There is no one amount of food that is just right for everyone who is the same height and weight. Different bodies use healthful foods differently. How does anyone know the right amount to eat? Probably the best way to know is to look for clues from your own body. Do you often feel too full after a meal? Eating food more slowly, chewing food well, and eating less may make you feel better. Does your scale or mirror tell you that you are heavier or thinner than you should be? If you are often hungry soon after meals, try thinking about what you are eating to make sure that your food choices are nutritionally correct. You can learn about nutritious foods in Chapter 5.

> What was your answer to *Early Checkup* number 3? (Do all people of the same height and weight need the same amount of food to feel their best?)

Eating well-balanced meals and nutritious snacks every day can be healthful and fun, too. Be a bit more daring and try some new foods, fixed in different ways.

Do you enjoy working hard around your home, school, and community? Do you find ways every day to exercise arm, leg, chest, and back muscles? Do you find it easy to get enough food and sleep every day?

Do you try sports and games just for the exercise and fun? Do you try sports and exercise that demand the most from you? Do you slowly build up to exercising and then, after exercising, slowly wind down?

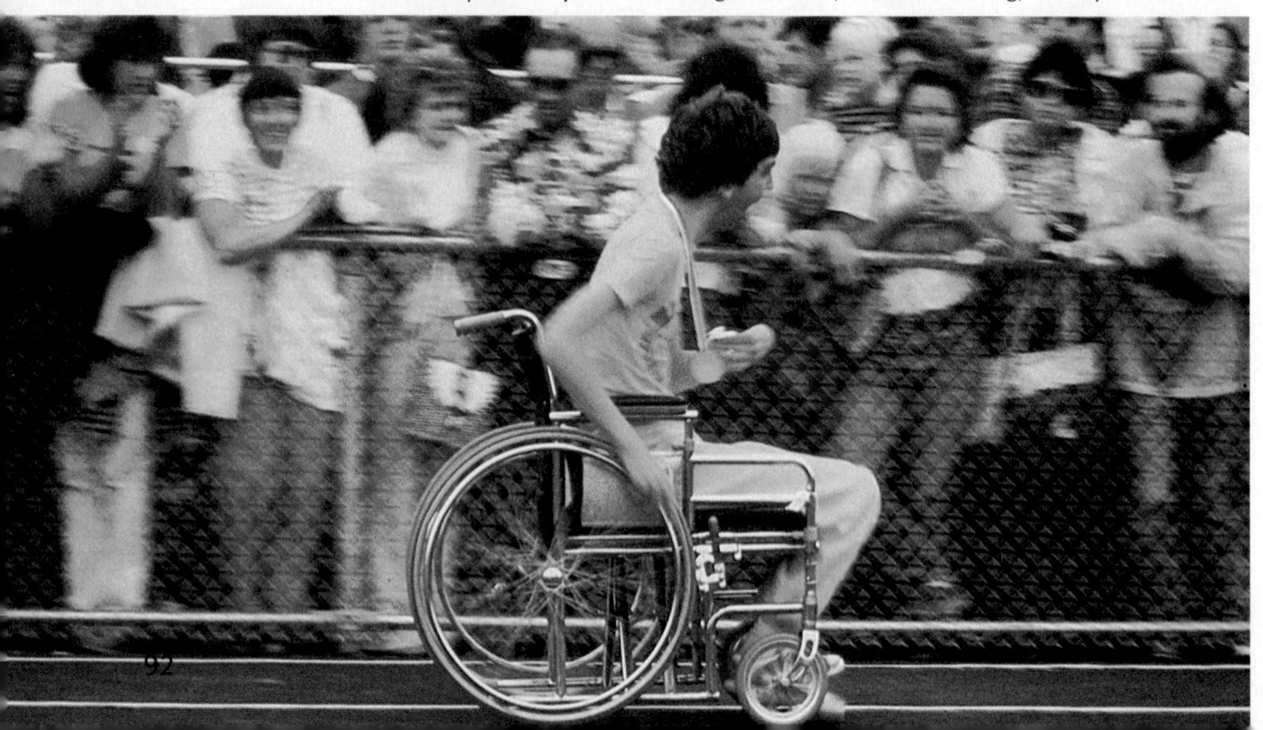

What Is the Best Way To Keep Fit?

flex
muscle tone
posture

How did you answer the questions under the pictures? If all your answers are yes, you are probably on the right path to fitness and good health. Fitness calls for daily exercise. Sports and special exercises are fine for fitness, but there are many other ways to get the daily exercise you need. Gardening, painting, cleaning, walking, running, and climbing are all ways to keep fit on your own. How many other fitness activities can you try?

What was your answer to *Early Checkup* number 4? (To be physically fit, must people do special exercises and play sports?)

People who are physically fit are about as healthy as their bodies can be. They feel well and they look well. People who are fit usually stand and sit with good **posture**. Good posture balances the body, keeping it straight but relaxed.

Fit people have firm, strong muscles that they can comfortably stretch and **flex**. Flexing a muscle is bending and shortening it. When a person's muscles remain in a partially flexed state, the person is said to have good **muscle tone**. People who are fit have strong hearts and lungs, too. They get the most blood throughout their bodies with the least strain on their hearts. Even people with special health problems, or who do not have full use of their bodies, often find ways to stay as fit as they can be.

Stress the idea that each individual has to select activities to suit that person's particular needs and interests. Many people prefer a formal exercise or sports program. Others prefer walking, biking, gardening, or other activities that use the body's muscles but are not undertaken for exercise alone. You may want to point out that, with adequate adult and medical guidance, children who were once considered "sickly" have been able to strengthen themselves and improve their health. One example to cite is President Theodore Roosevelt. He was a very sickly child who became stronger slowly through a carefully considered exercise program. As an adult, he was an unusually robust man.

Why Is Exercise Important?

Exercise helps more muscles in your body than just those you can feel. Exercise that makes your heart beat faster and moves blood more quickly through your body strengthens your heart and lungs. The same exercise makes you breathe more quickly and deeply. The lungs deliver more oxygen to the blood. The heart pumps more blood to the body cells that require more energy for the work they are doing. The stronger your heart is, the less work it must do to pump all that blood.

What was your answer to *Early Checkup* number 5? (Does exercise strengthen your lungs?)

You know that exercise helps people develop good posture and that this helps people look and feel better. Good posture also provides more room for organs like the lungs to work inside your body. Daily exercise even helps keep your brain healthy. Your brain is more alert when it is well supplied with oxygen.

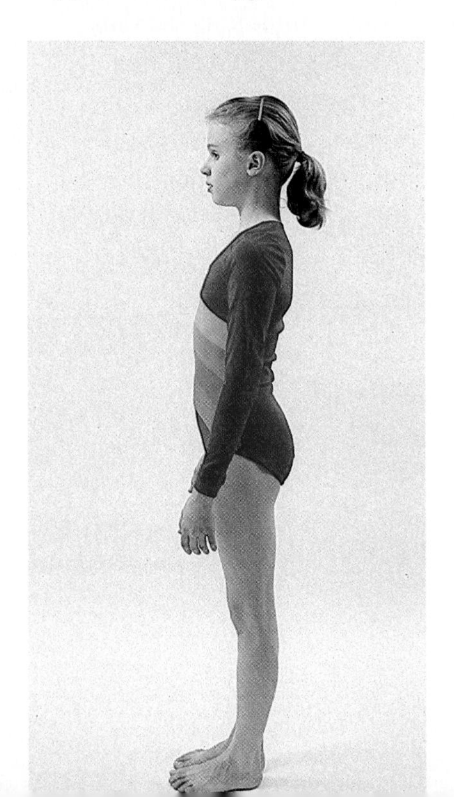

You may want to discuss the relationship between physical fitness and body efficiency. (*A well-trained athlete usually has a slower heartbeat rate [pulse], as well as a slower breathing rate, than people who are less "in shape." Because the athlete's heart has been strengthened by exercise, his or her heart can move more blood each time it pumps. Strong lungs are more flexible, so that each cycle of inhalation and exhalation delivers more oxygen to the body. In other words, a fit person's heart and lungs can do more work with less effort, and so with less strain, than those of an unfit person.*)

It is almost impossible to overstate the role of good posture. Perhaps one way of getting the message across to students is by pointing out how important posture is to the appearance of some of those people they admire in public life, particularly in sports. The role posture plays in self-image is very subtle. We tend to droop or slouch when our spirits are down. Sometimes making the effort to improve our posture can have a positive effect on our spirits.

Some posture problems, such as scoliosis (lateral curvature of the spine), require more attention than just an admonition to stand straight. Scoliosis can usually be corrected if caught at an early enough age. Many schools have early screening programs for scoliosis.

Exercise can also help people "work off" upsetting feelings. It can help them, for example, to forget what angers and worries them. Unhappy feelings can often keep people from achieving their best health and fitness. Do you have some favorite activity that helps you relax while you develop physical fitness?

aerobic exercise
cool-downs
warm-ups

Aerobic Exercises Strengthen Heart and Lungs

Chances are you are doing a lot of **aerobic exercise** each day. Aerobic exercises depend completely on oxygen to give your body energy. Such exercises increase the heart rate and breathing rate. This helps the body use oxygen more effectively, and strengthens the heart muscle. Running, jogging, and swimming are a few kinds of aerobic exercise. Everyone needs some aerobic exercise at least 3 times a week for about 20 minutes each time.

Warm-ups and Cool-downs Reduce Exercise Risks

Many exercises and sports demand a lot of sudden energy from the body. Even people who exercise every day should do **warm-ups** before beginning vigorous exercise. Warm-ups are simple exercises that stretch and flex the body's muscles, toning them for the job ahead. Warm-ups also help the heart and lungs get ready for more work. By warming up the body for exercise, people help lower the chance of hurting their muscles, joints, and bones.

What was your answer to *Early Checkup* number 6? (Do you need to prepare your body for vigorous exercise?)

After exercise, even if it has not been too vigorous, the body should be slowly brought to rest through some more simple stretching and flexing exercises. These are called **cool-downs**. The moderate exercise of a cool-down also lowers the heart rate and the chance of hurting the body in suddenly going from exercise to rest.

The following exercises may be used as warm-ups or cool-downs.

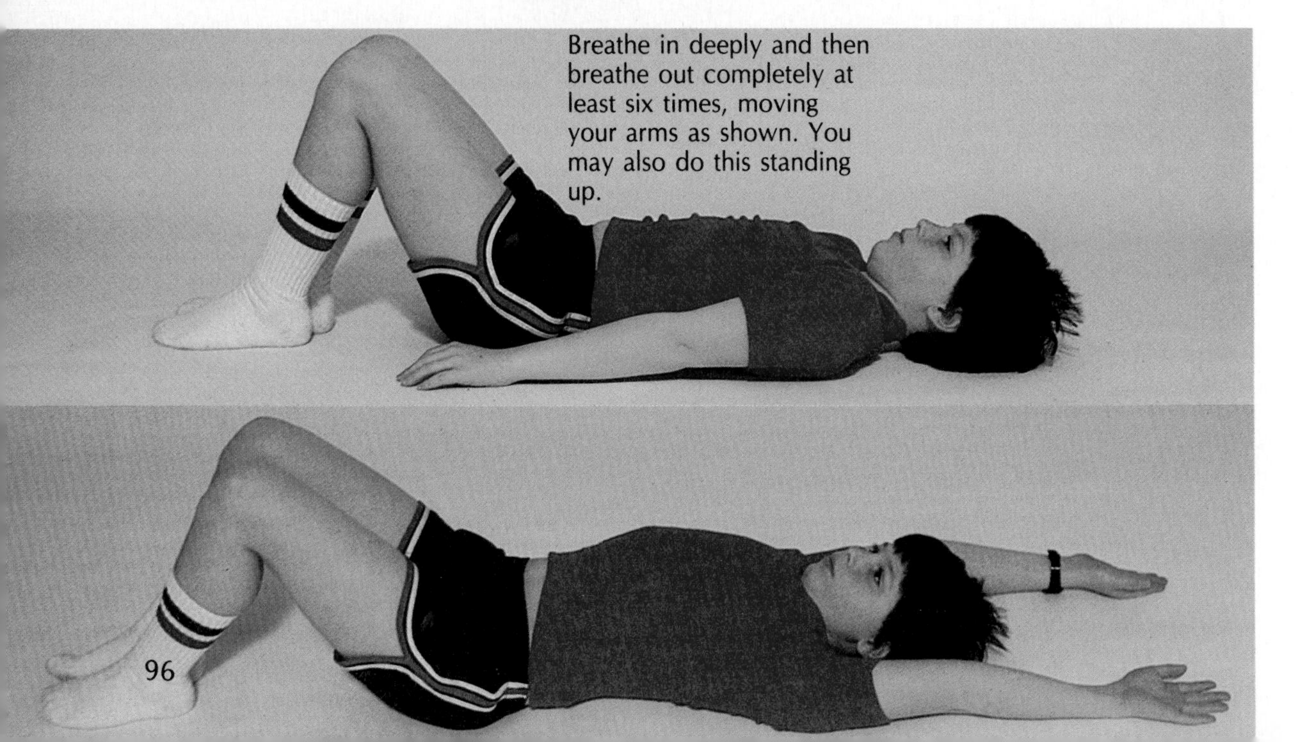

Breathe in deeply and then breathe out completely at least six times, moving your arms as shown. You may also do this standing up.

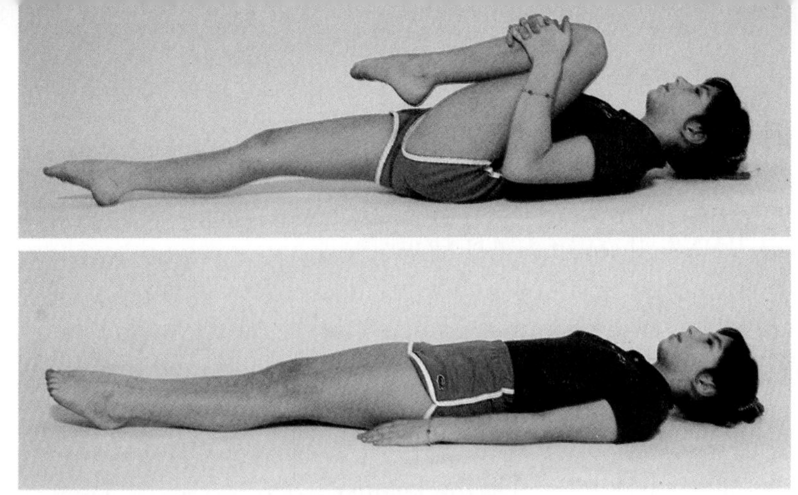

Pull up one knee as close to your chest as it will go, and then let your leg back down. Do the same with your other knee. Do this five times with each knee. This exercise is similar to jogging in place.

In this "roll-up," a person rolls down to the floor along the spine and then rolls back up along the spine. The muscles of the *abdomen* pull the body up. Roll-ups help strengthen the muscles that hold the back and spine in place.

What Have You Learned?

Number a piece of paper from **1** through **5**. Next to the numbers, write the words that are missing in these sentences.

1. Four major steps to good health are eating nutritious foods, getting enough __ and __, and keeping your body as __ as it can be.

2. During REM sleep, people often have __ that they remember.

3. What people do to keep clean, which also reduces health risks, is called __.

4. The way you stand or place your body for standing or sitting is called __. It can help make you look and feel better.

5. It is important to do __ before exercising and __ after.

Answers to *What Have You Learned?*

1. sleep; exercise (in either order); clean
2. dreams
3. hygiene
4. posture
5. warm-ups; cool-downs

A feeling of responsibility for one's own health can play an important role in the establishment of good health habits. Habits that children develop now may stick with them throughout life. The student's health responsibility includes correction of habits that cause unnecessary health risks, reinforcement of habits that reduce health risks, and an understanding that some health problems must be handled by more qualified people. One of the serious problems affecting young people is worrying about symptoms that may be part of a normal health pattern or that can be corrected easily. The stress created by worrying can sometimes be more serious than the symptoms. For that reason, and because early care of serious problems can reduce their effects, it is important to emphasize the need for students to speak to a parent, doctor, or nurse when they have reason for concern.

PLANNING YOUR OWN HEALTH RESPONSIBILITIES

Take Charge of Your Own Health

For much of your life up to now, others in your family have been largely responsible for your health. Adults in your family have made sure that you eat nutritious foods and that you get regular medical and dental checkups. Most likely, the older members of your family have taken care of cleaning the house and doing the laundry.

While there are many others who help you to stay healthy, no one can be more responsible for your body than you. Now that you are older, building health and fitness takes your own thought, time, and planning. For example, do you leave time every day for exercise, good nutrition, and personal health care? Do you arrange to finish homework, television, or reading early enough to get to bed on time?

There is more that goes into a good health plan. Your family and a doctor can help you understand certain health problems you may have. There are also other problems you are responsible for checking. For example, a mirror can tell you how clean and how well rested you look. A scale can tell you how quickly your weight is changing as you grow. Keep a record of your weight each week over the next few months. Show the record to your doctor and ask about it during your next checkup. Many young people gain weight quickly when they are growing quickly. However, if you are worried about being too thin or too heavy, talk with your family about it. They may be able to help you plan better eating habits.

Go up a flight of stairs or run down a street. Think about how you feel when you have been playing or climbing a lot of steps. Do you tire quickly? You may decide to build your fitness by slowly increasing your daily exercise. Think of how often you really feel well and at your best. If it is most of the time, you are probably following the right health plan.

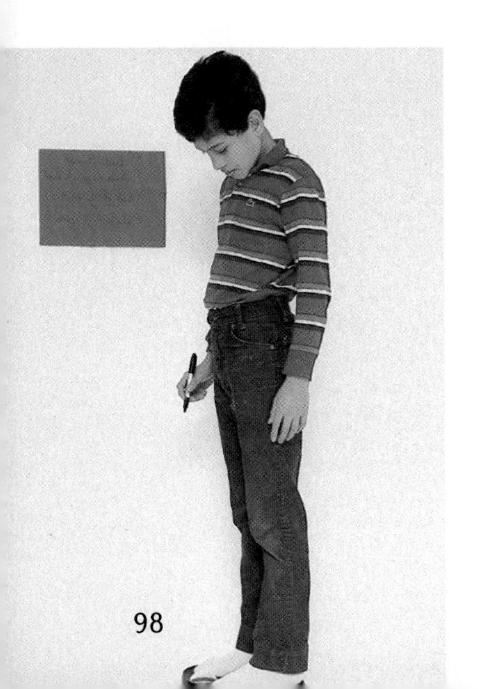

If you think it is not often enough, even though you are following a good health plan, talk with your family about the problem. Always tell your teacher, your school nurse, or an adult in your family if you think you have a fever, an injury, an unusual pain, or a tired feeling that you cannot explain.

For personal health plans to be effective for students of this age, privacy is essential. Often the interference of a well-intentioned adult or other child can upset a good resolution. Children may want to practice good health habits without letting others know of their intention.

On Your Own

Use the model chart to draw your own daily health plan. This plan is for you alone. You can change it as you follow it and as you come to know which changes make you feel well more often. You can share it with others or keep it to yourself.

Think of the time you now spend exercising and resting each day. How might you change the time spent to make yourself feel better? Everything you list under "Goal" becomes a health goal you should try to achieve. Under "Nutritious Meals," list some new and healthful foods you would like to try. These will also be health goals.

Remember, you should not be doing something every minute of the day. You should set aside time for relaxing every day. Use this chart only for a few weeks. By then, the responsibilities and goals will have become good health habits.

	Nutritious Meals	Exercise	Staying Clean	Tooth Care	
Mon.	Zucchini Fish Apples	20 min.	15 min.	5 min.	Actual Time
		30 min.	25 min.	15 min.	Goal
Tues.					Actual Time
					Goal
Wed.					Actual Time
					Goal
Thurs.					Actual Time
					Goal

preventive medicine

In most communities, medical care is available for people of varying means. That makes the medical checkup possible for virtually all children. Children of this age are usually advised to have a checkup at least once a year. You may want to point out that babies usually have checkups much more often than older children. The checkup for babies is a very important form of preventive medicine in two ways. First, correctible problems can be discovered early and solved with a minimum of time and worry. Second, immunizations can be administered. Without going into personal details, you may want to ask the students to enumerate some ways preventive medicine is important. Do not overlook the importance of the patient's conversation with the doctor. Such conversations are a good way of relieving a youngster's anxiety about visiting the doctor's office, and provide a good opportunity for the youngster to get health pointers.

Checkups Are Part of Every Health Plan

Checkups by a doctor are important even when you are feeling well. Having a doctor check your health when you are not sick is one kind of **preventive medicine**. It is a way of finding out if you have health problems before they become too serious. Many health problems can be corrected at an early stage. Preventive medicine can also teach people better ways to cut down on even more health risks. Instructions from the doctor should be added to your own health plan.

What was your answer to *Early Checkup* number 7? (Should a person who feels healthy skip a medical checkup?)

Even though other people may help you, in the end *you* are responsible for your health. A doctor can help you understand about your body and can give you advice. Then it is up to you to act on what the doctor says. You are also responsible for letting the doctor know exactly how you are feeling. It is your job to ask questions you have about your body. For example, suppose you talk with your doctor about a health problem that bothers you. The problem may be a skin rash or pimples. You may be worried about your size. Perhaps you are getting headaches or stomach aches from time to time. Maybe you have some other problem. Often a doctor's answers can help you understand that many other people your age have the same kinds of problems. You may also want to go over your daily health plan with a doctor at your next checkup.

Once in a while at a checkup, your doctor may give you an *immunization* shot, one to keep you from getting measles, for example. Immunization shots are another kind of preventive medicine. They reduce the risk of disease germs making you sick.

Your doctor will probably let you know how often you should have a checkup. If you think it is time for you to have a medical checkup, discuss it with the adults in your family.

What Happens at a Medical Checkup?

Often each new medical checkup seems different to people from the last one they had. Checkups do change. This may be because of some new way the doctor or medical team has learned to work.

The doctor often examines your ears, eyes, nose, and throat with special instruments and lights. The sound of your working heart and lungs will probably be checked with the help of a *stethoscope.*

The doctor checks for signs of future health problems. This checkup, plus immunization, can help you add to your daily health plan. For example, your doctor can tell you whether or not your weight seems right for your body and size.

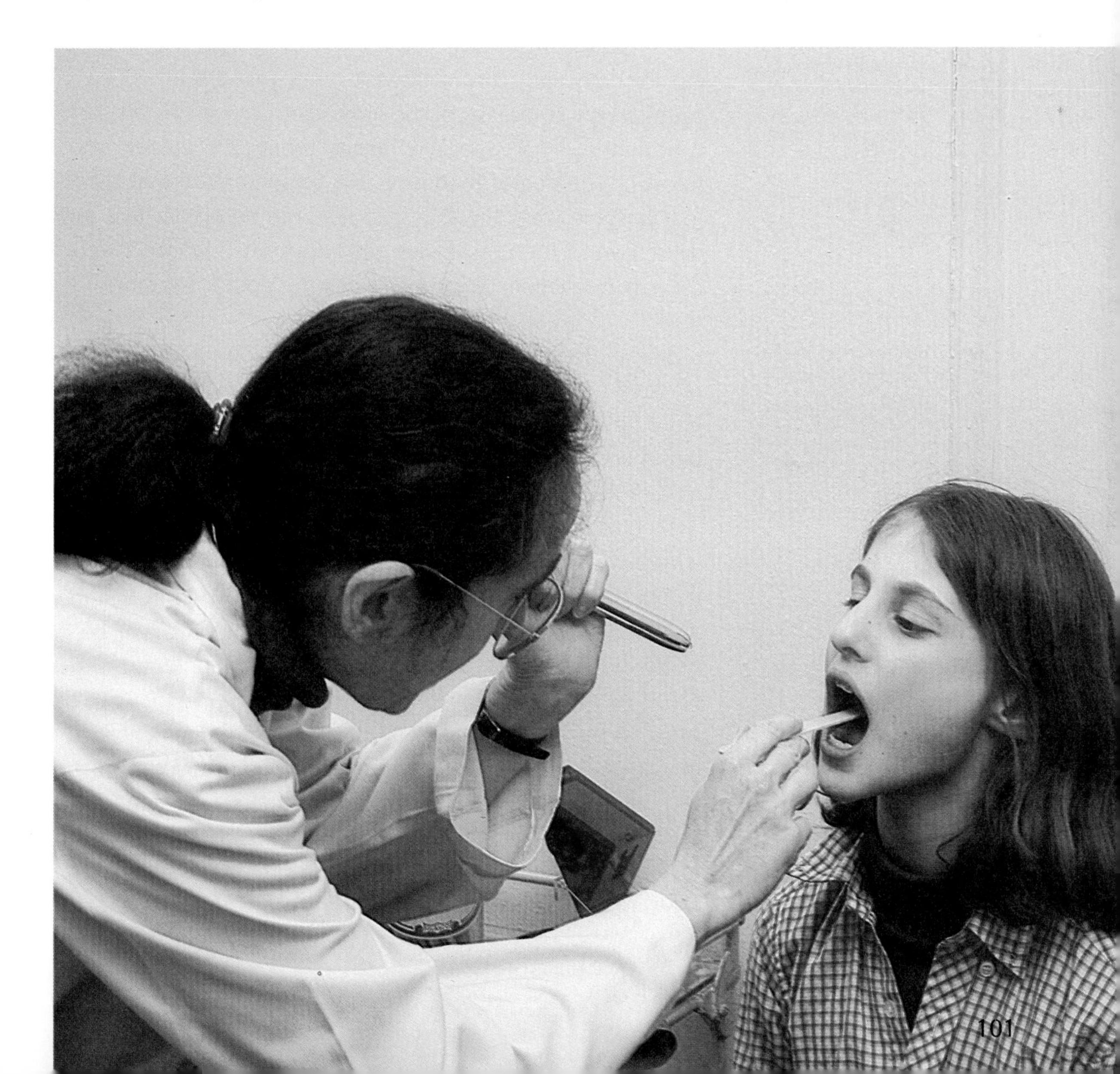

A medical checkup can be frightening if the patient has no idea of the reasons for the various instruments and tests. Many doctors and nurses forget how much most patients do not understand. They may welcome the opportunity to answer patients' questions. Students should be encouraged to ask about the various parts of a checkup.

The nature of the checkup may vary in several ways. More tests or fewer may be made at a specific checkup. In some medical practices, a nurse, medical assistant, or team of doctors may conduct the checkup. All these possibilities should be discussed with students.

Blood pressure is expressed as a function of two kinds of pressure: systolic (cardiac output) and diastolic (the artery's elastic resistance). The average adult blood pressure is 120/80. The first number is systolic pressure, the second, diastolic pressure.

The doctor or a medical assistant keeps track of your health history through a written record or chart. This chart covers your past health and any problems the doctor may want to check again.

Often the doctor will tap your knee with a light rubber hammer. Your leg will jerk a bit, which is a sign that your nervous system is working well. The doctor may also feel your *pulse* at your wrist or the side of your neck. Your pulse comes from the stretching of blood vessels and shows how many times a minute your heart beats.

The doctor might give you a *tine test.* This is a special test for detecting signs of disease germs that cause *tuberculosis,* a disease of the lungs that can be treated. For the tine test, small, specially treated prongs are pressed into the skin. The doctor then gives the person a card that shows four possible ways the skin may react to the prongs in a few days. Two of the possibilities need no further action. The other two reactions are signs to call the doctor for more tests.

Blood pressure is also checked. Your blood pressure is a measure of the force with which your heart is pumping blood through your blood vessels. In most cases, high or low blood pressure can be controlled through diet and special medicines.

To take blood pressure, a cuff attached to a gauge is wrapped tightly around the arm over an *artery.* Air is pumped into the cuff, slowing the flow of blood through the artery. When the sound of the heartbeat can no longer be heard through the stethoscope, the air is slowly let out. Blood rushes into the artery. This makes a sound that can be heard through the stethoscope. Now the measurement on the gauge is noted. The air continues to be released from the cuff, and the sound gets louder. When the sound stops, again the measurement on the gauge is noted. The two measurements indicate the blood pressure. If the second measurement is high, it may mean high blood pressure.

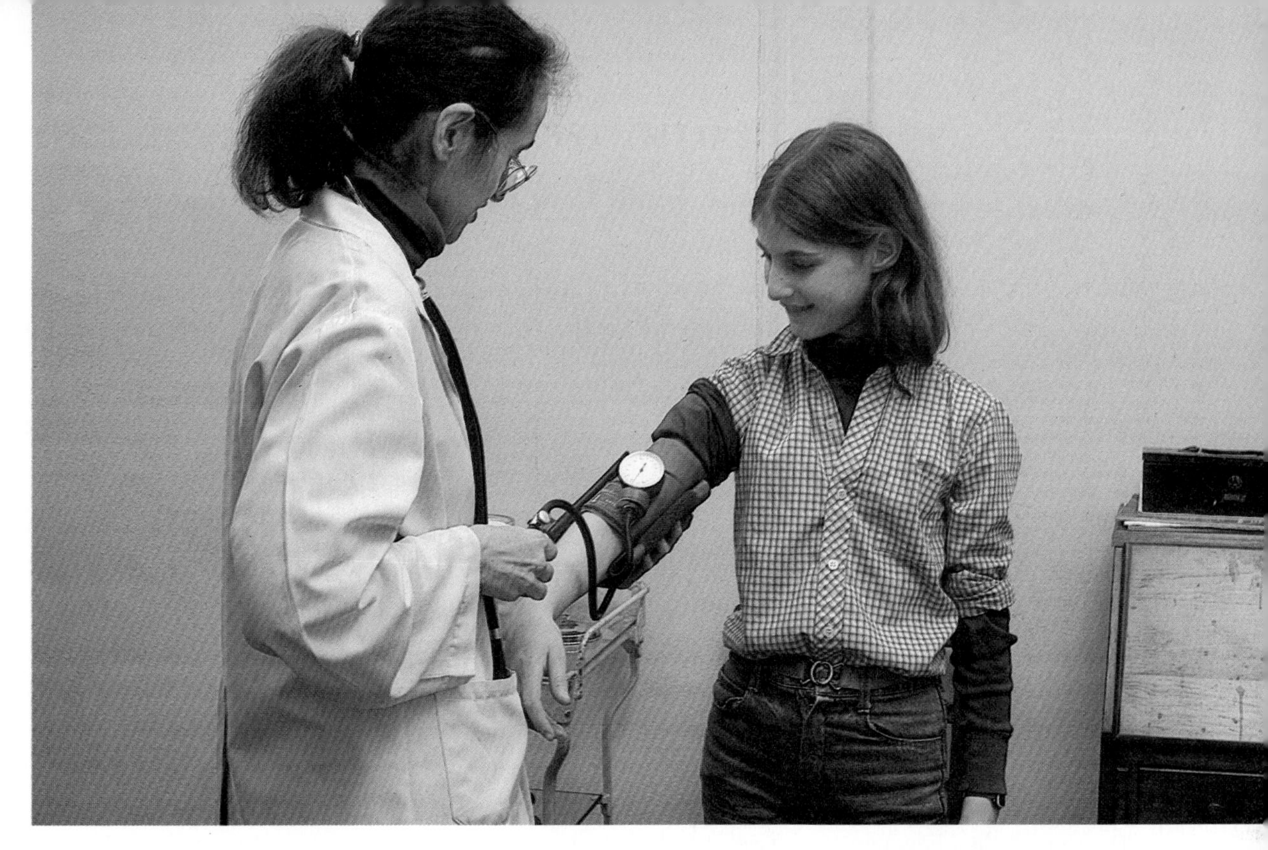

A special cuff is placed around the upper arm to check blood pressure. Air is pumped in to tighten the cuff, then let out to loosen it. A stethoscope is needed for checking blood pressure.

Something else the doctor may do is press your abdomen to check your *internal organs.* The doctor may also check glands in your neck and under your arms.

Finally, you may have to leave samples of your blood and urine to be tested at a laboratory. The results of these tests, together with many other details, give the doctor a very good picture of your health.

What Have You Learned?

Number a piece of paper from **1** through **3**. Next to the numbers, write the words that are missing in these sentences.

1. One way to take charge of your health is to make your own health __ and have regular __ by your doctor.
2. Immunization shots and discovering health problems before they are serious are two kinds of __ __.
3. Measuring the force of the heart pumping blood is measuring __ __.

Answers to *What Have You Learned?*

1. plan; checkups
2. preventive medicine
3. blood pressure

permanent teeth

HEALTHY TEETH HELP KEEP YOU HEALTHY

Make Tooth Care Part of Your Health Plan

Do you remember losing your first teeth? When they fell out, new teeth replaced them. The new teeth are your **permanent teeth**. Your permanent teeth are meant to last the rest of your life.

You had to take good care of your baby teeth. You have to take even better care of your permanent teeth. If these are lost, they will never be replaced by natural teeth.

Brushing your teeth in the way recommended by many dentists and the American Dental Association is an important part of daily tooth care. Follow two important steps before you brush. First, select the right kind of toothbrush. Most dentists say that a brush with soft bristles should be used. The brush should be small enough to reach all parts of your mouth. Second, choose a toothpaste that has a *fluoride* in it. A fluoride is a substance that helps prevent *tooth decay*. Your toothpaste should also have the American Dental Association Seal of Acceptance.

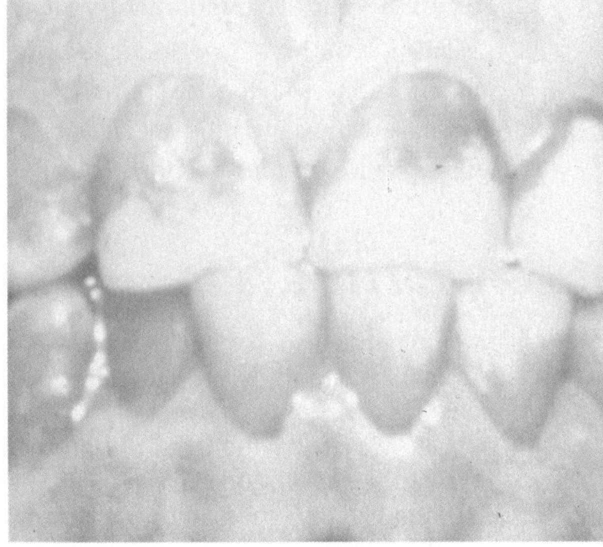

Chewing a *plaque-disclosing tablet* can show you where plaque still sticks to your teeth. The red areas need more brushing.

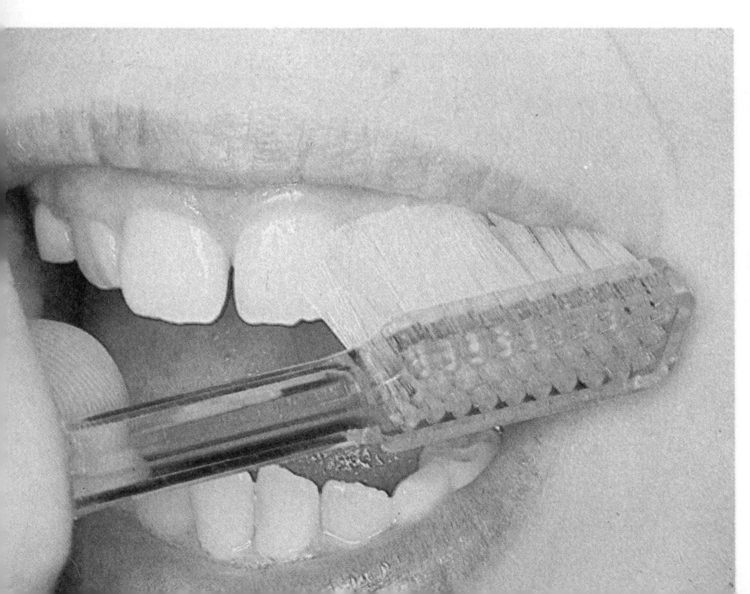

Place the head of the toothbrush beside your teeth, with the bristles at an angle against the gum line. Brush gently back and forth with short strokes. Clean both the inside and outside surfaces of your upper and lower teeth. Then brush the chewing surfaces. To brush the inside surfaces of the front teeth, tilt the brush and make several up-and-down strokes with the front part of the brush.

Another important part of daily tooth care is using *dental floss.* Flossing removes bits of food that brushing cannot reach. It also helps control *plaque.* Plaque is a sticky, colorless film on teeth. It contains bacteria that can harm the teeth and gums.

Sometimes you may find that you cannot brush or floss your teeth when you should. If you are out with your parents or on a field trip with your class, you will most likely not have your toothbrush with you. If this happens, rinse your mouth out well with water. Be sure to brush and floss carefully as soon as you can.

Break off about 18 inches (46 cm) of dental floss and wind most of it around one middle finger. Wind the rest around the other middle finger. Hold the floss tightly. Using your thumbs and index fingers, gently work the floss in between your teeth. Curving the floss into a C-shape, move it up and down against the sides of each tooth to remove the plaque that cannot be brushed away.

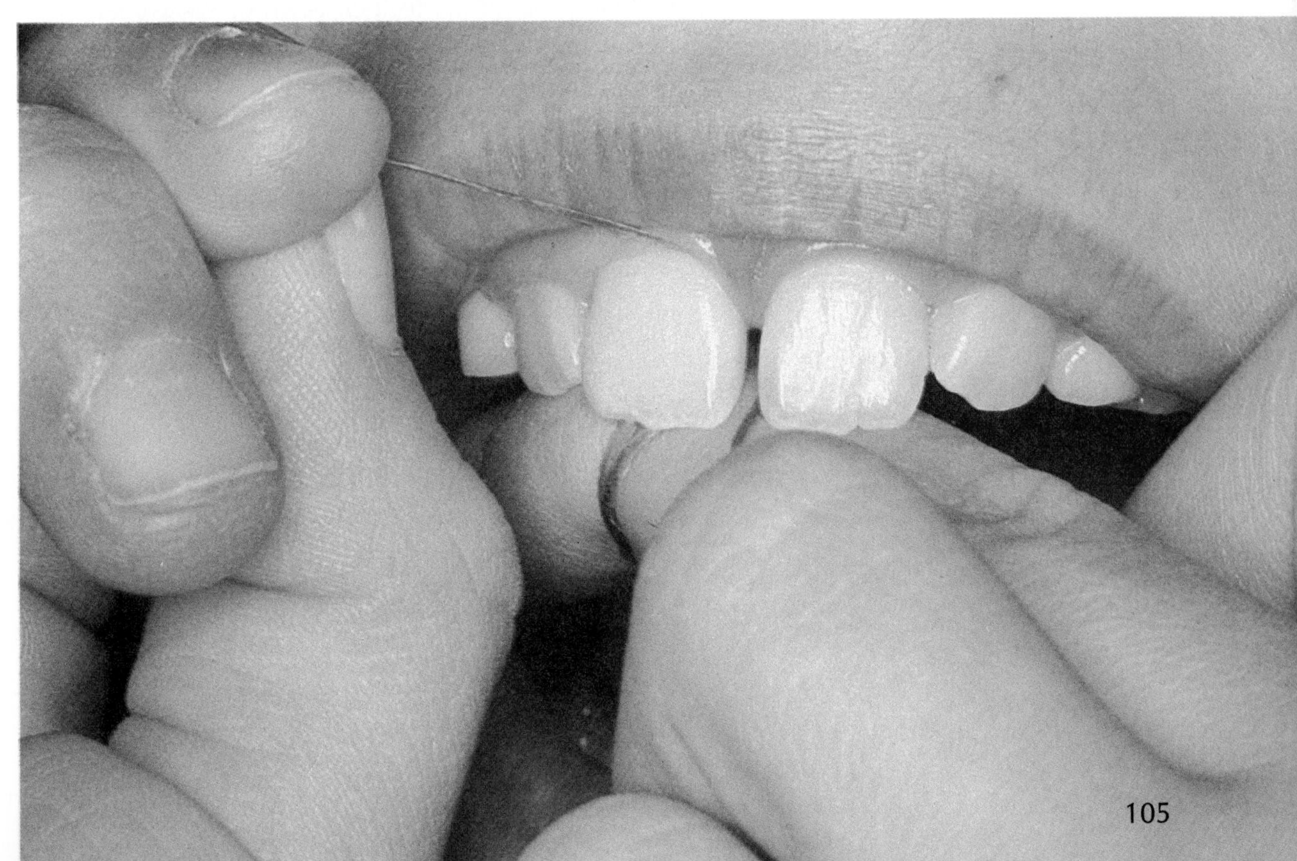

Children who wear braces often need positive reinforcement to encourage them to follow the necessary rules for orthodontia. It is not easy for a child with braces to refuse a chewy snack or an ear of corn; but to avoid tooth decay and keep the braces in good condition, the child must do so. One way to develop that strength is to concentrate on the improved appearance afterward.

Children should understand that orthodontic braces may be worn by adults as well as by children. If for any reason teeth cannot be straightened during childhood, they perhaps can be corrected later in life.

Teeth Can Be Straightened

Some people have problems with their permanent teeth. Front teeth may stick out too far. Perhaps teeth have grown in crooked or unevenly spaced. Some people are born with too many or too few teeth. Sometimes the bottom and top teeth do not meet properly to chew food. Sometimes problems like these affect the way people speak.

Many of these problems can be corrected by an *orthodontist.* An orthodontist is a dental specialist who corrects problems caused by crooked, crowded, or poorly spaced teeth. Some of these problems are corrected by special *braces* that are worn on the teeth. Different problems may require different kinds of braces. You may know children or adults who wear braces.

People who wear braces must be especially responsible about caring for their teeth. In addition to being very careful about regular brushing, they should avoid stringy or "chewy" foods that can get caught in the braces.

People who have problems with their teeth or who wear braces may be shy about smiling. They may not realize that a friendly smile is always welcome, and most people will not notice their braces. People are more likely to notice when a person does not smile often.

You can see how well an orthodontist can correct and straighten teeth. These are the same teeth before and after braces. People feel good about themselves when their teeth look good.

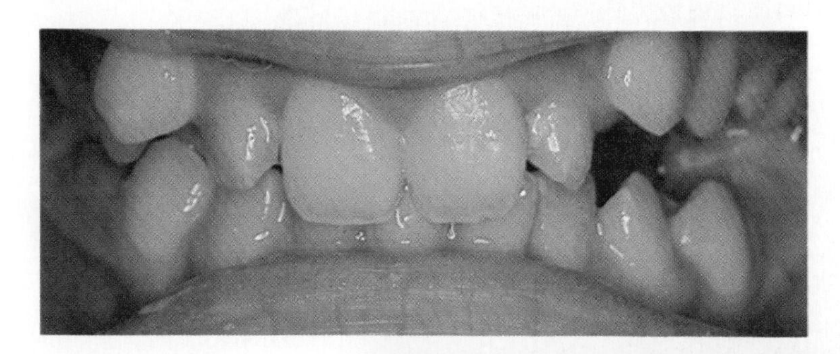

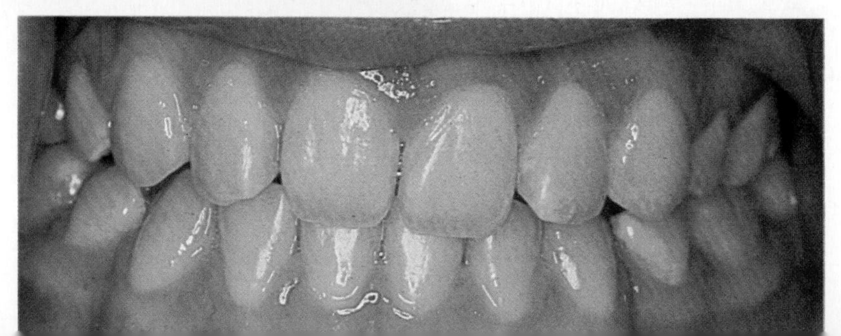

Reduce the Risk of Tooth Decay

cavities

If you think that colds are the number one health problem, think again. The most common health problem of all is tooth decay. Tooth decay is caused by plaque, an invisible film of bacteria that forms on teeth. The bacteria in plaque use the sugars in food to form acids. These acids can make holes in the hard enamel of the teeth. The holes are called **cavities**. If not treated, cavities will become deeper and will eventually destroy the affected teeth.

Many cavities can be prevented. Not eating sugar-rich snacks, and daily brushing and flossing, can help prevent tooth decay. Nutrients from milk, fruits, and vegetables keep your teeth healthy. It is also important to visit your dentist often. Cavities can be found and treated before they become too large. Your dentist may also put fluoride on your teeth.

What was your answer to *Early Checkup* number 8? (Can you do anything to reduce the risk of cavities?)

Another dental problem is *periodontal disease.* Periodontal disease can harm the soft tissues and bone that hold the teeth in the jawbone. If the gums are soft, red, or bleeding, this may be a sign of periodontal disease. At a checkup, the *calculus,* or hardened plaque, that has formed on your teeth can be scraped off. The removal of calculus helps reduce the risk of periodontal disease. Of course, regular brushing and flossing help prevent harmful plaque from collecting on your teeth.

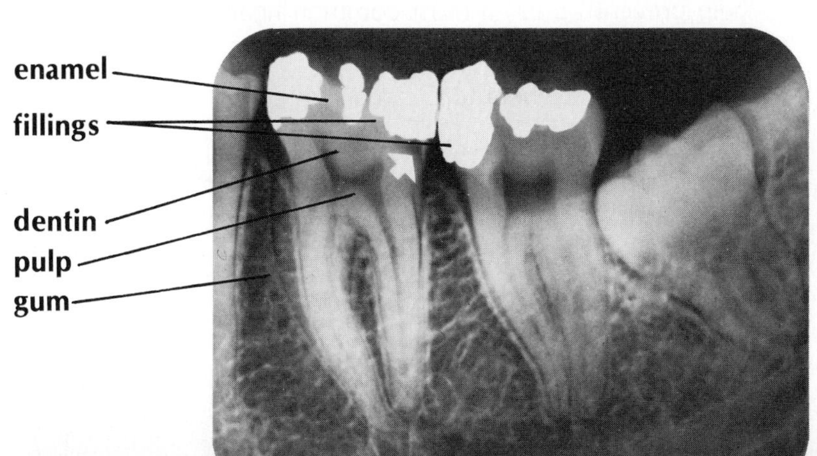

Even if a cavity has started, a dentist can fill it before it reaches through the *dentin,* to the *pulp,* or inner tooth. In the pulp, a cavity can be very painful. An *abscess,* or infection with pus, can form. Infections can travel to other parts of the body and make you sick. Many dentists apply fluoride gels or solutions to people's teeth during regular checkups. This preventive dentistry reduces the risk of tooth decay.

Try To Prevent Tooth Injuries

The best way to keep your teeth is to protect them from injury. You can reduce the risk of mouth injuries during rough games, sports, or other such activities by wearing the right safety equipment.

If some of your permanent teeth are knocked out in an accident, a dentist may be able to reattach them. It is important to place the unattached teeth in a clean, moist cloth and to get to a dentist as quickly as possible.

What Have You Learned?

Number a piece of paper from **1** through **4**. Next to the numbers, write the words that are missing in these sentences.

1. Preventive brushing, flossing, mouth-rinsing, and fluoride help prevent ___ ___, a most common health problem that causes ___ in the teeth.

2. Brushing and ___ help to clean a film called ___ from the teeth.

3. People can reduce the risk of tooth decay by avoiding foods with ___.

4. Calculus is removed from the teeth to reduce the risk of periodontal ___.

Answers to *What Have You Learned?*
1. tooth decay; cavities
2. flossing; plaque
3. sugar
4. disease

Learn More About It

If you are interested in learning more about sleep, dreams, and personal hygiene, here are some books to look for in your library. Your librarian can help you find others.

Gilbert, Sara. *Feeling Good.* New York: Four Winds Press, 1978. This is a book that will help answer some questions you may have about the way you look and feel.

Kozuszek, Jane Eyerly. *Hygiene.* New York: Franklin Watts, Inc., 1978. Keeping your body clean and free from disease is discussed in this book.

Lindsay, Rae. *Sleep and Dreams.* New York: Franklin Watts, Inc., 1978. Do you know why people walk, talk, and snore in their sleep? Do you know what to do when you have trouble falling asleep? Read this book and find the answers.

Do you want to find out more about caring for your teeth? You may want to write to the American Dental Association and ask for their booklets on good dental health for boys and girls. The address is

American Dental Association
211 East Chicago Avenue
Chicago, IL 60611

More To Do on Your Own

1. Try a new sport or exercise. Different sports and exercises stretch and strengthen different muscles. Notice which muscles are affected by the new sport or exercise. Does it make the muscles stretch or flex? What sort of warm-up exercises should you do before you start this activity? Ask your physical education teacher about good warm-up exercises. You may also want to go to the library and read about this new activity.
2. Select a nutritious food and learn to prepare it in ways you may not have tried before. Recipe books and some magazines are a good place to look. You may want to make a collection of recipes for this food and see if your family is interested in trying them.
3. Prepare a display that shows the correct way to floss or brush your teeth. Your display can be a poster with drawings or cutouts. Your display also can be a three-dimensional model made of clay; cardboard; pictures of toothpaste, toothbrushes, or floss; old toothbrushes and toothpaste tubes; or anything else you can think of.

Final Checkup

A. Number a sheet of paper from **1** through **10**. Next to each number, write the letter of the words that best complete each sentence.

1. Scientists who study sleep have learned that
- **a.** some people do not dream.
- **b.** people who dream cannot be awakened.
- **c.** there are different stages of sleep.
- **d.** some people have only good dreams.

2. Good personal hygiene
- **a.** is not necessary for health.
- **b.** means keeping clean.
- **c.** is only for adults.
- **d.** builds strong muscles.

3. Aerobic exercise
- **a.** strengthens the heart and lungs.
- **b.** does not need a warm-up.
- **c.** just refers to jogging.
- **d.** helps prevent gum disease.

4. You may feel more alert during active exercise because
- **a.** more oxygen is going to your brain.
- **b.** your muscles stretch and flex.
- **c.** it is good for your heart and lungs.
- **d.** you usually do it early in the morning.

5. Good posture
- **a.** is important only when you stand.
- **b.** means sitting, standing, and moving properly.
- **c.** does not affect the way you feel about yourself.
- **d.** is necessary for aerobic exercise.

6. Good preventive medicine includes
- **a.** getting regular medical checkups.
- **b.** eating healthful foods.
- **c.** getting enough sleep and exercise.
- **d.** all of the above.

7. Checking the pulse shows
- **a.** whether you have high blood pressure.
- **b.** if your nervous system is healthy.
- **c.** how many times per minute your heart beats.
- **d.** how deep a cavity is.

8. Plaque is
- **a.** used to prevent cavities.
- **b.** the substance that makes your teeth white.
- **c.** formed by brushing your teeth and flossing them carefully.
- **d.** a sticky, colorless film on teeth that can lead to tooth decay.

9. You should use a toothpaste that contains
- **a.** calcium.
- **b.** fluoride.
- **c.** plaque.
- **d.** dentin.

10. Food particles between the teeth that cannot be removed with a toothbrush
    (a.) can usually be removed with dental floss.
    b. need to be treated with fluoride by a dentist.
    c. will disappear by themselves.
    d. will always give you a cavity.

B. Number a sheet of paper from **1** through **10**. Write **true** or **false** next to the number for each of these ideas.

1. Eating nutritious foods, keeping your body and teeth clean, getting the proper amount of sleep, and engaging in regular exercise are all important health risks. false
2. Your heartbeat does not change while you sleep. false
3. Dreams do not occur during REM sleep. false
4. A mirror can tell you something about how healthy you are. true
5. People who must use a wheelchair cannot do anything to stay as fit as they can be. false
6. Cool-down exercises are usually not necessary after playing an active sport. false
7. Preventive medicine is a way of discovering health problems before they become serious. true
8. Taking pulse and blood pressure is a regular part of a medical checkup. true
9. If you lose a permanent tooth, another one will grow in its place. false
10. Regular use of dental floss is not important in preventing disease or reducing health risks. false

Write About Better Health

Write a short answer to each of these questions. Use complete sentences.

1. What are four important steps in reducing health risks?
2. Why are warm-up and cool-down exercises important parts of any active sports program?
3. What kinds of details are checked in a regular medical checkup?
4. How can following a regular plan of health-care activities make you feel good about yourself?
5. What kinds of problems do regular tooth brushing and flossing help avoid?

Model answers to *Write About Better Health* are provided in the chapter notes at the front of this *Teacher's Edition.*

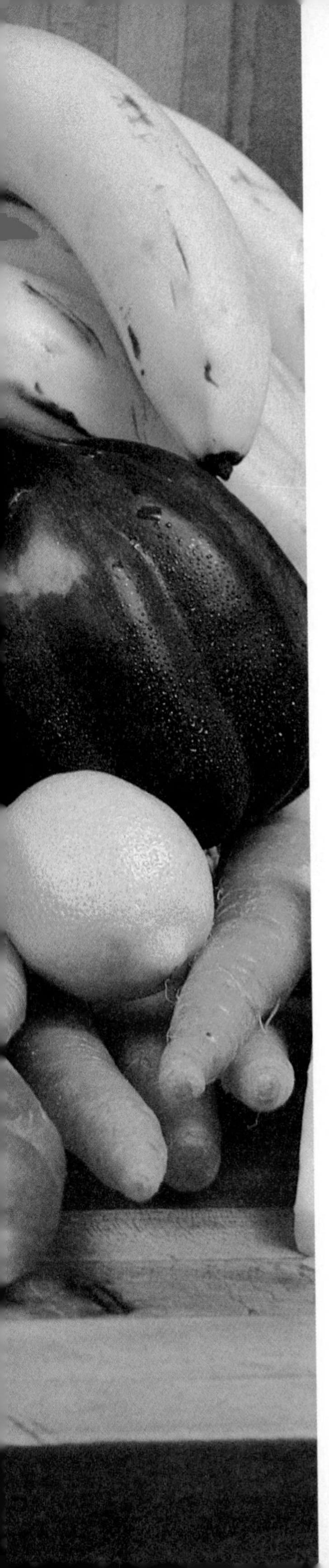

5 NUTRITIOUS FOODS FOR BETTER HEALTH

Long ago, people had little choice about what they ate. They were limited to plant foods they could find, or meat from animals that were raised or hunted. Today people can choose from thousands of different kinds of foods available in a single supermarket. In order to choose healthful, well-balanced daily meals, people need to know far more about foods than they ever needed to know in the past. To begin with, they need to learn how foods are used by the body.

LOOKING AHEAD

People who must plan meals for a family have an important responsibility. They must choose foods each day that provide the energy and materials needed to build healthy bodies. How do people make sure that their food choices are the most healthful for their families?

Members of a family are often responsible for planning some of their own meals. Do you choose some of the foods you eat for breakfast or lunch? The foods you choose to eat will affect how well you grow, how much energy you have, and how you feel. This chapter will help you make some food choices that can help build your health now and in the future. You will learn

- the building materials in food that are necessary for good health.
- how to choose from among different foods to have a balanced diet.
- how to determine your energy needs.
- ideas on getting to and staying at a weight that is right for you.

Here are some words that you may not have talked about in school before. You will learn more about them in this chapter. You can find all these words in the *Glossary* at the back of this book.

calories (kal′ər·ēz)
carbohydrates (kär′bō·hī′drāts)
digestion (də·jes′chən)
fat (fat)
ingredients (in·grē′dē·ənts)
minerals (min′ər·əlz)
nutrients (nü′trē·ənts)
nutritious (nü·trish′əs)
proteins (prō′tēnz)
vitamins (vī′tə·mənz)
water (wô′tər)

Early Checkup

Number a piece of paper from **1** through **8**. Answer each of these questions by writing **yes** or **no** next to the correct number on your paper. You can check your answers as you read this chapter.

1. Do people your age need more nutritious foods than many adults? yes
2. Can eating a lot of sugar give you lasting energy? no
3. Do parts of your body contain minerals such as iron? yes
4. Do some food package labels tell you how many calories the food contains? yes
5. Does the body begin to break down food before it reaches the stomach? yes
6. Is overeating the only reason people gain too much weight? no
7. Can being underweight lead to health problems? yes
8. Can losing or gaining weight too quickly be harmful to your health? yes

nutrients

NUTRITION—USING FOOD FOR GROWTH AND ENERGY

Every day, your body uses **nutrients** in foods you eat. Nutrients are the many different building materials important to your growth. Body *cells* use nutrients to build more cells as you grow. Some new cells replace others that wear out or are damaged by disease or accidents.

Your body also uses nutrients to produce energy. The different foods you eat must be changed into forms the cells can use—either for immediate energy or for energy the cells store for later use. Everything you do in life requires this energy. Your body uses energy to maintain its temperature and fight disease. When a cell divides to form new cells, it uses energy. You use energy to move, talk, think, breathe, eat, and even to sleep.

Carson enjoys making his own lunches. He reads a lot about nutrition to make sure each meal is well balanced, with different foods containing different nutrients.

Many different nutrients are needed for good health. This makes it important to eat a variety of foods every day. A daily diet that gives you all the nutrients your body needs for health is called a **nutritious** diet. By learning which nutrients they need every day and which nutritious foods they enjoy, people can plan a nutritious diet.

nutritious

Active people need a larger supply of nutritious foods each day than less active people. Young people need more of some kinds of nutrients than most adults. Young people need more energy because they are growing. They are also using more energy for daily exercise. People of any age need a nutritious diet to maintain their best health and energy and to do their best thinking.

What was your answer to *Early Checkup* number 1? (Do people your age need more nutritious foods than many adults?)

Active people need more energy from food. The harder you exercise, the more careful you should be to eat nutritious food.

carbohydrates

The "No Energy" Carbohydrate

Cellulose is a carbohydrate that comes from the tough cell walls in plants. Cellulose is sometimes called *fiber.* It is a nutrient that people cannot *digest* and use as a source of energy. However, it is important to a well-balanced, nutritious diet. It absorbs water and swells as it moves through the body. The bulk helps to slow the movement of food through your stomach and *intestines.* This gives your body a better chance to use more of the food. Fiber bulk fills you up and keeps you from overeating. It also gives the muscles of the stomach and intestines healthful exercise.

Healthful Meals Have Balanced Nutrients

Nutrients are divided into six groups. Eating nutrients from each group helps the body to use nutrients from other groups. This is called a well-balanced diet. It gives the body as much of each nutrient as it needs to make all the nutrients work for good health.

Carbohydrates Are Nutrients

Most fruits, nuts, vegetables, and grain products supply your body with the **carbohydrates** you need for energy. Carbohydrates are important energy-producing nutrients found in *starches* and *sugars.*

The nutrients called sugars are *simple carbohydrates.* The body changes them quickly to produce energy. Most fruits and some vegetables are good sources of simple carbohydrates and other important nutrients.

The energy from sugars is used up rapidly. Foods that have a lot of added sugar usually have very few other nutrients. This is why people should not eat foods that contain a lot of added sugar. They get enough energy from a

foods containing simple carbohydates

nutritious diet. The snack with added sugar usually contains few important nutrients for long-lasting energy. It also causes *tooth decay.* People who eat too many foods with added sugar may become easily tired and upset. This happens because their food choices lack the nutrients for longer-lasting energy.

Cellulose is only one of several kinds of fiber. Hemicelluloses, lignin, and pectin are others. Fibers absorb water as they move through the digestive tract. This provides bulk for the muscles of the stomach and intestines to push against. Interested students may enjoy developing a list of foods that contain fiber. Whole-wheat bread, bran, brown rice, and cereals made from unrefined wheat, rye, barley, and corn are the best sources. Beans, broccoli, Brussels sprouts, raw carrots, and other vegetables and fruits are good sources of fiber.

What was your answer to *Early Checkup* number 2? (Can eating a lot of sugar give you lasting energy?)

Starches are *complex carbohydrates.* They provide a steady flow of energy all through the day. The body takes a longer time to change these carbohydrates into energy. Complex carbohydrates are usually found in foods that contain many other nutrients. They are a good source of long-lasting energy. Many vegetables, nuts, and grain products are good sources of complex carbohydrates.

foods containing complex carbohydrates

fat
proteins

How Much Protein Do You Need?

People between ages eleven and fourteen need 1 gram (0.035 oz) of protein for each kilogram (about 2.2 lbs) of body weight. People between ages fifteen and eighteen need only 0.9 gram (0.31 oz) per kilogram of body weight. Active people need about the same amounts of protein as less active people. This is because the body uses very little protein to produce energy.

A person who eats a balanced diet of foods from each of the four food groups will get at least the minimum amount of protein the body needs to stay healthy.

Interested students may wish to research and share recipes for good-tasting foods having various protein combinations. For example, some good-tasting foods with various protein combinations include tacos, bean chowder, lasagna, pizza, and macaroni and cheese.

Ask the students for ideas on how fat can be reduced in a diet. Suggestions may include: *Eat lean meat, fish, and poultry; limit butter, cream, salad dressings, and shortening; broil, bake, or boil foods rather than fry them; limit the number of eggs you eat; drink low-fat milk, and eat cheeses low in fat.*

Proteins Are Nutrients

The body uses **proteins** to build cells for all its parts. Proteins are nutrients that become part of muscle, bone, skin, hair, teeth, the brain, and other body parts. Proteins also help keep *nerves* healthy and fight *infection.*

Meat, fish, poultry, eggs, cheeses, nuts, yogurt, milk, beans, whole grains, and rice are sources of protein. Many foods from plants do not by themselves give people enough protein. However, plants give you protein, especially when they are combined with other plant foods. In a balanced diet, more than one source of protein is eaten each day.

Fats Are Nutrients

Most people require only a small amount of **fat** in their diet. This is because the body itself produces and stores this nutrient. The body changes carbohydrates, protein, and unused food fats into body fat, which is stored for later use. Body fat is your reserve energy supply. Fat helps make skin soft and hair shiny. Fat also helps keep your body at the right temperature.

Fats can be found in such foods as milk, eggs, beef, nuts, and oil. Can you see why eating more carbohydrates, proteins, and fats than the body needs is harmful to good health? The body stores all of the extra amounts of these nutrients as fat. Too much stored fat can cause people to be overweight. Extra body weight causes *high blood pressure* and helps to cause *diabetes.* It also strains the heart and other body *organs.*

Have interested students research and report to the class on *cholesterol*—its sources and its effects on the body.

vitamins

The Cure-All Vitamin Fad

Doctors have found that too many extra vitamins may actually be harmful to good health. For example, too much vitamin C may cause *kidney* and *bladder* problems. Too much vitamin A may cause *liver* damage and bone growth problems.

Vitamins Are Nutrients

Most foods contain one or more **vitamins**. Vitamins do *not* provide energy. They also do not provide the material the body uses in building new cells. However, vitamins are important nutrients. They help the body use all the other nutrients in the food you eat. Some vitamins can be stored in the body fat. Other vitamins cannot be stored in the body. For good health, people must eat foods containing vitamins every day. A well-balanced, nutritious diet supplies most people with all of the vitamins they need every day.

Invite discussion of common myths about vitamins. Among those myths are the following: Vitamins provide energy; the more vitamins you take, the better off you are; organic or natural vitamins are better than synthetic vitamins; food does not provide enough vitamins. Explain that these myths have little medical or scientific evidence to support them.

Very few people suffer from vitamin deficiencies in America today. However, eating too much of one kind of food (e.g., one high in sugar or fat) over a prolonged period can lead to vitamin and other nutrient deficiencies.

These foods contain most of the vitamins listed in the chart on page 123. *The grapefruit contains vitamin C; the fish contains vitamins B and D; the collard greens contain vitamins A, B, C, E, and K; the potato contains vitamin C; and the yogurt with fruit contains vitamins A, Riboflavin, C, and D.*

On Your Own

Would a meal made from these foods contain all the vitamins on the chart on page 123? List each food you see here, along with the vitamins it provides.

Some Important Vitamins		
Vitamins	**Health Needs**	**Some Foods To Choose**
Vitamin A (stored by body)	good eyesight and healthy skin	green/yellow vegetables, yellow fruits, liver, eggs, milk
B Vitamins (not stored by body) thiamin riboflavin niacin pantothenic acid B_6 B_{12} biotin	making red blood cells; also needed for healthy skin, nervous system, muscles, and for use of carbohydrates	lean meats, liver, milk, eggs, peas, beans, whole grains, fish, green vegetables, corn
Vitamin C (not stored by body)	growth, healing of wounds, teeth and bone formation, use of iron	oranges, grapefruit, tomatoes, strawberries, broccoli, mustard greens, turnip greens, kale, potatoes
Vitamin D (stored by body)	teeth and bone formation, proper gland function	fresh fish, egg yolk, vitamin-D-fortified foods such as milk
Vitamin E (stored by body)	healthy cells, formation of red blood cells, use of other vitamins	vegetable oils, beans, eggs, whole grains, liver, fruits, vegetables, nuts
Vitamin K (stored by body)	to clot blood; aid in healing of wounds	spinach, lettuce, kale, cabbage, cauliflower, liver, egg yolk

minerals
water

Minerals Are Nutrients

Some **minerals** become parts of bone, muscle, and other kinds of body cells. Other minerals help carry oxygen to cells, control your heartbeat, and keep nerve cells healthy.

Milk products contain *calcium* for building bones and teeth. *Iron* helps build the oxygen-carrying red blood cells. It is found in liver, whole-grain cereals, egg yolk, fish, and green vegetables. The body also uses *sodium, phosphorus, potassium,* and other minerals such as *zinc, iodine,* and *copper.* Most people get all the minerals they need from foods in a well-balanced daily diet.

What was your answer to *Early Checkup* number 3? (Do parts of your body contain minerals such as iron?)

Hidden Salt Is a Health Risk

The body needs only tiny amounts of minerals like sodium, which is found in salt. Too much salt can contribute to high blood pressure and to heart and kidney disease. Even people who do not add any table salt to food may still be eating too much salt. Read food labels carefully. When you see "salt" among the first four contents listed on a food label, you will know that salt is a major part of that food.

Reading a food-content listing is an inefficient way to tell if a food is high in sodium. Food in which salt is listed far down the list of contents can still be high in sodium. That is because salt is not the only sodium source in processed foods. Sodium compounds are used as preservatives, flavor enhancers, stabilizers, and leavening agents. They are also used to improve texture and to preserve color.

Food-processing companies will soon be labeling sodium content in milligrams. Interested students may find information on the sodium content of foods in such publications as *Consumer Reports, Nutrition Action,* and *Current Health,* which their local school or library may carry.

Water Is a Nutrient

Every cell in your body is partly made up of the nutrient **water**. Water is also the major part of your blood, and carries other nutrients through your body. The water in *urine, sweat,* and your own breath helps to remove waste from your body.

These foods contain proteins, carbohydrates, fats, vitamins, minerals, and water, the six groups of nutrients. Each group helps your body to use others.

What Have You Learned?

Number a piece of paper from **1** through **5**. Next to the numbers, write the words that are missing in these sentences.

1. Six groups of nutrients in every well-balanced diet are —, —, —, —, —, and —.

2. Most healthy people do not need more — or — than they get from a nutritious daily diet.

3. Eating foods with added sugar can cause tooth —, a major health problem.

4. Extra carbohydrates are stored by the body as —, and can make a person overweight.

5. Being overweight can cause such health problems as heart — and high — —.

Answers to *What Have You Learned?*
1. proteins; carbohydrates; fats; vitamins; minerals; water
2. vitamins; minerals
3. decay
4. fat
5. disease(s); blood pressure

People Working for Your Health

Discuss with students how nutrition problems differ around the world in direct proportion to the availability of food. In some Third World countries in Asia, Latin America, and Africa, people are starving because there is not enough food. In these areas, people are suffering because there is not enough of the *right kinds* of food. These people suffer from such vitamin and mineral deficiencies as beriberi (a nerve disease from lack of B vitamins), rickets (a bone deformation from a lack of vitamin D), and pellagra (a skin rash, diarrhea, and sometimes dementia, from lack of niacin).

Dr. John Erdman is an assistant professor of food science and nutrition at the University of Illinois. Dr. Erdman researches and develops new food plants that grow quickly and are able to resist disease and bad weather. Such crops may someday feed hungry people all over the world. "These foods must be nutritious, pleasing to the taste, acceptable to the population, and inexpensive," says Dr. Erdman.

Soy-extended breads are eaten by people of some developing countries. Wheat flour is replaced by protein-rich soy flour when the breads are baked. "This doubles the protein value of the bread," Dr. Erdman explains.

The winged bean is another example of a protein-rich food that is being researched for use by developing countries. This plant grows best in humid tropics. Many other plant proteins will not grow in such a climate. "All parts of this plant are nourishing," Dr. Erdman says. "After research has been completed on the winged bean, it may supply protein, vitamins, minerals, and calories to many people living in developing countries."

Dr. Erdman received a Ph.D. in food sciences and nutrition from Rutgers University in New Jersey. He enjoys researching and testing food plants for use by countries that need them. "It's nice to know that my work can directly affect the lives of many people in the world," he says.

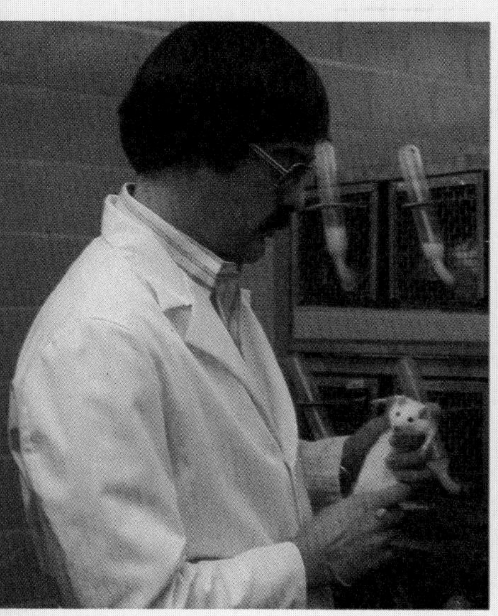

CHOOSING AND USING FOODS

Food Groups Make Choices Easier

You know that no single food can provide people with all the nutrients they need. A balanced, healthful diet calls for eating many different foods every day. To make choosing all those foods easier, think of them as being in one of four different groups. Combining foods from all four groups at each meal will usually give your body all the nutrients it needs to stay healthy.

After discussion of the chart, students may enjoy creating a large classroom chart showing their favorite foods in each food group, along with the kinds of nutrients each food provides.

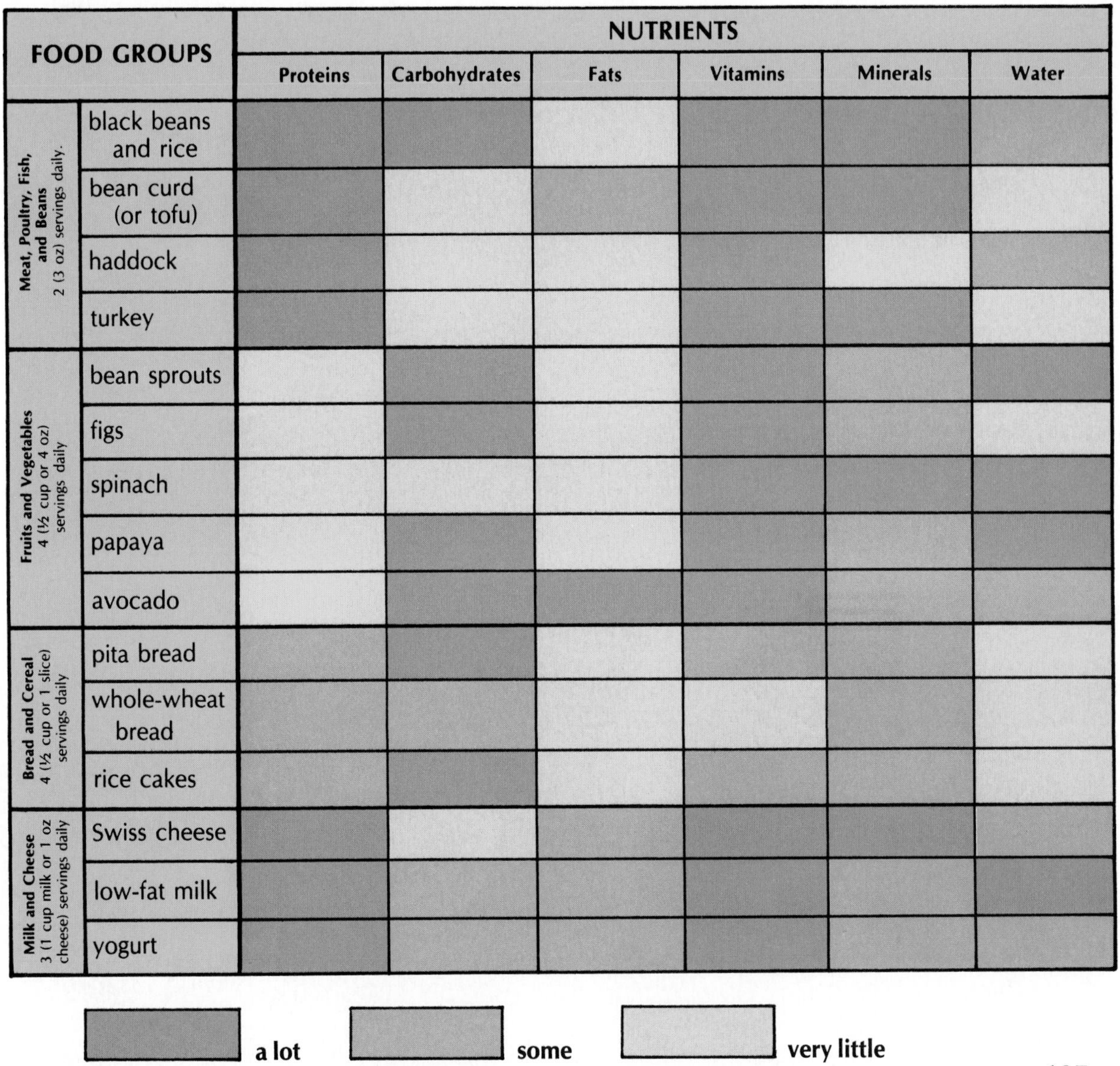

FOOD GROUPS		NUTRIENTS					
		Proteins	Carbohydrates	Fats	Vitamins	Minerals	Water
Meat, Poultry, Fish, and Beans 2 (3 oz) servings daily.	black beans and rice						
	bean curd (or tofu)						
	haddock						
	turkey						
Fruits and Vegetables 4 (½ cup or 4 oz) servings daily	bean sprouts						
	figs						
	spinach						
	papaya						
	avocado						
Bread and Cereal 4 (½ cup or 1 slice) servings daily	pita bread						
	whole-wheat bread						
	rice cakes						
Milk and Cheese 3 (1 cup milk or 1 oz cheese) servings daily	Swiss cheese						
	low-fat milk						
	yogurt						

a lot **some** **very little**

In discussion of these breakfast ideas, point out that many people limit themselves by thinking that only certain foods should be eaten at breakfast. Remind the students that it does not really matter what a person eats for breakfast—as long as the foods provide enough nutrients to get a good start on the day.

You Can Help Make Your Own Food Plan

Choosing a wide variety of foods can help make every snack and meal nutritious and more fun. Here are some breakfast and snack ideas that may be new to you. Each is low in sugar, fat, and salt. Can you figure out what nutrients each meal supplies?

You may find it fun to put together your own lunches or snacks. Lunch and snacks provide you with energy throughout the day. Remember a few steps for keeping food fresh and healthful.

- Keep hot foods hot.
- Keep cold foods cold.
- Reheat hot foods that have been refrigerated.
- Prepare everything with clean hands and utensils.
- Make sure all food is fresh and clean.

Supper gives you energy for homework and play in the evening. It also provides nutrients for your body to use while you sleep. What would make an exciting, healthful supper menu that is low in cost and yet has foods from each group?

Challenge the students to use their imaginations and to invent some interesting sandwich ideas. Some kick off suggestions could be: *peanut butter, cottage cheese, and raisins on whole-wheat bread; tuna fish and apple slices on rye bread; hummus made from chickpeas, with chopped tomatoes and bean sprouts in pita bread; refried beans rolled in a soft flour (or corn) tortilla, with chopped tomatoes, onions, celery, and green peppers added; whitefish with chopped celery and salad dressing.*

calories
ingredients

What Is U.S. RDA?

The term *U.S. RDA* on a food label stands for *United States Recommended Daily Allowances* of nutrients. The U.S. RDA for each food nutrient is based upon the recommendations of the *Food and Nutrition Board of the National Academy of Sciences* (FNB, NAS). For example, the FNB has determined that people need 18 milligrams (0.00063 oz) of iron each day. One serving of the spaghetti shown on this page provides 10 percent of this U.S. RDA. Do you see this on the label?

Read the Label

Most packaged foods are a combination of foods. The companies that prepare these foods are required by law to list the contents, or **ingredients**, on the package labels. Some companies also list the nutrients supplied by the food, the amount of each nutrient, and the **calories** the food supplies. Calories are units of heat energy in food. You will learn more about calories on page 135.

What was your answer to *Early Checkup* number 4? (Do some food package labels tell you how many calories the food contains?)

What are the main nutrients in this box of spaghetti? Which nutrients are present in such small amounts that no exact percentages are given?

NUTRITION INFORMATION PER SERVING

SERVING SIZE	2 OZ. DRY	PROTEIN CONTENT	8 GRAMS
SERVINGS PER CONTAINER	8	CARBOHYDRATE	42 GRAMS
CALORIC CONTENT	210	FAT CONTENT	1 GRAM

PERCENTAGE OF U.S. RECOMMENDED DAILY ALLOWANCE (U.S. RDA)

PROTEIN	10	RIBOFLAVIN	15
VITAMIN A	*	NIACIN	20
VITAMIN C	*	CALCIUM	*
THIAMINE	35	IRON	10

*CONTAINS LESS THAN 2% OF THE U.S. RECOMMENDED DAILY ALLOWANCE OF THESE NUTRIENTS.

INGREDIENTS:
DURUM FLOUR, NIACIN, FERRIC ORTHO PHOSPHATE (IRON), THIAMINE MONO-NITRATE AND RIBOFLAVIN.

Nutrition labeling is voluntary unless the company adds nutrients or makes a claim about the nutritional value of the food. About 40 percent of packaged foods now carry nutrition labeling.

Discovery—A New Pathway to Health

Less than 100 years ago, it was impossible to ship many foods over long distances. Storing foods without having them spoil was a serious problem. People had only one main way to prevent passing along disease germs in a package of food. This was to cook the food at a very high temperature and to store it in an airtight jar or can. However, this strong heating destroyed some of the important nutrients in foods, especially the vitamins.

All of this changed when scientists made two major discoveries. One was refrigeration—a way to keep foods fresh by storing them at low temperatures until they reached their destination. The other was a method of *fortifying* and *enriching* food. Enriching a food now replaced nutrients that had been lost in preparing the food. A fortified food had more nutrients added to it than the food had first contained. You have probably eaten bread enriched with niacin, one of the B vitamins. The milk you drink is probably fortified with vitamin D.

Today many chemical substances are often added to *preserve* foods, or to keep them from spoiling. Preservatives also help to keep the food looking and tasting good for long periods. The *Food and Drug Administration* (FDA) requires that food companies test these chemicals to be sure they are safe for eating. Several have already been taken off the market because they are dangerous. However, most have been proven safe. They enable people everywhere to buy nutritious foods for better health.

What Is in a "Natural" Food?

Some people might not eat the food in a can with a label marked "Ingredients —actomyosin, myogen, nucleoproteins, peptides, amino acids, myoglobin, lipids, linoleic acid, oleic acid, lecithin, cholesterol, sucrose, adenosine triphosphate, glucose, collagen, elastin, creatine, sodium nitrite, and sodium phosphate." Actually, this list gives nothing more than the chemical names for the natural ingredients of a sugar-cured ham. Not one chemical is an *additive*!

The ingredients listed for a sugar-cured ham are not additives. The list represents the inorganic and organic chemicals that are present naturally in this ham. Some students may be interested in learning more about food additives. Have them find out what additives are currently being tested for safety and what foods now contain these chemicals. For up-to-date information, students may write to the

Food and Drug
Administration
5600 Fishers Lane
Rockville, MD 20857

Other students may be interested in researching the chemicals that occur naturally in different fresh meats, grains, nuts, fruits, and vegetables. Have them compare their lists with ingredients on packages of similar, processed foods.

The Federal Trade Commission (FTC) plans to define *natural* food as a food that has been only minimally processed and contains no additives.

digestion

How Does Your Body Use Food?

Digestion is the changing of food so body cells can use it. Digestion begins in your mouth. As you chew, the food mixes with a liquid called *saliva.* The chemicals in saliva help change starches into sugar. Next time you chew a cracker or a piece of bread, notice the slightly sweet taste in your mouth. This is caused by the starch changing into sugar. Swallowing the food moves it down the *esophagus* and into the *stomach.* There stomach juices begin to change the protein found in food. The food is then pushed into the *small intestine.* More digestive juices break down the carbohydrates, protein, and fat in the food. These nutrients then move through the intestine walls and enter the *blood.* The blood carries the nutrients to the *liver.* This organ prepares fats, vitamins, and minerals for use by body cells. Extra nutrients are also stored by the liver.

What was your answer to *Early Checkup* number 5? (Does the body begin to break down food before it reaches the stomach?)

Any food that cannot be digested is passed into the *large intestine.* Water is removed from the undigested food. The remaining waste materials move into the *rectum* and leave the body through the *anus.*

Each cell in the body uses nutrients and produces waste. These wastes are removed by the blood and carried to the *kidneys.* The kidneys collect some wastes and pass them on to the *bladder.* These wastes leave the body in *urine.* Other wastes leave the body in *perspiration,* or sweat, and in your breath.

THE DIGESTIVE SYSTEM

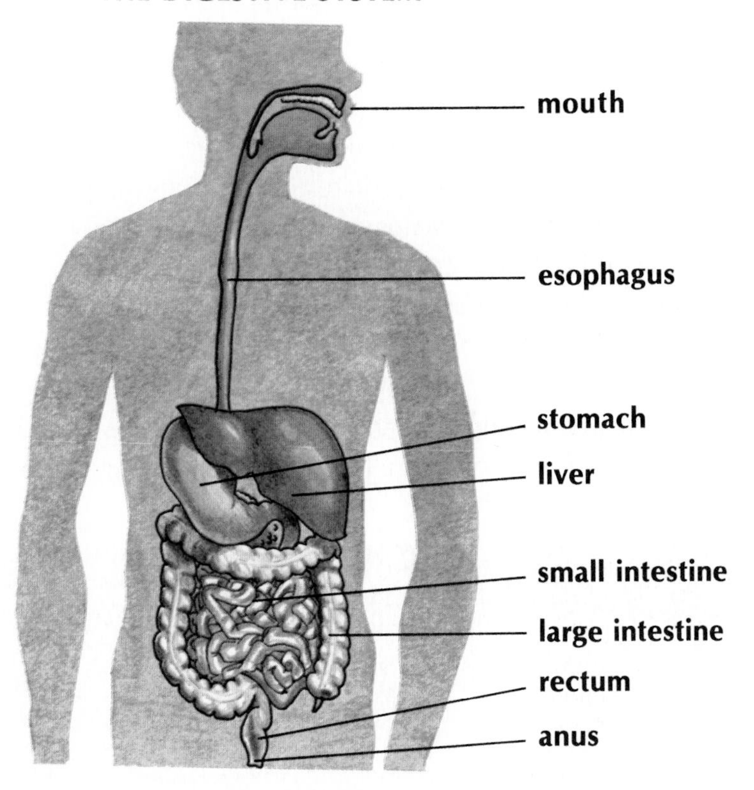

What Have You Learned?

Number a piece of paper from **1** through **4**. Next to the numbers, write the words that are missing in these sentences.

1. You can plan nutritious meals by choosing foods from all four __ __.
2. People eat many different foods because no single food can provide all of the __ they need for good health.
3. __is the process by which the body changes __ so that cells can use it. Blood carries __ from food to the cells, and carries __ away from the cells.
4. Food that is cooked at high temperatures for a long time may lose __. Scientists learned to __ foods, or put back the nutrients so important to health.

Answers to *What Have You Learned?*
1. food groups
2. nutrients
3. Digestion; food; nutrients; wastes
4. nutrients (vitamins); enrich

PEOPLE HAVE DIFFERENT FOOD NEEDS

How Much Energy Do You Need?

Every person's need for energy changes from day to day. No two people have exactly the same energy needs. How much energy each person requires depends on the person's age and size. It also depends on how quickly that person is growing and on the types of games or exercises she or he participates in during the day. For example, an active, growing young person often needs more energy than most adults. The same person may need different amounts of energy, depending upon changes in health and the weather. Why should these changes affect how much energy people need from time to time?

Do these people have exactly the same energy needs for the same activities?

How Is Food Energy Measured?

People gain energy from the nutrients in most of what they eat and drink. Different foods give your body different amounts of energy. The amount of energy in any food is measured in units called calories. The calorie is actually a measure of heat energy. Each calorie is the amount of heat energy required to raise the temperature of one kilogram (about one quart) of water by one degree *Celsius.* If a serving of food contains 250 calories, it contains enough energy to raise the temperature of 250 kilograms (62.5 gallons) of water by one degree Celsius.

Carbohydrates and fats usually supply more energy than other nutrients. You know that their unused energy is stored as body fat. When people use more calories of energy in one day than they eat, the extra calories come from the body fat. Eating more calories than the body is able to use can make people heavier than they should be. However, before going on a diet to eat fewer calories and lose extra weight, people should plan the diet with their families and especially with their doctors. Care must be taken to continue feeding the body all the nutrients it needs.

Snack Foods

Candy, potato chips, and other packaged and prepared snack foods often contain a lot of sugar and fat. Most of them are also low in other kinds of nutrients. People gain many calories but few really useful nutrients from these snack foods.

Different individuals use different amounts of energy for similar activities. The amount of energy a person needs and uses depends on many factors. For this grade level, the factors emphasized are growth rate, activity level, health, and weather. *Basal metabolic rate* (BMR) is also a major factor in determining a body's energy needs. Students will not read about BMR at this level. However, in the section where students compute their basic caloric needs (page 136), the results they get for their needs while at rest (but not asleep) reflect their BMR.

This person is 5 feet 10 inches (about 1.78 m) tall and weighs 150 pounds (about 68.2 kg). He eats about 1,800 calories of energy in daily meals and snacks. This is enough energy for this type of work. When he is more active, this same man may need more calories than when he is working at his desk. Where do the extra calories come from?

The term *calorie* as used by nutritionists is actually a shortened form of the term *kilocalorie*. A kilocalorie (or large calorie) is equal to 1,000 "small calories." (A small calorie is the amount of heat energy needed to raise the temperature of one *gram* |0.035 oz| of water by one degree centigrade.) The larger unit of measurement, the kilogram, is needed to measure the high heat potential in food.

On Your Own

Since no one is exactly like any other person, the amounts of energy you use in your daily activities are different from anyone else's. This means you require a different daily number of calories than anyone else does. You can get some idea of your own calorie needs. All it takes is a little math. First, determine how much you weigh in kilograms. To do this, multiply your weight in pounds by 0.45, because each pound is equal to about 0.45 kilogram. Multiply your weight in kilograms by 24 hours. This will tell you the smallest number of calories you need each day.

I weigh 88 pounds
multiply x045
440
352
I weigh 39.60 kilograms

My weight 39.60 kilograms
x 24 hours
15840
7920
I need 950.40 calories per day, sitting still, doing nothing.

Next, make a list of the activities you take part in during a day. Beside each activity, write the amount of time you spend doing it. Then use the following chart to figure out how many calories you use up as you do each activity.

Activity	Calories per Hour
reading, writing, eating, watching TV	80 to 100
preparing food, getting dressed, cleaning my room	110 to 160
walking moderately fast, doing carpentry, making my bed	170 to 240
walking fast, bowling	250 to 350
swimming, running, dancing, bicycling	350 and more

Daily Activity	Time It Takes	Calories Needed
Make bed	$\frac{1}{12}$ hour	$\frac{1}{12} \times 170 = 14.17$
Dress	$\frac{1}{12}$ hour	$\frac{1}{12} \times 110 = 9.17$
Make lunch	$\frac{1}{6}$ hour	$\frac{1}{6} \times 110 = 18.3$
Eat breakfast	$\frac{1}{4}$ hour	$\frac{1}{4} \times 80 = 20$
Bicycle to school	$\frac{1}{2}$ hour	$\frac{1}{2} \times 350 = 175$
Read, write, study	$2\frac{1}{2}$ hours	$2\frac{1}{2} \times 80 = 200$
Eat lunch	$\frac{1}{2}$ hour	$\frac{1}{2} \times 80 = 40$
Recess-play ball	$\frac{3}{4}$ hour	$\frac{3}{4} \times 350 = 262.5$
Read, write, study	3 hours	$3 \times 80 = 240$
Bicycle home	$\frac{1}{2}$ hour	$\frac{1}{2} \times 350 = 175$

Finally, add the calories from your activity list to the calories you figured out for your weight. The total will give you some idea of the number of calories you need from food each day. You may need more or fewer, depending on how fast you are growing.

Heavy but Not Overweight

People may be heavy but still not overweight. For example, some bodies have large bones and muscles but little fat. Bone and muscle weigh more than fat. If you wonder whether you are too fat, pinch the loose skin below your ribs. If there is less than an inch of loose skin between your fingers, you probably do not have too much fat for your age.

Some People Weigh More Than They Should

If people continue to take in more calories than they can use, they may become overweight. Being overweight can contribute to several kinds of health problems. Diabetes, heart disease, and high blood pressure are three illnesses that are more common among people who are overweight.

There are various reasons why people become overweight. Many people weigh more than they should simply because they eat too much. They may not be active enough to use enough of the calories they take in. Some people eat more than they should when they are worried or unhappy. Others may eat less, but eat too many foods that are high in sugar and fat. Still other people eat far less food than their weight would show. These people's body cells seem to turn more food into fat than other people's body cells do.

What was your answer to *Early Checkup* number 6? (Is overeating the only reason people gain too much weight?)

When machines do more of the work, people generally use up fewer calories. Often the result is more food energy being stored as fat.

Now Is the Time To Watch Your Weight

Being overweight or underweight can cause young people to have health problems when they become adults. Serious weight problems can also make people feel unattractive and unhappy about themselves. People who are unhappy about themselves often do not take care of their health properly. This can make their health problems even worse.

What was your answer to *Early Checkup* number 7? (Can being underweight lead to health problems?)

Nutritious Snacks Make Sense

A banana has 85 calories, a little protein, important minerals, and lots of vitamins A and C. It makes a more nutritious snack than a piece of fudge. One ounce (about 28.4g) of fudge has 115 calories and almost no nutrients. Do your snacks make health sense?

Are you satisfied with your appearance? Do you have plenty of energy and feel healthy? If you answered both questions yes, then you are probably at a good weight. Everyone is different. The right weight for you may not be the right weight for another person of the same age. This can make it hard to decide if you are at your *ideal weight.* If you are not sure, it may help to talk about your weight with your parents or a doctor.

Finding the right amount of nutritious food for the energy you need most of the time can be a giant step toward a healthy life. Getting enough exercise and rest each day lets your body use nutrients and calories in its own best way.

Weight Control and Health

If you are overweight or underweight, you may want to make and follow a weight-control plan.

1. Talk with a doctor. Determine what weight is best for you. Make sure you have no hidden health problems that might increase or get worse as you lose or gain weight. Work out a plan that will help you lose or gain weight slowly and steadily.
2. Ask your family to help you work out a daily diet. Make sure the diet includes foods from all four food groups and provides all the nutrients your body requires each day.
3. Plan to increase slowly and steadily the amount of exercise you get each day.

Stay away from diets promising "miracle" results. People who lose or gain weight too quickly can seriously damage their health.

What was your answer to *Early Checkup* number 8? (Can losing or gaining weight too quickly be harmful to your health?)

What Have You Learned?

Number a piece of paper **1** and **2**. Next to the numbers, write the words that are missing in these sentences.

1. Exercise helps you use up the __, or units of heat energy, in the food you eat. Part of this energy is stored in people as body __.
2. People may be __ just from eating too many foods that are high in sugar and fat. These foods give them some energy but not many longer-lasting __ for health and growth.

Answers to *What Have You Learned?*
1. calories; fat
2. overweight; nutrients

Learn More About It

Here are some books you may want to read. They can help you plan nutritious meals and snacks.

Paul, Aileen. *The Kids' Diet Cookbook.* New York: Doubleday & Co., Inc., 1980. This book offers simple suggestions for losing weight. Recipes, a calorie chart, and a record-keeping system are included to help make weight loss easier.

Pringle, Laurence. *Wild Foods.* New York: Four Winds Press, 1978. You may be surprised when you discover how many foods grow in the wilds. Recipes are included for your enjoyment.

Smith, Nathan J., M.D. *Food for Sport.* Palo Alto, CA: Bull Publishing Co., 1976. Whether you are an athlete or not, this book will provide you with a better understanding of nutrition.

You may find the following sources of value:

Bogert, George M. *Nutrition and Physical Fitness.* Philadelphia, Pa.: W.B. Saunders Co., 1979. This book presents a clear explanation of the ways in which the body utilizes nutrients for better health.

Fleck, Henrietta. *Introduction to Nutrition.* New York: Macmillan, Inc., 1981. The author explores the many facets of nutrition. Among them are the forces that determine food habits, and the effects that food processing, preparation, and storage have on the nutritive values of food.

More To Do on Your Own

1. Keep a food diary for a week. Write down everything you eat, including a stick of gum you might chew. At the end of the week, look over your diary. In general, did you eat a balanced diet? If you think you ate too many foods that are high in sugar or salt, note the times this happened. Then develop a plan to help yourself change your eating habits.
2. Watch TV at a time when many children's programs are shown (such as Saturday morning). Make a list of foods advertised in TV commercials. Then compare the foods on your list. Place a check mark beside each food that is high in sugar, salt, or fat. Draw a star beside each product that could be considered healthful.
3. Conduct a survey to find out what kinds of food additives are in your favorite packaged, prepared foods. As you read the labels, check for different kinds of information. Are any artificial flavors or colors added? Are any of the ingredients sodium (salt)? Do any of the words end in *ose* (possible forms of sugar)? Does the food contain ingredients that are probably additives? (Usually these are ingredients that have long, complicated names.) To help you in your survey, you may want to check your library for more information on food additives.
4. Look in magazines for articles or advertisements concerning diets that promise quick weight loss over a short time. Read the lists of suggested foods. Check to see if any particular nutrient seems to be left out. Note any dietary warnings.

Final Checkup

A. Number a sheet of paper from **1** through **10**. Next to each number, write the letter of the words that best complete each sentence.

1. The body uses proteins to
a. build new cells.
b. store vitamins.
c. improve eyesight.
d. carry wastes.

2. The two large groups of carbohydrates are
a. vitamins and oils.
b. fats and sugars.
c. sugars and starches.
d. minerals and fats.

3. Fat helps the body
a. store extra carbohydrates.
b. replace old, worn-out cells.
c. digest sugars.
d. burn up energy.

4. Vitamins B and C
a. can be stored in the body.
b. cannot be stored in the body.
c. are not important to building good health.
d. should always be taken in large amounts.

5. One of the minerals needed by the body is
a. calcium.
b. cellulose.
c. sugar.
d. fat.

6. A balanced, nutritious meal is made up of foods
a. that are all very low in calories.
b. that contain no sugars or fats.
c. that have a lot of salt in them.
d. from each of the four food groups.

7. A food package label will usually tell you
a. where the food was grown.
b. what percentage of each required nutrient the food contains.
c. exactly how much of each ingredient is in the package.
d. whether the food will help you reach your ideal weight.

8. The amount of energy you use is affected
a. only by how often you exercise.
b. only by your body size.
c. only by the amounts of food you eat.
d. by many different factors, such as age, size, amounts of exercise, and even the weather.

9. People become overweight
a. for many different reasons.
b. only because they eat too much.
c. only because they are born fat.
d. only because they never exercise.

10. People have poorly balanced, nonnutritious diets
    a. only in places where there is not enough to eat.
    b. only when they are eating too many calories.
    (c.) when there is not enough food and when they eat too much sugar and fat and too few other nutrients.
    d. only when they stop taking vitamin tablets.

B. Number a sheet of paper from **1** through **10**. Write **true** or **false** next to the number for each of these ideas.

1. Learning about calories is only necessary for people who want to lose weight. false
2. The two kinds of carbohydrates your body uses are starches and sugars. true
3. Some people have body types that use energy more slowly than others. true
4. Your body is able to use fats as an energy source even more quickly than it uses carbohydrates. false
5. People need large amounts of extra vitamins and minerals to stay healthy. false
6. Water is probably the least important nutrient needed by your body. false
7. Growing young people may need more calories per day than most adults. true
8. Sugars are a source of energy that does not last long and may cause people to feel tired, upset, and hungry when the energy is used up. true
9. People who are very overweight or underweight as youngsters may develop other serious health problems as adults. true
10. All food additives are harmful to people. false

Write About Better Health

Write a short answer to each of these questions. Use complete sentences.

1. List and explain three guidelines for preparing a healthful lunch.
2. Plan a meal that includes something from each of the four food groups. Indicate the group to which each food belongs. List some of the nutrients provided by each food in your meal.
3. Explain why many North Americans who eat poorly balanced, nonnutritious meals are also overweight.
4. Explain why being underweight may be as much of a health and social problem as being overweight.
5. List three important steps to take when planning a healthful way to lose or gain weight.

Model answers to *Write About Better Health* are provided in the chapter notes at the front of this *Teacher's Edition.*

6 YOU CAN LEARN THE SAFETY HABIT

See page 146 for possible student answers.

David enjoys helping in the kitchen. Each year he is able to do more of the actual cooking himself. As he learns more about how to prepare foods, he is also learning more about kitchen safety.

Can you find some safety practices in the photograph? Can you think of some other kitchen safety ideas?

LOOKING AHEAD

There are people who seem to have more than their share of accidents. These people spend a lot of money to have doctors treat their injuries. These people also miss many days of school, work, or play because of their accidents. Other people hardly ever have an accident. Why is there such a difference between people when it comes to having accidents and painful, expensive injuries?

Often the difference is in the attitude people have toward practicing good safety habits. The more people think about good safety ideas and the more they put these ideas to use, the fewer accidents they have. This does not mean that safety-minded people always avoid accidents, but safety-minded people are usually better prepared if accidents should happen. This makes them less likely to be hurt badly.

In this chapter you will learn how to become more safety-minded and how to form safety habits that may prevent you from having serious injuries.

You will learn

- how to stay safe at home or at play.
- how to be ready for fire and weather emergencies.
- how to deal with strangers.
- how to give emergency first aid.

Many rooms in the home present safety hazards of one sort or another. Often such hazards can be avoided by (1) becoming aware of them, (2) taking precautionary measures, and (3) practicing safety techniques under appropriate supervision.

As the students identify the safety precautions in the photograph, ask them to identify the possible consequences of *not* taking the necessary precautions.

1. *The boy is wearing oven-proof mittens to hold the hot dish, thereby avoiding serious burns on his hands.*
2. *An adult is supervising to ensure David is following safety practices, and to assist if necessary.*
3. *Alert students may also notice that David is wearing clothing that is appropriate for cooking. There are no loose sleeves or ties that can accidentally catch fire.*

Here are some words that you may not have talked about in school before. You will learn more about them in this chapter. You can find all these words in the *Glossary* at the back of this book.

antiseptic (an′tə·sep′tik)
conscious (kon′shəs)
first aid (fėrst ād)
panic (pan′ik)
puncture (pungk′chər)
risk (risk)
shock (shok)
unconscious (un·kon′shəs)

Early Checkup

How much do you already know about safety and first aid? Number a piece of paper from **1** through **7**. Answer each of these questions by writing **yes** or **no** next to the correct number on your paper. You can check your answers as you read this chapter.

1. Does being safe mean never taking a risk? no
2. Do people act as safely when they are upset as when they are calm? no
3. Are there dangers in the water that swimmers cannot see? yes
4. If someone bothers you on the telephone, should you hang up? yes
5. Do families need fire-escape plans and drills for their own homes? yes
6. Can people protect themselves from violent storms like hurricanes? yes
7. Are the most harmful skin burns the most painful kind? no

risk

Two of the main principles of safety-mindedness are (1) becoming more aware when safety is involved and (2) understanding when a risk is foolish and too dangerous.

YOU CAN REDUCE SAFETY RISKS

Many things people do in life involve taking a **risk**. A risk is anything someone does that may lead to being hurt. In a way, meeting new people is a risk. You may not like them, or they may not like you. Players in games run the risk that they may lose.

Most people accept such risks. Most people also accept certain safety risks. For example, they learn to roller-skate or to drive a bicycle, even though there is the chance of falling. People take the risk because practicing will help make the activity safer. They also decide that the risk itself is not too dangerous.

What was your answer to *Early Checkup* number 1? (Does being safe mean never taking a risk?)

You reduce the risk of injury when you know your body's limits. Waiting for someone to help you lift something heavy is playing it safe with your body. Knowing how to lift by bending your knees rather than your back is good safety planning, too.

However, some safety risks are foolish. A risk is foolish when there is a good chance that it can cause a serious health problem. Some risks may be foolish for one person but not for another. For example, an experienced ski jumper is taking a much smaller chance in a jump than a beginning ski jumper. However, even expert ski jumpers would increase their own risk by not taking good care of their skis.

It is important for students to understand when and for whom a risk is foolish. You may want to conduct a class discussion about this. Some risks may be recognized as foolish for anybody (such as running across a busy highway). Other risks may be foolish only for people who have had no preparatory training. For example, diving into a swimming pool is not a risk for an experienced swimmer who has learned how to dive. It can be a foolish and dangerous risk for someone who does not know how to swim.

People who care about safety consider others' safety as well as their own. They bike on paths or on the sides of roads rather than on sidewalks. They avoid play that can easily hurt people. They avoid dashing across the street without looking first, or when the light is red. Healthy, careful people have fewer accidents that break bones or cause sprains.

People who get enough sleep are helping to reduce their safety risks. Alert people have fewer accidents than people who are tired. People who do not drink alcoholic beverages take fewer safety risks. Drinking alcoholic beverages slows thinking and body movements. This can lead to accidents, especially among car drivers. Daily exercise and nutritious meals help reduce safety risks, too.

Do you read and obey safety signs and rules when you see them? Safety-minded people know that safety signs and rules are put there to reduce the risk of accidents.

For Your Protection

The best place for roller-skating or skateboarding is at a skating rink or park. Remember to wear a helmet and pads for protection.

Stay Safe on Wheels

Your bike should be the right size for you. When you sit, your feet should touch the ground. The handlebars, wheels, and seat should not be loose. The chain should be in good working order. Check the tires to see if they need air. Put tape over any sharp edges that could cause cuts. Night drivers should have a light on the front of their bikes. Loose pant legs should be tied, shirts tucked in, and shoes always worn. A *reflective* vest is useful and important for night driving. Some states require a light on the rear of the bike. Check if this is true in your area.

By law, there must be ten *reflectors* on a bicycle. The front of your bike should have a white reflector on it. On the back, there should be a three-inch (7.6 cm) red reflector. The front wheel should have a white or amber reflector on each side. Each side of the rear wheel should have a red or white reflector. Amber pedal reflectors should go on the front and back of each pedal.

Check your bike each time before driving it. Be sure to drive on the right-hand side of roads and follow all traffic signals. When you first learn to drive your bike, choose an area with no traffic and few people.

Check skateboards and skates, too, before using them. A skateboard should not have cracks or splinters. The surface should be rough to prevent your foot from sliding. The frame holding the wheels to the board should be firmly attached. Wheels should spin smoothly. Roller skates should fit comfortably. Check them for loose parts, sharp edges, and smoothly spinning wheels. Always choose safe places to skate.

Know Your Signals

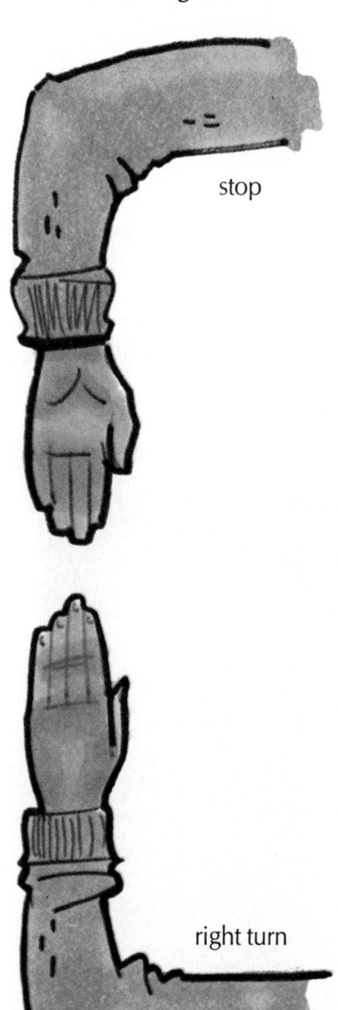

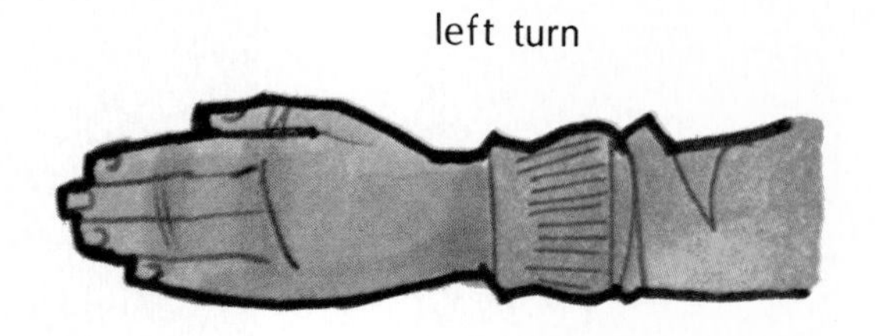

Stay Safe on the Ball Field

Before playing any active game, such as baseball or football, make sure you have enough room to run around in without bumping into people and buildings or coming near traffic. Ball fields, parks, and large, cleared fields are good places to play. Running games need a lot of space. For example, basketball courts need to have extra room on the sidelines to protect players who run out of bounds.

Use the proper safety equipment when you play. Baseball gloves, mitts, and helmets protect players. Wear the right shoes, too, for the game you are playing.

Rules make games safer and more challenging. Most rules forbid pushing and bumping that can cause accidents. Let bats and other equipment fall to the ground. Never throw them. After the game, put away balls, bats, and other equipment. Can you see how looking after sports equipment, on or off the field, helps to reduce safety risks?

People also seem to have more accidents when they are upset, worried, or under stress than when they are feeling calm. It is wise to avoid games and activities that involve risks when you are not calm. Talking problems over with your family can often make you feel better. Some warm-up exercises before a game can help to relax your mind and your body.

Discuss with the class the safety precautions motorbike drivers should observe. The local police can inform motorbike drivers where they can drive safely and legally. Precautions should include following all traffic signals, maintaining a safe speed, wearing a protective helmet, and being thoroughly familiar with the instructions for operating a motorbike before driving one. Stress that, like bicycles, most motorbikes are built to carry one driver and no passengers.

Discuss with the class the reasons why they should be taking precautions in the games and sports in which they participate. This may include why a batter must wear a helmet, why baseball players should wear gloves, or why players who wear eyeglasses should have special safety glasses.

What was your answer to *Early Checkup* number 2? (Do people act as safely when they are upset as when they are calm?)

Wear shoes or sneakers with soles that are not smooth and slippery. When you play running games, be sure your shoes let you move, stop, and turn easily.

More About Water Safety

There are other ways to reduce safety risks and increase the fun of swimming and other water sports. Swim in calm areas of the water, where waves are not high enough to knock you over or tire you. It is also wise to wait a while after eating before you swim. Surfboards should be used only in areas away from swimmers.

Stay Safe in the Water

The safest person in the water is someone who knows how to swim. However, whether you know how to swim or still have to learn, it is important to follow water safety guidelines.

Wherever you swim, always swim with someone nearby. Most public swimming areas have lifeguards. You should swim only when the lifeguard is on duty. At private pools or lakes, ask a friend to swim with you or just to stay nearby. Even the best swimmers sometimes need help.

Find out as much as you can about the water you plan to enter. Avoid fast-moving water and water with strong *undercurrents.* These undercurrents move swiftly below the surface, and can pull even good swimmers farther from the shore than they should be. Such currents often cannot be seen. Obey any signs *prohibiting* swimming.

What was your answer to *Early Checkup* number 3? (Are there dangers in the water that swimmers cannot see?)

H.E.L.P. stands for *Heat Escape Lessening Posture.* Emphasize that this position is to be assumed only when the person is wearing a PFD. Drownproofing is a procedure that should be followed only if someone is *not* wearing a PFD and is unable to swim to safety. Point out that even a nonswimmer is capable of either procedure.

Discuss the water safety of other people in the water. You might ask why playing roughly is particularly dangerous in water. Also, ask why it is important never to pretend that you are drowning or need help. Discuss how preparing for possible emergencies by keeping rescue equipment on hand contributes to safety.

Get a good idea of how deep the water is, and if the weather is about to turn bad. If rain or lightning begins, get out of the water immediately. If you are not feeling well, it is best not to swim. Sometimes people get muscle cramps while swimming. If this happens to you, get out of the water. If you cannot get out of the water easily, try ducking your head down in the water and rubbing the cramped area with your fingers.

If you are stranded in the water and you are wearing a *personal flotation device* (PFD), you should assume the *H.E.L.P.* position shown in the picture. This position keeps your body warmer in cold water. It is most important to keep your head above water.

Supervised pools and beaches are the safest places to swim. Read the posted rules, and follow the safety tips carefully. The following rules will often be included.

- Swim only when a lifeguard is on duty.
- Follow all instructions the lifeguards may give.
- Do not go into water that is over your head unless you swim well.
- Do not play roughly, push anyone underwater, or run near a pool.
- Dive only from the diving board.
- Make sure no people are swimming where you will dive.
- Keep glass objects away from a pool.

Drownproofing—Keeping Afloat in an Emergency

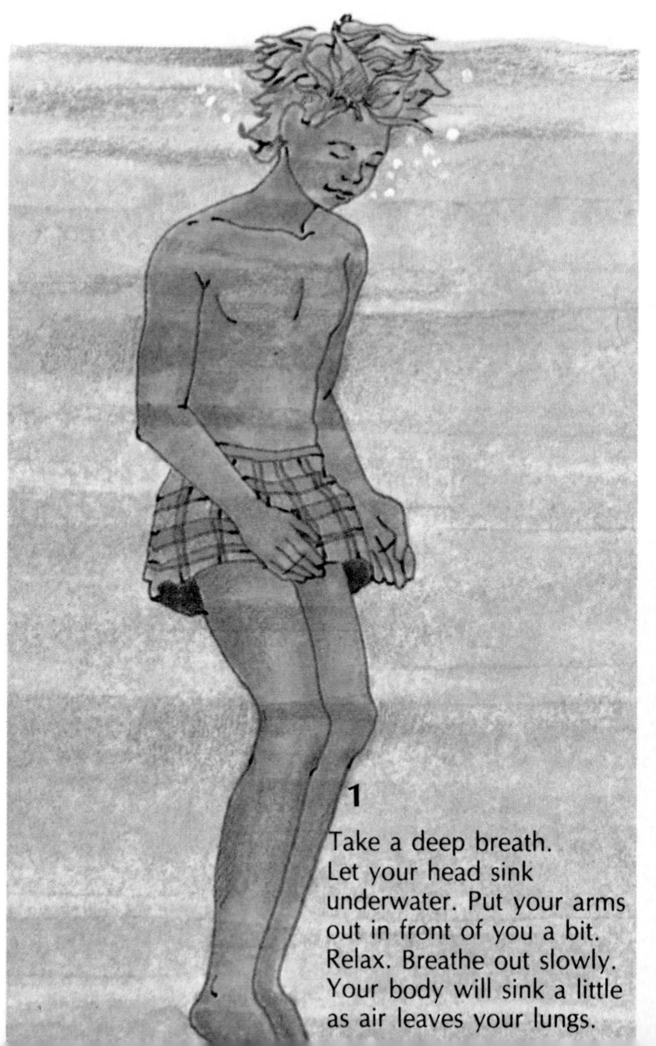

1
Take a deep breath. Let your head sink underwater. Put your arms out in front of you a bit. Relax. Breathe out slowly. Your body will sink a little as air leaves your lungs.

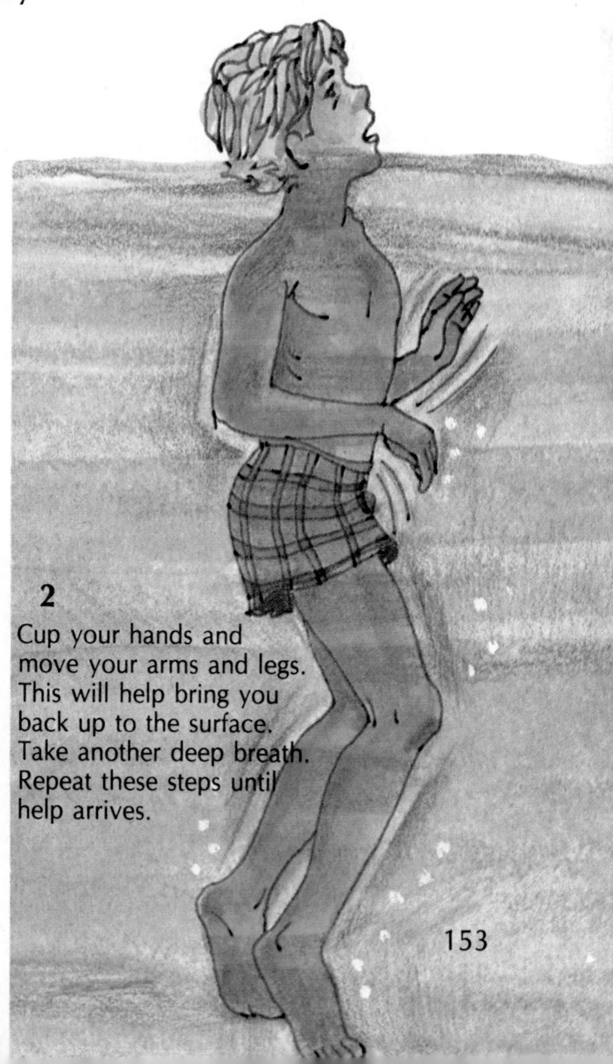

2
Cup your hands and move your arms and legs. This will help bring you back up to the surface. Take another deep breath. Repeat these steps until help arrives.

Stay Safe on a Hike

Every year people get lost on hikes. Often it is because they have left the marked trail and forgotten which trail will lead them out of the woods. Before starting a hike, study a map of the trails you will follow. You will encounter different trail-marking signs along the way, so learn what these mean ahead of time. Figure out about how long your hike will take. Write this information down—along with the trails you plan to follow—and leave it with someone who is not going with you.

Follow the marked trails you planned, being careful to look for the posted trail markings and to read them correctly. Stay with your group and do not go off by yourself. If the group does split up, agree to meet at a certain place and time.

A hiker's clothing. Comfortable, over-the-ankle boots that are "broken in"; socks; loose-fitting pants; a light rain parka; a sweater or coat for the cold; and a backpack. Keep your backpack as light as possible, and keep all your supplies here.

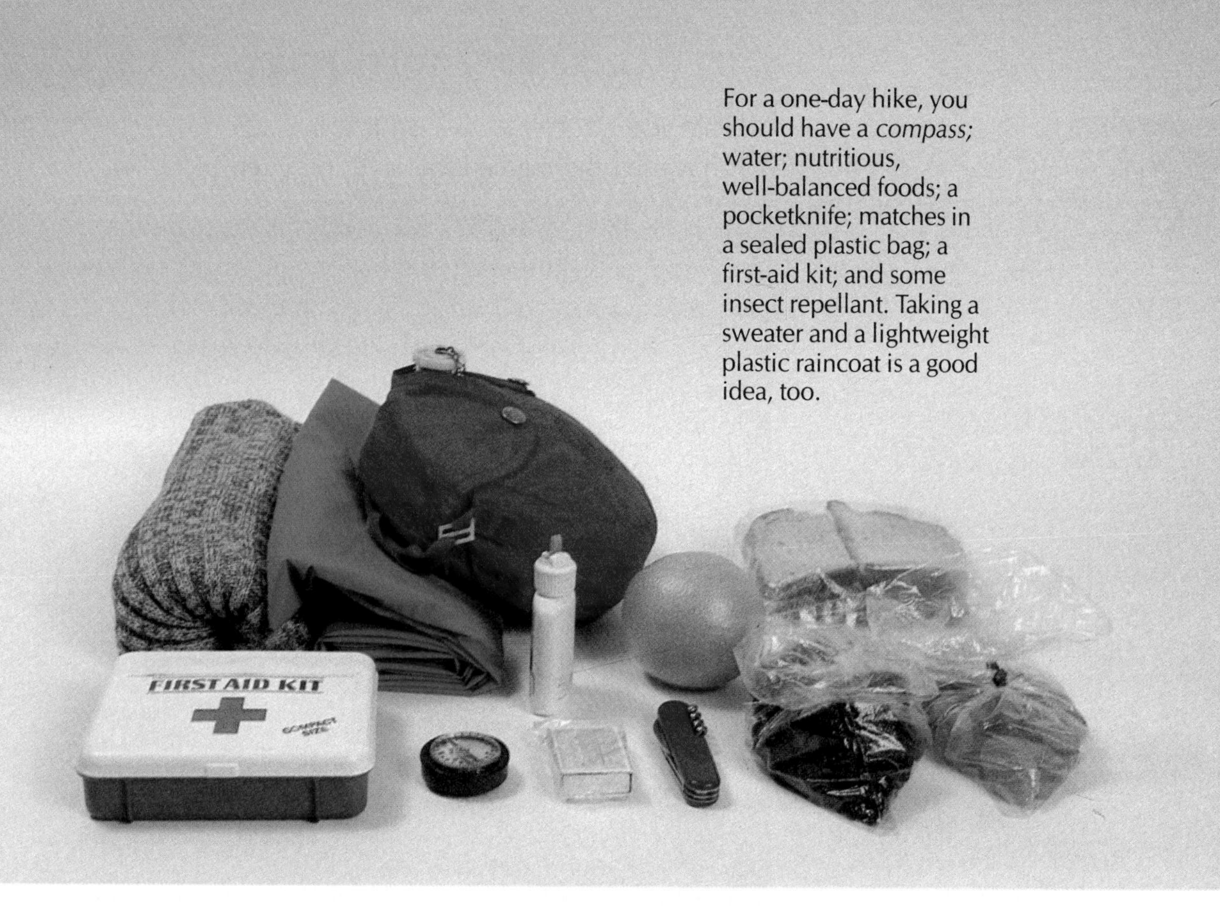

For a one-day hike, you should have a *compass;* water; nutritious, well-balanced foods; a pocketknife; matches in a sealed plastic bag; a first-aid kit; and some insect repellant. Taking a sweater and a lightweight plastic raincoat is a good idea, too.

What Have You Learned?

Number a piece of paper from **1** through **5**. Next to the numbers, write the words that are missing in these sentences.

1. On a bike that is the right size for you, your feet can reach the ___ when you sit on the seat.

2. When you check a skateboard or roller skates for safety, the wheels should ___ smoothly.

3. To reduce the ___ of injury, wear helmets and other safety equipment to ___ your body in certain games.

4. On a hike, the best place to carry supplies is in a lightweight ___.

5. Always have someone ___ when you swim.

Answers to *What Have You Learned?*
1. ground
2. spin (roll)
3. risk (danger, chance); protect
4. backpack
5. nearby (with you, close by)

YOU CAN BE PREPARED FOR EMERGENCIES

Know What To Do When You Are Alone

At some point, you and your family may decide that you are mature enough to stay home alone at times. You should have your own safety plan for when you are alone.

Decide with your family if you are to open the door to strangers. If strangers keep bothering you, call a neighbor or the police.

Discuss the aspect of using one's own judgment when dealing with strangers. Each situation in which children find themselves will be unique. They will have to make some decisions. You might ask, "Do you think it is always wise to let a stranger at the door know you are home alone? What would you do if you could not see the stranger?"

Who *are* "strangers"? Strangers can be people you have never seen, but they can also be people you have seen in your neighborhood and do not really know well. As with everyone you know, there are safe strangers and some who are not so safe. When a stranger bothers you on the street, do not be afraid to run away screaming. Find some people and run to them. Report to your family what the stranger looked like.

Sometimes strangers will make annoying telephone calls to people. It is best to hang up on such callers and to report the calls to your family. Never give a stranger your address or other information on the telephone.

When you give strangers directions, stand some distance away from them. Never accept a ride or a gift a stranger offers you. If the stranger bothers you, leave right away.

What was your answer to *Early Checkup* number 4? (If someone bothers you on the telephone, should you hang up?)

panic

What May Be the Most Important Kitchen Tool?

A small fire can often be put out with a home *fire extinguisher.* The best place for it is in the kitchen. Read and remember the operating instructions printed on the extinguisher. In a fire emergency, a fire extinguisher could be your most important kitchen tool.

Be Ready for Fire Emergencies

People are often injured in fires simply because of **panic**. Panic is a feeling of fear that makes people act unwisely. The first people to panic are usually those who have never planned for safety in a fire emergency. Panic makes it harder to protect yourself and harder for others to help you.

Many families practice a fire-escape plan. This helps to save lives every year. A good plan includes two ways out of every room in the home, where possible. It also includes a place outside the home where family members can meet. The first person to escape should call the fire department from a neighbor's home or a telephone booth. Calmly, the person should give the family's name and address, and the neighbor's name and phone number, or the number of the booth phone.

Schools and some families have regular fire drills to prepare for a fire emergency. Everyone must *cooperate* by following directions and staying with the group. In public buildings there are exit signs. You should always look for them in a theater, restaurant, or store.

What was your answer to *Early Checkup* number 5? (Do families need fire-escape plans and drills for their own homes?)

Discovery—A New Pathway to Health

At one time, a late-night fire could move through a home while everyone slept. However, that need no longer happen to a family. People with *smoke detectors* in their homes are awakened while there is still a chance to escape.

There are many kinds of smoke detectors, and they work differently. All of them make a loud noise when they sense smoke in the air.

Smoke detectors should be put up on ceilings or walls in hallways near the bedrooms. There the alarm will be sure to awaken people. The detectors should be tested every month, and their batteries should be replaced at least once a year.

One of the greatest dangers of fire is the damage smoke can do to the lungs. In a fire, the least amount of smoke is near the floor. Keep your head low and take a breath of air. Quickly stand up and feel the *top* of the door. If it is cool, crawl out of the room and escape.

You may want to point out that panic can be as life threatening as—or even more than—a fire or other emergency. When people force themselves to remain calm and to act rationally, they can make reasonable attempts to rescue themselves and others. Often when people panic, they run about wildly, using up valuable energy and time. It is not easy to stay calm in a crisis, but it is important to force oneself to do so. Fear is a normal reaction. However, it must not be allowed to interfere with the best interests of safety. Advance planning helps people act sensibly in cases of fire. That is one reason school fire drills are important. They help people know what to do before anything happens.

If the door is hot, do *not* open it. Instead, stuff rags or towels in the space around it to keep smoke out. Wet the rags if you can. Crawl to a window. If it is not high, climb out to escape. If it is high, call out for help.

Storm Watches—Storm Warnings

The U.S. Weather Service announces a *storm watch* when it feels a storm may form. It issues *storm warnings* when a storm has actually been sighted. Storm warnings are announced for the area where the storm may move next. Of course, there are other emergencies, such as *earthquakes,* that often cannot be predicted.

Avoid Dangers in Weather Emergencies

If you have ever been in a *hurricane* or a *tornado,* you know they are both violent storms.

Hurricanes usually begin over the ocean and move slowly toward land. They bring high winds, heavy rainfall, and rising tides, and can cause heavy damage. Radio and television reports warn people to leave their homes and move farther inland before the hurricane hits. At other times people are simply advised to make their homes safer from the storm. This means bringing loose objects from the yard and porch inside so they will not be blown around and cause damage.

Before a hurricane hits, it is often wise to clean out a sink or tub and fill it with water. Clean containers should be filled with water, too. The storm may damage the water supply or make it unfit to drink. It is also wise to stay indoors. Listen to a radio for storm announcements and instructions. Have a battery-powered radio and at least one powerful flashlight, in case the storm causes the electricity to go off.

What was your answer to *Early Checkup* number 6? (Can people protect themselves from violent storms like hurricanes?)

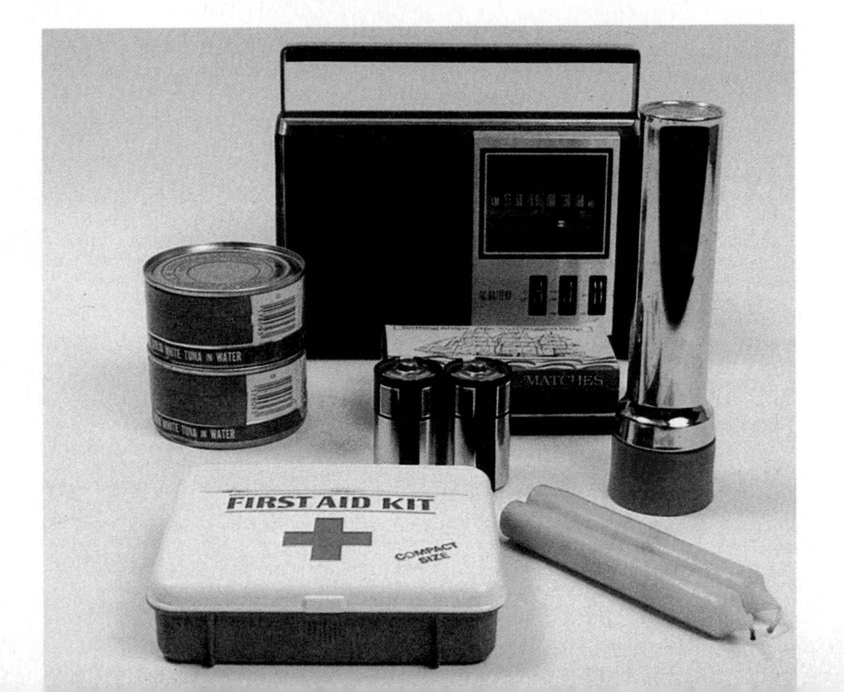

Reducing the risk of safety problems in a storm emergency includes having an emergency box or shelf at home with these supplies. Test the batteries once a month and replace them at least once a year.

Tornadoes strike suddenly. There is usually little time to prepare for them. Sometimes a state or regional weather bureau announces a *tornado watch,* but not exactly where it will strike. In a tornado the safest place to be is on the lowest floor of your home. If you are outdoors, lie down and protect your mouth, nose, and eyes from dust.

Use a Checklist for Home Safety

To many people, home may seem like the safest place to be, but it is where they have most of their accidents. Perhaps people become more careless in their homes because they are so used to them. The time to make your home safer is before an accident happens. The checklist on this page may help you to reduce risks at home.

Help Prevent Accidental Falls

- Keep toys and other objects off stairs and floors.
- Clean up spills right away.
- Use a stepladder, not a chair, to reach high objects.
- Do not run up or down steps.

Help Prevent Poisoning Accidents

- Store poisons in marked containers and away from food.
- Store poisons where small children cannot reach them.
- Keep safety caps on all medicines.
- Read the label carefully before using any product.

Help Keep Small Children Safe

- Store scissors, knives, and sharp objects where small children cannot reach them.
- Keep large plastic bags out of reach.
- Remove lids and doors from trunks and refrigerators that are no longer in use or are about to be discarded.
- Turn pot handles inward on the stove when cooking.

Help Prevent Fires

- Keep matches where small children cannot reach them.
- Keep paint, turpentine, and other substances that can catch fire in tightly closed metal containers.
- Keep long sleeves and curtains away from stove burners.
- Throw out old rags and newspapers.
- Replace old, frayed cords on electrical *appliances.*

At this time you may want to stress the importance of using emergency numbers only for true emergencies. Students should know that calling in a false fire alarm is a crime and also endangers other people's lives.

In talking about safety at home, you will want to be particularly careful not to infringe on a student's privacy. The "Make a Checklist for Home Safety" section is intended to make students aware of ways they can protect themselves and their families. It is not meant to question their family's safety-mindedness in any way. Students may want to discuss with their parents anything that seems unsafe at home.

On Your Own

When an emergency happens, it is important to be able to get help as quickly as possible. Every family should have a list of emergency phone numbers close to the telephone. Ask your family if you can make a list for your home.

With your family, discuss the numbers that are important for your emergency phone number list. Then make a list of those numbers. Some will be in the telephone directory. Decide where the list should be kept. If there are two phones in your home, you may want to have two copies of the list. Why would this be a good idea?

What Have You Learned?

Number a piece of paper from **1** through **5**. Next to the numbers, write the words that are missing in these sentences.

1. It is never wise to accept a ride or gifts from a ___.

2. It is important not to ___ when there is a fire emergency. There is less ___ close to the floor when there is a fire.

3. Many families have an ___ plan for fire emergencies. Some families even have fire ___ as you do in school.

4. The ___ may go off in a storm, so flashlights and a battery-powered radio should be in every home.

5. To reduce the risk of a poisoning accident, store poisons out of the reach of small ___ and away from where ___ is kept.

Answers to *What Have You Learned?*
1. stranger
2. panic; smoke
3. escape; drills
4. electricity (power)
5. children; food

antiseptic
first aid

It is important for students to understand that first aid is given to a person until professional medical care is available. Properly administered, first aid can save lives and prevent permanent damage. Good administration of first aid also includes remaining calm.

YOU CAN LEARN FIRST AID

Learn To Use a First-Aid Kit

First aid is immediate treatment given to injured or sick people before professional medical help arrives. People who know what to do in an emergency often save lives.

A first-aid kit at home should contain materials needed to treat emergencies, materials such as bandages and an **antiseptic**. An antiseptic is a chemical used to destroy disease germs that might cause infections in open wounds. The kit should be checked regularly to be sure everything is there and in good condition.

People Working for Your Health

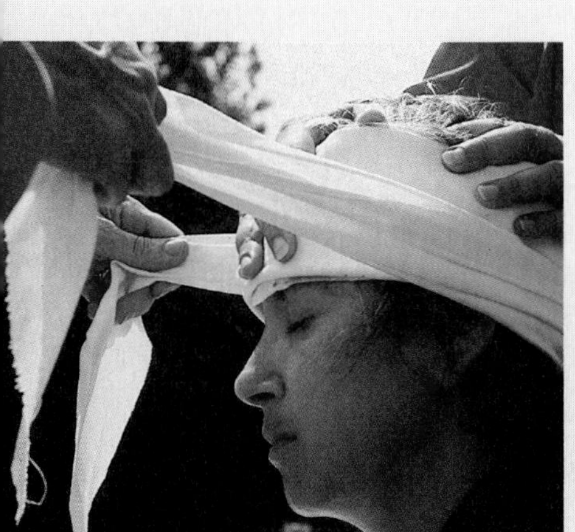

Foster Gibbons is a *paramedic* working out of St. Vincent's Hospital in New York City. In a big city like New York, emergency services are needed around the clock. Mr. Gibbons works the 4:00 P.M.-to-midnight shift. Always ready to respond to a call for help, he and his partner patrol the streets of downtown Manhattan in their ambulance. The area Mr. Gibbons patrols contains about one million people, so it is easy to see how badly his services are needed.

It was in high school that Mr. Gibbons became interested in learning how to give first aid. He had seen TV shows about paramedics and emergency services, and felt that this would be purposeful work in which to be involved.

Mr. Gibbons has his college degree, but it is not required in order to be a paramedic. What *is* required is more than 1,000 hours of course work and practice in giving emergency care. A paramedic must be able to evaluate how serious an accident victim's wounds are, diagnose what kind of care the victim needs, and administer the proper drugs and first-aid treatment. He and his partner must be prepared at all times to handle life-threatening emergencies such as heart attacks, pedestrian accidents, and drug overdoses. It is very demanding work, but Mr. Gibbons loves it. He says, "It lets me show my concern for other people. I feel I am excellent at what I do, and I play a very valuable role in the health-care team."

In the case of minor cuts and scrapes, first aid in the form of cleaning and bandaging the wound may be all that is necessary. Remind students, however, that they should always ask an adult whether further medical treatment is necessary.

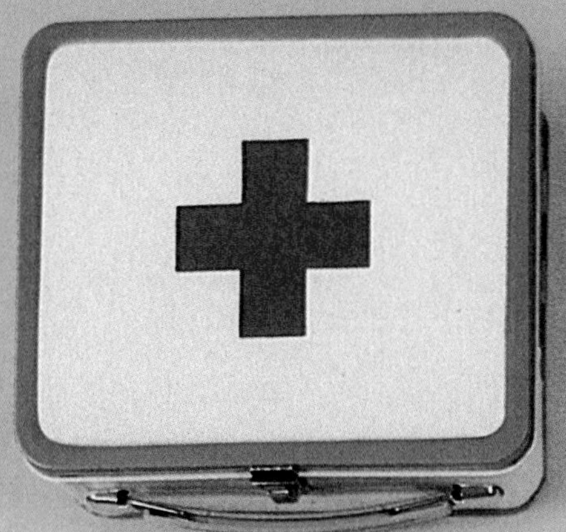

Tweezers—to remove splinters.

Cotton—to clean wounds, except open wounds.

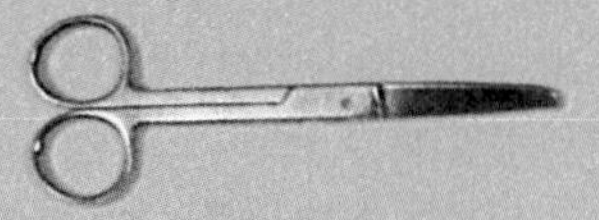

Scissors—to cut bandages and clothing.

Gauze bandages—to hold pads in place and to bandage large wounds.

An emetic—to make a person vomit in certain cases of poisoning (TO BE GIVEN ONLY BY AN ADULT).

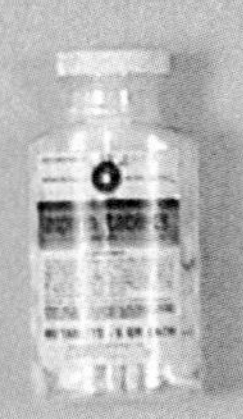

Aspirin—to ease pain and lower body temperature (TO BE GIVEN ONLY BY AN ADULT).

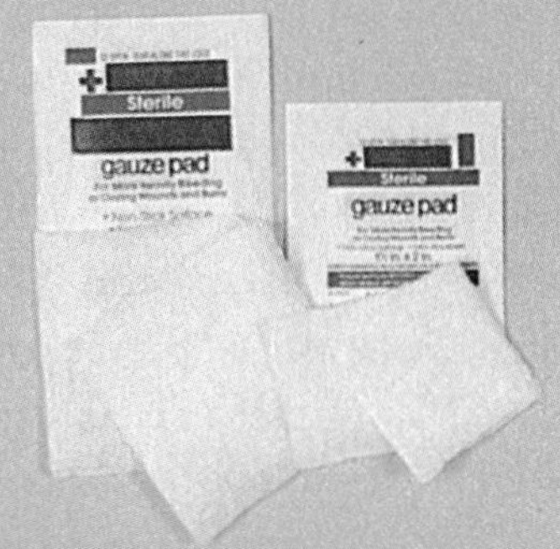

Large triangular bandage—to make an arm sling or to bandage a large wound.

Soap—to clean the area of the wound.

Gauze pads—to clean open wounds; help stop bleeding; and, taped in place, to cover wounds and help prevent infection.

Safety pins—to fasten large bandages such as a sling.

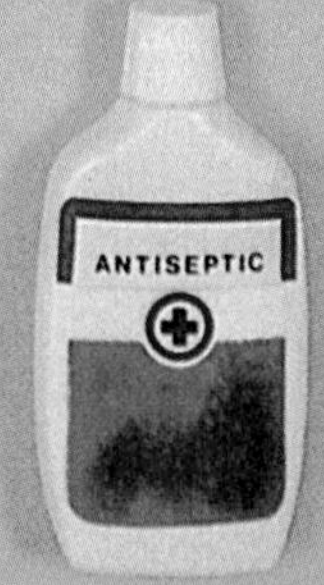

Adhesive bandages—to cover small cuts.

Elastic bandages—to bandage sprained ankles and wrists.

An antiseptic—to clean wounds and prevent infections.

conscious
shock
unconscious

Learn When First Aid Is Needed

Falls and Hard Blows

If someone falls or is hit by something hard, try to fill a plastic bag with some ice and then try to place this "ice bag" on the injury. The cold can help to keep the swelling down.

Avoid moving a person who may have broken bones. Try to get help by dialing "911" if your town has this emergency telephone service. If it does not, call the operator by dialing "0." Tell where you are and what has happened.

A person who has had an accident may be **conscious** or **unconscious**. Conscious people are awake, and can usually indicate where they feel pain and how the accident happened. Unconscious people are not awake, and this makes it difficult to know where they are injured. If it is possible, loosen tight clothing on the injured person. Do not pour water on an unconscious person or attempt to give the person anything to drink.

An injured person may go into **shock**. Shock happens because the heart beats more slowly and pumps less blood. A person in shock becomes weak, pale, thirsty, and may have cold, moist skin. The person may faint. Try to keep the person warm with a coat or blanket. Then get professional medical help quickly. If two people are with someone who has been injured, one can go for help while the other stays with the injured person.

If professional medical help does not come within an hour, you may give a half glass of water or juice to a conscious, injured adult every 15 minutes or a quarter glass to a conscious, injured child between two and twelve years old. If the person vomits, stop giving the liquid.

Look for a Special Health Tag

Sometimes people with special health problems wear bracelets or neck chains with tags that give medical information. For example, the picture shows both sides of the tag a *diabetic* would wear. If you find a person confused or unconscious, look for this tag. It will be worn around the wrist or neck. If you find one, read what it says. Then tell an adult.

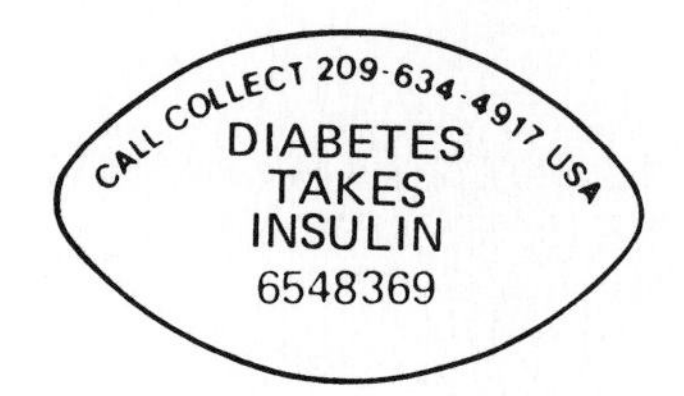

Discovery—A New Pathway to Health

One of the more common accidents is choking on food or choking on objects that have been swallowed by chance. Until recently, most people did not know what to do for a choking victim. Now, however, we know much more about how to save a choking victim than ever before.

Many choking victims can cough the object out. If a person is able to speak or make any noise from the mouth, encourage him or her to cough. *Do not* slap the back. Stay with the person to make sure that he or she is all right.

If a choking person cannot make any sound through the mouth, he or she is in serious danger. If the victim is conscious, stand in back of the person and bend her or his body so that the head is lower than the waist. Hold the victim's upper body with your hand and arm. With the heel of your free hand, deliver four sharp blows to the back between the shoulder blades. Follow this with four abdominal thrusts. For abdominal thrusts, wrap your arms around the victim's waist and make a fist with one hand. Place your fist with the thumb side toward the abdomen. Put your other hand on top of your fist. Your hands should be in a spot above the navel and below the breastbone. Press your fist into the victim's abdomen with a quick, forceful, inward and upward thrust. Repeat the steps until the object being choked on is dislodged. Each time you repeat the procedure, ask the victim if he or she can speak.

If the choking victim is or becomes unconscious, roll the person onto his or her side facing you. Deliver four sharp blows as described earlier, and then place the victim face up on a hard surface. Turn the victim's head away from you. Deliver four abdominal thrusts by placing the heel of one hand between the navel and breastbone, and the heel of the other hand on top of the first one. Apply an inward and upward thrust. Check the mouth for foreign matter. Repeat these steps until effective.

puncture

Removing a Splinter

Small splinters can sometimes be removed with a tweezer or the tip of a needle. First, clean the tool with alcohol. Next, use the tool gently to pull the splinter out. Then use an antiseptic to prevent infection. Some splinters may have to be removed by a doctor or nurse.

Cuts, Scrapes, and Punctures

Washing scrapes and cuts with soap and water—and then rinsing them thoroughly—will reduce the risk of infection. Cuts may bleed heavily. To stop heavy bleeding, press a gauze pad or clean cloth on the wound. Try to raise the bleeding area so that it is higher than the person's heart.

Nails, fishhooks, splinters, and other sharp objects can cause a **puncture**. Punctures are holes in the skin that may not necessarily bleed. You may need professional medical help to remove the object. Puncture wounds, especially when they do not bleed, can become infected. If your skin has been punctured by anything, or if a wound shows any sign of infection, tell your family. It may be important to have a doctor look at the wound.

If bleeding does not stop, tie gauze pads over the wound with a bandage, scarf, belt, or whatever you have. Tie it firmly but not too tightly, with the knot over the pads. Get an adult to help as soon as possible.

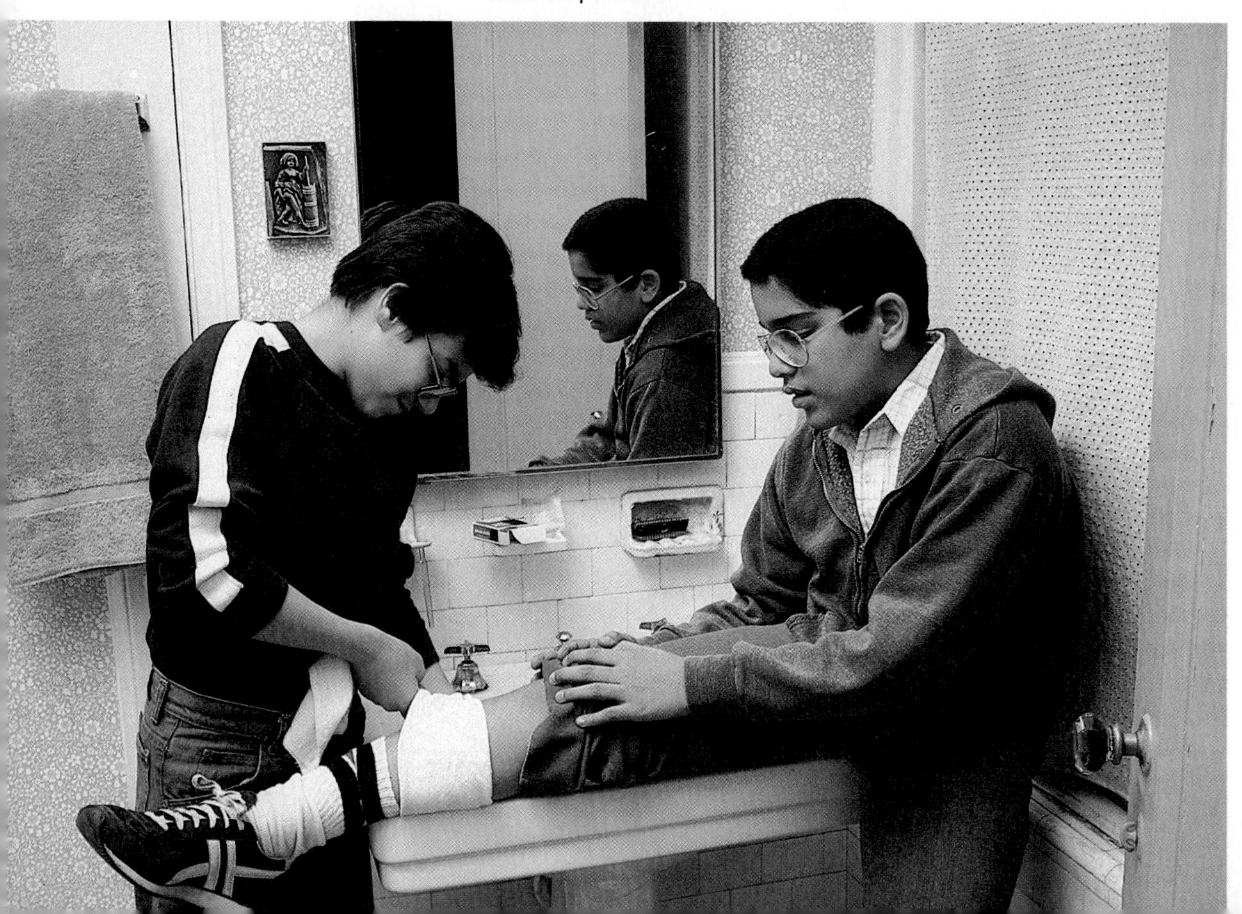

Burns

Skin with first-degree burns is red and painful, but without blisters. Soak the burned skin in cold water to stop the pain and reduce the redness. Do not use oil or ointment on these or any burns.

With second-degree burns, the skin blisters. Soak the affected areas in cold water for a long time—up to one hour. This may keep some blisters from forming. Dry the burns gently and bandage them. Do not break the blisters. Ask your family if they feel a doctor should look at these burns.

Third-degree burns may not hurt, but they are very serious. The skin is burned black, and white spots may appear. Do not put cold water on third-degree burns. Instead, cover the burns with a clean sheet, cloth, or piece of plastic. A doctor must care for third-degree burns right away. Call your doctor or an emergency room.

Caution students that *ice water* should never be used on a burn. Only cold tap water should be used.

Discuss with the class the special attention required for a puncture wound. You may want to point out that puncture wounds often do not bleed as severely as lacerations. Because bleeding is an effective aid in cleansing wounds, a puncture carries a particular risk of infection. These wounds must be cleaned thoroughly. In some cases a tetanus booster shot may be necessary.

What was your answer to *Early Checkup* number 7? (Are the most harmful skin burns the most painful kind?)

Poisons

A person who has swallowed poison may be unconscious or may be too young to tell you what the poison was. Look for the poison container and quickly call a poison control center, an emergency room, or a doctor. Have the container in your hand so you can read the label over the phone. The label will usually give you first-aid instructions. You can give the person water to help *dilute* the poison if he or she is conscious. When you have done all you can, wait with the person until help arrives.

What Have You Learned?

Number a piece of paper from **1** through **5**. Next to the numbers, write the words that are missing in these sentences.

1. A person who is weak, pale, cold, and thirsty after an accident may be suffering from ___.

2. A person who is injured in a fall should be kept ___. It is best not to ___ the person in case bones are broken.

3. A cut or scrape should be ___ to help reduce the risk of infection.

4. First-degree and second-degree burns should be treated by placing the burned area in ___ ___.

5. If someone is bleeding, ___ a gauze pad against the cut. The injured area should be ___ so that it is higher than the ___.

Answers to *What Have You Learned?*
1. shock
2. warm (calm, still); move
3. washed (cleaned)
4. cold water
5. press; raised (lifted); heart

Learn More About It

If you are interested in reading more about safety and first aid, here are some books you can look for in the library.

American Red Cross. *Standard First Aid & Personal Safety.* Garden City, N.Y.: Doubleday & Company, Inc., 1979. This book is a good source of information on first aid for all kinds of emergencies. Read it and be prepared to use what you learn.

Milton, Hilary. *Emergency! 10-33 on Channel 11.* New York: Franklin Watts, Inc., 1977. A family gets lost in a storm and uses a CB radio to get help.

Platt, Charles. *Outdoor Survival.* New York: Franklin Watts, Inc., 1976. Learn how to find your way with and without a compass, how to signal for help if you are lost, and how to prevent many kinds of outdoor accidents.

A good illustrated resource for first-aid procedures is:
Smith, Tony, and Breckon, Bill. *Accident Action.* New York: The Viking Press, 1979.

Information on water, bike, and fire safety is available from these organizations:

Public Safety Department
National Safety Council
444 North Michigan Avenue
Chicago, IL 60611

American National Red Cross
17th & D Streets, N.W.
Washington, DC 20006

More To Do on Your Own

1. Talk to a traffic police officer or a school-crossing guard about pedestrian safety. Ask about the most dangerous risks taken by pedestrians. Use what you learn to figure out how pedestrians can reduce their risk of accidents. Write down your ideas and compare them with those of some friends.
2. Learn how a compass works. Many Boy and Girl Scouts have compasses. You can make a simple compass by rubbing the tip of a sewing needle with a magnet. Rub in one direction only—from the center of the needle toward the tip. Then place the needle so it floats in a wide bowl of water. Which way does the needle point? Why does this happen?
3. You might want to learn more about giving first aid in an emergency. The Red Cross often gives first-aid courses. Look in the telephone book to see if there is a Red Cross first-aid course given near you.
4. Learn how to use the different kinds of bandages that are part of a first-aid kit. You might request permission to visit the school nurse's office and to ask the nurse to give you a demonstration. Later you can ask a friend to act as your "patient," and practice your first-aid skills.

Final Checkup

A. Number a sheet of paper from **1** through **10**. Next to each number, write the letter of the words that best complete each sentence.

1. People who follow a safety plan in their work and play
- **a.** need special Red Cross training.
- **b.** never have accidents.
- **c.** are taking risks.
- **d.** reduce the risk of accidents.

2. When you drive a bike at night,
- **a.** drive on dark streets to avoid traffic.
- **b.** wear light-colored clothing and reflector tape.
- **c.** wear dark-colored clothing.
- **d.** drive on the left-hand side of the street.

3. When you go swimming, you should
- **a.** wear a life jacket.
- **b.** swim only in public pools and at public beaches.
- **c.** have somebody nearby.
- **d.** swim in water with strong undercurrents.

4. Anyone caught in a room filled with smoke from a fire should
- **a.** stand on furniture.
- **b.** try to find the fire and put it out.
- **c.** call the fire department before doing anything else.
- **d.** try to leave by crawling to the nearest exit.

5. Hurricanes are storms that
- **a.** people can know about before they happen.
- **b.** strike without warning.
- **c.** hurt people no matter what they do.
- **d.** are never very dangerous.

6. An antiseptic is used to
- **a.** stop pain.
- **b.** clean wounds and prevent infection.
- **c.** stop bleeding and cover wounds.
- **d.** remove splinters that are not deep.

7. A person who is conscious
- **a.** is awake.
- **b.** seems to be asleep.
- **c.** needs to have water.
- **d.** does not need first aid in emergencies.

8. When a person is bleeding badly, it is best to try keeping the wound
- **a.** on the same level as the person's heart.
- **b.** lower than the person's heart.
- **c.** higher than the person's heart.
- **d.** bleeding as long as possible.

9. Cold water should not be used on a
- **a.** first-degree burn.
- **b.** second-degree burn.
- **c.** third-degree burn.
- **d.** burn of any kind.

10. If someone has swallowed poison, always
    a. call the poison control center or a doctor.
    b. make the person throw up.
    c. keep the person from throwing up.
    d. make the person eat something.

B. Number a sheet of paper from **1** through **10**. Write **true** or **false** next to the number for each of these ideas.

1. Knowing the limits of your own body can reduce the risk of accidents. true
2. It is safe to drive your bike on the same sidewalk with many pedestrians. false
3. Wearing helmets, gloves, and kneepads and elbow pads helps to make roller-skating and skateboarding safer. true
4. If you know how to swim, you are always safe in the water. false
5. People who do not know how to swim can still learn drownproofing. true
6. People who go on a one-day hike do not need to carry a backpack. false
7. Never give your name and address to someone who bothers you on the phone. true
8. Nobody knows where or when a tornado will touch the ground. true
9. Small children are safe around unused trunks or refrigerators as long as the lids and doors are closed. false
10. Puncture wounds do not always bleed. true

Write About Better Health

Write a short answer to each of these questions. Use complete sentences.

1. Why might someone who is tired or upset be less safety-minded than someone who is rested or relaxed?
2. What kind of preparations should a group make before going on a hike? Why are these preparations important?
3. Why does a family need to have an emergency fire-escape plan? What steps should be included in the plan?
4. What is the difference between a storm watch and a storm warning?
5. A family hears a weather report that tells about a hurricane moving toward their town. What should they do to prepare for this violent storm?
6. What would you do to help someone who has a wound that is bleeding badly?
7. Why is it important to try having the poison container in your hand when you call the poison control center after someone has taken poison?

Model answers to *Write About Better Health* are provided in the chapter notes at the front of this *Teacher's Edition.*

7 PREVENTING AND CONTROLLING DISEASE

The Mysterious European Plague

Not since the days of ancient Rome had the world known such a horrible disease. Now, in 1347, Europe was again in the grip of a mysterious, rapid spread of disease. People in the land that is today called Italy were dying by the thousands. The victims all showed the same *symptoms,* or signs, of the disease. Parts of their bodies swelled with *infection.* All had high fever and shivered with chills. Within 12 hours of their first symptoms, most were dead.

Doctors had given the disease a name. They called it *plague.* Most blamed hard times for the sickness. Many people were poor and getting too little to eat. This was part of the problem, but they could not know that the plague had really arrived aboard a spice ship from Asia. How could they dream that the disease was caused by invisible, living single-celled organisms called *bacteria*? The bacteria had been picked up by tiny fleas from rats on the ship. In turn, people bitten by the fleas were infected by the bacteria.

Within two years, the disease had spread from country to country, and even to the British Isles. By 1349, the deadly plague had killed more than a third of the people of Europe. Three centuries later, it would return to haunt the city of London.

Today the European killer is no longer a mystery. Doctors know the disease as *bubonic plague.* They know what the bacteria causing such diseases and plagues look like. Most important, they know how to keep these bacteria from ever causing another bubonic plague.

See the teaching notes on page 176.

The bubonic plague of the fourteenth century is the most dramatic example of a mass epidemic. It was called "Black Death," because extensive hemorrhages under the skin caused the skin to take on a blackish-purple hue. When the plague was at its worst, about 25 percent of the population of Europe died from it. (In this century, the influenza epidemic of 1917–18 actually caused more deaths worldwide. Because of the greater world population, the percentage of people killed was smaller.)

LOOKING AHEAD

Have you ever heard someone say, "I've never been sick a day in my life"? While this may not be exactly true, some people do seem to be ill less often than others. What is their secret?

Part of the reason some people stay healthier than others may be their *heredity.* They may have *inherited* certain healthful traits. However, most people who enjoy good health live in ways that help them *reduce their risk* of becoming ill. In this chapter, you will learn about different kinds of diseases that make people ill. You will also learn how everyone can reduce the risk of getting certain diseases. You will find out

- what causes many diseases and why some spread from person to person.
- some ways to help stop diseases from spreading.
- how some diseases can be prevented or controlled.
- what you can do to reduce the risk of becoming ill.

Here are some words that you may not have talked about in school before. You will learn more about them in this chapter. You can find all these words in the *Glossary* at the back of this book.

chronic (kron′ik)
communicable (kə·myü′nə·kə·bəl)
contagious (kən·tā′jəs)
disease (də·zēz′)
epidemic (ep′ə·dem′ik)
microbes (mī′krōbz)
noncommunicable (non′kə·myü′ nə·kə·bəl)

Early Checkup

Number a piece of paper from **1** through **8**. Answer each of these questions by writing **yes** or **no** next to the correct number on your paper. You can check your answers as you read this chapter.

1. Can diet, exercise, and rest help prevent some diseases? yes
2. Can cleanliness and proper washing stop the spread of some diseases? yes
3. Are some disease germs so small that they cannot be seen with an ordinary microscope? yes
4. If a disease is communicable, will you always catch it if you are near a person with that disease? no
5. Is it safe to drink water from a stream or lake that looks and smells clean? no
6. Is it safe to eat stuffing left inside a turkey after the turkey has been refrigerated? no
7. Are all diseases caused by disease germs? no
8. Are people whose parents have diabetes more likely to develop the disease than other people are? yes

Although the infectious agent for the plague was a bacterium carried by a flea that was carried by a rat, there is good reason to believe that the severity of the disease was attributable to poor diet resulting from the economic decline in the first half of the century. One of the themes of this chapter is that basic good health practices—diet, exercise, cleanliness, and rest—are our best defenses against disease. Therefore, in discussing the plague, you should point to poor diet as a determinant in the severity of the disease.

disease
microbes

Good Health Helps To Prevent Disease

A nutritious diet, low in fats and salt, reduces the risk of heart disease from *high blood pressure* and fat-clogged blood vessels. Regular exercise reduces the risk of heart and lung disease. It also helps reduce *stress*—emotional or physical strain that often leads to nervousness. People who are under stress for a long time are more likely to become ill than people who can rid themselves of stress. Rest and sleep help all parts of the body to grow in their own best way.

Here, disease is broken down into four major types: communicable (*microbe-based*), degenerative (*high-fat and salt diet, for example, over a long time*), environmental (*pollution, accidents*), and purely hereditary (*diseases like cystic fibrosis and sickle-cell anemia, for example*). These four types, however, do overlap. Degenerative diseases, for example, may be initiated by viruses or environmental conditions, and heredity undoubtedly plays a factor. The same is true of diseases such as the various forms of cancer, which are classified here as environmental. Some diseases that are purely hereditary, such as phenylketonuria (or PKU), a deficiency of a liver enzyme, can be cured by changing a baby's diet. Such a step is a change in the environment.

PREVENTING DISEASES

What Is Disease?

When any parts of the body are not working as they should, the body has a **disease**, or illness. Some diseases can be inherited. They are passed along from parents to their children. Some diseases are caused by a poorly balanced diet or problems in the *environment,* such as polluted water or air. Other diseases are caused by disease **microbes**. These are tiny bits of life, sometimes called *germs,* so small they can be seen only through a microscope. Parts of the body can also be hurt in accidents. In such cases, we talk about *injuries* rather than diseases, or illnesses.

There are so many kinds of disease that it is almost impossible to avoid them all. However, because so much is now known about what causes disease, there are many ways that people can reduce the risk of being ill.

Disease microbes can be kept from spreading when you cover your sneezes and coughs with a tissue. Eating balanced, *nutritious* meals and snacks and getting adequate exercise, rest, and sleep help the body stay strong enough to fight off many diseases. Being *immunized* against certain microbes helps keep people from getting the diseases they cause. Keeping the community's air and water clean helps prevent diseases of the digestive system and the lungs. People who do not smoke are helping to prevent lung and heart diseases. Following bicycle-safety and game-safety rules reduces the risk of injuries. These are a few ways people have learned to reduce risks to their health.

What was your answer to *Early Checkup* number 1? (Can diet, exercise, and rest help prevent some diseases?)

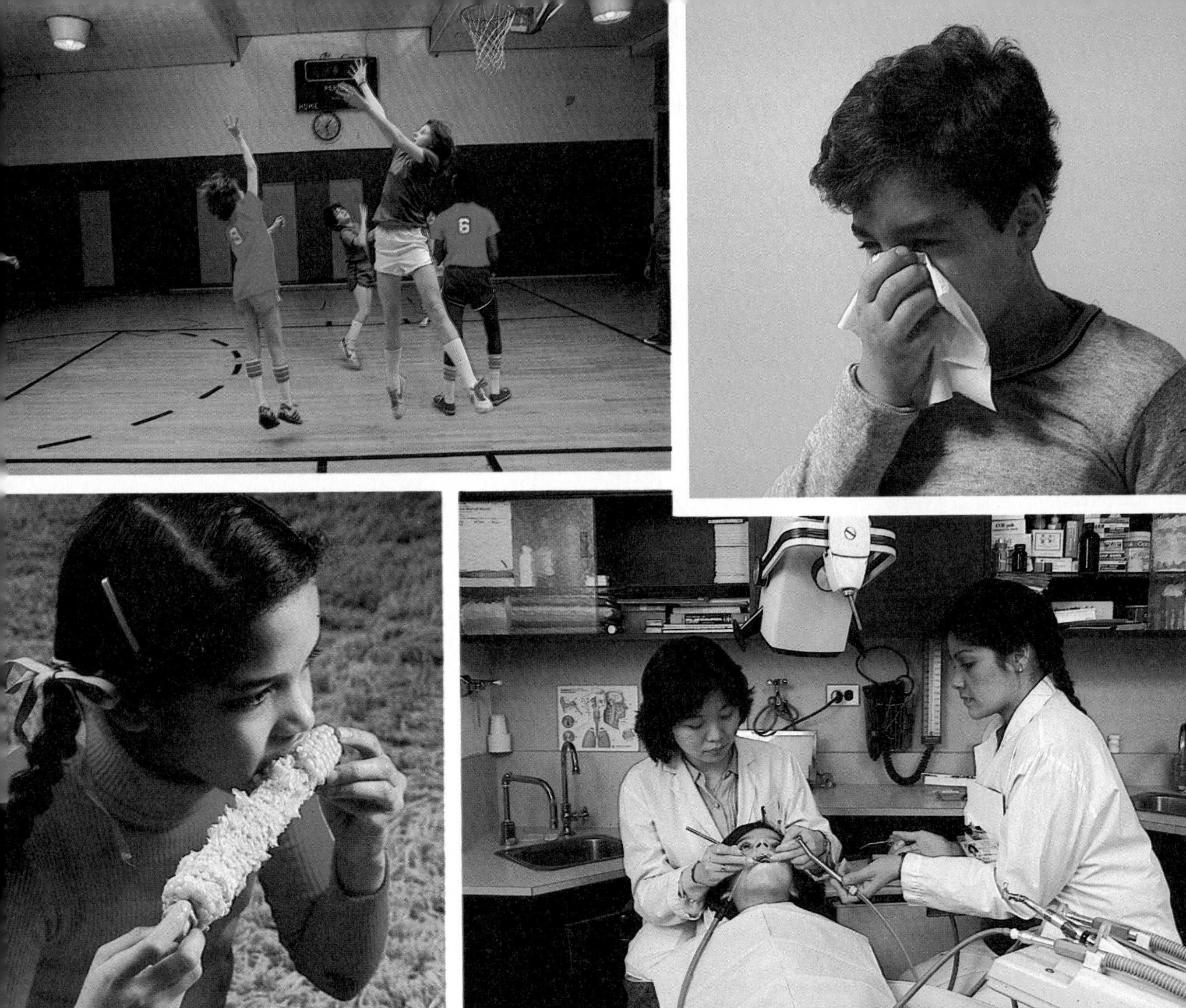

Is Reducing Disease Risks a New Idea?

Even before the nineteenth century, people were aware that certain diseases were communicable. They took various steps to combat these diseases, steps ranging from quarantine to burning corpses and contaminated bedclothes. Folk remedies often worked, even when the reasons given for the remedies were mistaken. Dairy farmers knew that once you had had cowpox, you would be immune to smallpox. In fact, it was from this folk knowledge that Edward Jenner got the idea that led to the smallpox vaccination.

Before the microscope was invented, people had no way of knowing that certain microbes caused some diseases. However, even then people tried to keep from becoming ill. For example, people in tropical areas found that a certain disease often struck those who lived near swamps. Many blamed the "bad air" around swamps for the disease. To reduce the risk of becoming ill, they closed their bedroom windows to keep out the "bad air." This did help to prevent the disease. Closing the windows worked for a reason they could not know. It helped keep the mosquitoes out. Certain mosquitoes carry microbes that cause the disease. Even today, people call the disease *malaria,* which means "bad air."

Even before people understood what caused some diseases, they learned to keep away from people who had certain illnesses. During times of plague, people tried to leave the more crowded cities to live in the country. They may not have understood why, but they knew that some diseases were spread from person to person. When no other reason could be found for a disease, some blamed "spirits" or the supernatural. Steambaths were used to sweat out the "evil spirits." Certain plants were used to drive them away. Some of these *remedies* did work, but not for the reasons people thought.

Many modern medicines are based on the natural drugs found in certain plants. Drug companies still study the plants used by ancient healers to discover new ways to cure disease. Many do not work at all, but some do. Today, for example, the periwinkle plant is used to make a cancer-fighting drug.

Discovery—A New Pathway to Health

By 1776, the time of the American Revolution, some scientists suspected that tiny "animals" caused certain diseases. They had seen some of the creatures through microscopes.

One hundred years later, in 1876, a young German doctor named Robert Koch found a way to test the "tiny animal" idea of disease. Koch's idea was that each creature is a different germ that can be recognized by its appearance under a microscope. If that kind of germ is found in the blood of people with the same disease, then that germ must cause the disease in a healthy person. To prove the idea, Dr. Koch would have to find just one kind of germ in animals with the same disease. He would then have to place that one kind of germ in the blood of a healthy animal.

No one had ever been able to grow a *pure culture* of germs. A pure culture is made up of just one kind of germ. Dr. Koch found a way, and he grew a pure culture of *anthrax* germs. Anthrax is a deadly disease that sick farm animals can pass on to people. By injecting healthy animals with his pure germ culture, Dr. Koch saw these animals become ill with anthrax. He had proved that certain microbes are the cause of certain diseases.

Koch went on to discover the microbes that cause *tuberculosis,* a lung disease, and *cholera,* a disease of the intestinal tract. He found a way to use anthrax germs to make a *vaccine* that immunizes cattle against the disease. He found a way to use live microbes to test for tuberculosis. Most important, Dr. Robert Koch proved an idea that would help people live healthier, longer lives. The idea is that *one kind of microbe causes one kind of disease.*

Traditional cures in prescientific societies often got good results with herbs such as foxglove (the source of digitalis). Because the body's natural antibodies were at work destroying germs, many folk cures *seemed* effective. Many patients got well even when nothing at all was done.

Toward the end of the seventeenth century, Anton van Leeuwenhoek became the first person to observe microbes through a microscope and report his discovery. Scores of years would pass before the relationship between microbes and disease began to be understood.

Stopping Diseases From Spreading

In 1847, Dr. Ignaz Semmelweis proved that diseases could be stopped from spreading in hospitals when floors, walls, beds, and instruments were washed with special chemicals. No one knew much about microbes at the time. At first, Dr. Semmelweis was thought to be a troublemaker for insisting that doctors clean their hands and instruments after treating each patient.

Doctors Have Learned To Prevent Some Diseases

Doctors were working to prevent disease even before Dr. Koch proved that microbes cause some diseases. Eighty years before, an English doctor named Edward Jenner had an idea that would wipe out one disease. In 1796, long before anyone knew that microbes can cause disease, Dr. Jenner made a *smallpox* vaccine.

Dr. Jenner wondered why people who had been ill with a less dangerous disease called *cowpox* never seemed to get smallpox. He knew nothing about microbes, but Dr. Jenner began injecting blood from people with cowpox into healthy people. When he later tried to infect these people with blood from people who had smallpox, he found they had become *immune* to the disease. Jenner called his discovery "vaccine," taken from a Latin word that means "from cows." Almost 200 years later, smallpox vaccine has helped doctors to wipe out the disease completely.

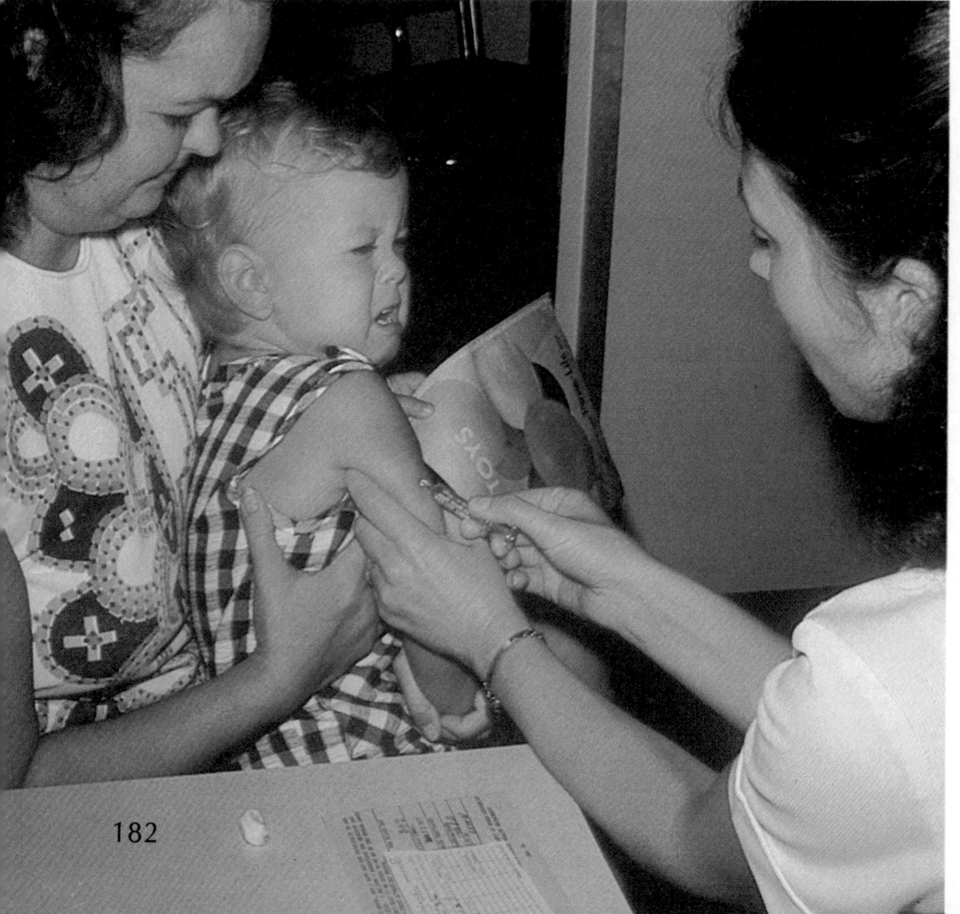

Fewer than 200 years after Jenner's discovery of smallpox vaccine, doctors also immunize people against such diseases as *polio, whooping cough, rubella* (*German measles*), *diphtheria, mumps,* and *tetanus*. The vaccines are made from weakened or dead disease microbes.

Jenner's work was successful where previous attempts had not been. Some people had tried to infect themselves with smallpox as a preventive measure. Some of them had serious cases of smallpox. Cowpox worked because it was a less virulent relative of the smallpox virus.

Students may not realize that smallpox was once one of the most feared diseases on earth. Not only did it frequently cause death, but it also left many victims who survived scarred for life. The eradication of smallpox is one of the major triumphs of medical history.

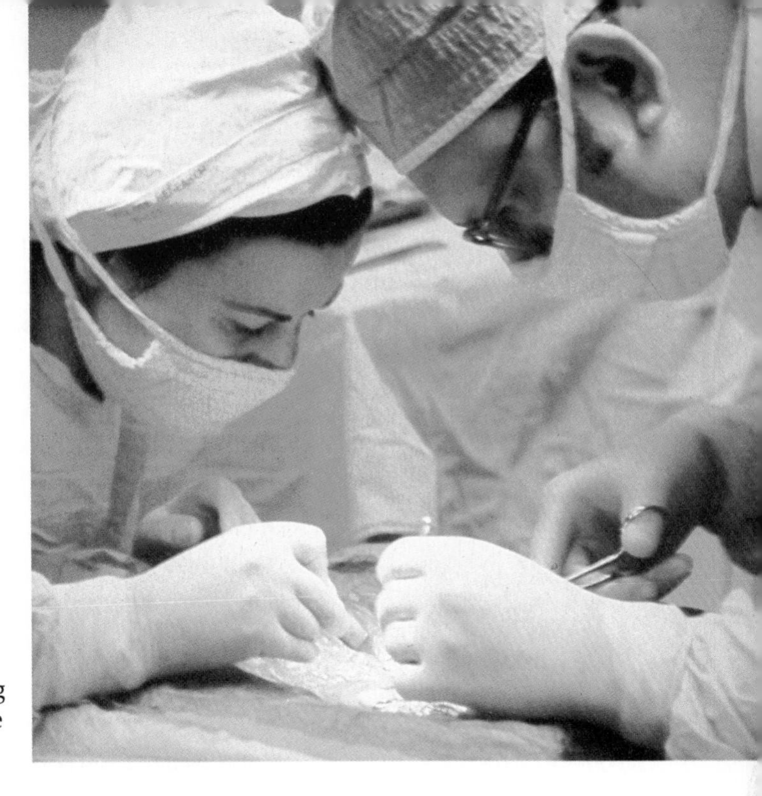

Dr. Joseph Lister, an English surgeon, showed doctors how clean operating rooms would prevent infections. It was in 1865, 11 years before Koch's work with germs. Today everything worn or used in a hospital operating room is *sterilized,* or made free of microbes.

What was your answer to *Early Checkup* number 2? (Can cleanliness and proper washing stop the spread of some diseases?)

What Have You Learned?

Number a piece of paper from **1** through **3**. Next to the numbers, write the words that are missing in these sentences.

1. If part of your body is not working as it should, you have an injury or a __.

2. Some diseases are __ by children from their parents. Other diseases can be caused by __ of the air or water. Still other diseases come from eating too few __ foods. A great many diseases are caused by __, which are invisible without a microscope.

3. The idea that some diseases are caused by germs was proved by __. He later found a way to use disease-causing germs to make a __, which provided immunity to the disease.

Answers to *What Have You Learned?*
1. disease (illness)
2. inherited; pollution; nutritious (healthful, balanced); microbes
3. Robert Koch; vaccine

communicable
contagious

Bacteria were once classified as plants because bacteria seem to share certain structural features with plant cells. For a while, later on, bacteria were considered to be *protists,* members of a biological kingdom different from the plant and animal kingdoms. Today, however, most biologists prefer to include bacteria in either the *prokaryote* or *monera* kingdoms.

Viruses are sometimes considered to be nonliving because they show no signs of life whatsoever unless they are inside a living cell. Today, however, research in genetics suggests that the essence of life is possession of DNA or RNA (nucleic acids), in which case viruses can be considered to be living.

Fungi are plantlike, but lack chlorophyll. This means they cannot use the energy of sunlight to produce food as green plants do. Fungi are either parasites or live on decaying matter.

COMMUNICABLE DISEASES

Microbes Cause Communicable Diseases

Many diseases caused by microbes are **communicable** diseases. That means the diseases can be spread by animal bites, by spoiled food and water, or by anything else carrying the disease microbes. Many communicable diseases are also **contagious**. Contagious diseases can be passed from one person to another.

Bacteria are one type of microbe. They are almost everywhere—in the air, the soil, foods, water, and on and in your body. Most kinds of bacteria do not cause harm. Many kinds are needed for people to live. However, the first disease-causing microbes ever discovered were bacteria. Some of the diseases caused by bacteria are anthrax, cholera, tuberculosis, certain *food poisoning,* and diphtheria.

Viruses are microbes much smaller than bacteria. While most bacteria can be seen with an ordinary microscope, viruses cannot. A special *electron microscope* must be used to see them. Where there is warmth, food, and water, bacteria *cells* grow and produce new cells. However, viruses produce more of their own kind only when they are inside the cells of living creatures. Scientists believe that just about all the known viruses cause diseases such as the common cold, the flu, smallpox, and *yellow fever.*

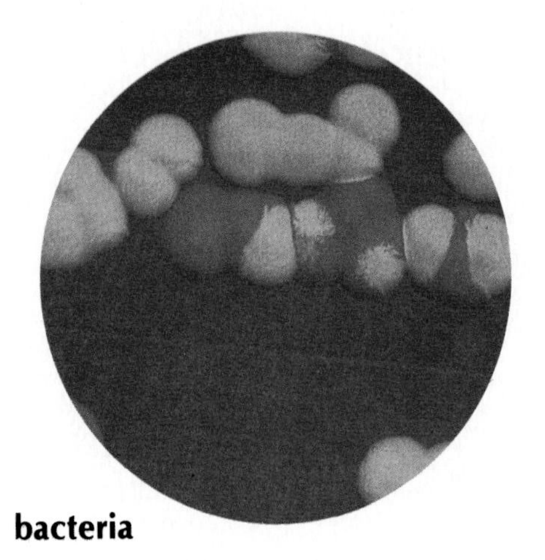

bacteria

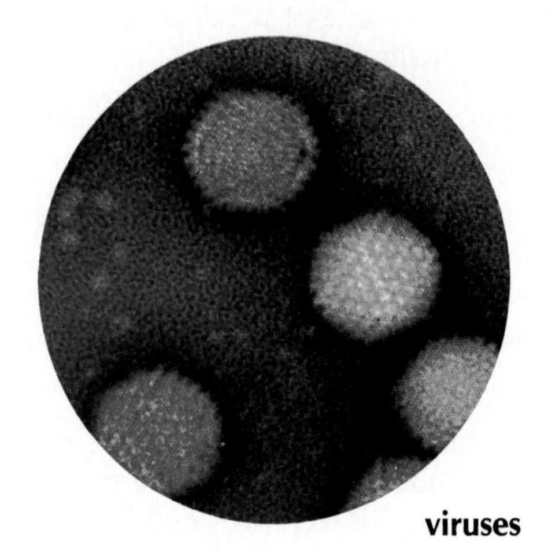

viruses

What was your answer to *Early Checkup* number 3? (Are some disease germs so small that they cannot be seen with an ordinary microscope?)

Fungi act in some ways like plants and are made up of one cell or many cells. Among the many-celled fungi are mushrooms and the molds you can see on some cheeses. Among the single-celled fungi are *yeasts*. Some of these fungi cause infections and diseases, such as *athlete's foot* and *ringworm*.

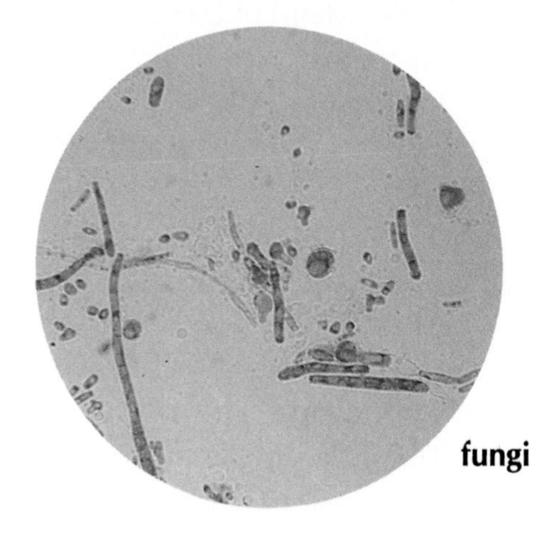

fungi

A *protozoan* is a small animal, such as the *amoeba*. Many protozoans live in water. Some cause health problems like *dysentery,* a disease of the digestive system, and certain *respiratory infections.*

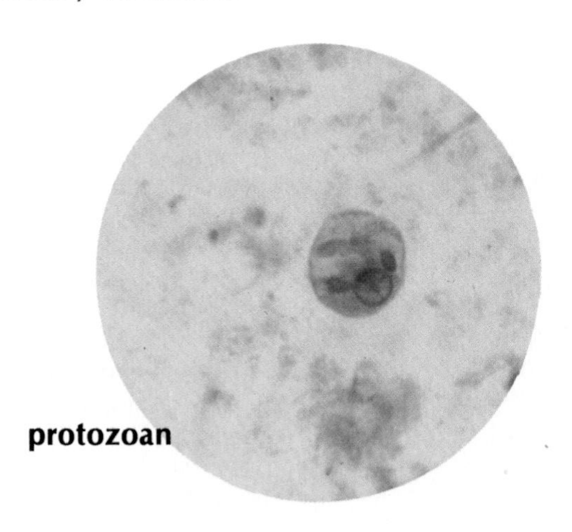

protozoan

Students have probably heard of "bacteria," "viruses," and "fungi" (the plural of "fungus"), but the word "protozoan" may be totally new to them. Even if the other words are familiar, the meaning of the words is unlikely to be. In fact, our knowledge of microbes has grown so fast in the past few years that it is hard to keep up with the latest interpretation of these tiny living things. (NOTE: The word "microorganisms" is often used instead of "microbes." Both words have the same meaning.)

Protozoans are single-celled animals. Unlike bacteria, protozoans have nuclei and considerable internal and external structure. In addition to amoebic dysentery, protozoans are responsible for the communicable but not contagious diseases of sleeping sickness and malaria.

Ask the class why only diseases caused by living things spread from one person to another (except certain viruses and the special case of hereditary diseases "spreading" from parent to child). Students should recognize that only living things *reproduce*. A small number of bacteria or other microbes can increase to millions of times their number, causing disease wherever they find a home in a living cell that offers them warmth, food, and water. Your class should be able to understand that refrigeration, which deprives food bacteria of warmth, helps keep food from spoiling.

epidemic

Other diseases that have animal vectors (carriers) of one kind or another include *brucellosis* (also known as *undulant fever,* carried by cattle, goats, and sheep), *dengue* (mosquitoes), *filariasis* (various insects), *malaria* (mosquitoes), *psittacosis* (also known as *parrot fever,* carried by birds), *rickettsial* disease (fleas, lice, and ticks), *schistosomiasis* (also known as *snail fever,* carried by snails), and *typhus* (lice).

Some Diseases Are Spread by Animals

This chapter began with the story of an **epidemic**. An epidemic is the quick spreading of a disease to large numbers of people. A microbe causes the disease, but the microbe is not spread from person to person. Bubonic plague is a disease that is passed on to people by animals. Rats become infected by the microbe. Fleas bite the rats and then pass on the disease microbes to people by biting them. There are many communicable diseases that sick people do not spread to other people. Many of these diseases are spread among people by animals.

What was your answer to *Early Checkup* number 4? (If a disease is communicable, will you always catch it if you are near a person with that disease?)

Certain animals, such as bats and dogs, may carry a disease called *rabies.* Only people bitten by animals carrying rabies will get rabies. These people will not pass the disease on to other people. The disease microbes that cause communicable diseases such as rabies, malaria, *typhus,* and bubonic plague are spread by the bites of animals, or their *saliva,* and by insect bites.

Once doctors had learned that some diseases are caused by microbes, it was possible to trace many communicable diseases to microbes in *ticks,* flies, snails, and mosquitoes.

Ticks are small relatives of spiders and usually live in woods or brush. They bite people to feed on blood. Ticks carry such diseases as *Colorado tick fever, relapsing fever, Rocky Mountain spotted fever,* and *tularemia.*

Discovery—A New Pathway to Health

Yellow fever is a disease that attacks the liver, kidneys, and digestive system. Its victims run a high fever and their skin takes on a yellow color. During epidemics, between 50 and 90 percent of people infected with yellow fever died. The disease is caused by a virus. People who survive yellow fever become immune to it and never get it again.

By 1881, yellow fever had caused epidemics that reached the tropical areas of Africa, many areas of South America, Cuba, and as far north as New Orleans, Louisiana. Doctors were puzzled about how the disease was spread. Often the family of a yellow fever victim would not come down with the disease at all. Somehow it was a communicable disease, but it did not seem to be contagious. Doctors tested the blood of people who had yellow fever. No bacteria that caused the disease could be found. Of course, what doctors of the time could not know is that the microbe that causes yellow fever is a virus. Their microscopes could not show them microbes so small.

Walter Reed also worked out in detail the transmission of typhoid fever.

A Cuban doctor, Carlos Juan Finlay, suggested that yellow fever might be reaching people by way of mosquito bites. In 1900, the U.S. Army put together a medical team to find the cause of the disease. The head of this medical group, Major Walter Reed, tested Dr. Finlay's idea that mosquito bites were the cause. He also tested the idea that yellow fever might be spread by the clothing or bedclothes of people with the disease. Some volunteers allowed themselves to be bitten by mosquitoes that had already bitten victims of the disease. Other volunteers wore clothing and slept in bedclothes taken from people with yellow fever.

The people bitten by mosquitoes came down with yellow fever. The others did not. One of the volunteers, an army doctor, died of the disease. Major Reed had proven Dr. Finlay's idea. He ordered programs to get rid of the mosquitoes. Yellow fever epidemics could be prevented. Today a vaccine is used to immunize people against yellow fever.

Some Diseases Are Spread by Water

Making Water Safe To Drink

Many campers and hikers buy special kits that make water safe to drink. They use the kits to filter the water and to destroy chemically any microbes that might get through the filter.

If you camp or hike, you know that you need to carry water even when you are going to be near a stream or lake. On long trips, campers either boil water drawn from nearby ground sources or treat it with chemicals before they drink it. Water, even when it looks clear and smells clean, may contain microbes that can harm people.

What was your answer to *Early Checkup* number 5? (Is it safe to drink water from a stream or lake that looks and smells clean?)

In this chapter, we have emphasized prevention of disease rather than symptoms. If students ask about the symptoms of some diseases mentioned, here is a partial list. Emphasize that only a doctor should ever diagnose any disease people suspect they may have and that many different diseases may cause similar symptoms.
BOTULISM: impairment of vision, speech, ability to swallow and breathe
CHICKEN POX: fever and skin blisters
CHOLERA: dehydration due to diarrhea and vomiting
COLORADO TICK FEVER: fever and chills
DYSENTERY: diarrhea and vomiting
HEPATITIS: fever, fatigue, and yellow skin
MALARIA: chills and fever
PLAGUE: swollen lymph glands, chills, fever, bleeding
RABIES: fever, fits
SMALLPOX: fever, rashes, vomiting
TUBERCULOSIS: fever, fatigue, coughing of blood
TYPHOID: headaches, fever, coughing, pink spots on body
YELLOW FEVER: fever, headaches, vomiting

Disease bacteria, such as those that cause *typhoid* or cholera, are often spread through drinking water. Harmful protozoans, such as the amoebas that cause a form of dysentery, also are spread by way of water. Microbes that cause disease often get into the water from human wastes. For this reason, *sewage*—the waste water from people's homes—is chemically treated before the water is returned to streams or lakes. Sewage that has not been treated nearly always carries disease germs.

Many scientists believe that sewage treatment can save even more lives than immunization programs. For example, the virus that causes one form of *hepatitis* may be carried in sewage water. If the sewage is not treated—that is, if the living bacteria are not killed—the hepatitis virus can thrive in the bacteria cells. Hepatitis is a disease of the liver that often causes the skin to turn yellow. The form of hepatitis that is spread by untreated water is also contagious. This means it can be spread directly from person to person.

In some less well-developed communities of Asia, Africa, and South America, people dump sewage in the same river from which they draw water for bathing and drinking. This often causes local epidemics of cholera and dysentery.

Why would swimming or fishing in polluted waters be a disease risk to people?

Typhoid, scarlet fever, and other diseases can also be spread by food. These diseases, however, are controlled primarily by local health departments, which try to keep people who have mild (or serious, for that matter) cases of the diseases from handling food. The emphasis in this book is on the diseases and practices that are more of an individual's responsibility: hepatitis, salmonellosis (food poisoning), and botulism, as well as swimming in waters with a high bacteria count or with known protozoans of disease-causing varieties. While protozoans normally do not cause disease, some protozoans in heavily polluted waters can cause fatal meningitis (inflammation of the covering of the brain).

Some Diseases Are Spread by Food

Water can become polluted when it contains untreated sewage. Harmful microbes can spread from the polluted water to the animals that live in it. For example, clams and oysters pick up small particles of sewage from the water. The sewage may contain the hepatitis virus. The virus remains and increases in the living cells of the clam's or oyster's body. People who finally eat these shellfish can develop hepatitis. The clams or oysters carrying the hepatitis virus look and taste just like clams and oysters that come from pure waters. Often animals carrying microbes that cause harm to people are not themselves made ill by these microbes.

Bacteria in food sometimes cause the food to spoil. It may begin to taste, smell, or look different. However, many harmful bacteria multiply in food without changing its appearance. People who eat such food can get food poisoning.

As a rule, foods that are moist and not kept cold can be poisoned by microbes. Bacteria multiply much more slowly at very low and very high temperatures. This is why meats are cooked at high temperatures and stored at low temperatures. When a turkey is cooked, the stuffing should be cooked separately. When the leftover turkey is refrigerated, the stuffing should be cooled separately. The turkey body is thick. It may keep a stuffing inside it from getting hot enough in cooking or cool enough in the refrigerator to slow the growth of bacteria. It is best not to eat stuffing that has been left inside a refrigerated turkey.

What was your answer to *Early Checkup* number 6? (Is it safe to eat stuffing left inside a turkey after the turkey has been refrigerated?)

Moist salads, such as chicken, tuna, potato, and egg salads, should always be stored in a refrigerator. They should never be eaten if they have been left in a warm place for too long.

Botulism is an extremely serious kind of food poisoning. It is caused by a poison that certain bacteria produce in improperly preserved or canned foods and in poorly sealed food containers. Bacteria that cause botulism produce a gas as they act upon food in the can. This gas may make the can bulge at the ends. Bulging cans should be reported to store managers right away. An early sign of botulism is double vision. Immediate treatment by a doctor is vital, since botulism can result in death.

Other Diseases Spread by Foods

Microbes do not cause all the diseases spread by foods. For example, certain harmful *worms* sometimes live in the bodies of animals. They are passed on to people unless the food has been well cooked. Pork, beef, and fish that have not been cooked enough can infect people with *tapeworms.* Pork that has not been cooked enough may carry the worm that causes a disease called *trichinosis.*

Discovery—A New Pathway to Health

A French scientist and doctor named Louis Pasteur discovered in 1862 that different harmless bacteria play important roles in making cheese and other foods. Pasteur's work with bacteria came long before Koch discovered that they cause certain diseases. Pasteur also discovered that certain harmful bacteria cause foods to spoil and rot. In fact, Dr. Joseph Lister used Pasteur's discoveries to show how surgeons once unknowingly helped to spread disease through unsterilized surgical instruments and clothing.

Pasteur was the first to try killing bacteria by slowly heating them without boiling. Pasteur wanted to find a way to kill harmful microbes in liquids like milk without ruining the flavor through boiling. Today almost all the milk sold in stores is *pasteurized.* It has been heated at a temperature lower than its boiling point but for a long enough time to kill harmful bacteria. This heating helps to reduce the risk of disease. Unpasteurized milk can carry diseases such as tuberculosis, *brucellosis,* and typhoid.

The Speed of a Sneeze

Germ-carrying droplets from a sneeze can travel 103 miles per hour.

Other diseases that are spread through the air in tiny droplets of water include diphtheria, German measles, mumps, (probably) polio, scarlet fever, tuberculosis, and whooping cough. (Smallpox would also be in the list if it still occurred.) Because of effective vaccines or treatments, these diseases are no longer common in the United States—although German measles (rubella) and mumps may occur in a community from time to time. Pinworms, unlike most worms that can affect people, are also airborne.

Some Diseases Are Spread Through the Air

Each time people *exhale,* or breathe out, they release tiny drops of water into the air. You can see these tiny drops by breathing on the cool surface of a mirror. A cough or sneeze lets out even more of these drops. People who are carrying microbes that cause colds and flu expose others to these infections. The viruses causing the infections travel through the air in the droplets exhaled by these people.

Some diseases, such as *chicken pox,* are contagious before any symptoms of the disease appear. Chicken pox microbes are often spread through the air. After the rash appears, a person with chicken pox spreads it by touching others or by touching objects also being used by others.

Diseases and infections that are spread through the air often travel quickly. Vaccines can protect people from diseases like the *measles.* However, no vaccines have yet been discovered for colds. Vaccines for flu are not always effective. When you have one of these diseases or infections, you also have the responsibility to try to stop it from spreading any further. What steps can you take to reduce the risk of spreading these diseases or infections?

On Your Own

Find out how close to the mirror you need to be to cause a fog to form when you exhale. The fog is caused by the droplets in your breath. Now cough a little bit. Do you have to be as close to get droplets on the mirror? Actually, the droplets from a cough or sneeze travel much farther than the mirror test will show. You can detect the droplets a little better if the mirror is cool.

The tiny droplets of water can be seen on a mirror even when breath cannot be detected in any other way. That is why mirrors are sometimes used to check the breathing of a person who is unconscious.

What Have You Learned?

Number a piece of paper from **1** through **5**. Next to the numbers, write the words that are missing in these sentences.

1. Until the __ was invented, doctors could not see __ or understand their role in causing certain diseases.

2. __ are disease microbes so small that they can be seen only with an electron microscope.

3. Yellow fever, malaria, rabies, and plague are caused by microbes spread to people by __. Yellow fever and malaria come from the bite of certain __, while some bat and dog bites spread a disease called __.

4. Any disease that can be spread to people is called a __ disease. If people do the spreading, it is __.

5. The method of killing bacteria by heating food to a temperature lower than the boiling point was invented by __.

Answers to *What Have You Learned?*
1. microscope; microbes
2. Viruses
3. animals; mosquitoes (insects); rabies
4. communicable; contagious
5. Louis Pasteur

chronic
noncommunicable

NONCOMMUNICABLE DISEASES

Some Diseases Are Not Spread by Microbes

You know that not all diseases are caused by microbes, so not all diseases are communicable. Less developed countries of the world are still troubled by epidemics from time to time. However, in more developed countries, such as Japan, Canada, the United States, and many European nations, people are having more serious problems with **noncommunicable** diseases. These are diseases that are not known to be spread by microbes.

Is a Microbe Really Responsible?

Some scientists are doing research to find out if many noncommunicable diseases actually may be started by viruses. Among these diseases or disorders are arthritis, *asthma,* cancer, diabetes, heart disease, *multiple sclerosis,* and *Parkinson's disease.*

Diseases such as *arthritis, diabetes, cancer, heart disease,* and certain diseases present from birth are noncommunicable. Some are inherited, while others happen for reasons not yet known. Some are caused by problems in the environment or by the unhealthful diets of people. Pregnant women who do not eat well-balanced meals, or who smoke or abuse other drugs, may cause health problems for the babies developing in their bodies.

What was your answer to *Early Checkup* number 7? (Are all diseases caused by disease germs?)

As noted also for communicable diseases earlier in this chapter, noncommunicable diseases often have degenerative, environmental, and hereditary components. Many may also be initiated or even directly caused by viruses. In no case, however, is it suspected that any of these diseases is ordinarily contagious. Children should be aware of this, as they are apt to think all disease is contagious and to worry about catching diseases from relatives when such worry is unwarranted.

Certain noncommunicable diseases are **chronic**. They will last a person's whole life because they cannot be *cured.* For example, arthritis and diabetes can be controlled by medicine. They cannot be cured. Most high blood pressure can be controlled by removing salt from a person's diet, staying at a normal weight, and getting enough exercise. There are also drugs to control high blood pressure. People who lower their risk of high blood pressure also lower their risk of heart disease. Even people whose families pass along *traits* for these diseases can help to lower their own risk through careful diet and regular exercise.

Cancer is a disease in which cells in one part of the body change and multiply wildly. While what causes cancer is still not known exactly, new treatments for certain kinds of cancer are working well.

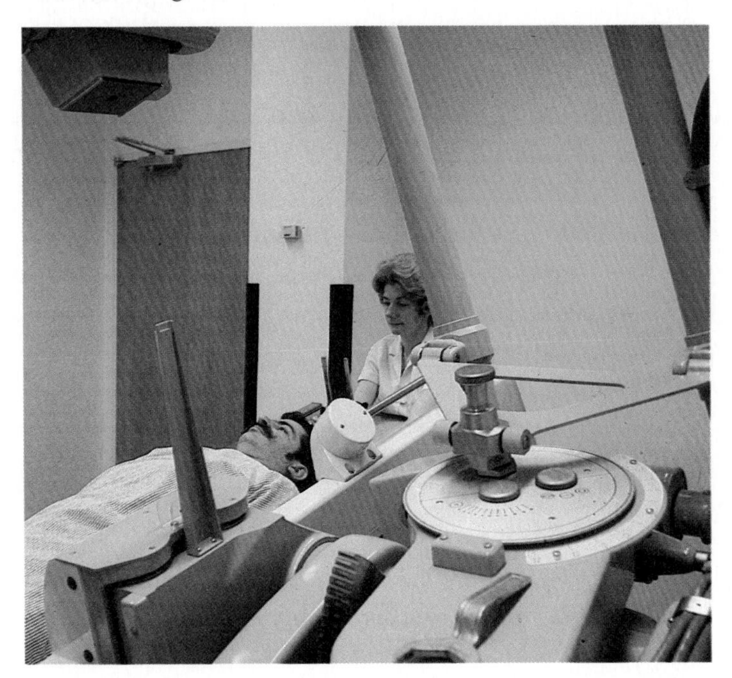

Certain cancers are treated with machines that aim *X-rays* at the cancer cells. The rays destroy the cancer cells, but few of the healthy cells around them.

People Working for Your Health

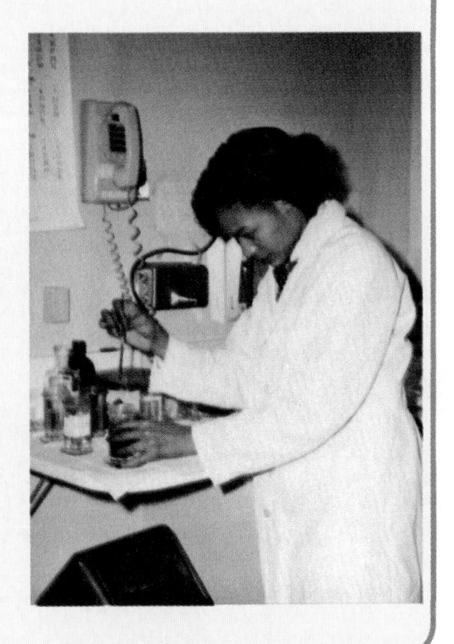

Ms. Kathy Threats is an assistant *lab technician* in a *histology* lab. Histology is the study of tissues. Ms. Threats prepares samples of tissue, taken from people who have skin cancer, for doctors to examine. After the tissue is removed in surgery, Ms. Threats cuts it into small pieces and freezes it in a special machine. Then Ms. Threats slices the tissue thinly and places it on microscope slides. After the slides have been prepared, a doctor examines the tissue under a microscope to see if any more cancer cells are present in the sample. Ms. Threats keeps records on each patient who has had surgery.

Ms. Threats has a college degree in *biological sciences.* In college Ms. Threats enjoyed her lab classes best. She likes to prepare the microscope slides. "It's very interesting," she says. "No two slides are alike. Every person's body is different."

How To Spot Diabetes

There are some early symptoms of diabetes everyone should know. Being thirsty all through the day, urinating often, and generally feeling tired may be diabetic symptoms. A doctor can quickly test the blood and urine to check for diabetes. People who suspect they may have it should consult a doctor who can perform these tests for diabetes. They should *never* try to perform tests for it on themselves. A doctor is trained to discover and treat this disease.

Diabetes Can Be Controlled

If you or someone in your family has diabetes, you know it is a noncommunicable disease. Diabetes seems to be an inherited disease. A person whose parent or grandparent has diabetes is often likely to get the disease. More than half of the people who have diabetes do not know they have it. This is because diabetes often begins with few symptoms. There is no cure for diabetes, but it can be controlled under a doctor's care. Sometimes people whose families have diabetes can reduce their own risk of having the disease. A well-balanced diet, an avoidance of foods with added sugar, and a regular exercise program can be very helpful in preventing diabetes.

What was your answer to *Early Checkup* number 8? (Are people whose parents have diabetes more likely to develop the disease than other people are?)

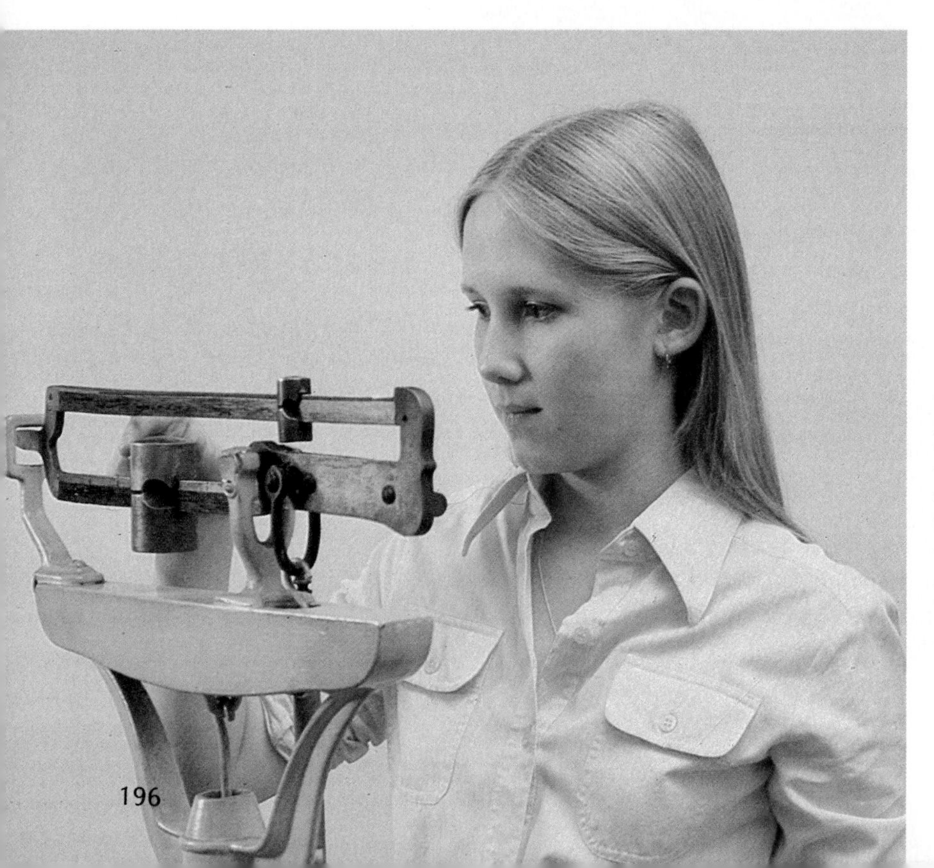

The best way to reduce the risk of diabetes is to avoid becoming overweight. Many doctors believe that a diet low in sugars and fats is especially helpful. Regular exercise helps move blood sugar into the muscle cells. This reduces the need for insulin in the blood.

No one knows exactly what causes diabetes, but somehow the body is not able to use the sugars and other *carbohydrates* from foods for energy. The *hormone,* or body chemical, that changes sugar to energy is called *insulin.* The body's insulin is made by certain cells in an organ called the *pancreas.* In a person with diabetes, these cells—*islets of Langerhans*—make too little insulin. Some people with diabetes daily take insulin that comes from animal glands. This extra insulin in the blood, along with proper diet and regular exercise, helps them change sugars to energy so that too much sugar does not remain in the blood. Other people control diabetes through careful diets or medicine other than insulin.

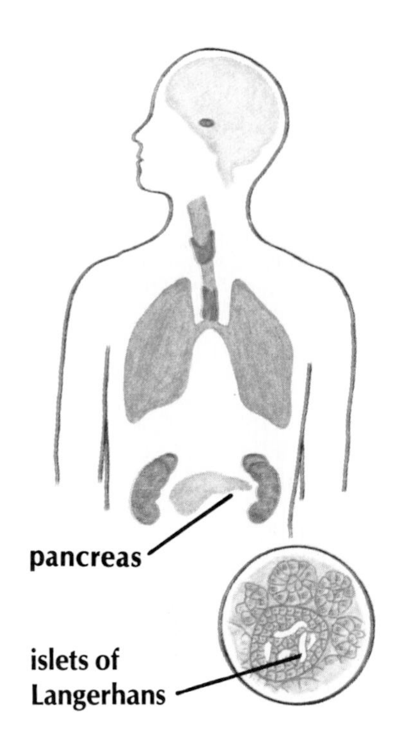

When there is too much or too little sugar in the blood, the body does not work properly. This can cause loss of consciousness. When a diabetic has too little insulin, the blood sugar gets too high. When too much insulin is taken, the blood sugar gets too low. Taking too much insulin can produce *insulin shock*, which can also lead to unconsciousness. In either case, prompt medical attention is required.

Discovery —A New Pathway to Health

Nobody understood what caused diabetes until 1921. In that year, two Canadian doctors, Drs. Frederick Grant Banting and Charles Herbert Best, under the direction of Dr. John James Rickard Macleod, discovered insulin. Drs. Banting and Macleod shared a Nobel prize in 1923 for their work. The discovery of insulin and its role enables doctors to treat diabetes successfully. People can now control their diabetes with insulin injections or oral medication. They can lead long, close-to-normal, healthy lives.

Frederick Banting

John Macleod

Heart disease is a noncommunicable disease. It can, however, be caused by communicable diseases in some instances. In particular, a throat infection caused by streptococci (strep throat) can lead to heart disease. So can advanced syphilis. Students who have severe sore throats should be checked by a doctor or nurse.

Heart Disease Is Our Number One Killer

Heart disease is the greatest health risk for most people. No one knows exactly how different diseases of the heart and *blood vessels* begin. However, doctors agree that eating nutritious, well-balanced meals and avoiding salt, fats, and added sugar help to reduce a person's risk of these dangerous diseases. Other important ways to reduce the risk of heart disease are to avoid smoking and to keep exercising vigorously on a regular basis.

A diet high in fats, especially animal fats, is connected with heart disease. Fats, especially *cholesterol,* are deposited in the blood vessel walls. These deposits can slowly build up and block blood flow in the blood vessels. If the amount of blood reaching the heart is reduced or stopped, the heart can become damaged.

In cigarettes, *nicotine* makes the heart beat faster and raises blood pressure. The gas *carbon monoxide* in cigarette smoke reduces the ability of the blood to carry oxygen.

What Have You Learned?

Number a piece of paper from **1** through **3**. Next to the numbers, write the words that are missing in these sentences.

1. One way to lower the risk of high blood pressure is to get rid of ___ in the diet.

2. Diabetes can be controlled by injecting ___.

3. A diet low in ___ may help prevent heart disease.

Answers to *What Have You Learned?*

1. salt
2. insulin
3. fat(s) (animal fats)

Learn More About It

Here are three books you may want to read. They tell about old and new discoveries for fighting disease.

Epstein, Sam, and Epstein, Beryl. *Secret in a Sealed Bottle: Lazzaro Spallanzani's Work With Microbes.* New York: Coward, McCann & Geoghegan, Inc., 1979. Read about the eighteenth-century discovery made by scientist Lazzaro Spallanzani that prepared the way for the future work of Louis Pasteur and others in their study of microbes.

Graham, Ada, and Graham, Frank. *Three Million Mice: A Story of Modern Medical Research.* New York: Charles Scribner's Sons, 1981. Learn about the scientists who study hereditary diseases and about the research animals that help them solve the mysteries of these diseases.

Silverstein, Dr. Alvin, and Silverstein, Virginia B. *The Sugar Disease: Diabetes.* Philadelphia, Pa.: J.B. Lippincott Co., 1980. This book will tell you about diabetes: its causes, the effect it has on the body, and its past and present treatment.

More To Do on Your Own

1. Choose one of the pioneers of the fight against disease who was *not* mentioned in this chapter, and prepare an oral report for the class. You can choose from such names as Christiaan Barnard, Clara Barton, Daniele Bovet, Alexis Carrel, Michael DeBakey, Paul Ehrlich, Sir Alexander Fleming, Galen, William Gorgas, Hippocrates, Charles Laveran, Anton van Leeuwenhoek, Élie Metchnikoff, Albert Sabin, Jonas Salk, and August von Wassermann.
2. The microbes that are spread by animals often have very complex life stories. Find out the life story of either the protozoan that causes malaria or the worm that causes *schistosomiasis.* Make a poster showing this life story.
3. Some people are born blind either because blindness is a trait they inherit from one or both parents or because of a disease the mother may have had before they are born. Today there is some hope that such people can be helped to see because of modern electronic devices that work directly on the nerves. Use the *Readers' Guide to Periodical Literature* in a library to find out about these new devices. Bring the article or a copy of it to show to the class.
4. Write a report on how you can prevent disease at home and at school.

Final Checkup

A. Number a sheet of paper from **1** through **10**. Write **true** or **false** next to the number for each of these ideas.

1. Some people are more likely to have certain diseases than other people are. true

2. Malaria is caused by bad air. false

3. At least one serious disease can no longer be found anywhere on earth. true

4. All dangerous diseases are caused by microbes. false

5. You can get yellow fever from the clothing of a person who has the disease. false

6. Untreated sewage usually contains microbes that can cause disease. true

7. You can tell if some food or water will make you sick by the way it looks or smells. false

8. A disease can be contagious before any signs of the illness appear. true

9. Nothing can be done to prevent or control diseases that are not caused by microbes. false

10. While cigarette smoking is bad for your lungs, it does not cause any other kind of harm. false

B. Number a sheet of paper from **1** through **10**. Next to each number, write the letter of the words that best complete each sentence.

1. A disease or illness occurs when
a. microbes are on the body.
(b.) a part of the body is not working as it should.
c. you are near a person who has some disease.
d. there are microbes in parts of the body.

2. Robert Koch showed that
(a.) some diseases are caused by certain microbes.
b. microbes cause all diseases.
c. proper washing can prevent the spread of microbes.
d. different microbes can cause a single disease.

3. Joseph Lister developed
a. the use of a vaccine to prevent smallpox.
b. a way to prevent anthrax.
(c.) ways to perform surgery that lowered the risk of disease.
d. all of the above.

4. One disease or disorder that can be caused by a protozoan is
a. cholera.
b. athlete's foot.
(c.) a form of dysentery.
d. botulism.

5. To reduce the risk of disease, scientists have
a. destroyed certain mosquitoes.
b. developed vaccines.
c. volunteered for medical experiments.
(d.) all of the above.

6. Typhoid, cholera, and hepatitis can be spread by
   a. water.
   b. air.
   c. animals.
   d. all of the above.

7. People can reduce the risk of botulism by
   a. filtering and treating drinking water.
   b. checking the appearance of foods.
   c. checking the appearance and condition of food cans and containers.
   d. refrigerating leftover foods.

8. Contagious diseases are
   a. also communicable.
   b. spread by animals.
   c. spread by water.
   d. spread by food.

9. The risk of some noncommunicable disease can be reduced by
   a. sterilizing hospital equipment.
   b. healthful eating, exercising, and not smoking.
   c. developing new vaccines.
   d. finding better ways to get rid of rats and mosquitoes.

10. The risk of getting diabetes is reduced by
   a. vaccination.
   b. checking the family history.
   c. maintaining a normal body weight.
   d. using insulin.

Write About Better Health

Write a short answer to each of these questions. Use complete sentences.

1. What are four ways that you can reduce your risk of getting a disease?
2. What are four different ways that people get communicable diseases? Name four ways people get noncommunicable diseases.
3. How can you show that a particular microbe is the cause of a disease?
4. What are four ways that disease can get from one person to another?
5. What are three typical features of noncommunicable diseases?

Model answers to *Write About Better Health* are provided in the chapter notes at the front of this *Teacher's Edition*.

CITY
AUTO
PARK

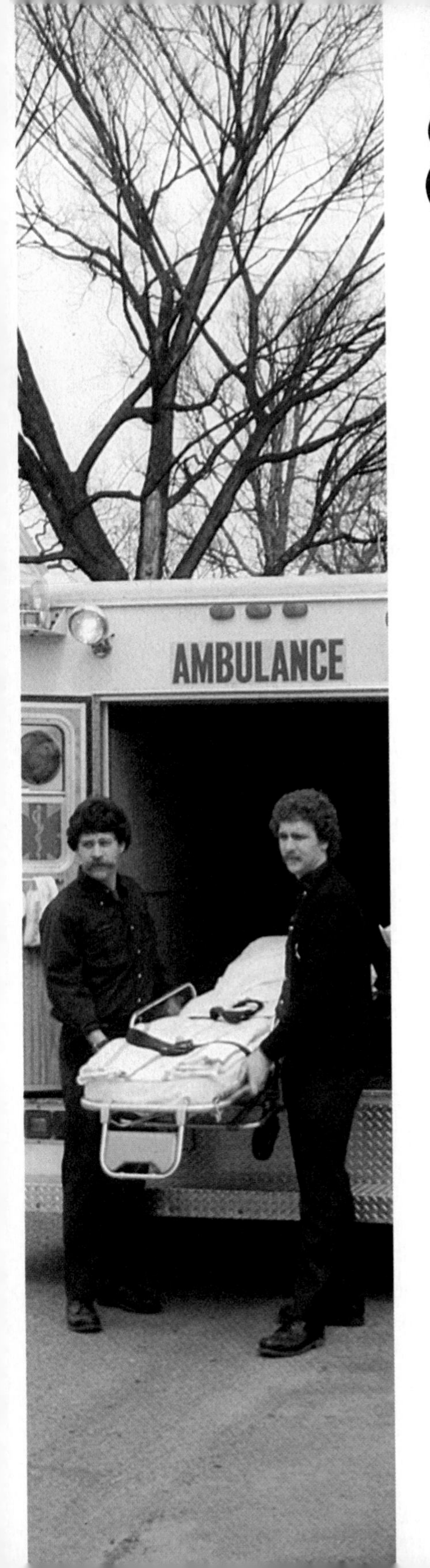

8 COMMUNITY ACTION FOR HEALTH AND SAFETY

This chapter deals with the concept of *risk reduction* as the major health goal of all community health services. Public health agencies and water and sanitation departments aim to minimize the risk of disease within the community. Police, fire, safety, traffic, and park departments aim to reduce the risk of accidental injuries. Discuss with students how a plan for risk reduction can help the population of a community to stay healthy.

The purpose of this introduction is to provide each student with a broader perspective from which the many modern health and safety services in the community can be identified, understood, appreciated, measured, and, above all, *intelligently used* by the greatest number of people.

Discuss the variety of health services pictured here as they relate to similar types of services available within your local community. Be certain students can identify and explain the services and are aware of their availability and location in their own community. Stress that while community governments can pass and enforce general health and safety laws, it is the responsibility of all people to reduce their own health risks through daily nutritious meals, exercise, and rest. It is also the individual's responsibility to seek out whatever community health services she or he may need.

The activities pictured on these pages are all going on right now somewhere in your own community. These people provide *health services.* Think about other services your family and neighbors use to reduce the risk of disease and accidents. List these services that help to reduce *health risks.* Check each one off as you read about it in this chapter.

communities
environment

LOOKING AHEAD

If you lived alone on a desert island, you might not face the health risk you do where you live now. There would be no other people to pass certain diseases on to you, nor any gases from cars and trucks to make the air unclean. You would never risk a traffic accident or sports injury.

Being alone, you would have to find your own *nutritious* food and fresh water. You would need to protect yourself from weather and wild animals. If you became ill, there would be no one to help you. You might have trouble just staying alive.

This is why people live and work together in **communities**. A community can be a village, a suburb, a city block, a neighborhood, or even a whole city. Together the people of a community can reduce more health risks than they could if they lived alone.

In this chapter, you will discover

- how people in a community help to protect each other's health.
- how communities work to keep their surroundings—called their **environment**—cleaner and more healthful.
- how a community deals with health emergencies and the special health problems some people must solve.
- people who have the job of helping to reduce a community's health and safety risks.

Here are some words that you may not have talked about in school before. You will learn more about them in this chapter. You can find all these words in the *Glossary* at the back of this book.

communities (kə·myü'nə·tēz)
conservation (kon'sər·vā'shən)
environment (en·vī'rən·mənt)
hazards (haz'ərdz)
natural disasters (nach'ər·əl də·zas'tərz)
pesticides (pes'tə·sīdz)
pollution (pə·lü'shən)
solid waste (sol'id wāst)
volunteer (vol'ən·tir')

Early Checkup

hazards
pollution

Modern machines and growing cities make life better, but they also cause many health and safety **hazards** for people. People share the hazards, or dangers, of traffic, noise, dirt, and disease. For example, without the proper safety measures, making energy from coal, gas, and oil can cause harmful chemicals to mix with air and water. This is **pollution**. *Nuclear energy* causes less air pollution. However, it may cause other hazards for a community.

Along with other *citizens,* people your age face all the health hazards in your community. You also share responsibilities with other citizens to reduce whatever health and safety risks you can in your community.

How much do you already know about the responsibilities people share in reducing a community's health and safety risks? Number a piece of paper from **1** through **6**. Answer each of these questions by writing **yes** or **no** next to the correct number on your paper. You can check your answers as you read this chapter.

1. Can a radio or TV station help the community reduce health and safety risks? yes
2. Do some people work for community health without being paid for their work? yes
3. Is the health department the only group that can protect a community's environment? no
4. Can destroying parts of the environment ever help to reduce a community's health risks? yes
5. Can one form of pollution sometimes cause another form of pollution? yes
6. Can noise harm your health? yes

natural disasters

COMMUNITIES WORK FOR HEALTH

Local Communities Help You Protect Your Health

The people in your neighborhood and in nearby neighborhoods are all part of your *local* community. People in your local community support and share schools, hospitals, and police, sanitation, and fire departments. Depending upon its size, a local community may have its own water, sewer, parks, and traffic departments. It may also have its own local health department, or it may share a health department with other communities.

A local health department works chiefly to reduce the risk of disease. It may have clinics where people are *immunized* against diseases like *polio, tuberculosis, diphtheria, whooping cough,* and *measles.* People who are immunized against such diseases rarely catch them, and so will not likely spread them to others. Health department inspectors check food stores to be sure meats, fruits, and vegetables are fit to be eaten. They make certain that restaurant and hotel kitchens are free of such disease-carrying animals and insects as rats and roaches. They keep close watch on air and water to be sure they contain as little pollution as possible.

Local health departments work in many ways to reduce the risks of health problems. They are able to teach people in the community how to keep their homes clean and free of animal *pests*—like rats, roaches, and mosquitoes—that carry disease germs. Health departments may also run programs for new parents on how to reduce health and safety risks for their children.

Local radio and television stations warn people of floods, earthquakes, and storms. These **natural disasters** are not the health and safety hazards they once were. Still, some people may be caught in such an emergency. Community health departments and citizen groups work to reduce any risks to

A Local Health Department at Work

When several people in one community got *food poisoning,* members of the local health department went into action. They learned that all the sick people had eaten in the same local diner. They checked the diner's kitchen and found a broken refrigerator. Foods were not being kept cold enough to prevent disease germs from growing on the food. They closed the diner until the owner stored food properly in a new refrigerator.

Have students suggest a list of possible local health regulations for food handlers that would help to prevent people from getting diseases through the foods they buy. These would include such rules as health checkups for workers; inspection for rats, mice, flies, or other pests that spread disease; washing hands after going to the toilet; and cleanliness in general. If you can, obtain your local health code to compare it with the list your class proposes.

The health department inspects for possible causes of disease.

health and safety. The *Red Cross* and local groups like the YMCA/YWCA often teach families first aid so they can be better prepared for emergencies.

Make sure that all the students know what to do in the kinds of emergencies that are likely to occur in your area. Emphasize the importance of radio and television in keeping people informed about measures to take. A battery-operated radio and at least one powerful flashlight are especially helpful, since electricity may be interrupted by the emergency.

What was your answer to *Early Checkup* number 1? (Can a radio or TV station help the community reduce health and safety risks?)

volunteer

People Support Their Community Services

The people in communities pay taxes to their local government. This is how they share the cost of hospitals and other special services that help make life happier and safer for them. Tax monies pay for accident prevention through traffic signs, traffic and street lights, better roads, and other safety measures. They also pay for emergency help when people become involved in fires, explosions, traffic accidents, and other life-threatening problems.

People vote for local governments they think will do the most to reduce health and safety risks in their community. People also give their own money and time to **volunteer** groups. Volunteers are people who work for a community without being paid.

What was your answer to *Early Checkup* number 2? (Do some people work for community health without being paid for their work?)

Margaret was hurt in a fall. Each week a volunteer drives her to a *physical therapist* in the community hospital. The therapist helps her do special exercises to strengthen her muscles. A visiting nurse comes to her home to work with Margaret there.

Kimi has gone back to school after being in the hospital. A volunteer teacher had helped her at the hospital. Her community has built a school with ramps and wide doors so that people in wheelchairs can get around more easily.

In some communities, volunteers help people who are ill by shopping for their food. They may come by for friendly "cheering up" visits, or to lend a hand with housecleaning. Volunteers in many communities drive people to and from hospitals and work. Many young people volunteer to help patients in hospitals by bringing them books and newspapers.

Often young people who cannot attend school are taught at home by special teachers. Some communities have passed laws that require schools, other public buildings, and streets to be built so that people who cannot walk can still use them. Sometimes volunteers participate in community programs that help adults with special health problems to learn new job skills and to find jobs.

Can you think of some volunteers who help the people in your community?

Volunteer organizations are an important way that even young children can participate in community health. Local organizations would probably be happy to supply posters or other information on how members of your class could work as volunteers.

After the Salk and, later, Sabin vaccines were introduced, the rate of polio fell so low that "The March of Dimes" seemed no longer needed. Since it had a large organization, however, "The March of Dimes" continued its work. Now the organization tries to prevent or cure diseases caused by heredity, such as Tay-Sachs and sickle-cell anemia, or diseases and deficiencies that can damage the fetus, such as VD, rubella, and malnutrition.

Health Care Goes Beyond the Local Community

Communities often solve local health problems with the help of state and national governments. For example, the *Food and Drug Administration (FDA)* is a national government group helping to protect people from medicines and foods that may be harmful. Volunteers from local communities also help national health groups. These groups work with doctors trying to find cures for such diseases as *cancer,* heart disease, *diabetes,* and lung disease.

Discovery —A New Pathway to Health

Do you know that a program called *"The March of Dimes"* was started by volunteers who gave money and time to find ways to prevent and cure a disease called polio? This disease, caused by a *virus,* used to strike young people and young adults. Many died or were left crippled by polio. In 1954, Dr. Jonas Salk found a way to immunize people against polio. Much of the money needed for Dr. Salk's study of polio came from people in small and large communities around the country.

Today almost no one gets polio, but "The March of Dimes" still uses volunteers. They now work to stop diseases that strike babies before or during birth. There are volunteers from communities all across the country who help health organizations, such as Alcoholics Anonymous, the American Red Cross, the National Association for Mental Health, and the United Cerebral Palsy Association.

Health Problems Around the World

High-speed, modern transportation often makes a health problem in one nation the problem of many nations. For example, suppose a Canadian, Mexican, and Italian visiting in Asia are infected with a little-known *influenza* virus. Before feeling ill, each traveler returns home by airplane. The plane carrying the Mexican makes a stop in Honolulu. The plane carrying the Canadian makes a stop in Los Angeles, while the plane carrying the Italian returns to Rome by way of London. Sneezing, coughing, and talking with people at their different stops, these three travelers leave a trail of Asian flu.

Today many diseases travel quickly throughout the world. This has caused the scientists of different countries to cooperate in working on certain health problems. International cooperation has brought doctors in every country vaccines to wipe out diseases such as *smallpox* and polio. Scientists from different countries have taught each other to control *malaria* and *yellow fever* by destroying the disease-carrying mosquitoes and their breeding areas. Doctors share ideas for treating emergency health problems in communities that are continents apart by using telephones and satellite television pictures.

While different nations share some of the same disease problems, the health needs of their communities may be quite different. The people living in *developed* nations usually live in communities where nourishing food, electricity, shelter, clean water, and modern medical care are available. They have refrigerators to keep food from spoiling, stoves and ranges to cook food, and clean places to wash dirt and disease *microbes* from their skin, clothes, and dishes. Developed nations have fast, safe, communication and transportation systems. All of these advantages offer people a *high standard of living.*

Although there are still families in our country who live without running water and electricity, the proportion is very small. The contrast between what we take for granted and what is available to most people in developing nations can be very sharp. (Of course, even in developing nations, there are people with very high standards of living.)

Canada and the United States, most of Western Europe, Australia, and Japan are among the world's developed nations. It is important to remind the students that many of the necessities and luxuries marking countries as developed did not exist about 100 years ago. They exist now because of the modern technology that has transformed much of the landscape and the way people live. Changes in medical knowledge and technology have been a major factor in these developments. Humanitarian impulses have brought advanced medical care to numerous countries that were not prepared to cope with the consequences of a decreasing death rate and higher survival rate into adulthood. Many of these countries must now face the problems caused by overpopulation and centuries-old concepts of family size.

Little Food for Many People

Every year the number of people in the world grows. Most of this growth is in developing nations. For example, almost half of all the people born each year are born in India, Brazil, and China. As doctors, farm experts, and engineers teach people in these countries better health and production skills, people are living longer lives. This also keeps the population growing. If populations of developing nations keep growing only half as quickly as they do now, by the year 2010 Mexico's population will have been doubled and India's population will have grown from 600 million people to almost a billion. You can see why the greatest need in developing nations is to produce more food.

Families in developed countries, such as the United States, Canada, Japan, and the European nations, have a high standard of living that allows most of them to build their own best health. This does not mean that every family can afford to buy all the food, clothing, cars, and pretty houses other families can afford. It simply means that people with a high standard of living can work to earn the money to pay for—or can learn the skills to produce—the food, clothing, and shelter needed to *survive.* Medical and dental care is available to help the people in every community build and keep their health.

However, not all countries of the world are developed. Many are still *developing.* In developing nations many people have no electricity. Often they live in dry regions without enough clean water to drink or raise food crops. Survival can be very difficult in many developing nations. At times there may be too little nutritious food or clean drinking water to keep people healthy.

In developing nations, such as India and certain countries in southeast Asia, South America, and Africa, many people

still suffer from diseases that are caused by too little healthful food. In India, Thailand, and the island of Jamaica, there is often too little *protein* in the diets of poor families. Young people may eat *starches* and sugar for growth and energy; but without enough protein from milk, meat, and beans, their stomachs can swell and their skin can peel. Too little protein can also cause brain damage. Young people in many Asian, African, and South American communities may survive, but they often grow slowly and suffer from diseases that come from drinking dirty water or from insects that breed in dirty water. Without well-balanced foods, their bodies have little strength to fight disease microbes.

The children in most developed nations are immunized against a disease called diphtheria. However, in developing areas such as parts of Africa, many starving children die of diphtheria during *droughts* (times when there is no rain). What can you guess about a community's standard of living when children are not *vaccinated* against disease and there is little or no food for survival?

International efforts are often aimed at dealing with the health problems of developing nations. Agricultural experts have attempted to improve food production in developing nations, technological teams have offered assistance in raising the level of technology in some developing countries, and emergency food supplies are often gathered from many countries to assist people in famine areas of developing nations. Still, the basic issue of improving sanitation and health practices remains a key factor in the health problems of developing nations.

Your students are probably most familiar with modern communities. It is important, however, that they become aware of communities elsewhere faced with life-threatening health risks, such as hunger or widespread disease from lack of basic sanitation facilities. Voluntary health organizations, supported by the citizens of all countries, attempt to provide for such poverty-stricken communities. Your students may enjoy a research project concerning such agencies. Classroom posters depicting the work of these organizations might be included in the project.

What Have You Learned?

Number a piece of paper from **1** through **4**. Next to the numbers, write the words that are missing in these sentences.

1. The local government has departments to reduce health and safety ___ in a community.

2. People pay ___ to share the cost of community health services. People also elect governments that will pass better health and safety ___. People also ___ to help others without being paid.

3. Some schools and other public buildings are built with ramps so that people in ___ can move about more easily.

4. Countries in which many people do not have enough food, clean water, and good housing are called ___.

Answers to *What Have You Learned?*
1. risks (hazards)
2. taxes (money); laws; volunteer
3. wheelchairs
4. developing

YOU CAN HELP PROTECT THE ENVIRONMENT

What Is the Environment?

Did you know that the word "environment" comes from words that mean "to turn in a circle"? If you turn in a circle, everything you see is part of your environment. The air around you that you cannot see is also part of your environment.

If your classroom were too warm or cold, or poorly lighted, your environment might make it harder for you to do well in school. If the air you breathe were always filled with dirt, smoke, and other harmful substances, you would be in danger of getting lung disease. Air that is polluted by dirt and chemical gases can also hurt the health of animals and plants needed by people for food. Every living thing in your environment depends upon every other part of the environment to stay healthy.

The local health, water, and sanitation departments help to keep the environment healthful. The federal government helps through the *Environmental Protection Agency* (*EPA*), but governmental and local groups cannot do the whole job. Every person in a community is needed to protect the local environment. No person is too young or too old to reduce the health risks of litter, noise, and other kinds of pollution.

Ask students to describe ways that they, as individuals, can help keep the environment both healthy (*functioning as it should in an ecological sense*) and healthful (*producing health benefits for the people who live in it*). Students should be encouraged to suggest and take such positive steps as planting a tree and picking up trash, as well as such "negative" steps as not making unnecessary noise and not burning trash.

The population of your community has certainly grown within the last 75 years. Ask students to list ways that this population growth affects the health of the environment. Changes in air, water, and land use should all be brought out.

What was your answer to *Early Checkup* number 3? (Is the health department the only group that can protect a community's environment?)

Many people have moved to this once-quiet community. More people can mean more car engines polluting the air and more rubbish on the streets. How can the people in this community reduce these health risks?

conservation

The students should understand that both renewable and nonrenewable resources must be conserved. Graphic presentations of ways to conserve these resources make good classroom posters, featuring such topics as keeping down school and home heat, avoiding excessive air conditioning, limiting car driving, growing your own food, and recycling.

Protecting the Environment Is a Community Job

Can you imagine owning something very valuable that you can use again and again but never use up? Some of your most valuable possessions can last in just that way when they are used wisely. There are parts of the environment that are *renewable.* People use air, water, animal and plant foods, and land—over and over again. These resources are renewable, but they should not be wasted or misused.

Other resources in the environment are *nonrenewable.* For example, once coal, oil, and natural gas are burned for energy, they are gone. They will not be renewed for millions of years. How long will it take to replace trees (still another natural resource) destroyed in a forest fire started by some careless camper?

In a farming community, soil is a valuable resource. To keep it from being washed or blown away, people plow around hills instead of just back and forth. This *contour plowing* helps keep the soil in place.

Through **conservation**, people can depend on having renewable and nonrenewable resources in the future. Conservation is saving parts of the environment for future use by people. People can conserve resources like water, oil, and trees by using them carefully. Conservation is also helping to protect parts of the environment like air and water to keep them healthful.

pesticides

Many communities have programs for *recycling* paper, glass, and metal cans. Recycling is a way of using them over and over again. People often separate these materials for recycling from their garbage.

Imagine a community in which there is a perfect *balance* of *natural* resources. The sun's energy is used, along with water and soil *minerals*, to produce food by green plants. Insects eat the plants. Small animals eat the plants and the insects. Larger animals eat the plants and the smaller animals. People eat the plants and the larger animals. Energy from the sun is thus being used for the health and energy of every form of life in the community.

Unfortunately, the natural balance is often upset by people. As there are more people, they need more homes, more machines, more food, and more clothing to survive and achieve a better standard of living. Trees and plants are cut down. There are fewer plants to feed the members of the community. Insects and animals must try to take their share from the food plants people need. To solve the problem, people often must harm one part of the environment to help save another part. For example, caterpillars and other insects may destroy food crops and trees. **Pesticides**, which are chemicals that kill insects, are sprayed on the plants. Insects are destroyed to save the crops and the trees needed by people for their health.

What was your answer to *Early Checkup* number 4? (Can destroying parts of the environment ever help to reduce a community's health risks?)

Water Conservation Is Often a Law

In some communities where there are droughts, or long spells without rain, there are laws against wasting water. Cars may be washed and lawns watered only at certain times of the week. Whether your community has a water conservation law or not, can you and people in your community find ways to save water? Can showers be shorter? Can water be turned off during tooth brushing? Are there other ways to save water?

solid waste

Solid wastes are unsightly, causing "visual pollution," but remind students that a solid waste like garbage can also cause a form of air pollution: bad odors. The main health problem regarding solid wastes, however, stems from water pollution. If untreated sewage or chemicals that leak from many solid wastes get into rivers, lakes, or other ground water, they can harm the ground water and its plant and animal life. If these wastes get into drinking water, they can cause dysentery and such diseases as salmonellosis and hepatitis.

People Can Prevent Solid Waste Pollution

There is one product every family in your neighborhood has. They produce it themselves. Every member of the family helps to make it every time a box or bottle is broken or thrown away. Except when it can be recycled, the product hardly ever does anyone any good. It can turn attractive neighborhoods ugly. It can make happy people unhappy. It is called **solid waste**.

When rubbish or other solid wastes, such as abandoned cars, are allowed to build up in a community, people face a problem called *solid waste pollution*.

There are people in communities whose job is to gather solid wastes from homes, stores, and factories. These are sanitation department workers, who bury, burn, or clean the solid wastes. Mines and factories often produce solid wastes that contain chemicals. These chemicals can pollute farming soil and community water supplies. The lives and health of water animals, plants, and people are threatened by solid wastes and the pollution they cause. Solid wastes can also attract insects and animal pests that carry and can spread disease throughout the community.

What was your answer to *Early Checkup* number 5? (Can one form of pollution sometimes cause another form of pollution?)

Waste water carries solid wastes from homes, schools, and offices through underground pipes to a community's sewage treatment plant. The water is cleaned for further use. Microbes break down harmful chemicals in sewage. *Aerators* supply the air that the microbes need to live. Solids are treated so they can be safely dumped in oceans, buried on land, or used as fertilizer.

Can even one family help to reduce the health risks in their community? See for yourself.

The Turners decided to make their home and their neighborhood look better by placing trash in sealed containers. At the same time, they helped to reduce some health risks for themselves and their neighbors.

Some of the solid waste problems come from measures originally designed to protect health. Packaging of foods is a fairly recent innovation. Not so long ago, everyone bought nearly all their food in unpackaged forms, such as spices from barrels or bins, vegetables from the counter, and meat from unwrapped pieces. Today, especially in modern supermarkets, everything comes with its own wrapper. The wrapper protects the food from contamination; but after the food is used, the wrapper becomes solid waste. Ask students what they would do to solve this problem. Some ideas that have been suggested by others are to:

- make packages that can be eaten;
- make packages that are biodegradable (that is, packages that quickly become part of the soil from the action of microorganisms);
- refuse to buy products that have excessive packaging;
- ask shopkeepers not to put purchases in a bag when there are only one or two items; and
- buy more things in large packages, so there is more per package of whatever may be needed.

The class may find still other solutions to this problem.

Noise Can Be a Health Risk

What pollutes the environment but cannot be seen? It leaves no rubbish, no chemical waste, no gases, and no soot. It can make people nervous, and make people who are ill feel even more sick. It can be a health risk to people with heart and stomach ailments. It can also harm the hearing of people who are around it too often.

Do you know why these people are wearing protective ear covers? Manufacturers of heavy machinery and airplane engines are trying to find ways to make their products run more quietly to prevent hearing loss.

Power tools make life easier for many families. Can you think of some ways people can use them so that neighbors are annoyed as little as possible?

The answer is, of course, noise. Anyone who has spent time near a place of construction knows that noise can pollute the environment. Often this kind of noise cannot be prevented, but every person can prevent other kinds of noise. People who play the radio or TV too loudly can turn it down. People can remember not to yell. People can also remember to talk more quietly so they do not annoy others. Car, truck, and motorcycle owners can make certain that their engines run as quietly as possible.

What was your answer to *Early Checkup* number 6? (Can noise harm your health?)

Could You Be a Noise Polluter?

If you answer "yes" to one or more of these questions, figure out how you can become less noisy.

1. Is your radio or TV ever louder than you need to hear it?
2. Do you yell to people in the street?
3. Do you use noisemakers on your bike?
4. Do you speak more loudly than you must?
5. Do you slam doors rather than just shut them?
6. Do you play your radio on the street?

A New World

What do television, computers, *DDT*, *penicillin*, nuclear power, rockets into space, microwaves, and jet airplanes all have in common? All of them came into use during or just after World War II — less than 40 years ago.

On Your Own

Modern inventions can make life easier and more comfortable. At the same time, such inventions may add health risks to the environment. By using some of these materials and machines less often, you may help reduce noise, air, and water pollution. Find out which of these inventions you need in your daily life and which ones you can do without.

Have a contest. Try not to use anything that has been invented during the last 150 years. The winner will be the one who, for just one day, uses the fewest materials and machines from the past 150 years. Here are some rules. You can make up some more of your own.

- No polyester or other *synthetics* can be worn. Wool, cotton, and linen clothes are all right.
- No food that has been frozen can be eaten. (Since you must eat nutritious, well-balanced meals, canned and refrigerated foods are allowed.)
- No radio, television, or electronic games can be played.
- No cars, buses, or trains that run only on electricity can be used for transportation.

If you like the idea of this *On Your Own* activity, you may want to ask anyone in the class who is interested to compete. Let the contestants report to the class and have the class vote on the winner. See the chapter notes at the front of this *Teacher's Edition* for more suggestions.

What Have You Learned?

Number a piece of paper from **1** through **3**. Next to the numbers, write the words that are missing in these sentences.

1. Everything around you is part of your ___.

2. Coal, oil, and natural gas are ___ resources. People must ___ them if they are to last. People also must not waste ___ resources, even though they can be used over and over again.

3. People are responsible for much of the sound, smoke, and chemicals that pollute the ___. Other health risks people can help reduce are ___ pollution and ___ pollution.

Answers to *What Have You Learned?*

1. environment
2. nonrenewable; conserve; renewable
3. air (environment); water; solid waste

Learn More About It

Here are three books that will help you learn more about protecting the environment.

Lyth, Mike. *The War on Pollution.* New York: Crane, Russak & Co., Inc., 1977. This book explains the different types of pollution found in the environment. It also shows what science, industry, and citizens can do to fight pollution.

Roth, Charles E. *Then There Were None.* Reading, MA: Addison-Wesley Publishing Co., Inc., 1977. This book describes how people have endangered many wildlife species. Ways to prevent this destruction are also presented.

Wise, William. *Animal Rescue: Saving Our Endangered Wildlife.* New York: G.P. Putnam's Sons, 1978. Learn about the people who have rescued thousands of animals from extinction.

More To Do on Your Own

1. Look up the name of your community in the white pages of the telephone book. Larger communities will list most or all of the departments and services within the government. (For example, one community of about 15,000 people has a number of departments listed—namely, building inspector, citizen's aid bureau, community development, court clerk, fire department, nutrition program, parking violations, police department, public works, recreation and parks, sewage treatment, tax collector, village clerk, village justice, village manager, and water department.) Think about which of these work for community health. Make a list of health functions for each of those departments.

2. Rubbish is solid waste. It can include wrappers, cans, and other packaging materials that have been scattered about the grounds, streets, and even floors. Most communities have a problem with litter. Make a poster or bumper sticker that will show how students can help keep your school free of litter.

Final Checkup

A. Number a sheet of paper from **1** through **10**. Write **true** or **false** next to the number for each of these ideas.

1. A local community health department often checks for health risks in food, water, and air. true

2. All health problems in a local community are caused by disease germs. false

3. People who must use wheelchairs all the time cannot go to school. false

4. Polio is a major health problem in most communities. false

5. Litter causes pollution on the land, just as chemical gases cause pollution in the air. true

6. People can do as much to prevent pollution as community laws can do. true

7. People in developing nations always have enough food to eat. false

8. All resources can be recycled, or used again. false

9. An important community health service is getting rid of solid wastes. true

10. Careless people are a major cause of health and safety risks. true

B. Number a sheet of paper from **1** through **10**. Next to each number, write the letter of the words that best complete each sentence.

1. Volunteers
- **a.** are paid for their work.
- **(b.)** are helpful in community hospitals.
- **c.** must be adults.
- **d.** work mostly in fire departments.

2. A family can prepare for an emergency by
- **a.** keeping an electric-powered radio handy.
- **b.** paying taxes.
- **c.** volunteering for "The March of Dimes."
- **(d.)** learning first aid.

3. In a community emergency, help is often provided by
- **a.** the recreation and parks department.
- **b.** the FDA.
- **c.** the local library.
- **(d.)** the Red Cross.

4. Each family in a community can be helpful in preventing
- **a.** noise pollution.
- **b.** solid waste pollution.
- **(c.)** both noise and solid waste pollution.
- **d.** natural disasters.

5. Most changes in a community's environment are caused by
- **a.** storm emergencies.
- **(b.)** the people who live in the community.
- **c.** buried solid wastes.
- **d.** water pollution.

6. Land is a resource that
   a. is nonrenewable.
   (b.) is renewable when carefully conserved.
   c. is renewable if there is no wind or rain.
   d. is nonrenewable if pesticides were used on it.

7. People prepare glass, cans, and paper for recycling by
   (a.) carefully separating them from garbage.
   b. never throwing them away.
   c. carefully placing all solid wastes in a closed container.
   d. squashing them with their feet.

8. A good way to reduce the health risk of solid wastes is to
   a. find new ways to package products.
   b. store them in closed containers until removed.
   c. improve their chemical treatment prior to final disposal.
   (d.) all of the above.

9. Noise pollution is a problem
   a. communities can do nothing about.
   b. caused by machines, not people.
   (c.) that can cause health risks.
   d. caused solely by loud portable radios.

10. Inventions discovered in the last 150 years
   (a.) occasionally may cause new health risks to communities.
   b. make work a lot harder.
   c. run on batteries only.
   d. were the result of volunteer organizations.

Write About Better Health

Write a short answer to each of these questions. Use complete sentences.

1. What are some of the services to the community provided by the local health department?
2. How can a community best help, and be best helped by, people with special health problems?
3. Can you give two examples of changes that can help and harm the environment at the same time?
4. What can a community do to reduce solid waste pollution?
5. What are three ways people can reduce noise pollution?

Model answers to *Write About Better Health* are provided in the chapter notes at the front of this *Teacher's Edition.*

ZAP!

9 MAKING DECISIONS ABOUT DRUGS

See the teaching notes on page 228.

People Decide About Drugs Every Day

Each time you watch television, listen to the radio, or read a magazine or newspaper, you encounter advertisements for products. You may not realize that many of those products are *drugs*. For example, can you tell which of the following items are drugs?

dandruff shampoo	cold capsule
diet candy	allergy pills
cigarettes	alcoholic drink
cola drink	coffee
sleeping pill	medicated skin cream
pain-killer	first-aid spray

Most people are surprised to learn that every one of these products contains one or more drugs. If most people are not aware that they are using drugs, how can they decide when a product may be a health risk?

Think about which of these products you or your family use. Can you name and describe the drugs they contain? If not, drug education will help you make better health decisions.

LOOKING AHEAD

All of the products mentioned in the chapter opener have one thing in common. Each contains one or more drugs. New drugs and new uses for drugs are being discovered and made available to the public nearly every day. However, public knowledge of what the drugs are and of how they affect the body lags farther and farther behind. The probability is increasing rapidly that, through ignorance, people will harm their health by using combinations of drugs meant to promote it. As a result, the unintentional misuse of legal drugs may become more of a problem and danger than the intentional abuse of illicit drugs. This is why the importance of *drug education* is stressed throughout this chapter.

Drugs are chemical substances that act with the body's own chemicals to change the way certain body parts work. Drugs are the active ingredients in medicines. Some drugs come from plants, animals, or minerals. Many more are made in laboratories and factories. Doctors use different drugs to diagnose, prevent, control, and cure diseases. However, drugs do not always improve the health of people. Some people use drugs for reasons that have nothing to do with their health. These people risk their health by using drugs just to experience the mind and body changes caused by the drugs.

How can people learn to make wise choices about which drugs can improve their health? How can they learn when to use them? Are drugs safe only when a doctor has ordered them? You will find answers to these questions in this chapter. You will find out how to gather the accurate information you need to make healthful decisions about drugs. You will also learn about

- why everyone needs to know more about how drugs help or harm health.
- four groups of powerful drugs that people should know about and understand.
- the serious health dangers of marijuana and other illegal drugs.

Here are some words that you may not have talked about in school before. You will learn more about them in this chapter. You can find all these words in the *Glossary* at the back of this book.

dependent (di·pen'dənt)
depressant (di·pres'nt)
hallucinogens (hə·lü'sn·ə·jenz)
narcotic (när·kot'ik)
prescription (pri·skrip'shən)
stimulant (stim'yə·lənt)
symptoms (simp'təmz)
tolerance (tol'ər·əns)

Early Checkup

Number a piece of paper from **1** through **7**. Answer each of these questions by writing **yes** or **no** next to the correct number on your paper. You can check your answers as you read this chapter.

1. Does your body always need the help of a medicine when you are not feeling well? no
2. Can people become ill from some helpful drugs sold at most drug counters? yes
3. Does taking extra amounts of a medicine help to cure a disease more quickly? no
4. Do people who are dependent on a drug feel ill when they stop taking the drug? yes
5. Does marijuana affect the user's brain? yes
6. Do smokers get sick more often than nonsmokers? yes
7. Is alcohol a type of food? no

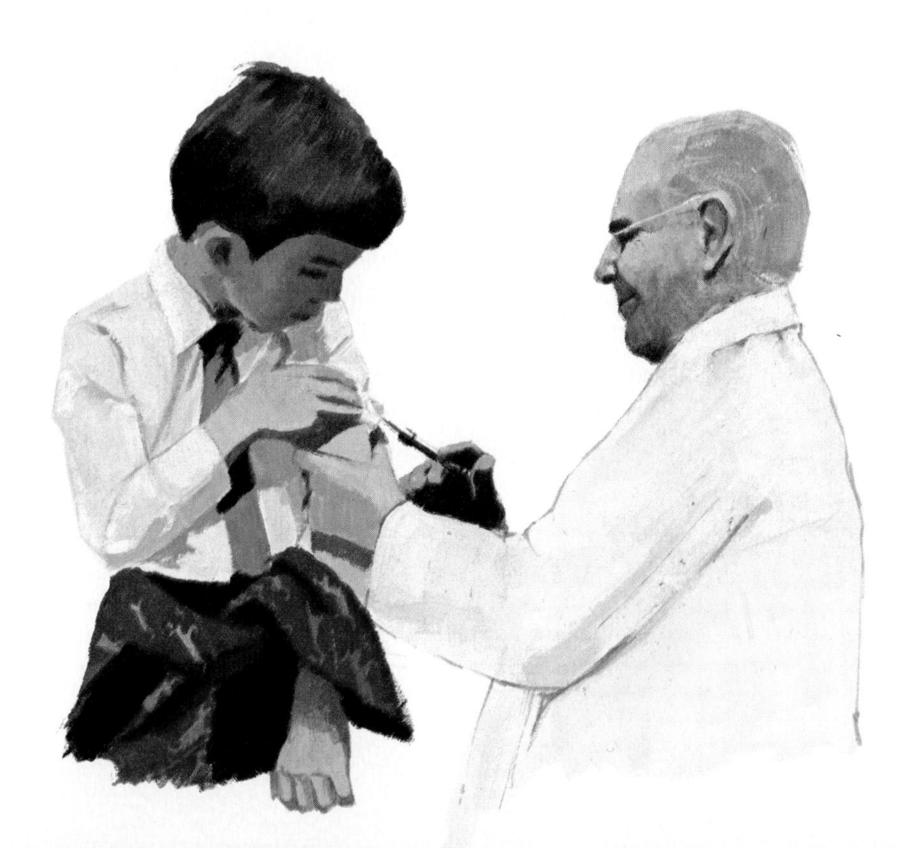

symptoms

People Are the Problem With Drugs

Drugs are made and sold to protect health, not to harm it. The only problem with drugs is the *people* who use them. When people have not learned to choose and use drugs safely, they make drugs a national health problem.

CHOOSING DRUGS FOR HEALTH

Can Drugs Change Disease Symptoms?

There are people who are sneezing today. Their noses are running. Some throats feel a little sore. These people may be feeling signals that their bodies are fighting some disease. Such signals are called **symptoms**. They may be symptoms of a cold, or the flu, or chicken pox. It may be that they are symptoms of an *allergy.*

When fighting a disease, the body uses a lot of energy. Nutritious foods and extra rest help to keep the body strong. However, such symptoms as a sore throat and coughing can make it difficult to eat and rest. This is a time to decide about using a helpful drug. It is also a time when people must know how to use the drug safely.

Some of the medicines people buy at a drug counter can ease the uncomfortable symptoms of a minor illness. Easing the symptoms will not cure the disease, but it may make the ill person more comfortable and able to rest, drink, and eat. That will help the body to fight the disease better and more quickly. However, choosing the right medicine without a doctor's help is not always an easy decision.

Sometimes using a drug to treat symptoms can cause more harm than the illness itself. For example, a ''cold medicine'' may simply hide symptoms of some other disease a doctor should know about. Getting rest and drinking fluids will help the body fight the cold itself. Sometimes the uncomfortable cold symptoms will disappear after several hours, and medicine will not be needed. If the symptoms remain, and no new symptoms develop, a mild cold medicine may bring temporary relief.

What was your answer to *Early Checkup* number 1? (Does your body always need the help of a medicine when you are not feeling well?)

The adults in a family should help younger people choose the right medicine. They should also help them understand when and how to use the medicine. These directions are printed on the label.

The same early symptoms that signal a cold may be followed by symptoms of a more serious illness. It can be important to wait a while and watch for changes before deciding to treat the symptoms with medicine.

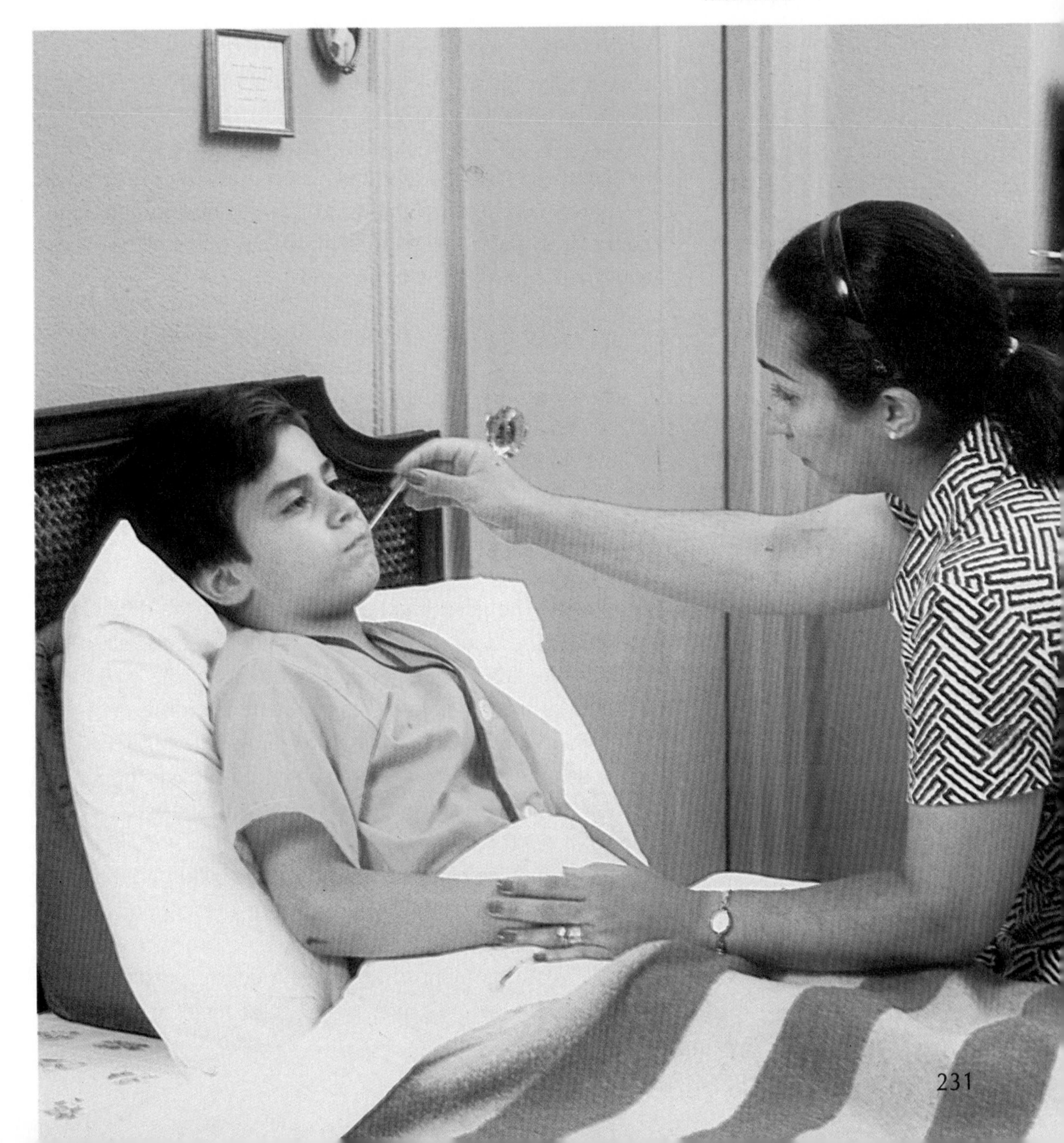

prescription

On the chalkboard, keep a running list of the kinds of information students find on the OTC drug labels. Emphasize that many people wrongly believe that OTC drugs are "harmless," because advertisements for OTC drugs are not required to provide the warnings that appear on OTC drug labels.

Usually a parent or other older family member is present when a doctor prescribes medicine for a young person. However, emergency situations arise when a young person requires medication, but a family member is not available. Point out to students that in such instances they should tell the doctor about drugs or medication they are taking, including over-the-counter drugs. It is important that students also inform the doctor of any allergic reactions they may have had in the past to drugs or foods.

DECONGESTANT/ANALGESIC

PRODUCT INFORMATION: For temporary relief of nasal congestion, headache, aches, pains and fever due to colds, sinusitis and flu.

NO ANTIHISTAMINE DROWSINESS

Dosage: Adults—TWO CAPSULES every 4 hours. Do not exceed 8 capsules in 24 hours. Children (6 to 12 years)—ONE CAPSULE every 4 hours. Do not exceed 4 capsules in 24 hours.

Warning: Do not give to children under 6 or use for more than 10 days, unless directed by a physician. Individuals with high blood pressure, heart disease, diabetes or thyroid disease should use only as directed by a physician. Do not take this product if you are taking another medication containing phenylpropanolamine.

This package is child-safe; however, keep this and all medications out of reach of children. In case of accidental overdose, contact a physician or poison control center immediately.

Formula: Each capsule contains 18 mg. phenylpropanolamine HCl, 325 mg. acetaminophen.

Also available in 48's

9692-925-36

What Is the Difference Between OTC and Prescription Drugs?

Many medicines—such as cold capsules, eye drops, nose sprays, aspirin, and first-aid creams—are *over-the-counter,* or OTC, drugs. Some soaps, diet aids, shampoos, and many health and skin-care products are also OTC drugs. Anyone can buy OTC drugs, just by going to a drugstore or supermarket.

OTC drugs are used to treat minor illnesses and health problems. However, certain OTC drugs may cause health problems to some people who use them. These problems are called *side effects.* Dizziness, sleepiness, and headaches are some side effects of many OTC medicines. In addition, certain people are allergic to some drugs, and can become seriously ill by using them.

What was your answer to *Early Checkup* number 2? (Can people become ill from some helpful drugs sold at most drug counters?)

The label on an OTC medicine gives several kinds of information. The label lists the *ingredients* of the medicine. It describes the symptoms the drug is supposed to relieve. An OTC label also lists possible side effects of the drug, and warns about the possible health problems the drug may cause when taken with certain other drugs. Some OTC drugs list the date after which the drug should no longer be used.

Many medicines can be bought only with the written order of a doctor or dentist. The written order is called a **prescription**. Medicines ordered by prescription are sold only by *pharmacists.* They are known as prescription drugs, or *Rx drugs.*

The kind and amount of medicine a doctor prescribes depend on the person's age, weight, past medical history, and present illness. The doctor may use different drugs for people with the same illness. Each prescription is different, and each person may find different directions on the prescription label. The prescription label does *not* list all the ingredients in the drug.

Doctors also usually tell their patients what changes to expect and what side effects to watch for. It is important to ask your doctor about the drug that is prescribed. It is also important to tell your family and a doctor right away if a medicine seems to be making you ill. It could mean that a drug that works well for others is not right for your body. Many people find it helpful to write down the doctor's advice about a medicine. They also ask the doctor and the pharmacist about any foods or other drugs they should not take while using the prescription medicine.

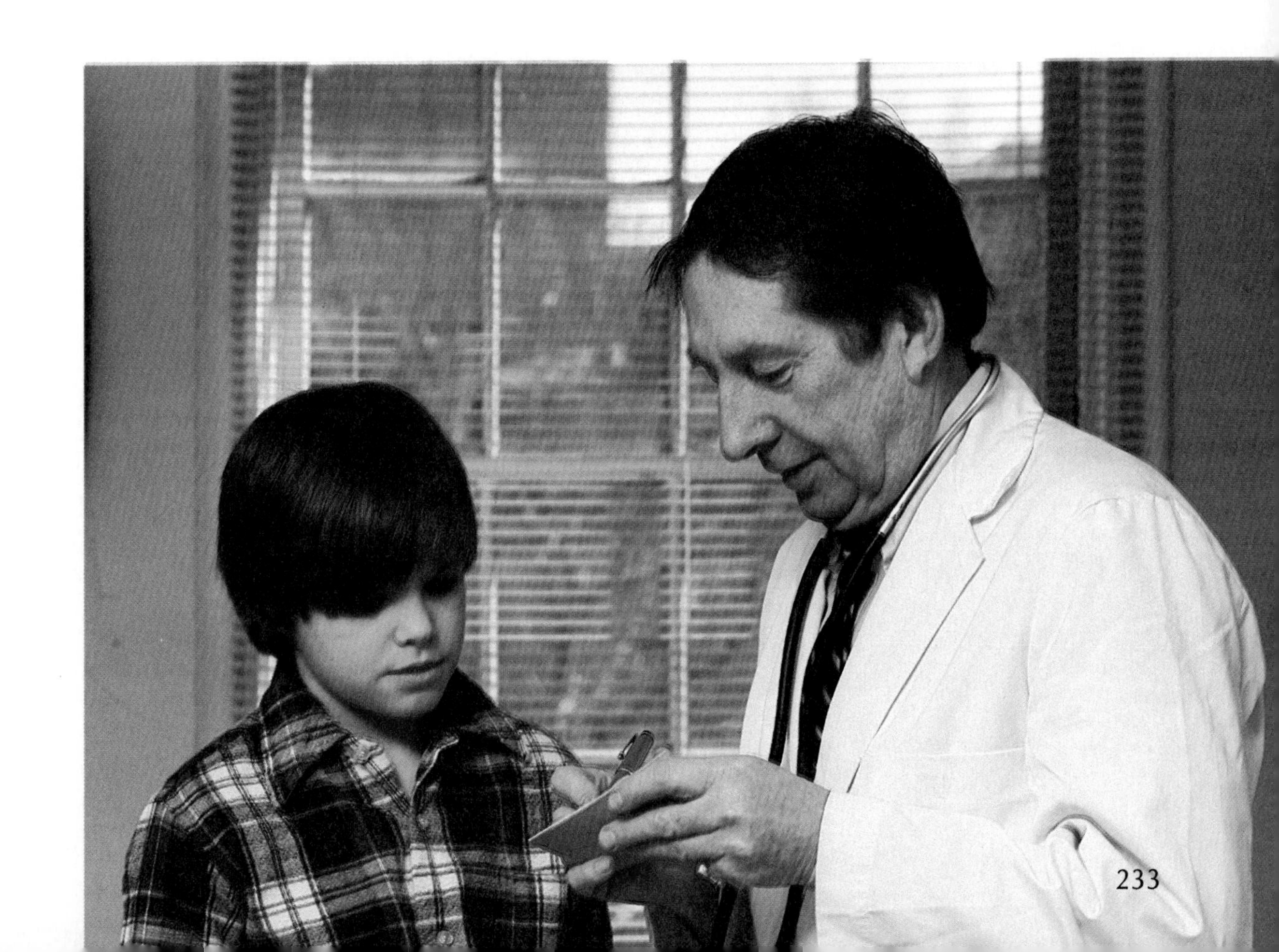

When Have You Had Enough Medicine?

Sometimes people stop taking a prescription medicine as soon as the disease symptoms go away. This is often unwise, since there may still be disease microbes in the body.
Always check with a doctor before you stop using a prescription medicine.

Why Should You Follow Directions?

The body has its own disease-fighting equipment. This is why people do not always need a doctor or medicines for some diseases. Healthy skin acts like a wall, keeping disease germs, or *microbes,* from entering the body, There are also chemicals in clean, healthy skin that destroy or slow the growth of disease microbes. A wet, sticky substance called *mucus* is made inside the nose. Mucus catches some microbes so they can be coughed or sneezed from the body.

Microbes that do get into the body are often destroyed by the *white blood cells.* People who eat balanced meals help to keep the body's disease-fighting equipment at its best. Getting enough rest and exercise helps, too. Sometimes, however, even healthy bodies may need more help in fighting more serious diseases.

The extra disease-fighting help your body needs comes from medicines that are usually selected by your doctor—or sometimes by your family. Making sure that a certain medicine can best help your body is now up to you. For example, reading the label and asking questions about the medicine help you to know more about how it will work best. Following the directions exactly will help to keep the medicine working safely.

To get the most help from a medicine, you must take it in the amount and at the time directed. When the directions say "one tablet every four hours," it may be harmful to your health to take the drug more or less frequently. Using a drug in any way other than has been directed is known as *drug misuse.* It does not make the user get well faster, and it may lead to serious new health problems.

Drug overuse means using more of a drug or using it more often than has been directed. This practice can cause health problems, too. Some people overuse nasal sprays, thinking they can prevent ever having a stuffy nose. Actually, too much of the spray can cause the delicate *nasal membranes* to swell. This only makes the nose feel stuffed up.

What was your answer to *Early Checkup* number 3? (Does taking extra amounts of a medicine help to cure a disease more quickly?)

Drug abuse means using a drug for no healthful purpose at all. Drug abusers may take sleeping pills, aspirin, or other drugs just for the feeling the drug may cause.

In discussion of the poster, emphasize that the last two drug-safety steps should be taken with or by the adults in a family.

There is much information available for young people about such drugs as antibiotics and sulfa drugs. You may want to have students research these prescription drugs, to give a report on how they were developed and on the diseases they combat.

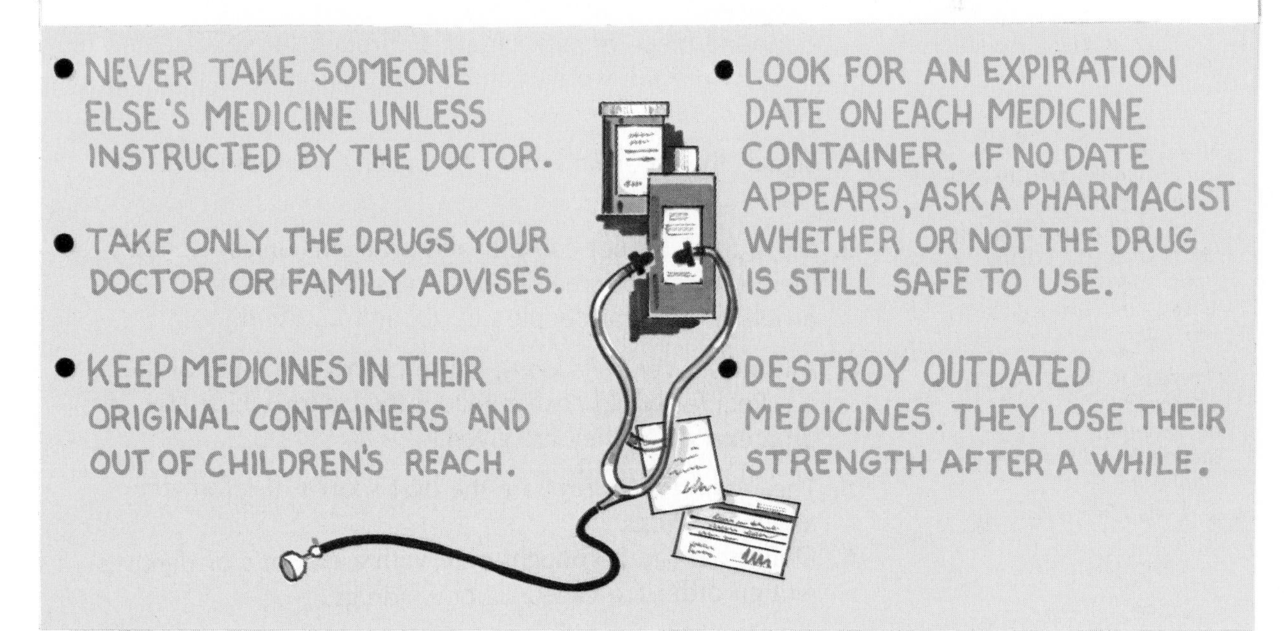

Discovery—A New Pathway to Health

This drug was used by Greeks more than 2,400 years ago to relieve pain and reduce fever. Hippocrates, the "Father of Medicine," prescribed it to patients in the form of the bark from a willow tree. In 1853, a German scientist named Charles Frédéric Gerhardt discovered that it was a chemical in the willow bark that was helping people. Since that time, this drug has been produced to relieve the pain and fever of people all around the world. Many doctors suggest it more often than any other medicine. If you have not yet guessed the name of this ancient "wonder" drug, it is printed upside down at the bottom of this page.

Emphasize to the class the need for a doctor's advice before taking more than one drug. No drug is of too little significance. Even aspirin or antacids can produce dangerous reactions when used in combination with other drugs.

What Have You Learned?

Drug *synergism* results when two or more drugs produce an effect greater than that of each drug alone. At times, the synergistic effects of drugs can be helpful. For example, a doctor may accelerate the activity of a drug by combining it with another. However, mixing drugs without a doctor's knowledge can lead to unexpected and serious results.

Answers to *What Have You Learned?*
1. symptoms
2. people; misuse; overuse; abuse
3. body; directions
4. labels
5. prescription; Rx

Number a piece of paper from **1** through **5**. Next to the numbers, write the words that are missing in these sentences.

1. Signals that your body may be fighting a disease are called __.
2. Most drugs do not cause health problems unless __ use them unwisely. Three reasons drugs cause health problems are that people __, __, and __ them.
3. All drugs, even mild ones, cause changes in parts of the __. People should always follow the __ for taking any drug exactly as they are given.
4. The __ on OTC drugs are the best source of information about the drugs.
5. Drugs that can be bought only with a doctor's or dentist's written order are called __ or __ drugs.

aspirin

UNDERSTANDING MORE ABOUT DRUG DANGERS

stimulant
tolerance

There are four groups of drugs that cause important changes in the nervous system. The body's control center—the brain—is part of the nervous system, so the chemical changes caused by these drugs affect the way a person thinks, feels, and behaves.

A few of these drugs are part of products some people use every day. Often people who use these products do not even know they are using a drug. Most drugs from these groups cannot be sold without a prescription from a doctor or dentist. Other drugs from these four groups are so dangerous that it is against the law for anyone to produce, sell, or buy them. However, even these most dangerous drugs are sold *illegally* by people of all ages.

Some people buy an illegal drug because they have heard about the changes it causes in the nervous system. They want to try the drug in order to feel its effects. Other people believe the drug will help them escape from problems they are having at home, in school, or with friends. Some even have said they used illegal drugs because it seemed like a "cool" thing to do. People who use drugs for reasons such as these are drug abusers.

How Do Stimulant Drugs Affect People?

Stimulant drugs speed up signals from the brain. These drugs make people feel more lively and awake. Doctors sometimes prescribe stimulant drugs, such as *amphetamines,* for a limited time to people who are having emotional problems. Doctors are careful to prescribe amphetamines in small amounts for a short time. This is because people build up a **tolerance** to stimulant drugs. Tolerance means that the body begins to need more of the drug in order to feel the same level of effect. Drug tolerance can cause people to overuse drugs.

Amphetamines come in capsule, tablet, liquid, powder, and lozenge form. Some common "street" terms for amphetamines include *bennies, pep pills, peaches, roses, dexies* (dextroamphetamines), *speed,* and *meth* (methamphetamine hydrochloride).

In addition to developing *tolerance* for stimulant drugs, people may also develop *dependence* on these drugs. The dependence caused by frequent use of amphetamines is not physical (addiction characterized by physical withdrawal symptoms). Rather, it is *psychological.* Users who are "high" on amphetamines feel as though they are tireless. When this "high" feeling wanes, they may become tired or depressed. This is known as "crashing." To counteract "crashing," the user often takes more of the drug.

Abuse of stimulant drugs, however, also can lead to other health problems. Abusers of stimulant drugs, particularly amphetamines, may suffer from malnutrition, poor motor coordination, irritability, and other physical, mental, and emotional impairments.

dependent
depressant

One Danger of Drug Misuse

Some people use amphetamines to stay awake and alert. Often the drugs work so well that their users cannot get to sleep when they should. They may start to use barbiturates to sleep at night. This dangerous misuse of drugs upsets the normal waking and sleeping patterns of the body. Mixing stimulant and depressant drugs can lead to serious illness or death.

Barbiturates and tranquilizers are classified as *sedative* drugs. They relax body muscles, relieve anxiety and tension, and induce sleep. Tranquilizers produce less of a sedative effect than barbiturates. However, improper use of either of these drugs can lead to psychological and physical dependence.

Barbiturates are taken in the form of capsules, tablets, or liquids. Some "street" terms for barbiturates are *downers, barbs, reds, blues, yellow jackets,* and *goofballs.* The effects of barbiturates and alcohol are very much alike. Speech becomes slurred, motor coordination is impaired, and sleep is often induced.

Abuse of the depressant drug *methaqualone* has risen sharply in recent years. Refer to the chapter notes for further information.

Coffee, chocolate, tea, and cola drinks have a stimulant drug called *caffeine* in them. Many people say they use these products for a quick "lift." The lift they feel comes from the effect of caffeine on the brain. It does not last long. A short rest, a little exercise, or a nutritious snack would be more healthful ways of getting quick energy. Interestingly, some people say they smoke because it calms them down. However, tobacco has *nicotine* in it, which is a stimulant drug. You will find out more about the effects of nicotine and tobacco later in this chapter.

How Do Depressant Drugs Affect People?

Depressant drugs slow signals from the brain. This causes muscles to relax. Depressants can also make people feel less tense or worried. Doctors often prescribe depressants, for a short time, to people who are nervous, upset, or having trouble sleeping. For example, *barbiturates* are very strong depressants that help people fall asleep. *Tranquilizers* are depressants used to calm people who are extremely nervous and upset.

Doctors are careful about prescribing depressant drugs because people can become **dependent** on them. A person who is dependent on a drug cannot stop taking it without feeling very sick. Doctors also prescribe small amounts of a depressant. Large amounts of these drugs can slow the signals from the brain too much. This can lead to *unconsciousness* and even death.

What was your answer to *Early Checkup* number 4? (Do people who are dependent on a drug feel ill when they stop taking the drug?)

Many people do not realize that *alcohol* is a depressant drug. Alcohol slows down the parts of the brain that control thinking, emotions, and behavior. That is why people often feel less shy and more talkative after drinking beverages that contain alcohol. You will learn more about the effects of alcohol later in this chapter.

Do you have some special ways to relax your mind at bedtime? Many people find it easy to fall asleep if they end their day with a quiet activity.

hallucinogens
narcotic

Heroin usually comes in the form of white or brown powder. It is often mixed with other substances to make buyers think they are getting more for their money. This increases the danger to buyers. They can never be sure of what they are getting. Some common "street" names for heroin include *horse, junk, smack, scag,* and *brown sugar.* (Heroin is sometimes "cut" with real brown sugar.)

Emphasize to students that drugs taken under a physician's supervision can be monitored for atypical effects on the patient. (Any medication can have unwanted side effects on a given person.) Moreover, the physician can see that the drug is discontinued before the patient becomes dependent on it.

Drug tolerance is a serious health problem. As a patient becomes increasingly tolerant to certain drugs, heavier doses are frequently used to achieve the same effect. High dosage levels can affect the heart and other muscles—and in some cases cause permanent damage and even death.

How Do Narcotic Drugs Affect People?

Narcotics are drugs that are made from the sap of the opium poppy plant. Today, most narcotic drugs can also be made in laboratories. There are some narcotic drugs that are so dangerous they are illegal to buy, sell, or use. Even narcotic drugs that are used to produce medicines are legal only when they are prescribed by doctors.

Narcotic drugs affect the brain and nervous system. They cause the heart rate to slow. They also slow the action of muscles and bring on drowsiness and deep sleep. Narcotics also relieve pain. For example, a narcotic called morphine is used in some medicines that lesson the pain of surgery.

Narcotics are dangerous because they have powerful effects on the brain even when they are taken in small amounts. Too much of the drug can cause unconsciousness and even death. People can also become dependent, or "hooked," on narcotics. For these reasons doctors prescribe narcotics to be used for very short periods of time. When narcotic medicines are prescribed they must be used under medical supervision.

Some people break the law by using illegal narcotics such as heroin. Every year a large number of these people become seriously ill or die from the effects of this illegal drug.

How Do Hallucinogens Affect People?

There is a group of dangerous drugs that are illegal for anyone to buy, sell, or use. These drugs affect the brain, causing people to see, hear, smell, and feel things that may not be real. These imagined sights, sounds, and smells are called hallucinations. The drugs that cause them are called hallucinogens.

A person having a hallucination risks serious injury. He or she may take foolish chances without realizing the dangers involved. Hallucinogens also speed up the action of the heart, increasing its workload. This can lead to heart and circulatory disease.

Marijuana and Other Illegal Drugs

One illegal drug in this hallucinogen group is called THC. This is the hallucinogen found in the leaves of the marijuana plant. People who use marijuana are breaking the law and harming their health. THC makes the heart overwork and slows the action of muscles. Marijuana affects the brain and reduces a person's ability to learn and remember. It also reduces the ability to work and play at sports with skill and safety. The chemicals in marijuana smoke damage the lungs and can cause diseases such as bronchitis, emphysema, and cancer.

Other illegal drugs in this group called hallucinogens are LSD and PCP. Both drugs are extremely dangerous because of their powerful effects on the brain. Like THC in marijuana, these drugs remain in the body for a long time after they are used. Their harmful effects on the brain can return unexpectedly.

What was your answer to *Early Checkup* number 5? (Does marijuana affect the user's brain?)

Stimulants	**Depressants**
amphetamines **nicotine** **caffeine**	**barbiturates** **tranquilizers** **alcohol**
Narcotics	**Hallucinogens**
codeine **paregoric** **morphine** **heroin**	**marijuana** **LSD** **PCP**

Marijuana contains more than 450 different chemicals. Research is just beginning to uncover the myriad ways in which these chemicals affect the body. The damage marijuana can cause to the respiratory and circulatory system, and to organs of all kinds, is already well documented. You might wish to assign a group of students to collect current articles about research on marijuana, and help these students design a way to share the information with the class. Some street names for marijuana include *grass, pot, tea, joints,* and *Mary Jane.*

LSD (lysergic acid diethylamide) is also known as *acid* and *sugar,* while PCP (phencyclidine) is called *angel dust, hog,* and *peace pills.* LSD may take the form of a tablet, capsule, or liquid. PCP comes as a tablet, crystal, or powder.

On Your Own

Boredom, curiosity, a need for independence, a need for excitement, relief from stress, peer pressure, a poor self-image, loneliness, rebellion, family/school problems, relationship problems, and the excitement of taking risks can contribute to drug abuse. You may want to have interested students write a report on the healthful alternatives to drugs as means of coping with the particular needs or problems.

Do you wonder why anyone would ever use drugs without the advice of a doctor? Do you wonder why people use products such as cigarettes that have dangerous drugs in them? Part of the answer is simple. Some people began to use cigarettes long before they discovered the dangers of the chemicals that were in them. Knowing that the drugs in the products can be dangerous has helped many people decide not to use them. Many people who drink alcohol have learned to use it more carefully. You may already have made some healthful choices about certain drug products yourself.

To make wise decisions about dangerous drugs, people need to learn more about them through drug education programs. People also need to understand themselves better. They need to think about healthful ways they can handle problems, instead of turning to drugs for solutions.

This chart lists some reasons different people have given for trying drugs. It also describes some of their emotions. At the far right are other, more healthful choices they might make. Copy the chart. Then see how many more reasons and emotions you can add, as well as other choices that would be more healthful than drug use.

Reasons for Using Drugs	Emotions	Healthful Choices
1. "I can't sleep at night."	The fear of being tired all the next day	Listen to soft music.
2. "Life is unexciting."	Feeling bored or lonely	Call a friend and plan a party.
3. "My friends all do it."	The fear of being left out	Talk to someone new, or make a new friend.
4. "I never have enough energy."	Not being able to keep up with others	Get more exercise.
5. "I can handle it."	Wanting to seem more adult	Get a part-time job and handle it responsibly.

People Working for Your Health

Frank White is the group supervisor of the Drug Enforcement Administration (DEA) in Fort Lauderdale, Florida. He works with other *narcotics agents* to track down drug dealers and stop drug traffic. To be a narcotics agent, it is necessary to have a college degree. The agents also attend 12 to 16 weeks of special training that includes learning about the law, *surveillance* methods, how to work with *informants,* and how to use self-defense techniques.

The main purpose of this kind of work is to keep drugs away from possible users by arresting the people who deal in drugs. This often involves working with an informant who has close contact with a drug dealer. Arrangements are made by the narcotics agent to buy drugs from the dealer. When the deal is made, the dealer can be arrested. The work is frequently very dangerous and requires a lot of back-up protection by other agents and the local police. After an arrest is made, the agent follows up the case by writing reports and testifying in court against the drug dealer.

Mr. White also fights drug abuse by talking to people in the schools and in the community. He feels that drug education is extremely important in helping people decide not to abuse drugs. Mr. White and the agents he works with are morally committed to "helping the youth of America by stopping drug abuse through education and enforcement of the law."

What Have You Learned?

Number a piece of paper from **1** through **5**. Next to the numbers, write the words that are missing in these sentences.

1. The four main groups of drugs that cause changes in the body's nervous system are —, —, —, and —.
2. Coffee, tea, and cola drinks contain a — drug called caffeine.
3. Drugs that slow down signals from the brain are —, such as barbiturates and —.
4. The body can become dependent on depressant and — drugs.
5. Hallucinogens are drugs that cause people to experience —.

Answers to *What Have You Learned?*
1. stimulants (stimulant drugs); depressants (depressant drugs); narcotics (narcotic drugs); hallucinogens
2. stimulant
3. depressants; tranquilizers
4. narcotic
5. hallucinations

DIFFICULT DECISIONS FOR THE FUTURE

What Should You Know About Smoking?

In a way, drug education programs work best with people your age. Fifty million Americans already smoke cigarettes. Half of them say they want to quit. You will have to decide whether or not you will take the risks involved in becoming a smoker. Knowing more about the risks people take by smoking will help you when you face this decision.

The longer people smoke, the greater is their risk of developing heart or lung disease. Tobacco *tars* are chemicals that turn sticky and brown when heated. These chemicals stick to throat and lung tissue, and can make cells unhealthy. *Nicotine,* the stimulant drug in tobacco, makes blood vessels narrow. As a result, the heart must pump harder to keep enough blood flowing through the body.

Invite students to give other reasons people may want to stop smoking. List their ideas on the chalkboard. The list may include: *stains on teeth; bad breath; stale-smoke smell in clothing, hair, and homes; smoker's cough; shortage of breath; low resistance to respiratory diseases; cancer of the lung, mouth, and bladder.*

What About Smoking Marijuana?

Some people think that because marijuana cigarettes do not contain tobacco, they are less dangerous to smoke. Recent research has shown that the chemicals in marijuana smoke cause more damage, faster, to the lungs and all body systems than those in tobacco smoke do.

See the chapter notes for more information on the long-term effects of smoking marijuana.

This is the healthy tissue of a nonsmoker's lung.

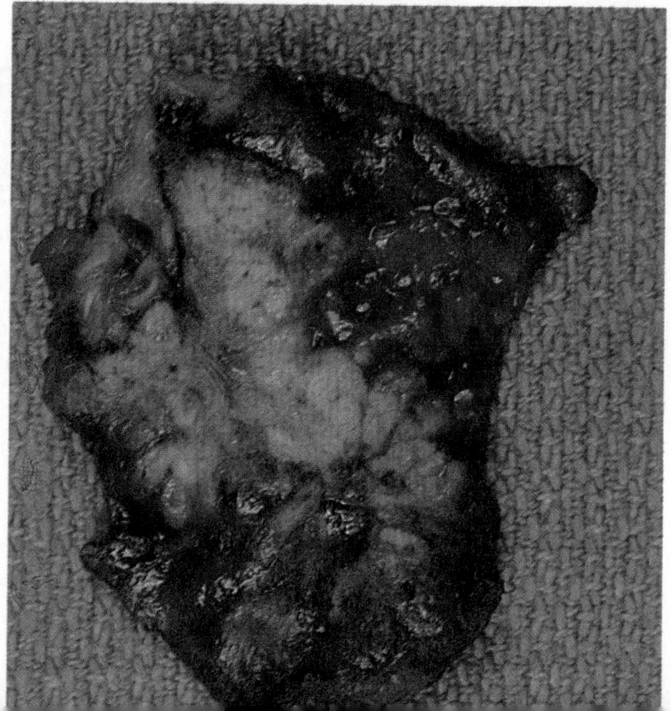

The tissue of this smoker's lung shows a disease called *cancer.* Chemicals in cigarette smoke can change healthy cells into ones that grow out of control, as in cancer.

Smoke from just one cigarette causes the tiny hairs in the air tubes leading to the lungs to move more slowly. These hairs, called *cilia,* then cannot sweep dust and disease microbes away from the lungs as they should. The result is that smokers are sick about 88 million more days each year than nonsmokers. Cigarette smoke has a gas called *carbon monoxide* in it. This gas is a poison that keeps the body from getting the oxygen it needs. For as long as six hours after a person has smoked, carbon monoxide stays in the body.

Smoking and Emphysema

A smoker's lungs can be harmed by the chemical gases in tobacco smoke. They can cause a disease called emphysema. In emphysema the air sacs of the lungs are damaged so that breathing becomes difficult. Emphysema victims gasp to get enough oxygen into their lungs.

What was your answer to *Early Checkup* number 6? (Do smokers get sick more often than nonsmokers?)

Smoking even affects nonsmokers. They breathe the tar, nicotine, and hundreds of other chemicals from a smoker's cigarette. Inhaling smoke can make the heart beat faster. It can also increase blood pressure and the level of carbon monoxide in the blood. Some people are also allergic to tobacco smoke. Their eyes water, and they begin to cough or sneeze.

Do these facts help you to make a healthful decision about smoking?

Tobacco Without Smoke Is Dangerous, Too

There is tobacco that is not sold for smoking. Some people chew or suck on tobacco. This smokeless tobacco can be very harmful because it contains chemicals that damage the mouth and stomach. The tobacco juice irritates the gums, stains the teeth and helps cause tooth decay. It also slows down the healing of mouth tissues, and it contains chemicals that are linked to heart and blood vessel disease and cancer.

Smoking causes an overinflation of the tiny air sacs, or alveoli, that make up the lungs. This brings about a breakdown of the cell walls so that many tiny air spaces become one large air space. The surface area vital for gas exchange in the lungs is drastically reduced. This condition is called emphysema. Emphysema can also result from bronchial irritation, asthma, allergies, lung infections, and air pollution.

Persons with emphysema do not use inhaled air efficiently. Their lungs cannot exchange fresh oxygen for used carbon dioxide fast enough to meet the needs of their bodies. Therefore, victims of emphysema are constantly gasping for air.

The continual "cigarette cough" that smokers experience is actually chronic bronchitis. This disease, caused by inflammation of the lining of the bronchi (the two main branches of the windpipe) and of the tubes leading from them, results in the production of large amounts of mucus.

Almost a million teenagers begin smoking each year. Most are aware of the health hazards of smoking, and many are not at ease doing it. Young people say they start to smoke because of the stress of adolescence, pressure from friends, boredom, or the need to rebel and feel independent.

On Your Own

Look around you, and you probably will find that most young people do *not* smoke. They have made a decision for better health. Why, then, do some of their friends start smoking? Have you heard any of these reasons before?

"It makes me feel grown up."

"It's the taste and the lift I like."

"I can quit anytime I want to. I just don't want to now."

"I eat too much if I don't smoke."

Students should be able to differentiate between the two types of dependencies that cigarette smoking causes. It is nicotine that causes physical dependence, which can result in nausea, headaches, and other physical symptoms when smokers try to quit. With psychological dependence, however, smokers feel they need a cigarette. For some, it becomes part of their daily routine. They feel lost without a cigarette in their hand. For others, a cigarette may seem comforting in moments of stress.

Make your own drug education poster. Use pictures of young people from newspapers and magazines, and write in an excuse for smoking. Then, next to that excuse, write in the facts about smoking. For example, the excuse that tobacco smoke "tastes good" is really a funny one. The fact is, hot tobacco smoke harms the mouth, throat, and taste buds on the tongue. The smoke increases the risk of gum disease. The "lift" people feel comes from nicotine—a drug that can make them drug-dependent. This is why many people find it hard to quit, whether they are sick or not. If you need further facts on smoking, ask a librarian for help.

What Should You Know About Alcohol?

Alcohol may seem like a food. It has many calories. However, it has no vitamins, minerals, or other food value. In addition, it is not digested in the same way as food. Alcohol is not a food. It is a drug that passes directly into the blood through the walls of the stomach and small intestine. The blood carries alcohol rapidly to the brain.

What was your answer to *Early Checkup* number 7? (Is alcohol a type of food?)

Alcohol is a depressant drug. It slows muscle movement and can cause people to lose their self-control. Some people cannot remember what has happened while they have been drinking. People who drink too much alcohol often think they can handle any situation. They do not believe that alcohol has changed their ability to move quickly, think clearly, and make sound decisions. Can you see why so many car accidents happen to people who have been drinking? Can you see why many states are passing stiffer penalties for drinking while driving?

It is often hard to know just how much alcohol is in a drink. Some people think that beer has less alcohol than wine and whiskey. That would be true if a serving of beer were the same size as a serving of whiskey. In fact, a 12-ounce (355-ml) can of beer contains the same amount of alcohol as a 5-ounce (148-ml) glass of wine or 1½ ounces (44 ml) of 80-proof liquor.

Two Kinds of Alcohol

The kind of alcohol in beer, wine, and other alcoholic beverages is *ethyl alcohol.* It is formed by the fermentation of sugar with yeast spores. The alcohol used medically is *isopropyl alcohol.* It is an antiseptic agent. It is poisonous and should *never* be taken internally.

Contrary to popular belief, alcohol is a depressant, not a stimulant. Alcohol affects those parts of the brain that regulate acquired behaviors, such as self-control. Like many other drugs, alcohol can have markedly different effects on people. The effects are often determined by the individual's own body chemistry.

Different people are affected by different amounts of alcohol. The effects of the drug depend upon a person's weight, mood, personality, and how much food is in his or her stomach.

Some adults celebrate at times by drinking small amounts of alcohol. Unless they have certain health problems, they are probably not harming their bodies. However, drinking too much alcohol for a long time can cause heart, liver, and brain damage. People who drink a lot of alcohol may develop a tolerance to the drug. They require more and more of it to feel the effect they want.

Taking alcohol along with cold tablets or other OTC drugs can make a person sleepy or dizzy. Taking alcohol along with tranquilizers or barbiturates increases the depressant action of the two drugs. Even a small amount of a tranquilizer taken with a small amount of alcohol can have a powerful effect. Death from drug overdose happens every day because people mix alcohol and depressants.

Many adults choose not to drink alcoholic beverages. Some have tried such drinks and do not like the way alcohol tastes or how it makes them feel. Others choose not to drink alcoholic beverages because they do not like what alcohol can do to harm their bodies and minds. Adults who do not drink alcoholic beverages enjoy life as much as, or more than, adults who do.

Sometime in the future, you will have to decide whether or not you will drink alcoholic beverages. If you decide not to, you will have an interesting time learning to handle questions and kidding from others. If you do decide to drink alcoholic beverages, you will be responsible for doing so in the most healthful way possible for you.

What Is an Alcoholic?

Alcoholics are people who become dependent on the drug alcohol. Their bodies need more and more alcohol to feel the same effect on the brain. When alcoholics try to stop drinking, they go through a *withdrawal* period that can be very painful. Alcoholism is a serious disease. Alcoholics should have medical help to withdraw from drinking.

The majority of alcoholics are not "down-and-out," skid row bums. In fact, of the ten million Americans who are alcoholics, only three percent are derelicts. The rest are people who work and have families. The reason most alcoholics go unnoticed is that they and their families conceal their drinking problems. Some alcoholics will not admit, even to themselves, that they need help.

Alcoholics need understanding and objective caring. There are many resources available to help alcoholics and their families. Practically every community has a chapter of *Alcoholics Anonymous*. *Alateen* groups comprise teenagers whose mothers or fathers are alcoholics. School counselors and religious organizations, as well as the National Council on Alcoholism, can help to refer people for proper treatment.

Inhalant abuse occurs frequently among young people because the substances producing the inhalants are inexpensive and easy to obtain. Almost anything in aerosol form can be used as an inhalant. The most commonly abused substances include paint, vegetable oil and hair sprays, glues, and paint thinners.

What Should You Know About Chemicals That Act Like Drugs?

In most homes, there are products such as hair sprays, paints, glues, lighter fluids, and window cleaners. All of these products give off *fumes,* or gases. Breathing these fumes, or *inhalants,* can cause a druglike change in the body and mind. Many affect the brain the way hallucinogens do. They can make people dizzy. Sometimes talking and walking become difficult. If used often, inhalants can cause lasting damage to the brain, nervous system, and respiratory system.

Sometimes people use an inhalant just to find out what it feels like. These people often want to show off by taking chances with their health. Breathing large amounts of such inhalants can cause motor-skill problems and permanent brain damage. It also can produce heart failure, suffocation, and sudden death. For these reasons, breathing inhalants, or challenging others to do so, is against the law.

Always store cleaning products out of children's reach. Sometimes small children inhale the fumes of a household spray or other cleaning product by mistake.

What Have You Learned?

Number a piece of paper from **1** through **3**. Next to the numbers, write the words that are missing in these sentences.

1. Lung cancer and emphysema are two diseases caused by __ in cigarette __.

2. A drug that many people think of as food is __.

3. Along with several other dangerous drugs, it is __ to buy, sell, or use marijuana.

Answers to *What Have You Learned?*
1. tars (chemicals); smoke
2. alcohol
3. illegal

Learn More About It

You can add to your understanding of drugs by further reading. Your library has books on the subject, written for people your age. Here are some titles you may find helpful.

Hydge, Margaret O. *Know About Alcohol.* New York: McGraw-Hill Book Company, 1978. The use and abuse of drinking alcohol are made clear in this book. Learn more facts about the effects of drinking.

Stwertka, Eve, and Stwertka, Albert. *Marijuana.* New York: Franklin Watts, Inc., 1979. The history, chemistry, use, and legal regulations concerning marijuana are among the subjects included in this book.

Woods, Geraldine. *Drug Use and Drug Abuse.* New York: Franklin Watts, Inc., 1979. This book discusses the difference between drug use and abuse. Both medicinal and nonmedicinal drugs are examined.

Interested students may wish to design and present a drug education program for other classes in your school. Posters, booklets, panel discussions, an assembly, and other means of communication could be explored in terms of time available, effort involved, and potential effectiveness.

More To Do on Your Own

1. Create an imaginary over-the-counter drug. Then draw or write a drug ad of your own that you think will educate people about your drug. For example, list all the side effects the drug may cause. Let the reader or TV viewer know the ways your drug may be dangerous, and the reasons people should still buy it.
2. Write a report about any drug that is prescribed by doctors to prevent, treat, or cure disease. Your school or community librarian can help you find articles and books on the subject of medicines.
3. Create an anti-smoking poster. Your poster may be original, or it might poke fun at a real cigarette ad you have seen in magazines. Make sure your poster states the facts about the effects of smoking on health, so the reader can come to an intelligent decision about smoking.

Final Checkup

A. Number a sheet of paper from **1** through **10**. Write **true** or **false** next to the number for each of these ideas.

1. Taking a drug for a headache or minor illness is not always necessary. true

2. A prescription drug label lists the ingredients of the drug. false

3. Prescription drugs are usually more powerful than OTC drugs. true

4. OTC medicines do not require prescriptions because they are always safe for everyone. false

5. Different people may have different reactions to the same drug. true

6. Amphetamines are drugs that slow the body's actions. false

7. People who overuse barbiturates can become dependent on them. true

8. Caffeine, the drug found in coffee, slows the actions of the body. false

9. Alcohol often makes people more talkative because it is a stimulant drug. false

10. Nicotine is not the only dangerous substance in cigarette smoke. true

B. Number a sheet of paper from **1** through **10**. Next to each number, write the letter of the words that best complete each sentence.

1. Undesirable reactions produced by drugs are called
a. symptoms.
b. alcoholism.
c. tolerance.
(d.) side effects.

2. Using drugs for nonmedical purposes is called
a. psychological dependence.
b. drug tolerance.
(c.) drug abuse.
d. physical dependence.

3. Medicines that can be purchased only with a doctor's written order are
a. stimulants.
(b.) prescription drugs.
c. hallucinogens.
d. OTC drugs.

4. Amphetamines cause people to
(a.) feel more energetic and alert.
b. have hallucinations.
c. feel relaxed and sleepy.
d. quit smoking.

5. Caffeine and nicotine are both
a. depressant drugs.
b. hallucinogens.
(c.) stimulant drugs.
d. narcotic drugs.

6. A slowing down of breathing, heart rate, and other body processes that can cause unconsciousness and even death may result when people drink alcohol and take
   a. hallucinogens.
   (b.) depressants.
   c. stimulants.
   d. narcotics.

7. Drugs slowing signals from the brain to the body, causing chemical changes that can permanently damage the brain, and causing people to have hallucinations are called
   (a.) hallucinogens.
   b. depressants.
   c. stimulants.
   d. narcotics.

8. Three dangerous substances found in cigarette smoke are
   a. caffeine, amphetamines, and nicotine.
   b. tars, PCP, and sedatives.
   c. carbon monoxide, morphine, and caffeine.
   (d.) nicotine, tars, and carbon monoxide.

9. The way alcohol affects a person depends on
   a. the person's weight, mood, and personality.
   b. what other drugs the person has taken.
   c. how much food is in the person's stomach.
   (d.) all of the above.

10. Nondrug products giving off fumes or gases that produce druglike effects are called
   a. OTC medicines.
   (b.) inhalants.
   c. barbiturates.
   d. alcoholic beverages.

Write About Better Health

Write a short answer to each of these questions. Use complete sentences.

1. How might common household products be abused? How might they harm your health?
2. Why are the reasons given by people for smoking poor excuses?
3. How are nonsmokers affected by cigarette smoking?
4. Why do some people try to escape their problems by using drugs?
5. How might teenagers avoid turning to drugs when problems arise?

Model answers to *Write About Better Health* are provided in the chapter notes at the front of this *Teacher's Edition.*

10 BETTER HEALTH FOR CONSUMERS

See the teaching notes on page 256.

"What a rotten skateboard!" said Ishi angrily, as he shut the door behind him.

Ishi's mother looked at her son. There was a bruise on his arm and his face was scraped.

"What happened?" she asked.

"One of the wheels came off my new skateboard," Ishi answered. "I fell, but I didn't hurt myself much . . . just some scrapes and bruises."

"Go wash them with soap and water," Ishi's mother told him. "I'll get the sales slip I saved when we bought the skateboard. That board is less than a month old! We're taking it back to the store. I purposely chose the model that was *guaranteed*."

Ishi was puzzled. "Can we do that, Mom? After all, I used it already."

"Yes," said his mother. "We bought it at Allesio's. That's a good store. They certainly don't want to sell products that may be dangerous. Mr. Allesio will return it to the manufacturer. That's the company that made the skateboard. Good manufacturers also want to know when there's something wrong with a product they're selling. No store or manufacturer is happy about returns, of course. But if they find out what's wrong, they may be able to correct the problem. That will help stop returns in the future."

"I never thought a skateboard was such a big deal," said Ishi. "I'll go wash my scrapes and bruises. Please don't leave without me. I'd like to learn more about this *return* business."

This story points out several characteristics of wise consumers. They buy reputable brands from reputable stores; they will return a defective product; they save such important items as sales slips and guarantees or warranties. Returning defective products is one means of alerting merchants and producers to problems with those products.

It is certainly bothersome and expensive for stores to receive returned merchandise. A store that gets too many returns on a product may stop selling that product. A manufacturer that gets too many returns may redesign the product.

Consumers should try to return faulty products, when possible. They must also be responsible about following directions for use and about admitting when they, not the product, are at fault.

LOOKING AHEAD

Many of the products you use every day can affect your health. For example, by wisely choosing and using food, clothing, soap, toothpaste, and sports equipment, you can help to build better health.

In this chapter you will find ideas for choosing products and services that offer good health value.

You will learn

- what health values to look for in products and services you buy or use.
- how product labels can help consumers.
- how advertising can help consumers.
- how consumers can be helped to protect themselves from unsafe products and services.

Here are some words that you may not have talked about in school before. You will learn more about them in this chapter. You can find these words in the *Glossary* at the back of this book.

brand name (brand nām) **effective** (ə·fek′tiv)
consumer (kən·sü′mər) **myths** (miths)

Early Checkup

How much do you already know about your responsibility as a consumer? Number a piece of paper from **1** through **6**. Answer each of these questions by writing **yes** or **no** next to the correct number on your paper. You can check your answers as you read this chapter.

1. Should only the people who actually *buy* products be called consumers? no
2. Can consumers believe the information they read on health product labels? yes
3. Do consumers have any protection from false health information in advertising? yes
4. Are extra vitamins needed for most people with normal health? no
5. Can the government help to protect consumers from dangerous health products? yes
6. Can consumers become so wise that they do not need help to protect their health? no

Some stores and some manufacturers will not take back defective products. Wise consumers quickly learn to avoid them. Later in this chapter, students will learn about some other alternatives for consumers who buy faulty products. They will also learn how to investigate products before buying them.

Although people have always been consumers, problems of modern consumers are different from those of our ancestors who hunted and gathered their own food, made their own clothing, and frequently had no medical resources except herbs. We are fortunate to have an enormous variety of health products and services. That variety, however, makes choice more difficult.

An interesting way to start the chapter would be to have one or more students take the part of the mythical "two-thousand-year-old person."

Some topics to ask the "two-thousand-year-old person" about might include

- how much product choice people had a long time ago compared with today.
- how and why product packaging has changed.
- the first consumer-safety group (a group to test the safety and efficiency of spears, arrows, herbal remedies, etc.).
- safety problems and safety "labeling" in the Stone Age.

This activity can be not only fun but instructive, for it introduces the consumer health concerns that are the major themes of this chapter.

YOU CAN BE AN EFFECTIVE CONSUMER

consumer

What Is a Consumer?

Anyone who uses or buys products or services is a **consumer**. This means that everyone is a consumer part of the time. Think about just a few of the choices you make as a consumer.

- Which shoes should I wear for the game?
- What should I eat for breakfast and lunch?
- Should I buy the regular or the giant tube?
- Is the bruise serious enough to show to a nurse or doctor?

The Better Business Bureau Helps Consumers

People often call the *Better Business Bureau* to find out if it has received complaints about some store, product, or service. The bureau is supported by local business people who want to stop any unfair or dishonest practices that cheat consumers. Most telephone directories have a listing for "Better Business Bureau."

What was your answer to *Early Checkup* number 1? (Should only the people who actually *buy* products be called consumers?)

Many consumer decisions can help or harm a person's health. For example, the breakfast cereal you ask your family to buy may contain added sugar. The sugar can help cause *tooth decay*.

You Can Make Good Decisions

It is not always easy to make the wisest consumer decision. There are so many health questions to keep in mind. Does the product work well? Will it break easily? Is it safe for everyone in the family? Does the health value seem worth the price? Do I need it? Where can I get more information?

This shield shows that the American Dental Association has accepted a product for the care of teeth and gums.

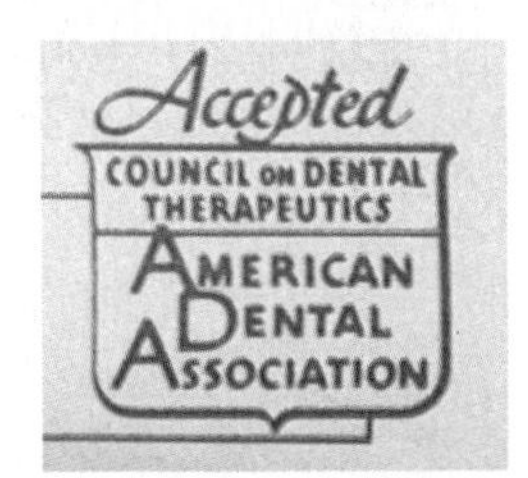

Of course, consumers also think about how well they like a product, as well as how healthful it may be. For example, two different brands of *fluoride* toothpaste may cost about the same amount of money. Both may be approved by the *American Dental Association* (ADA) as being good for preventing tooth decay. In that case, both may be good products. When products are equally good, the consumer may choose the toothpaste that tastes best. This makes building good health more fun, since teeth should be brushed several times a day.

When choosing sneakers, wise consumers ask, "Do they fit well?" "Are they well made?" "Will they last?" "Is the price right?" "Am I paying more for the product name than for its *value?*"

Lead the children through the parts of the fruit drink label. Not all vitamins and other nutrients must be listed on a food label, but some manufacturers go beyond legal requirements and list all nutrients. For certain products, such as catsup or mayonnaise, the Food and Drug Administration has agreed that if certain standards are met (e.g., how many tomatoes are used per pint of catsup), ingredients do not have to be listed. Your local library may have copies of the FDA standards. If not, you may write:

Food and Drug
Administration
Office of Public Affairs
5600 Fishers Lane
Rockville, MD 20857

Read Your Labels

Labels can give important information for making consumer decisions. There are national laws that manufacturers must obey when they label food, clothing, and many other health products. The information printed on the labels must be honest. Food *ingredients* must be listed on can, bottle, or box labels. Ingredients are the different materials used to make the product. The ingredients must be given, in order, from the greatest to the least amount used.

What was your answer to *Early Checkup* number 2? (Can consumers believe the information they read on health product labels?)

What is the major ingredient of the fruit drink? What other health information is on the label?

Most clothing must also have labels that tell what kind of cloth was used to make it. The label should also tell how to clean the clothing. Other health products list directions for use, how long the product will keep, and any warnings about how the product may be unsafe.

The cautions on over-the-counter (OTC) drug labels are intended *to provide instructions for use, to indicate when the product is or is not suitable, to warn of inappropriate uses, and to alert consumers to any safety or health hazards they may risk in using that product.*

Care labels attached to clothing may simply provide information on how to make the clothing last longer. *In the case of flame-resistant materials, however, following directions can be the critical difference between maintaining and losing the ability to resist fire.*

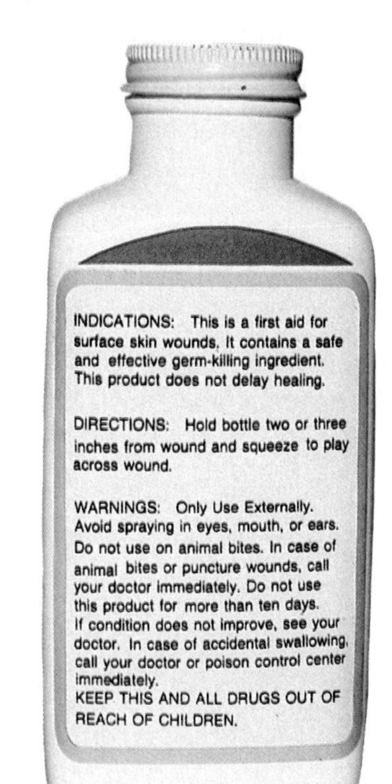

Antiseptics and other health products you buy without a *prescription* often have usage and warning labels. What can you learn from this label?

Most clothes carry labels explaining how to care for them. Why does this product have to be washed with a detergent and no soap or bleach?

brand name

"Hidden messages" are used by almost all advertisers to make their ads more effective. There is nothing wrong with hidden messages, but the students should learn to separate such messages from the real information the ads contain. Many ads cater to psychological needs and desires. Buying for psychological needs is often harmless, as in the case of a shampoo. Sometimes, however, psychological buying patterns can cause people to take economic and health risks. (*Buying products to increase popularity or to "fit in" better can lead to spending money unwisely. At its extreme, successful advertising psychology motivates individuals to purchase cigarettes, alcoholic beverages, and over-the-counter drugs.*)

What Does Advertising Tell You?

Just as labels can give the consumer product information, so also can *advertising.* Think of all the advertisements you find in newspapers and magazines, as well as on signs and billboards. Other advertisements are the commercials on radio and television.

Advertisements can be helpful to consumers. They tell people about new products and services. They also help to show consumers the differences between similar products and services. Most products are given a **brand name** by the companies that make them. Advertisements help consumers remember the brand of products they like to use.

Not all advertising helps consumers make wise choices. Does the fact that famous people like some brand of food help the consumer know more about its health value? Is a skin cream healthful because a beautiful actress says she uses it? To make people want to buy their brand, companies give consumers more than health information. They try to make people think they will be more attractive, more popular, or otherwise better off for using their brand.

Does this ad contain useful health information about shampoo? Can some brand of shampoo make all people who use it look like the people in this picture? If these people were smoking the same brand of cigarettes would it be a sign that the brand being smoked is healthful?

The *Federal Trade Commission* (FTC) is a government agency that helps to protect consumers from false advertising. The FTC tests the information in advertisements to make sure it is truthful. If it is not, the advertisement must be changed.

What was your answer to *Early Checkup* number 3? (Do consumers have any protection from false health information in advertising?)

On Your Own

Learn to listen carefully to the information that advertisements give you about products. Do the advertisements give enough useful facts to help you decide which brands to buy or use?

Look through the advertisements for health products and services in a magazine or newspaper. Choose five that you think give important information to consumers. Choose five more that do not. Number each advertisement and write down the number of points you would give it for the information it contains. Give a zero to the ad with no useful health information and up to 5 points to the ad with a lot of useful health information. You may score some as having 0,1,2,3,4, or 5 points. Score the same way to show how much—or how little—you like the ad.

Without showing your scores, ask a friend or someone in your family to score the same advertisements.

Compare your scores. Do different people feel the same way about the same advertisements?

How many of these advertised products do you or your family use? Have these advertisements helped you to decide to buy or use these products?

Encourage students to discuss the extremely important role advertising plays in our society. Ask them to picture a world with no advertising at all. Shoppers would miss knowing where the bargains are. If you needed a particular product or service, you could not check a free advertising circular or the telephone directory's Yellow Pages, or find it advertised in the local newspaper. New products would have little chance of making their way into the economy.

Students often believe that advertisers try to trick them with misleading claims. Discuss the purpose of advertising (*to persuade people to buy a certain brand*). Encourage students to read or to listen to ads critically. For example, ask what an advertiser is saying in an ad that claims, "No product is better." (*The advertiser hopes the consumer will think, "This product must be the best." However, all that "No product is better" really means is that there may be a number of products that are about equal in quality.*)

myths

Some People Believe Myths About Products

Have you ever heard or read the kind of stories people call **myths**? Myths are tales and ideas that people sometimes believe are true even when there is no proof supporting that belief. For example, some people believe that the only good way to clean teeth is with an electric toothbrush. Is this a fact or a myth?

Most dentists seem to agree that a regular toothbrush with soft, straight bristles can clean teeth as well as any electric toothbrush.

"My mouthwash prevents colds."

A myth is often based partly on facts. Some mouthwashes do kill harmful *germs.* However, no mouthwash can kill enough germs to prevent disease.

"Any food marked 'natural' is better for my health."

"Natural" foods are often no better for your health than less expensive foods of the same kind. Salt and sugar are "natural," but you would not want too much of them added to foods.

"Protein shampoo feeds my hair with nutrients."

Proteins, such as those found in eggs or milk, are *nutrients.* However, hair is not living *tissue.* It does not use foods that are placed directly on it.

"I take a lot of extra vitamins. They make me extra healthy."

Most people get all the *vitamins* they need in a well-balanced daily diet. If you think you need extra vitamins, ask your family or doctor.

What was your answer to *Early Checkup* number 4? (Are extra vitamins needed for most people with normal health?)

What Have You Learned?

Number a sheet of paper from **1** through **5**. Next to the numbers, write the words that are missing in these sentences.

1. Wise consumers get all the __ they can before choosing health products or services.

2. Some important questions a wise consumer asks about health products and services are about how __ they are for a family to use, how __ they work, and how __ they will last.

3. The __ ingredient listed on a food label is the major one used in making the food.

4. Companies use __ in newspapers and magazines. These tell consumers more about new products and help consumers remember __ names of the products.

5. A story that may be based on some facts, but is not proven, is called a __.

Answers to *What Have You Learned?*
1. information (facts)
2. safe; well; long
3. first
4. advertisements; brand
5. myth

effective

Wise Consumers Protect Each Other

Wise consumers do more than simply return products that are not safe or effective. They help protect other consumers by reporting the unsafe or ineffective product to a government agency. Agencies responsible for each kind of product can often be found in the telephone directory. They may not know about unsafe or ineffective products until consumers report them.

WHO PROTECTS THE CONSUMER?

Health Products Must Be Safe and Effective

The *Food and Drug Administration* (FDA) is a government agency that protects the health of consumers. The FDA makes sure that the information given on the labels and packages of health-care products is truthful. The FDA also tests many health products before they are sold. For example, medicines must be tested *before* they can be sold. The FDA checks them to make sure that they are safe and **effective** for consumers. An effective product is one that does what it is supposed to do. Even when a drug is effective, the FDA may prevent its use because the drug may be dangerous to many people. For example, a drug may be effective in relieving the *symptoms* of a cold, but it might also cause damage to another part of the body. The FDA also checks toothpastes, lipsticks, and some shampoos. These products do not have to be approved before they are sold unless their manufacturers claim that the products change the users' health.

What was your answer to *Early Checkup* number 5? (Can the government help to protect consumers from dangerous health products?)

People Working for Your Health

Every day, Ms. Eileen Douglas helps people become wise consumers. Ms. Douglas is a reporter for New York City's WINS television station program, *Inflation Fighter.* On this consumer information program, Ms. Douglas reports on the best buys for such daily needs as food and clothing. She talks with consumer experts, and with consumers themselves, to find out the best ways for people to save money every day.

Ms. Douglas has a college degree in political science. During her last year at college, she reported the news for a television station in her town. After college, she began working for station WINS. Ms. Douglas enjoys giving consumer information to her television viewers. "I am one of the first people to know the facts," she says. "It's fun to pass those facts on to everyone else."

Consumers Are Protected by Their Government

Wise consumers protect themselves best by staying well informed about health products and services. However, even wise consumers sometimes need the aid of health professionals. There are government agencies that help to protect the health and safety of all consumers.

- The *U.S. Department of Agriculture* checks the quality of any meat and poultry being transported from one state to another.
- The *FDA* checks other foods, including pet foods.
- Each state has a *consumer protection agency* for the people in that state.
- The U.S. *Consumer Product Safety Commission* works to keep products that might be unsafe from being sold.
- The *U.S. Postal Service* can refuse to accept products that are dangerous or make false claims.

What was your answer to *Early Checkup* number 6? (Can consumers become so wise that they do not need help to protect their health?)

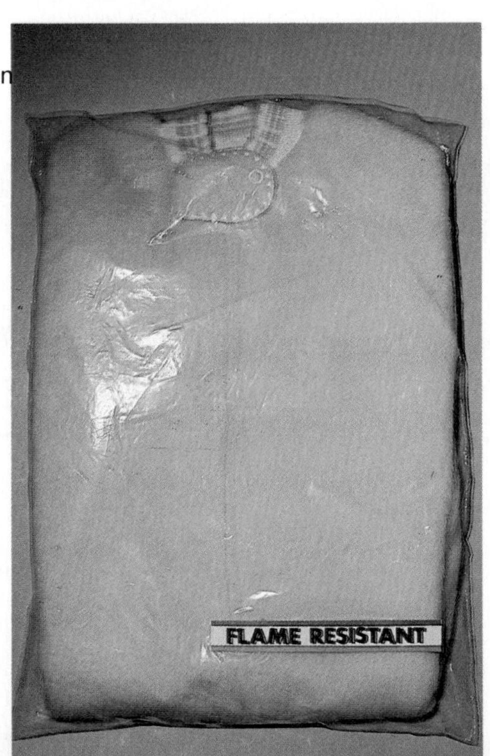

The U.S. Consumer Product Safety Commission requires that children's sleepwear be made of fabric that does not burn easily. Do you think such laws help protect consumers?

The Consumer Product Safety Commission was founded in 1970. It is especially concerned with products that affect children's safety, such as dangerous toys and furniture, and caps on aspirin and other medication bottles that can be easily removed by children. It is generally believed that the work of the commission has saved thousands of children's lives.

The commission acts mainly on consumer complaints about unsafe products. While letters or complaints from individual class members might not be appropriate, a group letter of complaint about some unsafe product could be addressed to:

Director, Office of Communications
Consumer Product Safety Commission
Washington, DC 20207

In addition to the broad-based agencies mentioned in the student's book, there are many specialized organizations that help the consumer: the Securities and Exchange Commission for stocks and bonds; the Interstate Commerce Commission for problems with buses, trucks, or (in some cases) railroads; the Civil Aeronautics Board for most consumer problems with airlines; and so forth. Besides these federal agencies, the locally run Better Business Bureaus help consumers handle complaints.

Health Professionals Must Be Licensed

When you think of health professionals, do you picture only doctors and nurses? Think of how many others in your community provide health services for consumers.

Often young people visit a *pediatrician,* who is a doctor specializing in children's health. Some people go to doctors in clinics or have a *family doctor.* Adults often get their health care from an *internist.* Internists offer preventive health care and treat diseases. Every type of doctor and dentist must receive a professional license from the state in which she or he practices. Next time you go for an examination, look at the license on the wall. That license took the doctor or dentist a long time and a lot of training to get.

These people are all health professionals.

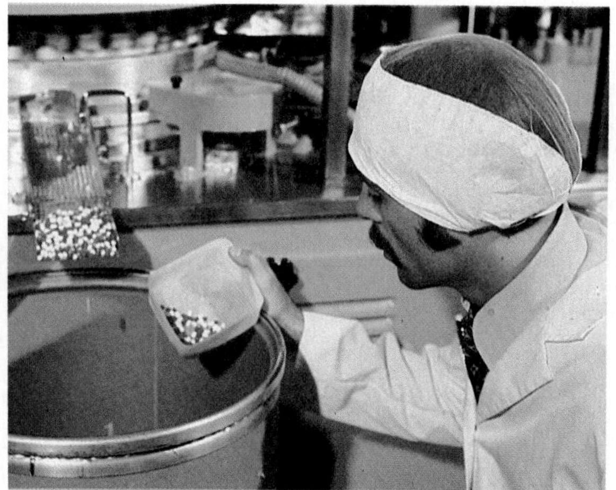

What Have You Learned?

Number a piece of paper **1** and **2**. Next to the numbers, write the words that are missing in these sentences.

1. Before they can be sold, drugs are checked by the FDA to see that they are safe and ___.
2. The U.S. Department of Agriculture checks the quality of ___ and ___.

Answers to *What Have You Learned?*
1. effective
2. meat; poultry

Learn More About It

The catalog and magazine listed here will help you become a wise consumer.

Consumer Information Center. *Consumer Information Catalog.* This free list of all federal publications for consumers is published four times a year. For a copy, write to

Consumer Information Center
Pueblo, CO 81009

Consumers Union. *Penny Power.* This magazine helps young people learn how to become better consumers. See if your library has copies. For your own subscription, write to

Penny Power
Box 1949
Marion, OH 43305

More To Do on Your Own

1. *Consumers Union* is an organization that helps consumers by testing brands and reporting on the results of the tests in a magazine called *Consumer Reports.* Look at some recent issues of *Consumer Reports* in a library. See if you can find the reports on some products or services you use. You may find reports on foods, radios, or bicycles. Some reports show how often repairs are required. Does any report help to change your mind about the product? Does any make you feel even better about the product you use?

2. You often get more product for your money when you buy a larger size. However, sometimes you do not. Choose any three items of a brand that comes in at least three sizes. (Some products to look at can include toothpaste, shampoo, soap, milk, bread, or apple juice.) Find the price of one ounce (or one gram) in each size. To do this, divide the price by the number of ounces (or grams). The price for one ounce or gram is called the *unit price.* Make a chart that shows what you discovered.

3. Find out about health care in your community. Ask your family, friends, and teachers, "Where do people in this area get health care?" Ask, "Why do people choose different ways to get health care?" Some health-care options to think about are *fee-for-service* doctors, *prepaid medical groups, clinics,* and hospitals. Find out what health care is available for people who have little money. Ask about *health insurance* in your community. You may want to make a simple map or chart that shows the different kinds of health-care services available near where you live.

Final Checkup

A. Number a sheet of paper from **1** through **10**. Next to each number, write the letter of the words that best complete each sentence.

1. Every day a consumer
a. buys products.
b. makes choices.
c. returns items to a store.
d. buys services.

2. An example of a health product is
a. toothpaste.
b. shampoo.
c. soap.
d. all of these.

3. For a health product, the most important information a consumer should have is
a. how the product tastes.
b. how much the product costs.
c. how well the product works and how safe it is.
d. how the product is advertised.

4. If two products are about the same in most ways,
a. there is no way to choose between them.
b. you should buy the one you like best.
c. you should buy the one that is advertised most.
d. you should buy both.

5. Labels that tell what is in the products are used on
a. foods only.
b. clothing only.
c. foods and clothing.
d. foods, clothing, and toys.

6. A consumer who pays attention to advertising
a. will never learn anything useful.
b. will sometimes learn useful information.
c. will always make wise decisions.
d. will become more popular.

7. Advertising claims are checked by
a. the Federal Trade Commission (FTC).
b. the Food and Drug Administration (FDA).
c. both the FTC and the FDA.
d. neither the FTC nor the FDA.

8. Product safety is checked by
a. the U.S. Consumer Product Safety Commission.
b. the Food and Drug Administration (FDA).
c. the U.S. Postal Service.
d. all of the above.

9. Myths about products
a. are not based on any proof.
b. help you make wise consumer decisions.
c. never confuse people.
d. are approved by most doctors.

10. In every state a dentist must have
   a. a nurse.
   (b.) a license.
   c. a label.
   d. an assistant.

B. Number a sheet of paper from **1** through **10**. Write **true** or **false** next to the number for each of these ideas.

1. You become a consumer only when you buy something. false
2. One of the most important things a consumer can have is information. true
3. All products list their ingredients on the label. false
4. There is no way to check products before buying them. false
5. Advertisements always have helpful information. false
6. Some shampoos have ingredients that feed your hair. false
7. Health professionals need licenses from their states. true
8. The FDA makes sure that drugs are safe and effective before the drugs are allowed to be sold. true
9. No one checks pet foods to make sure that they are safe for pets. false
10. Each state has its own consumer protection agency. true

Write About Better Health

Write a short answer to each of these questions. Use complete sentences.

1. What are some good reasons for making a consumer choice? Which two reasons are most important for health products?
2. What four kinds of information can you often find from reading labels?
3. What kinds of information can you get from advertising?
4. How can you change your habits to become a wise consumer?
5. Name four government agencies that help protect the health and safety of consumers. What is the special job of each one?

Model answers to *Write About Better Health* are provided in the chapter notes at the front of this *Teacher's Edition.*

GLOSSARY

This *Glossary* lists all the words that appeared in your text in **boldfaced** type. Some other words you may need are also included.

Right next to the word, you can find the way it is pronounced. The pronunciation is in parentheses ( ) right after the word itself. If you are not sure how to say a particular sound in the pronunciation, look at the pronunciation key. It appears throughout this *Glossary*.

Small dots in the pronunciations help you see how to separate syllables. a dark mark (′) shows which syllable gets the main stress. In some words, a lighter mark (′) shows a syllable that is also stressed, but not as heavily as the main one.

PRONUNCIATION KEY*

a hat, cap
ā age, face
ä father, far

b bad, rob
ch child, much
d did, red

e let, best
ē equal, be
ėr term, learn

f fat, if
g go, bag
h he, how

i it, pin
ī ice, five

j jam, enjoy
k kind, seek
l land, coal
m me, am
n no, in
ng long, bring

o hot, rock
ō open, go
ô order, all
oi oil, voice
ou house, out

p paper, cup
r run, try
s say, yes
sh she, rush
t tell, it
th thin, both
ᴛʜ then, smooth

u cup, butter
u̇ full, put
ü rule, move

v very, save
w will, woman
y young, yet
z zero, breeze
zh measure, seizure

ə represents:
a in about
e in taken
i in pencil
o in lemon
u in circus

*From SCOTT, FORESMAN BEGINNING DICTIONARY
By E. L. Thorndike and Clarence L. Barnhart.

abdomen (ab′də·mən), the part of the body where the stomach, intestines, and other digestive organs are located.

abscess (ab′ses), a pocket of pus resulting from an infection.

abuse (ə·byüz′), to use something, such as a drug, for reasons other than it is meant to be used.

additive (ad′ə·tiv), a substance added to food to change or improve it.

adrenal (ə·drē′nl), having to do with a gland in the body that regulates blood pressure, heartbeat, and energy.

aerator (er′āt·ôr), a device that supplies oxygen.

aerobic exercise (er′ō′bik ek′sər·sīz), any exercise that helps the body use more oxygen and improves the circulatory system.

aging (ā′jing), changes in the characteristics of a living or nonliving thing that happen over time; the process of growing older.

alcohol (al′kə·hôl), a colorless liquid used in whiskey, wine, and other beverages. Alcohol is a depressant drug.

allergy (al′ər·jē), an unusual reaction of body tissue to certain substances such as drugs and foods.

amphetamine (am·fet′ə·mēn), a stimulant drug that speeds up the activity of the body, lifts mood, and decreases appetite.

antiseptic (an′tə·sep′tik), a substance that stops or slows the growth of germs. Antiseptics are used to fight infection.

anus (ā′nəs), the opening at the lower end of the digestive system through which solid wastes pass out of the body.

artery (är'tər·ē), a blood vessel or tube that carries blood from the heart to the other parts of the body.

arthritis (är·thrī'tis), a noncommunicable disease that causes inflammation of joints in the body.

asthma (az'mə), a noncommunicable disease that causes breathing difficulty and a cough.

atrium (ā'trē·əm), either of the two upper chambers of the heart that receives blood from the veins and in turn forces it into the ventricles.

bacteria (bak·tir'ē·ə), tiny plants that can be seen only with a microscope and sometimes cause disease.

barbiturate (bär·bich'ər·it), a drug used to relieve pain, relax tension, and bring on sleep.

bladder (blad'ər), a sac in the body that stores the urine it has received from the kidneys.

blind spot (blīnd spot), the point on the retina where all the nerves of the eye join to form the optic nerve.

blood (blud), the red fluid that circulates through the veins and arteries.

blood pressure (blud presh'ər), the force with which blood pushes against the inner walls of the arteries.

blood vessel (blud ves'əl), a tube through which blood flows throughout the body. Arteries, veins, and capillaries are blood vessels.

botulism (boch'ə·liz'əm), a serious type of food poisoning caused by certain bacteria produced in foods that are not canned or preserved properly.

brain stem (brān stem), a part of the brain that connects the cerebrum and spinal cord and carries signals between them.

brand name (brand nām), the unique name that a company gives to its product so that consumers can remember and distinguish it from other products.

bronchial tube (brong'kē·əl tüb), one of the two main branches of the windpipe, each leading into one of the lungs.

caffeine (kaf'ēn'), a stimulant drug found in tea, coffee, chocolate, and cola drinks.

calculus (kal'kyə·ləs), a hard substance that forms when plaque is not removed from the teeth.

calorie (kal'ər·ē), a unit for measuring heat energy. Each calorie is the amount of heat energy it takes to raise the temperature of one kilogram of water by one degree Celsius.

cancer (kan'sər), a disease in which certain body cells grow uncontrollably and destroy healthy cells.

capillary (kap'ə·ler'ē), one of the many hair-thin blood vessels that are at the ends of the veins and arteries.

carbohydrate (kär'bō·hī'drāt), a nutrient made by green plants that provides the body with energy.

carbon monoxide (kär'bən mo·nok'sīd), a colorless, odorless, and poisonous gas that is found in the fumes of automobile engines.

cavity (kav'ə·tē), a hole in a tooth caused by tooth decay.

cell (sel), a small unit of living matter of which people, plants, and animals are made.

cell membrane (sel mem'brān), a thin layer of tissue that surrounds a cell.

cellulose (sel'yə·lōs), a carbohydrate that comes from the tough cell walls of plants. Cellulose is a nutrient that the body cannot digest or use as a source of energy.

cerebellum (ser'ə·bel'əm), the part of the brain that controls the coordination of the muscles.

cerebrum (sə·rē'brəm), the part of the human brain that controls speech, the ability to think, and voluntary muscle movements.

chicken pox (chik'ən poks), a contagious disease that occurs most often in children. A symptom of chicken pox is a skin rash.

cholera (kol'ər·ə), a serious, infectious disease of the intestinal tract caused by a microbe. Its symptoms include vomiting, cramps, and diarrhea.

cholesterol (kə·les'tə·rol'), a fatty substance that is found in the blood and tissues of the body.

chromosome (krō'mə·sōm), one of several threadlike bodies located in the nucleus of each body cell. Chromosomes carry genes that contain the traits passed from parents to children.

chronic (kron'ik), lasting for a long period of time or coming back again and again, as a chronic disease.

cilia (sil'ē·ə), tiny hairlike parts of the lung that help remove foreign substances.

circulatory system (sėr'kyə·lə·tôr'ē sis'təm), the heart, blood, and blood vessels all working together to carry blood throughout your body.

a hat	**i** it	**oi** oil	**ch** child	ə = a in about
ā age	**ī** ice	**ou** out	**ng** long	ə = e in taken
ä far	**o** hot	**u** cup	**sh** she	ə = i in pencil
e let	**ō** open	**u̇** put	**th** thin	ə = o in lemon
ē equal	**ô** order	**ü** rule	**ᴛʜ** then	ə = u in circus
ėr term			**zh** measure	

communicable (kə·myü'nə·kə·bəl), easily passed on to others by animal bites, spoiled food and water, or anything else carrying disease microbes.

communication (kə·myü'nə·kā'shən), giving or exchanging thoughts, feelings, and information through words or actions.

community (kə·myü'nə·tē), a group of people who live in the same place.

complex carbohydrate (kəm·pleks' kär'bō·hī'drāt), a nutrient found in foods, such as nuts and grains, that provides long-lasting energy.

conscious (kon'shəs), being alert and aware of one's actions and surroundings.

conservation (kon'sər·vā'shən), the protection and careful use of the environment.

consumer (kən·sü'mər), a person who buys or uses products and services.

contagious (kən·tā'jəs), catching; passed from one person to another.

cool-down (kül'-doun'), a type of exercise that helps the body go from a state of activity to a state of rest.

cytoplasm (sī'tə·plaz'əm), the living jellylike material within a cell that is located outside the nucleus.

DDT (dē·dē·tē'), an insect poison used to kill lice, flies, mosquitoes, and other pests.

dental floss (den'tl flôs), a thin thread, usually waxed, that is used to clean between the teeth.

dentin (den'tən), the hard, bonelike material underneath the enamel of the teeth. Dentin makes up the main part of a tooth.

deoxyribonucleic acid (DNA) (dē·ok'sə·rī'bō·nü·klē'ik as'id), any of a group of acids found primarily in the nucleus of cells. DNA carries the traits that are passed on from parents to children.

dependable (di·pen'də·bəl), reliable; trustworthy.

dependent (di·pen'dənt), needing a drug. People who are dependent on a drug become ill when they stop taking it.

depressant (di·pres'nt), a kind of drug that slows down body activity and relaxes muscles.

dermatologist (dėr'mə·tol'ə·jist), a doctor who is specially trained to treat the skin and its diseases.

diabetes (dī'ə·bē'tēz), a noncommunicable, genetic disease in which the body cannot use food sugars for energy because of a lack of insulin.

diaphragm (dī'ə·fram), the large sheet of muscles and tendons at the floor of the rib cage, separating the chest cavity from the abdominal cavity.

digestion (də·jes'chən), the changing of food by the mouth, stomach, and intestines for use by the body.

digestive system (də·jes'tiv sis'təm), the many body parts that work together to take in and process food for use by the body.

diphtheria (dip·thir'ē·ə), a disease of the throat that causes fever and the formation of a membrane that coats the air passages.

disease (də·zēz'), illness or sickness.

dominant (dom'ə·nənt), the stronger of two genes that has the ability to block out a weaker, or recessive, gene.

drought (drout), a long period of dry weather caused by little or no rain.

drug (drug), any substance that changes how the body and mind function.

dysentery (dis'n·ter'ē), an infectious disease of the digestive system that causes severe diarrhea.

emotion (i·mō'shən), a feeling, such as love, hate, sadness, or fear.

emphysema (em'fə·sē'mə), a disease that causes the air sacs in the lungs to grow in size and makes breathing difficult.

endocrine gland (en'dō·krən gland), a gland that produces a hormone. The pituitary, adrenal, and thyroid glands are endocrine glands.

enriching (en·rich'ing), replacing nutrients that have been lost in the preparation of a food.

environment (en·vī'rən·mənt), the air, water, land, and all the living and man-made things that surround and influence us.

epidemic (ep'ə·dem'ik), the quick spreading of a disease to large numbers of people.

epidermis (ep'ə·dėr'mis), the outer layer of the skin.

epileptic seizure (ep'ə·lep'tik sē'zhər), a loss of consciousness and convulsions that occur in people who have epilepsy, a disorder of the nervous system.

esophagus (ē·sof'ə·gəs), the tube that connects the mouth with the stomach.

fat (fat), a substance found in the bodies of animals and plants. Fats are nutrients that, when eaten, provide the body with energy.

fertilized egg cell (fėr'tl·īzd eg sel), a cell in a mother's body that develops into a baby.

fiber (fī'bər), a carbohydrate that comes from the tough cell walls of plants. Fiber is a nutrient that the body cannot digest or use as a source of energy.

first aid (fėrst ād), immediate treatment that is given to an injured or sick person before trained medical help arrives.

flex (fleks), to bend; to shorten a muscle.

fluoride (flůr'īd), a chemical that is added to toothpaste and water to prevent tooth decay.

food poisoning (füd poi'zn·ing), an illness caused by the eating of foods that are polluted by bacteria or harmful chemical substances.

fortifying (fôr'tə·fī·ing), adding nutrients to a food that it did not initially contain.

fume (fyüm), vapor, smoke, or gas given off by a substance.

fungi (fun'jī), a group of plants without green leaves, such as molds, mildews, and mushrooms. Fungi is the plural of fungus.

gene (jēn), a chemical substance that is part of a chromosome. Genes are passed from parents to children and determine what traits are inherited.

germ (jėrm), a tiny plant or animal that may cause disease.

German measles (jėr'mən mē'zəlz), a contagious disease that causes a fever and red spots on the skin; also known as rubella.

goal (gōl), something a person wants and works hard to achieve.

growth hormone (grōth hôr'mōn), a substance produced by the pituitary gland that controls the growth of the body.

growth spurt (grōth spėrt), a period of sudden, quick growth that occurs at different times for different people.

hallucinogen (hə·lü'sn·ə·jen), a drug that causes a person to see, hear, feel, taste, or smell things differently than they really are.

hazard (haz'ərd), a possible source of harm or danger; risk.

heart disease (härt də·zēz'), a sickness that occurs when the heart or part of the heart does not function properly.

hemoglobin (hē'mə·glō'bən), the substance in the blood that gives it its red color. Hemoglobin carries oxygen from the lungs to the tissues and carbon dioxide from the tissues back to the lungs.

hemophilia (hē'mə·fil'ē·ə), an inherited illness of males in which bleeding is difficult to stop.

hepatitis (hep'ə·tī'tis), a disease of the liver that can make the skin turn yellow and the liver become inflamed.

heredity (hə·red'ə·tē), the passing on of traits from parents to children through genes.

high blood pressure (hī blud presh'ər), a disease of the circulatory system that is caused in part by stress, being overweight, smoking, and eating foods that are high in salt and fat.

hormone (hor'mōn), a chemical that is produced by the glands of the body and causes changes in parts of the body.

hygiene (hī'jēn'), a system of rules for keeping well; personal cleanliness.

immune (i·myün'), protected from disease by antibodies that fight the disease-causing microbes.

immunization (im'yə·nə·zā'shən), the use of weakened or dead disease microbes to make the body produce its own protection against disease.

infection (in·fek'shən), a disease or condition in people, animals, or plants caused by the spreading of disease germs.

influenza (in'flü·en'zə), flu; a contagious disease caused by a virus.

ingredient (in·grē'dē·ənt), a part of a mixture; one thing that goes into making something else.

inhalant (in·hā'lənt), a substance giving off fumes that, when breathed in, produce a druglike effect.

inherited (in·her'it·ed), received certain traits from one's parents.

injury (in'jər·ē), harm done to a person or thing, which often occurs in accidents.

insulin (in'sə·lən), a hormone produced in the pancreas that enables the body to use sugar.

a hat	i it	oi oil	ch child	ə = a in about
ā age	ī ice	ou out	ng long	e in taken
ä far	o hot	u cup	sh she	i in pencil
e let	ō open	u̇ put	th thin	o in lemon
ē equal	ô order	ü rule	ᴛʜ then	u in circus
ėr term			zh measure	

internist (in·tėr′nist), a doctor who gives preventive health care to people. Internists also treat diseases.

islet of Langerhans (ī′lit ov lang′ər·hanz), one of a group of small endocrine cells that secretes insulin.

kidney (kid′nē), one of a pair of organs in the body that removes wastes from the blood.

lab technician (lab tek·nish′ən), a person trained to perform tests in a laboratory.

large intestine (lärj in·tes′tən), the part of the intestine that receives undigestible food and water from the small intestine.

liver (liv′ər), a large organ in people and animals that helps the body use food and removes wastes from the blood.

LSD (el·es·dē), a very strong drug that produces hallucinations. LSD is short for lysergic acid diethylamide.

malaria (mə·lar′ē·ə), a disease spread by certain mosquitoes. Its symptoms include high fever and body weakness.

marijuana (mar′ə·wä′nə), a drug made from the leaves of the hemp plant. Marijuana is smoked for its effects on the mind and body.

measles (mē′zəlz), a virus-caused disease, most often of children. Symptoms include fever and a rash of red spots on the skin; also called rubeola.

medulla oblongata (mi·dul′ə ob′long·gä′tə), the lower part of the brain stem that contains nerve centers to control involuntary functions such as breathing and blood circulation.

microbe (mī′krōb), a tiny animal or plant, especially a disease germ, that is too small to be seen without a microscope.

mineral (min′ər·əl), a substance that is neither plant nor animal. Minerals are nutrients that are important to the health of muscles, nerves, blood cells, teeth, and bones.

misuse (mis·yüs′), the incorrect use of something.

mucus (myü·kəs), a wet, sticky substance in the nose, mouth, throat, and other body organs that keeps germs from getting inside the body.

multiple sclerosis (mul′tə·pəl sklə·rō′sis), an incurable disease of the brain and spinal cord. Its symptoms include speech problems and poor muscle coordination.

mumps (mumps), a contagious disease that is caused by a virus and occurs most often in children. Its symptoms are a swelling of the glands in the neck and difficulty swallowing.

muscle tone (mus′əl tōn), a condition that occurs when the muscles remain slightly flexed.

myth (mith), a story or idea that is not supported by fact or by scientific research.

narcotic (när·kot′ik), a habit-forming drug that causes drowsiness or sleep, dulls the senses, and reduces pain.

nasal membrane (nā′zəl mem′brān), the thin lining of the nose that produces mucus.

natural diasaster (nach′ər·əl də·zas′tər), an event, caused by nature, producing loss of lives and destruction of property. Tornadoes, floods, hurricanes, and earthquakes are natural disasters.

nerve (nėrv), a fiber or fibers that connect the brain or spinal cord with different parts of the body.

nervous system (nėr′vəs sis′təm), the brain, spinal column, and nerve fibers receiving and interpreting signals to control all the activities of the body.

noncommunicable (non′kə·myü′nə·kə·bəl), not spread by disease microbes. Diseases such as arthritis, diabetes, and cancer are noncommunicable.

nonrenewable (non·ri·nü′ə·bəl), not able to be replaced.

nucleus (nü′klē·əs), the "control center" of most plant and animal cells. The nucleus is needed for the cells to grow and divide.

nutrient (nü′trē·ənt), a substance found in foods that keeps body cells healthy.

nutritious (nü·trish′·əs), healthful; nourishing.

optic nerve (op′tik nėrv), either of two nerves that connect the eye to the brain.

organ (ôr′gən), a group of body tissues that work together to do a particular job. The heart, lungs, and eyes are organs.

orthodontist (ôr′thə·don′tist), a dentist who specializes in straightening and adjusting teeth.

over-the-counter (OTC) (ō′vər ᴛʜə koun′tər), having to do with kinds of drugs and medicines that can be bought without a doctor's prescription.

overuse (ō′vər·yüs), using a drug or other substance more than has been recommended.

pacemaker (pās′mā′kər), a special group of cells in the heart muscle that help to maintain a normal heartbeat.

pancreas (pan′krē·əs), a large gland near the stomach that produces insulin and a digestive juice.

panic (pan′ik), a loss of control of one's actions caused by fear or fright.

paramedic (par′ə·med′ik), a person who is trained to help doctors or to give emergency medical treatment.

Parkinson's disease (pär′kin·sənz də·zēz′), a nerve disease that can occur in older people. Its symptoms include trembling of the fingers and hands.

pasteurized (pas′chə·rīzd′), heated at a temperature less than boiling, for a long enough time to kill harmful bacteria.

PCP (pē·sē·pē), a very strong hallucinogenic drug, made from phencyclidine.

pediatric endocrinologist (pē′dē·at′rik en′dō·krə·nol′ə·jist), a doctor trained to treat children with problems or diseases related to the endocrine glands.

pediatrician (pē′dē·ə·trish′ən), a doctor who specializes in the care and development of children.

penicillin (pen′ə·sil′ən), an antibiotic made from a mold. Penicillin is used to treat diseases caused by various bacteria.

periodontal disease (per′·ē·ō·don′təl də·zēz′), disease of the gums that causes redness, bleeding, and swelling.

permanent teeth (pėr′mə·nənt tēth), the set of 32 teeth that replaces the primary teeth. Permanent teeth will not grow back if lost.

perspiration (pėr′spə·rā′shən), sweat; a watery fluid given off through the pores in the skin.

pesticide (pes′tə·sīd), a chemical used to kill insects. Pesticides save crops and trees from being destroyed by certain insects.

pharmacist (fär′mə·sist), a person licensed to prepare and sell prescription drugs.

physical (fiz′ə·kəl), having to do with the body.

physical therapist (fiz′ə·kəl ther′ə·pist), a person trained to help people with disabilities to use their muscles through exercise and massage.

pituitary gland (pə·tü′ə·ter′ē gland), an endocrine gland located at the base of the brain. The pituitary gland produces hormones that control growth.

plaque (plak), a film of bacteria and food particles that forms on the surface of the teeth.

plaque-disclosing tablet (plak dis·klōz′ing tab′lit), a tablet that leaves a coloring on plaque and shows where teeth need further brushing.

polio (pō′lē·ō), a serious disease, usually of children, that causes paralysis and sometimes death.

pollution (pə·lü′shən), the poisoning or spoiling of the environment by litter, untreated wastes, gases, and loud noises.

posture (pos′chər), the way in which the body is held or positioned.

prescription (pri·skrip′shən), a written order from a doctor for making and using a medicine.

preventive medicine (pri·ven′tiv med′ə·sən), regular checkups, immunizations, and good health practices that keep people from getting sick.

protein (prō′tēn), a nutrient that the body uses to build healthy new cells, keep nerves healthy, and fight infection.

protozoan (prō′tə·zō′ən), a very small animal that can be seen only through a microscope. Protozoans are types of microbes.

pulmonary artery (pul′mə·ner′ē är′tər·ē), the blood vessel that takes waste-filled blood from the heart to the lungs.

pulmonary vein (pul′mə·ner′ē vān), the vein that brings blood containing oxygen from the lungs to the heart.

pulp (pulp), the soft inner part of a tooth, where the nerves and the blood vessels are.

pulse (puls), the regular beat of the arteries as blood is pushed through them by the heart.

puncture (pungk′chər), a hole made by a pointed object.

a hat	**i** it	**oi** oil	**ch** child	ə = a in about
ā age	**ī** ice	**ou** out	**ng** long	ə = e in taken
ä far	**o** hot	**u** cup	**sh** she	ə = i in pencil
e let	**ō** open	**u̇** put	**th** thin	ə = o in lemon
ē equal	**ô** order	**ü** rule	**ᴛʜ** then	ə = u in circus
ėr term			**zh** measure	

quality (kwol′ə·tē), a characteristic or trait.

rabies (rā′bēz), a serious disease that causes death if not treated. People can get rabies if they are bitten by an animal that has the disease.

recessive (ri·ses′iv), the weaker of two genes that can be blocked out by a stronger, or dominant, gene.

rectum (rek′təm), the lowest part of the large intestine through which wastes leave the body.

recycling (rē·sī′kəl·ing), processing something so that it can be reused.

red blood cell (red blud sel), one kind of cell found in the blood. Red blood cells carry oxygen from the lungs to the cells and tissues in the body.

reflector (ri·flek′tər), a piece of red, yellow, or white plastic that light bounces off of, making it possible for others to see an object at night.

reflex (rē′fleks), an involuntary action, such as sneezing, blinking, or shivering, that occurs in response to signals received from nerve cells.

relapsing fever (ri·lap′zing fe′vər), any of several infectious diseases in which there is a high body temperature that keeps returning.

REM sleep (rem slēp), a stage during sleep in which the sleeper's eyes move a lot and dreams take place.

renewable (ri·nü′ə·bəl), referring to a supply of something that is never used up and can be refilled or replaced.

respiratory infection (res′pər·ə·tôr′ē in·fek′shən), a disease of the respiratory system caused by a virus or germ.

respiratory system (res′pər·ə·tôr′ē sis′təm), the nose, trachea (windpipe), bronchial tubes, and lungs working together to bring oxygen to and remove wastes from the blood.

ringworm (ring′wėrm′), a contagious disease caused by microscopic fungi. The infection causes a round ringlike shape on the skin.

risk (risk), a chance of getting hurt or losing something; danger.

rubella (rü·bel′ə), see German measles.

rubeola (rü·bē·ō′lə), see measles.

Rx drug (är·eks drug), a prescription drug, sold only by a pharmacist.

saliva (sə·lī′və), a liquid produced by glands in the mouth. Saliva helps to digest food in the mouth.

schistosomiasis (shis′tə·sō·mī′ə·sis), a disease caused by worms that is passed on to people who bathe in waters that are poisoned by these worms.

sewage (sü′ij), waste water that runs from sinks, toilets, and bathtubs into underground sewer pipes.

shock (shok), a dangerous condition brought on by a severe injury, great loss of blood, or emotional upset. Shock causes a sudden drop in blood pressure that leads to unconsciousness.

sickle-cell anemia (sik′əl sel ə·nē′mē·ə), a genetic blood disease in which the red blood cells change from a round to a sickle shape and prevent oxygen from getting to body tissues.

side effect (sīd ə·fekt′), an unwanted or unexpected effect that occurs when using a drug or medicine.

simple carbohydrate (sim′pəl kär′bō·hī′drāt), a nutrient that the body quickly changes to produce energy. Most fruits and some vegetables contain simple carbohydrates.

small intestine (smôl in·tes′tən), a long winding tube in the digestive system that receives food from the stomach.

smallpox (smôl′poks′), a contagious disease caused by a virus. Its symptoms are high fever and red spots on the skin.

social (sō′shəl), having to do with people as they live together in a group.

spinal cord (spī′nl kôrd), a thick cord of nerve tissue that extends from the brain through the spine and down the back.

starch (stärch), a complex carbohydrate that is stored in plants such as potatoes, wheat, rice, and corn. Starches are a good source of long-lasting energy.

sterilized (ster′ə·līzd), made free of microbes.

stimulant (stim′yə·lənt), a substance or drug that temporarily increases the activity of the body.

stomach (stum′ək), a baglike organ in the digestive system that receives food from the mouth.

storm warning (stôrm wôr′ning), a warning given when a bad storm has been sighted and is likely to hit a certain area.

storm watch (stôrm woch), a warning given when the weather conditions are likely to produce a bad storm.

stress (stres), emotional strain that causes people to feel excited, anxious, worried, or angry.

symptom (sim'təm), a signal given by the body in response to some disease, infection, or change.

system (sis'təm), a group of separate parts working together as a whole.

taste bud (tāst bud), any of a group of cells in the tongue that sense whether something is sweet, bitter, salty, or sour.

Tay-Sachs disease (tā·saks də·zēz'), a rare, hereditary, and currently incurable disease of the nervous system that starts in infants and causes early death.

tetanus (tet'n·əs), a disease that causes spasms and stiffness of the muscles.

thyroid (thī'roid), a gland that regulates body processes and growth.

tissue (tish'ü), a group of similar cells that work together to do the same job.

tolerance (tol'ər·əns), a condition in which more and more of a drug is needed to produce the same effect.

tooth decay (tüth di·kā'), rotting of a tooth, caused by germs and bacteria.

trachea (tra'kē·ə), windpipe; the tube that connects the throat to the lungs.

trait (trāt), a quality such as hair color or eye color that may have been passed from parents to children through genes.

tranquilizer (trang'kwə·lī'zər), a drug used to relax muscles, lower blood pressure, and reduce nervous tension.

trichinosis (trik'ə·nō'sis), a disease caused by a harmful worm that can live in the intestines and muscles of people and certain animals. Its symptoms are headache, chills, fever, and muscle soreness.

trust (trust), belief in the honesty or truthfulness of a person or thing.

tuberculosis (tü·bėr'kyə·lō'sis), a disease that destroys body tissue. Tuberculosis most often occurs in the lungs.

typhoid (tī'foid), an infectious, often fatal, disease that causes high fever and inflammation of the intestines.

typhus (tī'fəs), a serious disease that is spread by fleas, lice, or mites. Its symptoms are high fever, weakness, and dark-red spots on the skin.

unconscious (un·kon'shəs), not able to feel or think; not aware of one's surroundings.

urine (yůr'ən), the liquid waste that has been removed from the blood by the kidneys.

vaccination (vak'sə·nā'shən), a shot given as protection against a disease.

vein (vān), a blood vessel or tube that carries blood from any part of the body to the heart.

ventricle (ven'trə·kəl), one of the two lower chambers of the heart that receives blood from the atria.

virus (vī'rəs), the smallest germ that is known. A virus is too small to be seen through most microscopes.

vitamin (vī'tə·mən), a substance that is necessary for good health. Vitamins help the body use nutrients in foods.

volunteer (vol'ən·tir'), a person who works without pay.

warm-up (wôrm-up), an exercise that is done to prepare the body gradually for more vigorous exercise.

water (wô'tər), a nutrient that helps the body use other nutrients. Water in the blood mixes with other nutrients and carries them to the cells of the body. The water in urine, sweat, and the breath helps to remove wastes from the body.

white blood cell (hwīt blud sel), one type of cell in the blood. White blood cells attack and kill germs.

whooping cough (hüp'ing kôf), a disease, most often of children, that causes loud coughing.

withdrawal (wiᴛʜ·drô'əl), the physical and emotional discomfort that occurs when people suddenly stop taking a drug or other substance to which they are addicted.

X-ray (eks'rā'), a ray that can pass through a solid object and show what the inside looks like.

yellow fever (yel'ō fē'vər), a serious disease that is spread by the bite of a certain mosquito. Its symptoms are a high fever and yellow skin.

INDEX

A **bold-faced** page number means you will find a picture on that page.

Acknowledgements

Cover photograph by James L. Ballard

Caulderon Press, by Victoria Beller-Smith—14, 18, 21, 23, 25, 27, 30, 32, 33, 43, 45, 84, 85, 101, 103, 116, 118, 119, 121, 122, 125, 128, 129, 130, 148, 156, 157, 168, 169, 179, 239, 266

Caulderon Press, by Michal Heron—41, 179, 208, 232

Caulderon Press, by Barbara Kirk—30, 57, 90, 94, 96, 97, 98, 151, 155, 160, 165, 179, 192, 233, 249, 259

Caulderon Press, by Lynn Thompson—44, 91, 131, 135, 136, 158, 258, 260, 261, 267

Caulderon Press, by Karen Wunderman—149

Jerry Cummings—83, 147, 229, 257

Donald E. Schlegel—69, 70, 74, 250

Gerald Smith—53, 67, 72, 73, 74, 75, 133, 140, 150, 152, 153, 159, 167, 170, 235, 246, 264, 265

Lynn Thompson—48, 137, 197

Ira Adler—54

Air India—189

American Association of Blood Banks—47

American Cancer Society—244, 268

Copyright by the American Dental Association. Reprinted by permission.—104, 105, 107

American Petroleum Institute—215, 218

American Society of Microbiology—184

James L. Ballard—10, 38, 62, 80, 112, 144, 174, 202, 226, 254

Baylor College of Medicine—53

Victoria Beller-Smith—16, 50, 57, 117, 179, 196, 209, 231

Richard Blumberg—126, 212

Peter Bruegel: *The Tower of Babel* (Detail), Kunsthistoriches Museum Vienna, Photo Saskia/EPA—174

Photography by Carolina Biological Supply Company —41, 47, 51, 66

Photo courtesy of Celanese Corporation—268

Centers for Disease Control, Atlanta, GA 30333—182, 185

Cold Spring Harbor Laboratory—Research Library Archives—184

Cosmos Soccer Club—45

Culver Pictures—52, 236

Raphael David, M.D.—49

Dr. E.R. Degginger, FPSA—65, 108, 115

Joseph A. DiChello, Jr.—57

Drug Enforcement Administration—243

DuPage Pathological Associates—244, 245

Eli Lilly & Company—180, 220

Dr. John Erdman—126

Food and Drug Administration—268

Girl Scouts of the USA—17, 33

Michal Heron—13, 15, 164

Junior Achievement—87

March of Dimes Birth Defects Foundation—210

Medic Alert Foundation International—166

Courtesy of Memorial Sloan-Kettering Cancer Center —195

Pictures courtesy of Montefiore Hospital and Medical Center, New York—88, 89

The National Center for Atmospheric Research is sponsored by the National Science Foundation.—161

National Library of Medicine—181, 197

Parke-Davis, Div. of Warner-Lambert Co., Morris Plains, NJ 07950—191

Police Athletic League—28, 45, 95

Photograph courtesy of Reynolds Aluminum Recycling Company—217

Schwinn Bicycle Company—262

Courtesy of Dr. George Silling—106

Special Olympics, Inc.—134

Texas State Department of Highways and Transportation—56, 138

Kathy Threats—195

Photo by UNICEF—92

United States Department of Agriculture—92, 139, 177, 186, 207, 216, 221

USDA—Soil Conservation Service—190

University of Rochester—183

Walter Reed Army Medical Center—187

Courtesy of Howard L. Ward, D.D.S.—periodontist—104

Courtesy Carl Zeiss, Inc., New York—46

Bernard Zeller—154

83 84 85 86 87 / 9 8 7 6 5 4 3 2 1